EAST ASIA AND LATIN AMERICA

EAST ASIA AND LATIN AMERICA

The Unlikely Alliance

Edited by
Peter H. Smith, Kotaro Horisaka,
and Shoji Nishijima

ROWMAN & LITTLEFIELD PUBLISHERS, INC.
Lanham • Boulder • New York • Oxford

ROWMAN & LITTLEFIELD PUBLISHERS, INC.

Published in the United States of America
by Rowman & Littlefield Publishers, Inc.
A Member of the Rowman & Littlefield Publishing Group
4501 Forbes Boulevard, Suite 200, Lanham, Maryland 20706
www.rowmanlittlefield.com

PO Box 317, Oxford OX2 9RU, United Kingdom

British Library Cataloguing in Publication Information Available

Library of Congress Cataloging-in-Publication Data

East Asia and Latin America : the unlikely alliance / edited by Peter H.
Smith, Kotaro Horisaka, and Shoji Nishijima.
p. cm.
Includes bibliographical references and index.
ISBN 978-0-7425-2386-0 —ISBN 0-7425-2376-4 (pbk :
alk. paper)
1. East Asia—Foreign economic relations—Latin America. 2. Latin
America—Foreign economic relations—East Asia. 3. United
States—Foreign economic relations. 4. Globalization. I. Smith, Peter
H. II. Horisaka, Kotaro, 1944– III. Nishijima, Shoji.
HF1600 .5 .Z4 L294 2003
337.508—dc21

2002014223

Printed in the United States of America

∞™ The paper used in this publication meets the minimum requirements of American National Standard for Information Sciences—Permanence of Paper for Printed Library Materials, ANSI/NISO Z39.48-1992.

Contents

Tables and Figures

Tables

Figures

Acknowledgments

THIS BOOK HAS A LONG HISTORY. As a result we owe thanks to countless people—colleagues, students, staff, and professional associates throughout the world.

The volume emerged from a multiyear project on the topic "Latin America and the Pacific Rim" organized by the Center for Iberian and Latin American Studies (CILAS) at the University of California, San Diego, and co-sponsored by UCSD's Graduate School of International Relations and Pacific Studies (IR/PS). The program included residential fellowships for mid-career professionals from Asia and Latin America, intensive seminars and workshops, and major international conferences. Many of the chapters in this book began as research papers by visiting fellows. Other contributions are from senior scholars who took part in the project in one way or another.

We want to acknowledge the special role of the project's International Advisory Board, whose members were Kotaro Horisaka (Japan), Kim Kiwhan (Korea), Olga Pellicer (Mexico), Pasuk Phongpaichit (Thailand), Gilson Schwartz (Brazil), and Alberto van Klaveren (Chile). Lawrence Krause of IR/PS also made outstanding contributions to the overall effort.

For financial support we thank the Ford Foundation, the Center for Global Partnership, and various entities within the University of California. For their intellectual and moral support we express special gratitude to Cristina Eguizábal of the Ford Foundation and Rikimaru Takahashi of the Center for Global Partnership.

We wish to thank Seiichi Katayama, director of the Research Institute for Economics and Business Administration at Kobe University, for graciously hosting a meeting of all the program fellows in October-November 2000. We also thank Sophia University and the University of Chile for hosting special workshops in late 1999.

Martin G. Hoffman provided professional assistance with the editing of early drafts. As the project developed we came to rely extensively on the substantive knowledge and editorial talents of Natalia Porto and Kati Suominen, at the time both graduate students at UCSD.

The CILAS staff at UCSD was instrumental in all stages of the project. Nora Bodrian helped with grant proposals, grant reporting, grant expenditures—and still more grant proposals. Florencia Quintanar, now embarked on a diplomatic career, worked many overtime hours in order to make arrangements for visiting fellows from overseas. Erik Lee and Apha Thirakaroonwongse assisted with myriad details, as did students and friends from throughout UCSD. With tenacity, skill, and good humor, Caroline Awbrey pulled the manuscript together in its final stages.

We could not have done this without them.

Peter H. Smith, La Jolla, California
Kotaro Horisaka, Tokyo, Japan
Shoji Nishijima, Kobe, Japan

INTRODUCTION: THE GLOBAL ARENA

East Asia, Latin America, and the Changing World Order

WE LIVE IN A PERPLEXING WORLD. Instead of the "new world order" that was expected to emerge in the aftermath of the Cold War, we see disorder and uncertainty. In economic terms, the widely heralded process of "globalization"—so often depicted as a panacea—has promoted growth but has also divided the world into winners and losers, while punctuating the decade of the 1990s with cataclysmic economic crises. In geopolitical terms, the global distribution of power is highly uneven and ultimately unstable. The United States emerged from the Cold War as the world's "sole remaining superpower," but its preeminence looked precarious: As one prominent analyst predicted, a multipolar redistribution of power is almost certain to take shape in the early twenty-first century, and the United States will have been "the first, last, and only global superpower."[1] And on September 11, 2001, terrorist attacks on New York City and Washington, D.C., claimed more than three thousand American lives, destroyed entire buildings, provoked a military response reaction from the United States, and sowed anxiety and fear. What will the future bring?

Countries around the world looked on with apprehension. What could they do? In particular, what could the less powerful do? What do they want, and how can they best promote their interests?

This book is about the societies and governments of two major world regions—Asia and the Americas, or, more precisely, East Asia and Latin America. It explores their interconnections, interests, and goals. It examines how they have responded to common problems—especially the economic crises of the 1990s—and how they have pursued the goals of economic development.

It evaluates their diplomatic and economic (or, better said, geoeconomic) initiatives to promote cooperation and collaboration. It explores their relationships to major powers, especially the United States, and it illuminates the ways that leading regional powers—including China and Japan—are likely to expand or constrict their opportunities for transregional collaboration.

By focusing upon these regions, this volume sheds light on efforts by less powerful countries to shape the world in accordance with their interests. Toward this end, the book addresses three key questions:

1. What are the predominant interests of countries in these regions? What do they have in common?
2. What kind of partnership are they now constructing? What are the current possibilities, and what is the long-term potential?
3. What could be the impact of such a partnership? What importance might it have?

These are large questions, and they do not admit easy answers. They demand a multifaceted, interdisciplinary approach, and they require an exercise of the imagination.

Why These Regions?

Connections between Asia and Latin America have not attracted much attention. There is a massive scholarly literature about Asia and "the West," of course—especially about relationships between Japan or China and the United States—but there is very little published work on linkages between Asia (as a region) and the Americas (as a region). This focus therefore makes our book distinctive. But what is the underlying rationale?

One basic factor is size. These are large and important regions. Their combined population is around 2.3 billion people, nearly 40 percent of the world's total. (China is the world's largest country, Indonesia is fourth, Brazil is fifth.) Moreover, their combined economic output is approximately 27 percent of the gross world product. (Japan accounts for nearly 14 percent of the world output; the rest of East Asia accounts for 6.3 percent, and the Latin American share hovers around 6.7 percent. As of 1999, the United States was producing 28–29 percent of the global GNP.)[2] These are substantial areas, and their relative significance—economic as well as demographic—is bound to increase over time.[3]

A related consideration concerns standing in the world arena. Most countries in Asia and Latin America occupy the middling, or lower-middling, echelons of international power. Unlike much of sub-Saharan Africa or South Asia, they are not the poorest of the poor or weakest of the weak. Nor do they depend on global demand for a single commodity, like petroleum-exporting countries of the Middle East. They have substantial resources, human and natural, they have expansive possibilities for future development, and they are capable of exerting international influence—within limits.

To demonstrate these points, table I.1 displays the relative position of countries in East Asia and the Americas on economic rankings developed by the World Bank.[4] With the conspicuous exceptions of Japan, Canada, and the United States, the largest number of countries—and most large countries—fall into the "middle income" categories (with GNP per capita figures between $756 and $9,265 at 1999 levels). Three Asian nations—China, the Philippines,

TABLE I.1
East Asia and the Americas by Income Level, 2000

	East Asia	Americas
Low Income:	Cambodia	Haiti
	Indonesia	Nicaragua
	North Korea	
	Myanmar	
	Vietnam	
Lower-Middle Income:	China	Bolivia
	Philippines	Central America*
	Thailand	Colombia
		Cuba
		Dominican Republic
		Ecuador
		Paraguay
		Peru
Upper-Middle Income:	South Korea	Argentina
	Malaysia	Brazil
		Chile
		Mexico
		Panama
		Uruguay
		Venezuela
High Income:	Japan	Canada
	Hong Kong	United States
	Singapore	
	Taiwan	

*Excepting Nicaragua, which is in the low-income category.
Source: Adapted from World Bank, *World Development Report 2000/2001: Attacking Poverty* (New York: Oxford University Press, 2001), pp. 334–335.
GNP per capita cutoff levels are as follows: low income, $775 or less in 1999; lower-middle income, $756–$2,995; upper-middle income, $2,996–$9,265; high income, $9,266 or more.

and Thailand—fall in the "lower middle-income" bracket, as do eleven nations of Latin America. Two Asian countries—South Korea and Malaysia—are in the upper-middle income group, as are seven countries of Latin America. In sum, the classifications yield two insights: one is that countries at the middling range are likely to have a good deal in common with each other; another is that both regions are internally unequal, or heterogeneous, with member countries in all income levels from lowest to highest.

As members of the global community, nations of these regions necessarily confront the presence and influence of the world's dominant power, the United States. They confront regional powers: In this capacity Latin America once again must deal with the United States, while countries of East Asia must deal with Japan—and China to a rapidly increasing extent. (In this regard, Japan occupies a singularly complex position: It is a close ally of the United States, but also a natural rival; it is part of Asia, but also one of the richest countries in the world.) They also confront a daunting array of social, economic, and political challenges.

Largely in response to these realities, nations of Asia and Latin America are looking for new partners. Their idea is to broaden economic and political networks, expand room for maneuver, enlarge the menu of plausible options, and, in so doing, diminish the global influence of the United States. At the regional level as well, Southeast Asia and China are seeking to reduce their dependence upon Japan, just as nations of the Southern Cone are striving to mitigate the hemispheric hegemony of the United States. These are classic acts of balancing in international relations. Clear examples are the efforts by countries (and groups of countries) in both regions to reach out to the European Union.

And in keeping with this overall strategy, East Asia and Latin America are now looking toward each other. As will be explained in subsequent chapters, they are seeking to strengthen economic ties—through trade and investment, through cross-membership in multilateral organizations (such as APEC, the forum for Asia-Pacific Economic Cooperation), and through formal bilateral agreements. They are sharing information and ideas about such common experiences as the imposition of drastic neoliberal policy reforms and the currency crises of the 1990s. And most recently, they have established a new organization—the Forum for East Asia–Latin America Cooperation (FEALAC)—in order to identify, define, and promote mutual understanding, interests, and goals.

What difference can this possibly make? It is our belief that an East Asia–Latin America partnership will be significant in several ways. First would be a positive effect on the well-being of citizens in the two regions—on their attitudes and outlooks, as well as on their immediate economic prospects. Second, consolidation of an Asian–Latin American alliance would constitute a positive step toward globalization "with a kinder face"—in particular, a globalized world that would operate on the basis of internationally accepted rules, rather than exertions of raw power. And third, effective cooperation between Asia and Latin America could provide a model for transregional and transcultural partnerships among other regions of the world; in particular, it could revive the ideals of South-South cooperation. In this sense, an Asia–Latin America axis could stimulate a broader, more inclusive series of networks linking all (or virtually all) of the world's societies into a genuine global community.

Really, Now . . .

What is the basis for such cooperation? What do Asia and Latin America see in one another, and what is the foundation for their rapprochement?

Ties between the two regions are deeper and stronger than most people think. The connection dates back to the sixteenth century, when the Manila galleon began ferrying spices, silks, and other goods between two Spanish colonies—Mexico and the Philippines, which itself became a hybrid society composed of Asian and Iberian cultural influences. As long ago as the late nineteenth century, Japanese workers began migrating to Latin America, especially to Brazil, Peru, and Mexico. At the same time, Chinese coolie laborers helped build railroad networks in Peru, Cuba, and Mexico (they also laid much of the track on the transcontinental railway in the United States). Nearly a century later, Peru elected a son of Japanese immigrants (Alberto K. Fujimori) as president of the nation, a development that unleashed "Fujimori fever" throughout Japan in the early 1990s; it was sadly ironic that, after his fall from power and grace, he would claim political refuge in Japan.[5] Meanwhile, the Japanese community in Brazil, especially in the megalopolis of São Paulo, would flourish as a visible and successful case of cross-cultural assimilation.[6] And when Japan began to import migrant labor, in the late 1980s and early 1990s, it opened its doors to *dekasegi* from Brazil, "returning workers" who were descendants of Japanese emigrants. Best estimates suggest that well over one million people of Japanese descent are now living in Latin America[7] and more than 250,000 *nikkeis* from Latin America are living in Japan.

To a considerable extent, these migratory waves laid the basis for significant economic relationships. Fully one-tenth of Latin American exports go to East Asia (in fact, Japan is the largest single overseas market for Chile). Around 2–3 percent of Asian exports head for Latin America—a figure that is modest but likely to rise in the future. Japan has invested heavily in Latin America, Korea has begun to follow suit, and Taiwan has focused especially on smaller countries of Central America and the Caribbean.[8] For most of the 1990s Japan was the largest single source of foreign economic aid to Latin America; it is now second only to the United States. Japan is also the second largest user of the Panama Canal, after the United States, and it has consistently expressed strong interest in plans to widen the canal. Reflecting its expanding interests and role in the region, Chinese shipping also relies on the canal and a China-based firm (Hutchison Whampoa) has secured the management lease for the terminal ports. Moreover, the economic crises of the 1990s—and their spillover effects from one region to another—heightened the need for knowledge, insight, and understandings about each other.

Political transformations have also shaped the mutual agenda. Patterns of democratization and/or liberalization in both regions have given rise to shared concerns about processes of transition and consolidation. In South Korea, Taiwan, and Mexico, dominant-party regimes have given way to open competition and opposition victories. In Indonesia, a regime that was at once bureaucratic and personalistic (under Suharto) collapsed in the wake of a currency crisis; throughout the Southern Cone of South America, by contrast, transitions from military to civilian leadership were relatively smooth. The recent experience of Vietnam might well portend the future of Cuba (as well as of North Korea). Comparisons of this sort have not only begun to stimulate a good deal of cross-regional academic research. They have also led policy makers in the two regions to seek practical lessons from one another with regard to social policy, institutional design, and governance.

Unfortunately, they share another common bond—the presence of terrorist threats. There have been bombings of Jewish facilities in Buenos Aires, a nerve agent attack on the Tokyo subway, kidnappings and assassinations in Colombia, violent attacks on UN personnel in Indonesia. Radical Islamic groups are taking hold in the Philippines and in the tri-border area of Argentina, Paraguay, and Brazil. Osama bin Laden's Al Qaeda network is said to have cells in more than sixty countries, including some in East Asia and Latin America. During 2000 there were 193 terrorist incidents in Latin America and scores throughout East Asia.[9] Clearly, there exists a need for close communication between the governments of these two regions.

And as a result of all these factors, there are cultural linkages as well. Shared experiences—social, economic, political—have stimulated scholarly research on Asian–Latin American interconnections and interactions. Academic research centers and teaching programs have blossomed in Mexico, Brazil, Japan, and more recently in Korea and China. Brazilian telenovelas have acquired popular followings in China while Mexican telenovelas have penetrated Philippine and other Asian markets. Sushi bars and dim sum restaurants are commonplace in Lima, São Paulo, and Mexico City, and Latin American cuisine—from Brazilian churrascarias to Mexican taquerías to the ubiquitous U.S.–based Taco Bell chain—has gathered a substantial following in Asia. The quintessentially Latin American game of soccer has become the leading sport of China and other Asian countries. Similarly, Latin American music—and U.S.–based Latino music—has surged in Asian markets with the popularity of such stars as Ricky Martin, Jennifer Lopez, and Caetano Veloso.

In short, East Asia and Latin America have common histories, traditions, and interests. They face some common problems. They have sufficient resources to exert a significant and growing impact on the shape of the post–Cold War order. By joining together, they can increase their influence by a significant margin. Whether they will do so is another question.

Approaching the Issues

This book has four substantive sections. After this opening statement (and the companion essay that follows), part I examines the nature and strength of the underlying economic connection between East Asia and Latin America. Part II offers long-term assessments of developmental strategies in East Asia and Latin America, with particular emphasis on the economic role of the state. Part III explores the economic crises of the 1990s, perhaps the most conspicuous (and least welcome) experience shared by the two regions. Part IV turns to geopolitical issues and ways that leading powers might (or might not) affect prospects for closer collaboration between countries of East Asia and Latin America. The volume concludes with a policy statement about the nature of Asian–Latin American cooperation, prospects for its development, and its potential impact on the global arena.

Notes

1. Samuel P. Huntington, "The Lonely Superpower," *Foreign Affairs* 78, no. 2 (March/April 1999): 37. For an alternative view see Stephen G. Brooks and William C. Wohlforth, "American Primacy in Perspective," *Foreign Affairs* 81, no. 4 (July/August 2002): 20–33.
2. Calculated from data in World Bank, *World Development Report 2000/2001: Attacking Poverty* (New York: Oxford University Press, 2001), table 1, 274–275.
3. One forecast projects that China will have the world's largest economy as early as 2025. See commentary in the *International Herald Tribune*, May 23, 2001, 8.
4. As the table makes clear, we speak of "East Asia" in a broad and inclusive sense of the term.

5. Moreover, Fujimori has successfully claimed Japanese citizenship, something he never acknowledged during his public career in Peru.

6. Ruth Corrêa Leite Cardoso, *Estrutura familiar e mobilidade social: Estudo dos japoneses no Estado de São Paulo* (São Paulo: Kaleidos-Primus, 1998).

7. See Iyo Kunimoto, "Japanese Migration to Latin America," in *Japan, the United States, and Latin America: Toward a Trilateral Relationship in the Western Hemisphere*, eds. Barbara Stallings and Gabriel Székely (Baltimore: Johns Hopkins University Press, 1993), 99–121.

8. In exchange for diplomatic recognition, as explained in chapter 15 of this volume.

9. U.S. Department of State, *Patterns of Global Terrorism 2000* (April 2001); see also *Patterns of Global Terrorism 2001* (May 2002). This point is further developed in chapter 16.

1

The Challenge of Globalization: Strategic Options for Developing Economies

Lily M. Bravo Castillo

WE FIND OURSELVES IN THE MIDST OF profound and qualitative changes in the international political economy. Among their myriad consequences, these transformations are demanding "new instruments, new public policies and new rationales" for actions by nation-states and their legitimization.[1] In this respect, the dramatic changes caused by the so-called information technologies and technological revolution since the 1960s have been one of the main promoters of this new international political economy. These changes are also reshaping the world's industrial organization and revamping the state's role in economic development.

Placing these considerations within the context of the larger process that has come to be known as "globalization," we can view the state as an institution (or set of institutions) whose purpose is to attenuate the uncertainties and complexities of these transformations. Globalization is assumed by many to be a positive phenomenon because it increases the volume of exchange and the income of participating economies, thereby improving the quality of life for most people within those areas. But as the process accelerates, the accidents that accompany it are becoming ever more serious and frequent. This is especially true in the case of international financial crises, which have led many analysts and policymakers to regard globalization as an essentially negative development. In the great majority of capitalist societies, economic disparity is increasing. Stock market disorganization and economic contraction are creating unemployment, leaving people without a social safety net.

The goal of this chapter is to assess the impact of globalization on sovereign states and their strategies for economic development. At the same time, it seeks to outline a series of strategic options available to developing economies for coping with the demands and new realities of global change. I write from the perspective of Latin America, but I regard my arguments as relevant to East Asia as well.

For purposes of this analysis, globalization shall be understood as the simultaneous effect of three major trends: (1) the internationalization of trade and production, (2) increases in capital mobility, and (3) expanding flows of knowledge and information (ranging from basic communication to technology transfer). This conceptualization makes it possible to identify three important variables that affect the degree of integration of national economies with the global economy: (1) technology, (2) trade and capital mobility, and (3) strategic alliances and network forms of organization. The management of these three variables will define the role of the state in the economic development of a nation and its integration with the global economy. Thus, the process of globalization and the accompanying changes in world politics mean that the nation-state's role and institutions are changing dramatically, in both their domestic and external spheres and in their forms of action. They also signify the need to reformulate public policies in accordance with demands for equitable development and sustained growth.

A Paradigm Shift in the International Political Economy

Globalization refers to a world in which societies, cultures, polities, and economies have, in some sense, come closer. On this basic level, it refers to growing interaction and interdependence between the various units that constitute the global system.[2] Processes are multidimensional, encompassing various activities and their effects on countries, regions, multinational enterprises, international organizations, public and private organizations, and social groups and movements. Commonly applied with an economic emphasis, the concept tends to focus attention on specific actors (companies, transnational financial agencies) and processes (technological innovation, transformation of the productive system, and the creation of worldwide networks in different fields) at the expense of others.

Within this broad framework, however, there is no substantial agreement as to how globalization should be understood and conceptualized with respect to either its dynamics or its structural consequences. In recent literature, debates have taken place among three schools of thought: the Hyperglobalists, the Skeptics, and the Transformationalists.[3]

For the Hyperglobalists, globalization defines a new era in human history in which traditional nation-states have become anachronistic, even irrelevant units in the global economy.[4] Economic globalization brings with it the "de-nationalization" of economies by means of transnational networks of production, trade, and finance. This perspective emphasizes an economic logic and the principle of global competition. National governments are limited to acting merely as entities of global capital transmission, or as intermediary institutions between powerful and impersonal forces of governance at local, regional, and global levels. Economic globalization is constructing new forms of social organization that are supplanting, or eventually will supplant, traditional nation-states as the principal economic and political units in world society. For this school, globalization is principally an economic phenomenon.

The Skeptics, in contrast, maintain that the contemporary process of globalization is neither historically nor qualitatively new. On the contrary, it merely represents a greater degree of interaction between predominantly national economies. Empirical evidence—especially relating to trade and investment—shows that contemporary levels of economic interdependence are by no means unprecedented. According to the Skeptics, national governments, not market forces, are the chief architects of globalization. Moreover, internationalization does not provide a panacea—it reflects and ratifies deeply rooted patterns of inequality and hierarchy in the world economy, which in structural terms has changed only marginally over the last century. Such inequalities contribute more to the advance of fundamentalism and aggressive nationalism than to the emergence of a global civil society. Additionally, the Skeptics observe, economic activity is paving the way for the emergence of three large financial and trade blocs: Europe, the Asia-Pacific area, and the Americas. Globalization and regionalization are perceived as contradictory tendencies, and this underlying tension is bound to result in discord and conflict.[5]

For the Transformationalists, globalization is the principal driving force behind the rapid social, political, and economic changes that are structuring societies and the modern world order.[6] Globalization is responsible for a "massive upheaval" of social and economic institutions, as well as of the world order. The direction of the upheaval remains uncertain. Governments and societies throughout the world are faced with the need to adapt to a world in which a clear distinction between international and domestic, between internal and external affairs, does not exist. Globalization is a historic, long-term process that is characterized by contradictions and significantly affected by short-term and situational factors. Globalization is associated with new forms of global stratification in which some states, societies, and communities are becoming more integrated into the workings of the global order, while others are being marginalized. The reformulation of the patterns of global stratification is related to a growing deterritorialization of economic activity as production and finance have continued acquiring global and transnational dimensions. Globalization is reconstructing, or carrying out a "re-engineering" of, the power, roles, and authority of national governments.

In short, the intensity of global transactions, the increase in international trade, and the simultaneous tendencies toward integration and fragmentation produce societal demands for greater degrees of predictability—or, at least, a narrowing of the boundaries of uncertainty. Meeting this demand requires the development of governance capabilities. This can be accomplished to the extent that the state is capable of acting appropriately on the domestic level and in international concert for adopting supranational measures.

Issues and Challenges

As a market phenomenon, globalization acquires its basic impetus from technological progress and particularly in the capacity of this progress to reduce the costs associated with transporting and moving goods, services, capital, information, and individuals. Dramatic increases in the scale of technology in many industries (in terms of cost, risk, and complexity) have rendered even the largest national markets too small to be meaningful economic units.[7] National markets are no longer the main entities of the world economy. National markets are *fused* transnationally rather than linked across borders.

For developing countries, an issue of considerable concern is the possibility that they could find themselves disconnected from global technological development trends, which is related to the marginal role that they already play in the generation of technological knowledge. In point of fact, strategic alliances formed to exploit and develop technology are largely limited to the participation of large companies based in the Organization for Economic Cooperation and Development (OECD) countries. Therefore, developing countries should assign greater importance to the *application* of technologies available internationally. Other vehicles, such as international trade in capital goods and foreign direct investment, are better suited to effecting technology transfers to developing countries than strategic alliances.

Trade and capital mobility also affects the degree of integration of national economies with the international economy. This leads us directly to what has been defined as market globalization, which refers to the increase in the flows of capital, goods, and services across national borders. Market globalization can be measured in terms of the volume of *trade and capital flows,* which indicate differences in the breadth and extent of the integration of countries and regions around the world.

Since the end of World War II, trade has expanded consistently and steadily among industrialized economies, at a pace three to four times faster than the growth of domestic product. As a consequence, these economies have become more and more dependent on trade, which has prompted them to become more integrated under one international trade order. World trade in 1999 has been valued at approximately $10.6 trillion per year, an increase of 2.5 times over the total amount recorded for 1986. In recent decades developing economies have been increasing their participation in and benefits from international trade. A great deal of the expansion of trade in the last decade has taken place between the newly industrialized countries of Asia and Latin America and the advanced economies.

This increasing dependence on trade influences the economic policy of all nations. Governments are forced to create or provide suitable environments for enhancing the competitiveness of national producers in international markets. Nations that have engaged in open-market policies must compete successfully in international markets or else their prospects and potential are dim. Unemployment will rise and economic growth will slow down.[8] In other words, the implication of greater trade integration for governments is that the cost of closing their economies increases, which in turn restricts the range of options available to governments for managing internal economic dislocations. When the economic activity of a country depends increasingly on foreign trade, the dependency of such a country upon the actions of others increases as well. This also means that, with market globalization, states must concern themselves more with the stability of international relations and maintaining economic openness.

Capital mobility represents another form of market globalization. More than $1.2 trillion dollars change hands every day, reflecting an increase in trade and investment across borders. However, the bulk of these exchanges are speculative monetary transactions and arbitrage.

At the same time, this globalization of financial markets is limiting the economic autonomy of the modern state and transforming the nation-state system. Investors are becoming less and less concerned with national borders as they seek the most profitable opportunities. The process by which capital mobility influences economic policy can be stated in the following terms: the easier it is for asset holders to move their capital offshore, the stronger the incentives for governments to pursue policies that will increase rates of return on domestic investments. In particular, capital in portfolio investments can rapidly flow out of a nation in anticipation of exchange-rate depreciations. Foreign exchange markets are volatile and tend to react dramatically to small changes in fundamentals (interest rates, budgetary balances, and inflation). States thus run the risk that their economic decisions may lead to an unsustainable increase or decrease in the value of their currencies. Additionally, if a government wishes to seek a loan in the international capital market, it must follow policies that maintain investor confidence. This creates a structural incentive for governments to implement conservative macroeconomic policies, placing an enormous priority on low inflation and lesser importance on growth and employment.

In addition, the rapid growth in foreign direct investment (FDI) has led to major changes in the global economy. Over the last few decades, FDI flows have grown at an annual rate of 11 percent. This increase has not only been in terms of the amount of the flow but also its geographic expansion and diversification. During the 1980s, FDI was mainly concentrated among industrialized areas such as Japan, North America, and Western Europe; in the 1990s, by contrast, developing regions in Asia and Latin America played host to larger flows of FDI and also a greater number of investors.

Still another consideration relates to the presence and strength of strategic alliances. The motivations for such alliances are multiple and complex. Key factors include (1) the need to compete in the most desirable markets; (2) the importance that the economic activity of companies within national boundaries still holds for local governments, where promotion policies oriented toward local industrial sectors favors the establishment of alliances with national or regional leaders; (3) the hope of reducing the costs of competition; and, most important, (4) the increasing cost, risk, and complexity of modern technology. In addition, globalization has prompted the expansion and evolution of corporate production beyond the reach of the individual firm, thus promoting the expansion of transnational corporate activities. As a consequence, this expansion of corporate production and business is creating for national economies a different mode of integration with the international economy that goes beyond the traditional pattern of economic interdependence and the cross-border exchange of goods and services.

With increasing frequency, large multinational corporations are associating with their competitors to form joint ventures in order to share the burden of cost and risk, as well as to guarantee market access. The more internationalized these corporate activities become, therefore, the greater the corporate interest in maintaining an open and stable global economy—whether between states, regions, and/or blocs. In short, this trend is causing national economic identity to become less precise, undermining governmental capacities for clear decision-making that would favor economic nationalism.

Finally, the recent proliferation of transnational strategic alliances represents a fundamental change in the organization of international economic transactions, which are being transformed from markets and/or hierarchies (trade and multinational corporations, or MNCs) into postmodern global networks. A 1992 OECD report defines a "network" as a distinctive form of organization, representing a type of arrangement with its own specific, distinctive features that henceforth must be considered in its own right.[9] In this sense, the emergence of international strategic alliances signals the replacement of integrated transnational hierarchies by global networks, that is, a cooperative and reciprocal organization of economic transactions. And although trade and capital flows are relevant considerations, the most important flows across transnational networks are intangibles: knowledge and information.

Strategic Options for Developing Economies

Globalization has far-reaching economic and political effects. The question is whether contemporary actors—citizens, firms, governments—are likely to be freer, better off, or safer than they would otherwise be. There can be no clear or precise answer to this question. It is my contention, however, that there is still opportunity for governmental initiation and implementation of policies that allow the state to assure domestic well-being and position itself properly in the external arena. I refer to such macropolicies or "grand policies" as *strategic options,* defined by Peter Smith as "opportunities for (and variations of) relatively long-term, consistent policies . . . to protect and promote the interests of nation-states."[10]

My purpose is to outline a series of the grand policies available for two developing regions, East Asia and Latin America. Both areas have been deeply affected by contemporary processes of economic globalization. They have also endured the painful experience of currency crises—with extensive aftershocks from the Mexican crisis of 1994–1995, the Brazilian crisis of 1999, and the ubiquitous Asian crisis of 1997–1998. Shocks in one region also proved to have substantial effects in the other, and to this extent countries and citizens in the two areas now have a shared economic destiny.

In the aftermath of these shocks, nations of Asia and Latin America must pursue the same general objectives: (1) seeking macroeconomic stability and reducing vulnerability; (2) improving productivity and increasing international competitiveness; and (3) protecting the poor, that is, avoiding social disintegration. Success in achieving these objectives will depend upon the policies implemented both within the internal arena and with respect to the region's ties to the external environment. We therefore must turn our attention to identifying the necessary prerequisites for implementing successful policies within the framework of globalization.

International analysts and investors evaluate emerging economies according to a series of criteria, such as (1) level of development, (2) growth potential, (3) the degree of internal and external macroeconomic equilibrium, (4) political risk and the credibility of economic policy, and (5) the state of the banking system. These criteria make it possible for us to establish the prerequisites for emerging economies that wish to join the club of globalized economies. First are benchmarks for domestic macroeconomic performance. It is desirable to maintain steady and sustained annual growth rates of at least 5 percent (a rate that would depend also on the growth of the world economy as a whole); to control inflation, posting a one-digit annual rate; and to keep public finances under control, avoiding a public-sector deficit. The qualitative variables that account for the public perception of political risk, the credibility of economic policy, and the state of the banking system are also important. Developing economies that enjoy a good reputation in international markets are those supported by their strong macroeconomic fundamentals, political stability and clean banking systems—as in Taiwan, Hong Kong, and Chile.

Second, the evolution of the exchange rate in the medium term is an important factor for determining the stability of developing economies. In this sense the degree of external financial vulnerability is also relevant, expressed by the importance of an economy's current account deficit and the strength of its external position (that is, the relationship between international reserves and short-term foreign debt). Argentina, Mexico, Uruguay, China, and India are relatively solid economies, but they are vulnerable because of the high degree of foreign debt and their potential for experiencing foreign trade imbalances.[11]

Taking into account these prerequisites and their own relative position in the international context, Latin American and East Asian economies might consider four kinds of strategic choices: (1) openness versus closure, (2) needs for financial regulation, (3) a "third way" for social policies, and (4) the possibility of open regionalism.

Openness and the Closed Alternative

Commercial and financial globalization have a disciplinary impact on governments. Economic openness brings with it the promise of greater economic growth and an increase in living standards, but also restricts government policy choices. This makes it difficult for governments to apply Keynesian policies and utilize stabilization instruments within the national economy. It also has created new incentives for making use of microeconomic measures to help in the management of the economy—such as deregulation and research and development. But the opening of the national economy is the result of conscious state policies—policies that can be changed, although the cost of doing so may be high or increasing.

In the case of trade, countries that opt for openness must take into account the interconnection between technological innovation, financial markets, and productive activity. Exports really matter to the extent that they contribute to productive development, stimulating higher levels of investment and production and the full utilization of productive capacity, in this way generating productive employment. Thus, developing economies need to create spaces for improving their position in world trade. To do so they need to invest in human resources, education and training, and public infrastructure; develop stronger markets; create a stable macroeconomic environment; and establish and strengthen long-term capital markets, improving access to capital for new small and medium-sized companies.

Those countries that require foreign capital and foreign investment for growth and employment must constantly respond to the demands of foreign markets. To a great extent, the nature of financial, social, and governmental institutions determines the degree of success attained by this process.

A consequence of this overall process is that labor finds itself at an increasingly greater disadvantage in relation to capital. The globalization of financial markets has granted capital holders a wider range of available options, but labor continues to be much less mobile. The result has been a decrease in the political power of labor among advanced industrialized societies, and lower labor influence in the industrialized economy.

The Asian crisis prompted some emerging economies to reconsider certain issues associated with openness policies. The most radical reaction, a kind of protest in the face of globalization, has been that of "deglobalization." The proponents of "deglobalization" challenge the development model itself and "the institutionalization of exports and foreign capital as the twin engines of economic growth." They hold that the "fundamental flaw" of the model is that it encourages indiscriminate integration into the global economy and an overreliance on foreign capital for development. Deglobalization of the domestic economy, then, means "its reorientation toward greater reliance on the internal market; greater dependence on domestic capital resources; closer cooperation with neighboring economies to create protected regional markets"; and, ultimately, "a lower rate, and more benign pattern, of growth that would generate less income inequality."[12] This position has gained strength from the public protests carried out by groups that identify globalization as the culprit for social inequality. These protests have accompanied a number of international summits and meetings, such as the Millennium Round in Seattle, the Americas Summit in Quebec, and even the Governors Meeting of the Inter-american Development Bank in Santiago, Chile.

Financial Liberalization and the Regulatory Framework

While increases in the international trade of goods and services have far outstripped the growth of domestic production, the movement of capital around the globe has grown even faster than that of trade. From 1980 to 1990, the volume of cross-border equity transactions grew from $120 billion a year to $1.4 trillion.[13] It is precisely the "hypermobility" of capital that is argued to have undermined the ability of nation-states to control their national currency and other important economic variables. Facilitated by the development of new communication technologies, capital flows represent the most quintessentially globalized form of economic activity.

After decades of applying controls on capital movements, the international activities of domestic financial institutions, and the entry of foreign financial institutions into their countries, developing economies in recent years have opened their financial systems by liberalizing capital flows and the rules governing the international operations of financial intermediaries. For such liberalization policies to produce optimal results, however, developing economies need to make adequate preparations. If such a policy is premature and poorly conceived, its costs can be very high—since the liberalization of capital accounts can erode domestic financial controls, eliminate a tool of industrial policy and of patronage, and reduce opportunities for governments to finance themselves through the sale of bonds at interest rates lower than those prevailing on world markets.[14]

Knowledge of how to confront large-scale foreign capital inflows is therefore crucial. Of course, this also depends on the nature of the capital flows. If capital enters an economy as FDI and generates new productive capabilities and facilities, it can have a more positive impact on the economy. But if capital flows enter an economy in the form of dollar-denominated bank deposits or through the purchase of existing shares in the stock market, thereby creating pressures for a monetary revaluation (that is, the strengthening of the domestic currency) and disincentives toward internal investment, while at the same time stimulating consumption, they can be highly risky. Under such circumstances, increasing monetary policy autonomy by applying mechanisms that impede the excessive entrance of capital, especially short-term capital, can be an optimal policy: as examples we can cite the 30 percent reserve requirement tax applied by Chile and Colombia, or the taxes imposed in Brazil. In the specific case of Chile, the Central Bank has sought to dissuade the entrance of short-term and speculative capital flows in favor of foreign direct investment.

Any such measures should contribute to broadening and not limiting the access of developing economies to capital flows, especially long-term ones. In this sense, it is important that any new measures do not discourage FDI flows toward developing economies, since they contribute not only a more stable source of capital flows, but also provide technological and managerial know-how and better access to markets.[15] Moreover, any change in financial architecture should be based on the concept of nondiscriminatory membership (where developing economies can actively participate in decision-making). It should also enhance transparency and the disclosure of information, strengthen financial systems in both national and global economies, and include appropriate burden-sharing mechanisms for handling international financial crises.

The solution may not necessarily mean creating new institutions, but may instead involve a number of reforms to existing ones designed to structure and discipline financial operations and transactions. This managed approach would eschew the heavy hand of international regulation, while maintaining the element of risk essential to capitalism without removing the safety net provided by the IMF.[16] These reforms have already been formulated and they include improving the supervision of financial institutions, instituting Western-style accounting practices for banks and corporations, and the opening of markets to foreign investment. Such has been the case in the recovery process of the East Asian economies. Following the crisis experienced by these economies, since 1999 the region has witnessed a return of capital inflows. The need to continue attracting this type of financing, but upon a more stable basis, has forced the modification of the legal framework regulating investment in South Korea, Thailand, and Indonesia. The goal of these modifications is to continue the opening process and promote the entrance of foreign capital in the banking and financial sectors in order to encourage the establishment of institutions with a greater degree of sophistication for capital management, thereby avoiding new speculative bubbles.

The Neoclassical Model and the "Third Way"

Under the new international economic order, the most important challenge for the world economy will be to make globalization compatible with national sociopolitical stability, which means ensuring that international economic integration will not lead to national social disintegration. Among developing economies, options ranging from the establishment of a basic social safety net to Keynesian policies of the type that fulfill social welfare functions can provide the answer for avoiding social disintegration. Considering differences in the level of development among developing economies, policies that implement the liberalization of trade and capital, competitiveness, and harmonization with international standards can have different or even opposing effects. While in advanced developing economies these policies can increase growth potentials and social mobility among workers, in less advanced countries they can undermine social cohesion where low-skilled or less-educated workers are concerned. Consequently, it is within these developments (and many others, of course) that social policies come to play an important role in the state's response to the demands imposed by globalization.

Today we are confronted with two possible models for the formulation of social policy: the neoclassical model and the "emerging" model, also known as the "Third Way," which is still under construction and presents an end-of-the-century critical alternative to neoclassicism. The term "Third Way" appeared in the international vocabulary during the Cold War, as developing countries sought to establish paths that would be distinct from both capitalism and communism. The phrase then reemerged in the political sphere of the mid-1980s and came to characterize major changes espoused by Social Democratic parties in Europe, the Democrats in the United States, and the Labour Party in the UK.

The neoclassical paradigm conceives of a state in retreat within the context of increasing globalization and capitalization. It holds that the social sphere is better served by the market than by the state, since the market is considered to be the most efficient mechanism for resource allocation. Deregulation and privatization not only create greater efficiencies, but also generate greater degrees of individual freedom. For its part, the emerging model emphasizes notions of human security, mutual vulnerability, sustainability, and democratic governance. Whether or not the latter perspective becomes the paradigm of the twenty-first century will depend upon the nature of the neoliberal crisis and the crisis of modernity in general.

It took decades for Latin America to adopt the neoclassical paradigm. Early in the twentieth century key countries of the region, especially in the Southern Cone (Argentina, Chile, and Uruguay), established social policies well before most industrialized Western nations did so. The application of these social policies—regarding education, health care, labor rights, and social security—thus predated eras of induced development and industrialization. This approach, called the "distributive model" by Jorge Nef, was divided into three stages. The first ran from the first part of the century to the Great Depression of the 1930s; during this period, social policies helped to transform a manifest social conflict into a progressively institutionalized competition. The second stage began with the application of import-substitution industrialization strategies in the late 1930s and lasted well beyond World War II; during this era, social policies were transformed into a populist component of projects for economic reactivation and induced industrialization. The last stage started with the Cuban Revolution and lasted only briefly, until the Alliance for Progress in the 1960s; during this final stage, social policy came to be a component of a counter-insurgency strategy.[17]

The distributive model sought to implement deep structural changes through programs for urban property reform, land reform, and the equitable redistribution of income and wealth. The alliances that began to flourish between middle- and lower-class sectors were also important. Many changes were promoted by the union movement, which exerted "bottom to top" pressure and persuaded centrist governments to pass legislation favorable to it. Unfortunately, these alliances began to face serious contradictions characteristic of class-segregated societies, while distributive policies and strategies became unreachable utopias typical of what came to be labeled the "far" left. Finally, the model was plunged into crisis and ultimately extinguished. The welfare state and the import-substitution strategy experienced a sharp loss of prestige as a result of the successive economic crises of the period between the 1960s and the 1980s.

Within this context, a new model emerged as a product of intense internal social conflict and the external pressures of the Cold War. Political and economic crises led to the shattering of democratic institutions and to the emergence of authoritarian regimes. These new governments established repressive states based upon the so-called Doctrine of National Security, whose principal function was to contain social protest and demands and to dismantle populist (and representative) mechanisms for policy formation. In this model, the continuance of economic liberalism was sustained by the elimination of economic and political democracy. It was within this context of liberalization and growing repression and militarization that a new paradigm of social market policy arose: the neoclassical model.

Public policies associated with this model focus on structural adjustment, while its principal tenet is the unrestricted operation of the market and macroeconomic equilibrium. The social effects of this approach in Latin America were class polarization, national disintegration, and the extreme concentration of power and wealth. Neoclassical policies on these matters had a strong impact upon civil society. On the one hand they drastically reduced the ability of the state to confront increasing demands and problems. On the other, they increased social tensions between the elite and the masses, increasing social fragmentation among winners and losers. For example, the increase in crime in the region served as an indicator of this growing contradiction. Ultimately, economic interdependence and the region's need to integrate itself into the international economy have led to a further subordination of the nation and to a loss of sovereignty. Both developments could provoke national disintegration, combined with an integration of powerful minority social groups.

At the start of the twenty-first century, it is evident that in Latin America the neoclassical development model has failed to produce tangible benefits for the immense majority of the population. With the election of new leaders in recent years—such as Fernando Henrique Cardoso in Brazil, Ricardo Lagos in

Chile, and Fernando de la Rúa in Argentina—the Latin American region has begun its search for an alternative "third way" to guide growth and development strategies. The keystone of this new approach rests upon the concepts of equal opportunity, personal responsibility, and the mobilization of citizens and communities. Public policies must shift from a focus on wealth redistribution toward greater emphasis on wealth creation. This perspective also entails fiscal discipline, health care reform, investment in education and training, social security and labor welfare programs, and plans for urban renewal and public safety.

The Third Way implies a thorough, ongoing program of policy modernization. It seeks to modernize the state and the government, including state welfare, the economy, and other societal sectors. According to the Third Way, "modernization" means reforming social institutions in order to meet the demands imposed by globalization. Modernization is not exclusively identified with economic development.[18]

Within this process of modernization, the four spheres of power, government, economics, and civil society are equally important, and each one must consider solidarity and social justice as central priorities. A democratic order, as well as an effective market economy, depends upon a flourishing civil society. The emerging model proposes the construction of a new social contract based upon the slogan, "no rights without responsibilities." In the economic sphere, it seeks to reconcile mechanisms for economic growth with the structural reform of the welfare state. The development of both human and social capital is considered vital for economic success. This type of paradigm requires a high level of social investment in education, health care, social security, communications, and infrastructure. It also depends upon a balance between regulation and deregulation on both the national and transnational level. The benefits of the markets and the activities that take place within them are acknowledged. Markets have, or can have, beneficial outcomes that go beyond productive efficiency. A successful market economy has an important "hidden curriculum."[19] The market mechanism sends continuous feedback to producers, sellers, and consumers, which provide an empirical basis for policy formation and decision-making. Notwithstanding, the markets are not free from failures or the effects of external events, and this is where the "visible hand of the state" is required.

From a social perspective, the Third Way seeks to promote a diverse society based upon the principle of equality. This is achieved by maximizing equality of opportunity. The recognition of these premises and their incorporation into social policy must be realistically adapted to the inexorable realities of globalization. For those that count themselves within the Transformationist camp, the state-centric system coexists with an equally powerful, though more decentralized, multicentric system. These two spheres of world politics have overlapping elements and concerns, and their norms, structures, and processes tend to be mutually exclusive, thus giving rise to a set of global arrangements that are new and possibly enduring, as well as extremely complex and dynamic.[20]

Despite its association with the Western world, the fact is that a number of Asian countries applied something very close to the Third Way with respect to their social policies. The post–World War II Asian development process, with Japan at the forefront, was based upon the project of the "developmental state" (this is particularly true in the cases of Japan, South Korea, Hong Kong, Taiwan, and Singapore). While there are many critics of the developmental state concept, it was undeniably crucial in the promotion, orientation, and assurance of economic growth, industrialization and technological modernization, and development in its very broadest sense. The development strategy consisted of a combination of fundamental and interventionist policies to achieve rapid accumulation of human and physical capital. The Asian economies under consideration maintained the highest GDP growth rates in the world for a full three decades and gained substantial global market share, transforming in the process their economic structure and social safety net. What is more, although exploitation and oppression were integral parts of the development process, economic growth advanced equally on all fronts (with respect to salaries, health care, education, and housing), with significant improvements in the quality of life of the population as a whole.[21]

In order to achieve this growth, East Asian economic leaders established the principle of shared growth, promising that all groups would benefit as the economy expanded. Therefore, leaders had to obtain the support of economic elites for their pro-growth strategies. Next they persuaded the elites to share the benefits of growth with the middle class and the poor. Lastly, in order to assure the cooperation of the middle class and the poor, leaders demonstrated that these socioeconomic classes would benefit from future growth.[22] Among the mechanisms utilized to achieve this end, the following were among the most significant: comprehensive land reform programs (South Korea and Taiwan), rice and fertilizer pricing policies to assure increases in rural incomes (Indonesia), and the introduction of wealth-sharing programs (in Malaysia, to improve the lot of ethnic Malays relative to ethnic Chinese). Hong Kong and Singapore undertook massive public housing programs, and other economies assisted workers' cooperatives and established programs to encourage small and medium-size enterprises.

Building human capital was also at the heart of the developmental strategy. The Asian economies in question focused spending on education and training, first by providing universal primary education and later by increasing the availability of secondary education. In this sense, education policies contributed to more equitable income distribution, since government served large segments of the population that otherwise would have lacked access to education through their education policies.

Globalization and Regionalism

The debate over globalization versus regionalism has its origin in the dichotomous relationship between globalization and fragmentation. As we have already seen, globalization entails changes in both the intensity and scope of international interactions. With respect to its intensity, to a certain extent globalization overlaps ideas related with integration, interdependence, multilateralism, and openness. The scope of globalization points to the "geographical spread of these trends and is cognate with globalism, spatial compression, universalization and homogeneity."[23] For its part, fragmentation represents an opposite tendency that also displays two dimensions. One of these suggests disintegration, autarky, unilateralism, closeness, and isolationism, with the other dimension indicating a tendency toward nationalism or regionalism, spatial distension, separatism, and heterogeneity.

Just as the end of the Cold War provided increased impetus for globalizing tendencies in the discussion on the new world order, the 1990s saw a resurgence of fragmentationist tendencies. Fragmentation may affect the international economic arena by encouraging the formation of regional groupings. However, in comparison to previous regional economic groupings, it is less probable that the current tendency toward the creation of such blocs will lead to a repetition of the clashes of the 1930s, since contemporary regionalism is more open and trade-driven and is offset by the transnational nature of finance and production. Current regionalist tendencies are less threatening: "open regionalism means that policy is directed towards the elimination of obstacles to trade within a region . . . while at the same time doing nothing to raise external tariff barriers to the rest of the world."[24]

By 1999 there were around eighty regional agreements in force that offer privileged access to the markets of countries that make up their membership. The most prominent are the European Union (EU), the North American Free Trade Agreement (NAFTA), and the Common Market of the South (MERCOSUR, composed of Argentina, Brazil, Uruguay, and Paraguay). In fact, nearly all of the 130 members of the World Trade Organization (WTO) belong to at least one regional trade agreement. Japan, South Korea, and Hong Kong were the only exceptions. It is interesting to note that during the year 2000 each of these three countries initiated conversations with other countries or groups oriented toward undertaking studies on the feasibility, advantages, and disadvantages of signing free trade agreements. Japan has begun studies for establishing negotiations with the Association of Southeast Asian Nations (ASEAN) economies, New Zealand, South Korea, Singapore, and even Chile in the Latin American region. For its part, aside from its conversations with Japan, South Korea has successfully concluded negotiations for a free trade agreement with Chile as well.

Virtually all of these regional trade agreements arose mainly in response to the liberal orientation of the global economy. Today's economic regionalism has a very limited political agenda. Most regional agreements are focused on expanding trade within their respective blocs by means of internal tariff reduction and the elimination of external barriers. The current movement toward economic regionalism responds to three impulses. First, the regional agreements of the 1980s and '90s have emerged as an economic strategy for developing nations. The result is that both developing economies and developed economies have reached similar points of view and adopted similar policies toward market liberalization. This consensus has made it easier to coordinate governmental policies with respect to economic issues and fluctuations in the world economy. Second, regional trade agreements have proven themselves to be faster and simpler mechanisms for eliminating trade barriers than negotiations undertaken within a multilateral framework. States that have common borders have more immediate trade barriers to address, and therefore regional negotiations offer greater probabilities for making progress and attaining rewards. Finally, public debt and budgetary deficits have constrained the possibilities for implementing Keynesian policies in many developing countries. In this sense, monetary policy might also have a relevant role to play in the more internationalized economies. Thus, regional trade agreements could become very attractive because they provide political leaders with the ability to attribute certain levels of economic growth to their governmental policies. That is, regional trade agreements can be the fastest and most effective vehicle for immediate benefits.

As each of these motivations suggests, regional strategies are fully compatible with continued global economic openness. Regional accords represent clear efforts to widen and expand domestic markets through the creation of larger economic spaces. Therefore, they should be looked upon as public policy tools and not public policy objectives, since the ultimate goal is a "more gradual" integration with the globalized economy and not merely attaining membership within a regional bloc. Nonetheless, it is sometimes argued that membership in institutionalized regional integration schemes like the EU and NAFTA is a necessary precondition for the economic success of developing economies. This implies that they face the risk of being left behind, isolated from the dynamic of growing globalization. Clearly not all developing economies have participated in globalization: to date, economic dynamism has been regionally concentrated. But while the type of regionalism represented by the EU, NAFTA, and MERCOSUR is widely interpreted as contributing to global free trade, dissenting arguments see them as a trend toward the subdivision or fragmentation of the world economy, and as vehicles for pursuing the limited interests of their members to the detriment of nonmember countries.[25]

An alternative to the traditional view of regionalism and its trade blocs is "open regionalism" (OR). Open regionalism's main objective is achieving the integration of national economies into global markets. Based upon a regional foundation, it posits taking advantage of complementarities and the opportunities offered by the geographic and cultural proximity that characterizes the nations of the same region. In this sense, OR appears as another strategic option for certain groups of nations facing the challenges and opportunities of globalization. OR can also widen and deepen multilateral commitments in a regional context, and thus become a building block for multilateral openness.[26]

Movements toward regional integration accelerated sharply in Latin America during the 1990s. A proliferation of regional, subregional, and bilateral agreements is bringing about the gradual liberalization of mutual trade and growing economic and political cooperation. The region's objectives include greater and improved integration into the international system, improved international competitiveness, and the promotion of joint liberalization. This renewed tendency toward regionalism has its roots in a variety of factors. First is the historic decline of Latin American participation in international financial and trade markets, a decline aggravated by the possible global tendency toward the creation of regional megablocs formed around the United States, the European Union, and Japan. Second is the perception that, within the context of growing internationalization, the national markets of Latin America are too small and fragmented. Third is the strong association that has emerged in Latin America between regionalism and democratization.[27] We can see an affirmation of this linkage in the fact that the new schemes of regionalism, such as MERCOSUR, have established democracy as a precondition for joining and maintaining active membership.

In the case of East and Southeast Asia, the tendency toward the formation of a regional bloc, though equally deep-rooted, has had a less formal history than that of Latin America. The most institutionalized subregional grouping is ASEAN, which dates back to the 1960s. In percentage terms, inter-ASEAN trade barely grew during the 1980s, creeping from a mere 3.2 percent of total trade in 1980 to the only slightly higher level of 4 percent in 1990, with much of this trade not governed by preferential trade rules.[28] This can be explained by the fact that ASEAN was not primarily conceived as a vehicle for close economic integration, but rather as a nondiscriminatory political and economic subregional grouping. In this sense, while it may not provide the primary economic framework for its members, its political functions and traditions of cooperation have been important for conflict resolution and collective decision-making. In recent years ASEAN has faced significant challenges from other countries in East Asia—among them rapid industrialization, increases in foreign capital flows, and liberalization in the commercial and financial sectors. The response has been to create a relatively formalized, market-oriented ASEAN free-trade area (AFTA).

Liberalizing tendencies have given rise to equally innovative groupings elsewhere in the region, such as the Greater South China Economic Zone (including Hong Kong, Macao, Guangdong, Fujian, and Taiwan); the Growth Triangle (Singapore, Batam Island in Indonesia, and Johor Province in Malaysia); a Baht Zone in the border areas of Thailand, Laos, and Cambodia; and possible cooperation in the Sea of Japan that includes China, the two Koreas, and Russia. These initiatives have been taking form thanks to policies of deregulation and the easing of national rules for foreign direct investment, as well as the relocation of productive sources within the region. These informal economic zones share four salient characteristics. First, each one forms a natural economic territory that cuts across national boundaries, in which trade with neighbors has been initiated at some time or another in the past. Second, each contains both a center and a periphery, where the growth of the center tends to be constrained by its limited areas and labor force. These pressures on the center are transmitted to the periphery through trade, investment, and labor movements. Third, no formal agreements are made between the governments concerned, though in some cases we can note free trade zones established by local governments in the periphery in order to accelerate the transfer of industries from the center. Fourth, each one of these informal subregional economic zones, with the exception of the Growth Triangle, is located along borders between market and ex-centrally planned economies. In the beginning, trade and investment exchanges were severely restricted between the sides. With the end of the Cold War and the adoption of liberal reforms in the socialist economies, these border zones started to show signs of economic vitality, with the cross-border movement of goods, services, investment, and people all increasing.[29] The most significant difference that characterizes these zones, especially in comparison with NAFTA and MERCOSUR, is that they do not involve formal mechanisms for managing and directing the process of ongoing economic integration.

Transnational initiatives and organizations emerging from Asia have been conceived more on trans-Pacific terms than on exclusively regional grounds. One of the principal reasons for this is the importance of the U.S. market for

Asian economies. By the same token, U.S. trade is increasingly concentrated in Asia as well. Moreover, such institutions as the East Asia Economic Caucus, the Pacific Trade and Development Conference, the Pacific Basin Economic Council (PBEC), and the Pacific Economic Cooperation Council (PECC) constitute networks of public and private actors but not formal intergovernmental organizations, and therefore they lack decisional authority. Instead they have promoted the formation of transnational networks.

By far the most significant regional mechanism is the Asia Pacific Economic Cooperation (APEC) forum that includes Australia, New Zealand, the United States, Canada, Mexico, Chile, and Peru, as well as most East Asian economies. Established in 1989, APEC has become the principal locus for intergovernmental dialogue on economic policy issues. APEC displays a series of particular characteristics that make it different from other integration schemes, especially those in the West. Worth singling out is its strong emphasis on the concept of open regionalism, which translates into two principles: a commitment to nondiscrimination and the willingness to consider new members. Another feature is the reliance on voluntarism. Negotiation takes place only among the "like minded," and does not affect all sectors, with the result that the organization tolerates very different speeds of liberalization and reform.[30] Compared to formal free trade agreements, such as NAFTA, and other formal forms of integration like the European Union or MERCOSUR, member economies have not displayed keen interest in close policy coordination. Perhaps the fact that the region did not face a severe crisis until the 1997–1998 period also explains why the desire to create a regional organization with greater degrees of commitment and institutionality remained limited.

APEC is further restrained by the economic and political heterogeneity of its membership. On a political level, East Asia still bears witness to the Cold War. One of the factors that has the greatest impact upon APEC is the accommodation of China and Taiwan within one organization. In addition, certain regional fears are still visible with respect to the roles and influence that Japan and the United States could exert over other Asian economies. Last but not least, the ASEAN countries fear that their integration efforts could be diluted by inclusion in a wider organization. And in economic terms, East Asian nations remain highly diverse—much more so than countries of Latin America. Singapore and Hong Kong are free ports. In Korea and Taiwan initial trade and exchange reforms date to the early 1960s, but industrial policies have formed integral parts of their growth strategies. For its part, China is a reforming socialist economy that still possesses a substantial array of discretionary controls and will probably undergo significant future reform.

Conclusion

Globalization can be conceived as a process that does not have a single, fixed, or determined destination, whether it is understood in terms of a perfectly integrated world market, a global society, or a global civilization. A priori, there is no reason to suppose that globalization should simply evolve in one direction or be understood in relation to one ideal condition (perfect global markets). Furthermore, whatever the interpretation of globalization applied (that of the Hyperglobalists, the Skeptics, or the Transformationalists), there is no single recipe for policies and strategic options that developing economies should follow in order to cope with the demands that globalization imposes upon them.

Unfortunately, there is a certain inclination among developing nations to understand globalization merely as the global diffusion of Western modernity, which is to say, Westernization. They tend to equate globalization with the spread of Western capitalism and Western institutions. As a result, it should be emphasized that globalization is a process and not a singular condition. It does not reflect a linear development logic, nor does it presuppose or prefigure a world society or a world community. On the contrary, globalization reflects the emergence of interregional networks and systems of interactions and exchange. Within this process, a complex transnational interconnection takes place that affects the relationships between communities, states, international institutions, nongovernmental organizations, and multinational corporations that, in turn, make up the world order. Globalization involves individual actions as well as institutional interactions.

How can developing areas respond to this phenomenon? Both East Asia and Latin America, in different phases and under different circumstances, have based their development strategy on externally oriented growth. Consequently, both regions receive ample benefits from advances in the liberalization of global trade. These benefits are not merely limited to an improvement in their terms of trade, but relate to the creation of jobs, access to greater degrees of technology and technological innovation, and incentives for productive activities, to cite but a few examples. This leaves governments with the task of defining and implementing mechanisms that permit the constant improvement of the country's position in world trade. This is possible by means of the formulation of consistent, coherent, and updated plans on social and educational matters, as well as public infrastructure.

While trade openness can bring with it great benefits, financial openness can become a double-edged sword if an adequate infrastructure, promotion policies, and clear safeguards are lacking. The Asian crisis of 1997–1998 serves as a bitter and recent reminder of this truth. But the occurrence of such a calamity in relatively open economies does not mean that the solution lies in closing the economies. Latin America and East Asia both depend upon foreign capital for financing their growth and development, and closing their economies to these capital flows would imply a greater economic and social cost. As a result, it would be better for emerging economies to take note of the lessons to be learned.

One of first lessons is to recognize the importance of exercising a certain degree of supervision over the magnitude of capital flows that come from abroad. Unchecked growth and a lack of control over short-term net foreign debt and liquid liabilities result in a greater degree of vulnerability for the host economy.[31] Furthermore, the creation of mechanisms that promote productive investment over speculative investment is highly desirable. In contrast to short-term flows, long-term capital flows translate into productive investments that tend to increase the receptor's capacity to efficiently absorb them. The central point is not to eliminate foreign capital inflows, but to prevent them from dominating local markets

Another issue relates to the opening of the capital account. Experiences ranging from the Latin American debt crisis of the 1980s to the Asian financial crisis of the 1990s demonstrate that indiscriminate opening brings with it elevated costs in those economies that have not developed strong, stable, and competitive financial systems. For those emerging economies facing pressure to liberalize their capital account, an optimum policy for carrying out this process would be a gradual and selective opening oriented toward the long term, adjusted to the consolidation of other reforms of a structural nature. In this sense, the quality and maturity of the financial and banking sectors is of extreme importance, as well as the existence of measures aimed at reducing the vulnerability of the emerging markets to the volatility of capital flows. Successful illustrations are the *encaje* rates used by both Chile and Colombia, which affect the relative price of short-term and speculative capital flows by effectively placing a tax upon them that is not shouldered by long-term capital flows.

Social policies are put to the test during situations of economic and/or financial crisis. The lower socioeconomic strata, especially the poor, almost always bear the largest burden at such times. At present, social policies are awash in uncertainty. Under the neoliberal model, it has not been possible to create a social safety net that is sufficiently comprehensive for mitigating the negative impacts of globalization. In the case of Latin America, the result has been an increase in crime, greater social vulnerability, as well as the risk of producing profound disillusionment with politics. In this sense, pursuit of the Third Way could make it possible to combine social solidarity with economic dynamism. This approach still lacks a firm theoretic base, however, as it essentially represents a combination of benevolent intentions with a critique of neoliberal failings. It is primarily a rationalization for political compromise between left and right, in which the left moves closer to the right.[32] Perhaps the economic miracle registered by the Northeast Asian economies could provide a basis for drawing lessons for creating more equitable social foundations, greater social mobility, and more egalitarian opportunities.

Globalization is a fact. So is regionalization. International tendencies demonstrate that these phenomena are not necessarily mutually exclusive. The most conspicuous example of regional integration is the European Union, but it is undeniable that this is a phenomenon happening all over the world—in Asia, Latin America, Africa, and Eastern Europe. In Latin America, the integration movement has led to the initiation of negotiations for the creation of a Free Trade Agreement of the Americas, or FTAA, that would stretch from Alaska to Tierra del Fuego. Simultaneously, a multiplicity of regional, bilateral, and even trilateral agreements have emerged, and extraregional agreements are also under negotiation. The Asian nations are also following this tendency and even Japan, one of the most reluctant countries with respect to this type of formal integration, is exploring whether or not to enter into free trade agreements with neighboring or Pacific Rim economies. For developing countries, regional groupings can be an effective tool that allows them to achieve a gradual insertion within the globalization process. The challenge is to achieve a mode of insertion that builds upon existing capacities, generates productive investment, and facilitates participation in and access to technological progress and scientific creation.

Globalization has spawned criticism and occasional protest. Beneficial or not, however, the process is here to stay and evolve. Events such as the terrible attacks on the World Trade Center in New York and the Pentagon in Washington, D.C., represent assaults upon the very heart of economic/financial globalization and U.S. national security. Whether or not the attack truly came in response to economic transformations led by the West, and chiefly by the United States, it certainly made a horrible but effective use of key elements in the process (information technology, capital mobility, strategic alliances, and informal networks). The international community's response to September 11 and the U.S.–led campaign against terrorism will not deter, divert, or change the process of economic globalization; developing economies still need to devise appropriate strategies in light of new economic realities. The international economic contraction, the financial crises, the 9/11 attacks, and the war against terrorism mean that developing economies are facing new challenges and vulnerabilities as they struggle to cope with the demands of globalization.

Notes

1. Hernán B. Gutierrez and Claudio M. Rojas, "La institucionalidad pública chilena y su contribución al desarrollo regional en el marco de la globalización," *Estudios Regionales*, no. 10 (Universidad del Bío Bío, December 1998): 1.

2. Carlos J. Moneta, "Los procesos de globalización, reflexiones sobre su concepción y efectos sobre la evolución del sistema mundial," *Estudios Internacionales*, no. 106 (1994): 175.

3. D. Held, A. McDrew, D. Goldblatt, and J. Perraton, *Global Transformations: Politics, Economics, and Culture* (Oxford: Polity Press, 1999), 3.

4. Kenichi Ohmae, *El fin del estado nación* (Santiago: Editorial Andrés Bello, 1997), 5.

5. D. Held, et al., *Global Transformations*, 6.

6. See Anthony Giddens, *The Consequences of Modernity* (Stanford: Stanford University Press, 1990); and James N. Rosenau, *Turbulence in World Politics: A Theory of Change and Continuity* (Princeton: Princeton University Press, 1990).

7. Stephen J. Kobrin, "The Architecture of Globalization: State Sovereignty in a Networked Global Economy," in *Governments, Globalization, and International Business*, ed. John H. Dunning (London: Oxford University Press, 1997), 149.

8. Geoffrey Garret, "Capital Mobility, Trade, and Domestic Markets," in *Internationalization and Domestic Politics*, eds. Robert O. Keohane and Helen V. Milner (New York: Cambridge University Press, 1996), 89.

9. Organization for Economic Cooperation and Development, *Technology and the Economy: The Key Relationship* (Paris: OECD, 1992), 78.

10. Peter H. Smith, "Strategic Options for Latin America," in *Latin America in the New International System*, eds. Joseph S. Tulchin and Ralph H. Espach (Boulder: Lynne Rienner, 2001), 35–72, with quote on 36.

11. SELA, "La crisis asiática: Riesgos y oportunidades para América Latina" (paper presented at international seminar on The Globalization of Financial Markets and its Effects on the Emerging Economies, Santiago, Chile, March 1999), 4–5.

12. Walden Bello, "The Answer: De-Globalize," *Far Eastern Economic Review* (April 29, 1999).

13. Ray Kiely, *Globalisation, (post-)Modernity, and the Third World* (London: Routledge, 1998), 11.

14. Stephan Haggard and Sylvia Maxfield, "The Political Economy of Financial Internationalization in the Developing World," in *Internationalization*, 10.

15. Stephany Griffith-Jones, "A New Financial Architecture for Reducing Risks and the Severity of Crises" (paper presented at international seminar on The Globalization of Financial Markets, Santiago, Chile, March 1999), 9.

16. Richard N. Haass and Robert E. Litan, "Globalization and its Discontents: Navigating the Dangers of a Tangled World," *Foreign Affairs* 77, no. 3 (May /June 1998): 4.

17. Jorge Nef, "Estado, poder, y políticas: Una visión crítica," in *Cambio social y políticas públicas*, ed. Raúl Urzua (Santiago: Centro de Análisis de Políticas Públicas, Universidad de Chile, 1997).

18. Anthony Giddens, *The Third Way and Its Critics* (Cambridge: Polity Press, 2000), 32.

19. Giddens, *The Third Way,* 35.

20. Rosenau, *Turbulence in World Politics,* 11.

21. Manuel Castells, "La era de la información, economía, sociedad y cultura," *Fin del Milenio,* vol. III (Mexico: Siglo Veintiuno Editores, 1999), 275.

22. A World Bank Policy Research Report, *The East Asian Miracle: Economic Growth and Public Policy* (New York: Oxford University Press, 1993), 11.

23. Ian Clark, *Globalization and Fragmentation: International Relations in the Twentieth Century* (New York: Oxford University Press, 1997), 1.

24. Clark, *Globalization and Fragmentation,* 189.

25. Rafael Urriola and Andrés Rebolledo, "Regionalismo, multilateralismo, y coordinación en la integración económica," in *Globalización, América Latina, y la diplomacia de las cumbres,* ed. Francisco Rojas (Santiago: FLACSO-Chile/McGraw-Hill, 1998), 108.

26. CEPAL, *El regionalismo abierto en América Latina y el Caribe: La integración económica al servicio de la transformación productiva con equidad* (Santiago: CEPAL, 1994).

27. Alberto van Klaveren, "América Latina: Hacia un regionalismo abierto," *Estudios Internacionales,* no. 117 (January-March 1997): 64, 66.

28. Fiona Butler, "Regionalism and Integration," in *The Globalization of World Politics, an Introduction to International Relations,* eds. John Baylis and Steve Smith (New York: Oxford University Press, 1999), 416.

29. For more detailed information about subregional informal economic zones, see *Economic Dynamism in the Pacific,* ed. Grahame Thompson (London: Routledge, The Open University, 1998), 163–182.

30. Stephan Haggard, "Regionalism in Asia and the Americas," in *The Political Economy of Regionalism,* eds. Edward Mansfield and Helen Milner (New York: Columbia University Press, 1997), 44–45.

31. Ricardo Ffrench-Davis, "Globalización de la volatilidad financiera: Desafíos para las economías emergentes," in *Crisis financieras en países "exitosos,"* ed. Ricardo Ffrench-Davis (Santiago: McGraw-Hill, 2001), 12.

32. Giddens, *The Third Way,* 11.

PART I
THE ECONOMIC CONNECTION

WHAT IS THE NATURE OF THE ECONOMIC CONNECTION between East Asia and Latin America in the face of rapid transformations in the global economy? How solid is the economic foundation of this potential partnership?

To begin the study of such questions, Sayuri Kuwabara traces trends and oscillations in recent flows of capital from Japan to Latin America. Historically Japan has shown relatively modest interest in Latin America, but conditions changed during the 1990s. Latin America accounts for about one-tenth of total foreign direct investment (FDI) outflows from Japan, with Mexico and Brazil the principal destinations. Portfolio investment has also surged in recent years, and Japan has been a leading source of official development assistance (ODA) for the region. Kuwabara suggests that free trade agreements could provide a potentially powerful mechanism to attract additional Japanese FDI into Latin America, as well as to solidify the existing capital flows.

Taik-Hwan Jyoung assesses the status and future of economic relations between South Korea and Latin America. Korea's economic engagement in Latin America has increased massively in the past few years. The country's investors have in particular sought out the Latin American market after the increase in Korean labor costs in the late 1980s, and as Korean firms have developed strategies to take full advantage of globalization. With its expanding middle classes and its industrial complementarities, Latin America was becoming an increasingly desirable site for investment. Outward FDI to Latin America suffered from Korea's financial crisis of the late 1990s. On a positive note, though, Latin America became an attractive export market in the face of the post-crisis devaluation of the *won*.

Shoji Nishijima and Akio Hosono analyze current and imminent "modes of economic integration" between the two regions, with special attention to governmental policy and the recent surge of interest in free trade agreements (FTAs). They examine the economic logic of bilateral FTAs and their recent evolution. And as they demonstrate, Japan has embraced the FTA concept to the point where it is exploring the possibility of bilateral agreements with Chile and Mexico. Moreover, Japan's active participation in the Forum for East Asia–Latin American Cooperation (FEALAC) provides further evidence of its growing interest in Latin America and of its hopes that interregional accords can serve as building blocks for a new economic world order.

To round out this section, Kotaro Horisaka adds an insightful discussion of decision-making processes in private business firms and their surprising impacts on regional economic integration and on connections between Asia and Latin America. As governments have retreated from the center stage of economic planning, the movers of investment capital—the private business firms—have stepped to the foreground. Liberalization of trade and investment regimes as well as ever-heightening competition in both Asia and Latin America have unleashed important intraregional cross-border investment flows and alliances. Moreover, some Asian companies have taken the additional step of moving toward integration with Latin America, creating cross-regional production links as part of their global network. Further development of such ties will require close collaboration between business and governments in both regions.

Taken together, the essays in this section leave two clear impressions. One is that the economic relationship between East Asia and Latin America is already rather deep. The other is that this relationship is bound to intensify within the near future.

2

Capital Flows from Japan to Latin America

Sayuri Kuwabara

HISTORICALLY, JAPAN HAS SHOWN MODEST INTEREST in Latin America. Following World War II, however, Japan began to expand its involvement in Latin America by implementing policies revolving around economic interactions and migration. During the 1960s and 1970s, Japan's private sector greatly increased its activities in the region to become a prominent investor and trader. After the debt crisis of 1982, while the private sector's interest toward the region receded, the Japanese government continued to increase its economic assistance to the region as part of its official development assistance (ODA) policy and extended its support and financial contributions to solve Latin America's debt problem.

In spite of their growing importance, little has been known about capital flows from Japan to Latin America, and little scholarly attention has been paid to the topic. Recent research has been largely oriented toward explanations of Japan's outward foreign direct investment (FDI) or ODA policy toward developing countries in Asia. This chapter provides a comprehensive survey of capital flows from Japan to Latin America in the 1990s with a view to understanding why the Japanese private sector retreated from the region while the government committed its official funds to help Latin America's economic development. The essay traces the roots of the problem to Japan's exceptionally prolonged economic stagnation in the post-bubble period and to characteristics of the Japanese corporate system. It is my expectation that, once the Japanese economy returns to a course of self-supported recovery, private capital flows from Japan to Latin America will be reactivated. One would also anticipate that the level of ODA provided to the region will be maintained unless the government changes its use of ODA as a principal foreign policy tool.

The chapter is structured as follows. An opening section describes the recent development of the Japanese economy as the background for the Japanese private sector's retreat from international financial activities. A subsequent section analyzes financial flows from Japan, both in aggregate terms and with regard to private and public components. Although this essay mainly covers the 1990s, the role of Japan in solving the Latin American debt problem is explained in light of its importance. A final section offers some proposals that deem the reactivation of capital flows from Japan to Latin America useful.

The Japanese Economy

Japan's economic performance was lackluster through most of the 1990s. Along with rapid expansion in the real economy, there was alarmingly high inflation in land and stock prices. When monetary policy was tightened in 1990 in an effort to puncture the excesses of the so-called bubble economy, stock prices fell sharply and economic growth began to decelerate. The balance sheets of many financial institutions deteriorated as they became burdened by huge amounts of non-performing loans. Declining consumer and business confidence led to a prolonged downturn in the economy. Real GDP growth decelerated to just 0.3 percent in 1993, largely on account of business investment. There was a mild recovery in 1994–1995, but this fell far short of initial expectations.

After another short-lived recovery in 1996, the economy plunged back into recession in late 1997. The downturn was initiated by a larger-than-anticipated fall in household spending after the April 1997 consumption tax hike and cuts in public investment. Further downward pressure came from a reduction in domestic bank lending, propelled by the desire to strengthen balance sheets in advance of the "Big Bang" financial reforms and the impending overhaul of bank regulation, as well as from the disruptive impact of the failure of a major bank and two large securities firms in November 1997. The Asia crisis compounded this weakness through its impact on external demand, as well as undermining confidence more generally. As a result, GDP declined by 1.1 percent in 1998. Following a modest recovery in 1999, the economy strengthened in early 2000 and, thanks to the buoyant world economy, real GDP grew by 1.5 percent for the year as a whole.

Responding to increasing evidence of weak activity, the government acted to inject substantial fiscal stimulus. Policy packages involved spending on public works, income tax cuts, credit guarantees for bank loans to small and medium-sized enterprises, incentives for housing construction, and so forth. The Bank of Japan has continued to ease monetary conditions by cutting interest rates and supporting credit intermediation, while other government financial institutions have also been mobilized to relax financing constraints. In spite of these expansionary policies, the economy picked up only modestly. The private sector's propensity to spend declined and the government's attempt to boost output growth through fiscal stimulus had only a temporary effect. The unemployment rate reached 4.7 percent in 1999, the highest rate in the post–World War II period.

Despite these oscillations, Japan has had a current account surplus ever since fiscal year (FY) 1981. But the size of the current account surplus both in absolute terms and in relative terms to GDP has fluctuated sharply, mainly reflecting changes in trade surplus. The income balance has also persistently been a surplus because of an increase in the country's net external assets. In contrast to its trade and income balances, Japan has had a deficit in its service balance and net current transfers for two reasons: First, a growing number of Japanese citizens took advantage of the sharp appreciation of the yen after the Plaza Accord of 1985, and second, there was an expansion in overseas grant aid.

Japan's capital and financial accounts typically run large deficits. Movement in capital and financial accounts was also volatile during much of the 1990s, partly reflecting worries on the part of foreign investors about the state of Japan's economy and, more recently, Japanese institutional investors chasing higher returns on overseas financial markets. Although the financial account deficit fell by nearly 75 percent between 1993 and 1996—reflecting the corresponding easing in the current account surplus—it rose again sharply in 1997–1998 as there was a very sharp increase in short-term loan assets, which pushed up the "other investment asset" category. To a large extent, this reflected increased loans by Japan's banks to their subsidiaries and to other Japanese companies in Asia as the region's deepening financial crisis made Western banks reluctant to lend. Net outflows fell sharply in 1999, reflecting both the reversal of substantial short-term bank outflows, as well as increased foreign purchases of equities as the economy turned around.

With the exception of 1990, when it was overtaken by the newly reunified Germany, Japan has held the position of the world's largest net creditor nation. The growth in net overseas assets is the result of a huge current account surplus and a capital and financial account deficit that less than offset that surplus.

In order to forecast future developments in current account balances, and thus, the position of Japan as a net exporter of capital, it will be useful to analyze investment-saving (I-S) balances, as current account surplus equals aggregate net saving by definition. It is widely believed that Japan's current

TABLE 2.1
Japan: Selected Economic Indicators, 1992–2000

	1992	*1993*	*1994*	*1995*	*1996*	*1997*	*1998*	*1999*	*2000*
Real GDP Growth Rate (%)	1.0	0.3	0.6	1.6	3.9	0.9	−0.3	−1.3	0.5
Inflation (CPI, annual average, %)	1.7	1.2	0.7	−0.1	0.1	1.8	0.6	−0.3	−0.6
Unemployment Rate (annual average, %)	2.2	2.5	2.9	3.1	3.4	3.4	4.1	4.7	4.7
General Government Balance (% of GDP)	1.5	−1.6	−2.2	−3.5	−4.2	−3.2	−4.5	−6.8	−8.0
M2 + CDs (end of year, % change)	0.6	1.1	2.9	3.2	2.9	3.8	3.9	2.6	2.2
Bank Lending (end of year, % change)	2.5	0.5	−0.2	2.1	−0.4	0.0	−4.7	−5.9	−3.8
Exchange Rate (average yen/dollar rate)	126.7	111.2	102.2	94.1	108.8	121.0	130.9	113.9	107.8
Interest Rates (3-month CDs, average, %)	4.3	2.8	2.1	1.1	0.5	0.5	0.6	0.1	0.2

Source: International Monetary Fund.

TABLE 2.2
Balance of Payments and International Investment Position of Japan, 1991–2000 (US$ billions)

	1991	*1992*	*1993*	*1994*	*1995*	*1996*	*1997*	*1998*	*1999*	*2000*
Current Account	68.20	112.57	131.64	130.26	111.04	65.88	94.35	120.70	106.87	116.88
(as of % of GDP)	(2.0)	(3.0)	(3.1)	(2.8)	(2.2)	(1.4)	(2.2)	(3.2)	(2.5)	(2.5)
Trade Balance	96.08	124.76	139.42	144.19	131.79	83.56	101.690	122.39	123.32	116.72
Service Balance	−41.79	−43.96	−43.08	−48.06	−57.36	−62.24	−54.15	−49.42	−54.16	−47.62
Income Balance	25.96	35.60	40.41	40.23	44.29	53.55	55.74	56.57	49.84	57.63
Net Current Transfer	−12.04	−3.83	−5.10	−6.11	−7.68	−9.00	−8.83	−8.84	−12.14	−9.83
Capital Account	−1.20	−1.30	−1.46	−1.85	−2.23	−3.29	−4.05	−14.45	−16.47	−9.26
Financial Account	−67.66	−100.28	−102.21	−85.11	−63.98	−28.10	−118.05	−116.76	−31.11	−75.54
Direct Investment	−30.33	−14.63	−13.71	−17.18	−22.47	−23.24	−22.86	−21.35	−9.96	−23.30
Portfolio Investment	45.71	−27.36	−69.85	−27.44	−26.26	−33.81	32.13	−39.18	−27.48	−35.97
Financial Derivatives	−1.32	−2.58	−1.03	0.23	−10.32	−7.33	−3.39	−0.85	5.10	−14.36
Other Investments	−81.73	−58.68	−17.63	−40.72	−4.94	36.29	−123.93	−55.39	1.22	1.22
Net Errors & Omissions	−7.73	−10.38	−0.50	−18.03	13.78	0.64	34.31	4.36	16.97	16.87
Overall Balance	−8.39	0.62	27.47	25.27	58.61	35.14	6.57	−6.16	76.26	48.95
Net International										
Investment Position	684.34	514.85	612.04	690.32	817.6	891.02	958.73	1153.64	829.12	1157.93
Assets	2006.51	2035.24	2180.04	2424.24	2632.86	2652.61	2737.45	2986.33	3013.60	3012.17
Liabilities	1622.17	1520.39	1568.84	1733.92	1815.26	1761.59	1778.72	1832.69	2184.48	1854.24

Source: IMF, *International Financial Statistics.*

account surplus will shrink but will not turn into a deficit. According to one private think tank's projection, Japan's current account/GDP ratio will stay at 2.3 percent in 2005 and will decrease to 0.4 percent in 2025.[1] The disaggregate projection for I-S balances is as follows. The net savings ratio in the household sector will decline gradually as a result of the aging of society, although the short-term outlook for private consumption remains weak and the net household saving ratio remains high because of uncertainty stemming from corporate restructuring and high unemployment. The corporate sector had a net investment position for most of the 1990s. However it will return to an excess saving position in the future as business fixed investment is likely to shrink because of a decline in the growth potential of the Japanese economy. At the same time, Japanese firms will be forced to increase overseas investment instead of investing domestically. As for the general government sector, during the 1990s, there has been a substantial deterioration in public finance, with the I-S balance swinging from near-equilibrium to a net investment of nearly 9 percent of GDP, because of the stagnation of tax collection associated with an economic slowdown and stimulatory fiscal policy. Given the slow progress of fiscal consolidation, although the fiscal deficit will begin to decline, it will not shrink very quickly. Furthermore, the social security surplus, which is used partly to finance the investment of local government and public corporations, continues to shrink rapidly from a peak of 3.7 percent of GDP in 1990 to 1.2 percent of GDP in 2000. A further deterioration of public finances is likely to result from the rapidly aging population, which should eventually turn the social security surplus into a deficit. In the short- to medium-term, however, Japan will continue to have the largest current account surplus, and thus be the largest capital exporter in the world, as a projection prepared by the IMF shows.[2]

Capital Flows to Developing Countries

In Japan, financial flows to developing countries are divided into four categories: official development assistance (ODA), other official flows (OOF), private flows (PF), and grants by private nonprofit agencies.[3] Recent trends in official flows have included an upturn (likely temporary) in aid flows, and the launching of an enhanced debt-relief program for heavily indebted poor countries (HIPCs).

Trends in recent private capital flows to developing countries have undergone three fundamental changes. First, Japanese firms' and financial institutions' retreat from lending activities and portfolio investments abroad to levels last seen in the early 1990s is evident. This reflects their need for business restructuring as well as heightened risk aversion after the events of 1997–1999 in international

TABLE 2.3
Financial Flows to Developing Countries, 1994–2000 (US$ millions)

	1994	*1995*	*1996*	*1997*	*1998*	*1999*	*2000*
Official Development Assistance (ODA):							
Bilateral grants	5,423	6,434	5,576	5,039	4,949	5,539	5,813
Bilateral grant assistance	2,403	2,973	2,396	2,018	2,168	2,340	2,109
Bilateral technical assistance	3,020	3,462	3,181	2,021	2,782	3,199	3,705
Bilateral loans	4,257	4,123	2,780	1,574	3,657	4,959	4,959
Bilateral ODA Total	9,680	10,557	8,356	6,613	8,606	10,498	9,640
Contributions to multilateral institutions	3,788	4,170	1,252	2,823	2,126	4,888	3,779
ODA Total	*13,469*	*14,728*	*9,608*	*9,435*	*10,732*	*15,385*	*13,419*
Other Official Outflows (OOF):							
Export Credits (over 1 year)	616	939	−185	−374	1,620	−755	−1,552
Direct investment and others	614	3,793	1,930	4,733	8,560	7,242	−3,052
Finance to multilateral institutions	2,070	1,021	−67	121	2,076	1,231	−252
OOF Total	*3,300*	*5,753*	*1,678*	*4,480*	*12,257*	*7,718*	*−4,855*
Private Flows (PF):							
Export Credits (over 1 year)	1,701	3,079	−1,427	−3,452	−3,905	−2,292	−358
Direct investment	7,437	9,497	8,338	15,126	11,613	7,882	6,191
Other bilateral securities and claims	5,263	10,434	22,061	9,017	−3,037	−4,546	478
Finance to multilateral institutions	2,870	−35	−581	−1,411	−4,579	−4,114	−52
PF Total	*11,531*	*22,975*	*28,392*	*19,280*	*92*	*−3,070*	*6,259*
Grants by Private Voluntary Agencies	*213*	*216*	*232*	*223*	*203*	*261*	*231*
Total Official and Private Flows	*28,513*	*43,671*	*39,910*	*33,418*	*23,282*	*20,294*	*15,053*

Source: Ministry of Finance.

financial markets. Second, the reduction in private capital flows also reflects a collapse in demand for external financing in rapidly adjusting countries in East Asia and elsewhere. Third, and in marked contrast, FDI flows, which remained resilient during this crisis, have now become the single largest item of more stable long-term capital flows from Japan to developing countries.

Official Development Assistance (ODA)

For Japan, ODA is an integral part of the nation's foreign policy, and is essentially based on economic and diplomatic foundations.[4] To address the plight of the many people who are still suffering from poverty in developing countries, as stated in its ODA Charter, Japan supports the "self-help efforts" of developing countries to enable their "economic take-off." The philosophy of Japan's ODA is largely based on the country's own postwar experience. To rebuild its economy after World War II, Japan obtained loans from the World Bank to develop its core infrastructure and industry.

Until the early 1970s, almost all development assistance was directed to Asian countries, partly because of the U.S. government's pressure to make financial contributions to the capitalist countries of Asia in the context of the Vietnam War, and partly because of Japan's efforts to expand its markets (figure 2.1). Much of the assistance was tied-aid loan and was used to purchase goods and services from Japan. With the growing importance of its role in the world economy, the Japanese government started to increase the ODA budget in the mid-seventies. At the same time, it diversified the destination of ODA and increased the share of untied loans. Since the late 1970s, several ODA doubling plans

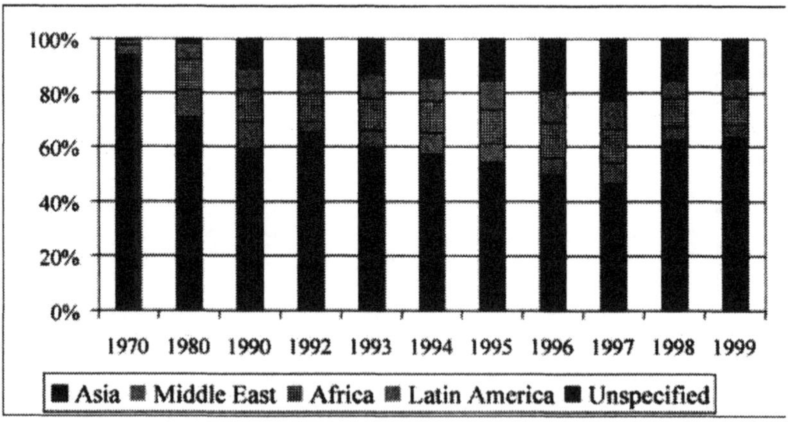

FIGURE 2.1
Regional Distribution of Japan's Bilateral ODA, 1970–1999
Source: Japan's ODA: Annual Report 2000.

(1978–1980, 1981–1985, and 1986–1992), helped by the rise of the yen, made Japan a major aid donor.[5] After continuous expansion, in 1997 the aid budget was cut by 10 percent in the context of overall fiscal reform. However, the further cut was frozen and a new tied-aid loan facility to help Asian countries affected by financial crisis boosted aid volume in the next two years. Thus, in 1998, Japan's bilateral ODA disbursement increased to US$8.6 billion, up 30.8 percent from the previous year, and to US$10.5 billion in 1999, up 22.0 percent from the previous year. In recent years there have been increasingly strident calls to review and reduce Japan's ODA budget, however, especially in light of the weakness of the economy and the growing need for fiscal reform.

According to the Development Assistance Committee (DAC) of the OECD, Japan was the second largest donor to Latin America following the United States in 1998, accounting for 12 percent of total bilateral and multilateral aid to the region. Moreover, the number of Latin American countries to which Japan was the largest donor more than doubled, from 5 in 1993 to 12 in 1994, and further increased to 17 in 1997. A breakdown by recipient country reveals that Mexico and Brazil are major destinations of Japan's increased ODA to Latin America. The Japanese government maintains that one of the important points to be considered for the concession of economic assistance is the economically and politically important roles played by those countries, although it does not state what these roles specifically entail for those countries. A substantial part of the increase in Japan's ODA to the region has been offered to poor nations like Bolivia, Paraguay, and the Dominican Republic, where many Japanese immigrants and their descendants live. Other major recipients of Japan's ODA in the region have been relatively low-income Central American countries that are frequently hit by natural disasters.

Other Official Flows (OOF)

In addition to ODA, economic cooperation through the Japan Bank for International Cooperation (JBIC), or the former Export-Import Bank of Japan (JEXIM), is another major component of official flows.[6] The financial facilities offered by JBIC include export loans, import loans, overseas investment loans, and untied loans. JBIC also provides guarantees to private financial institutions, short-term loans designed to finance the external transactions of the governments of developing nations (bridge loans), and equity participation in the overseas projects of Japanese companies. The JBIC's financial activities focus on projects in developing countries where local private financial institutions cannot cover financing on their own. Because JBIC's mandate is the support of internationalization for Japanese companies, and JBIC is required by its statutes to cofinance with private financial institutions, the bank plays a significant role in supplementing and encouraging financing in the private sector.

As for the geographical distribution of JBIC's operations, nearly half had been destined for Asia and Oceania, but Asia's share increased to more than 60 percent in 1997 and 1998, reflecting increased support to Asian countries. Latin America has been the second largest destination of JBIC's overseas financial activities.

JBIC's recent financing activities with Latin America were characterized by support for a variety of projects that promoted exports and contributed to improvements in the environment for foreign direct investment, mainly by upgrading infrastructure. Because of JBIC's main role as a catalyst of private capital flows to developing countries, the major destination of economic cooperation through JBIC's financial activities are relatively large and advanced economies in the region, such as Argentina, Brazil, Chile, Colombia, Mexico, and Peru.

Japan and the Latin American Debt Crisis

With respect to official flows, the role played by the Japanese government in solving the Latin American debt crisis in the 1980s deserves special mention. The Japanese government extended its support and financial contributions to U.S. initiatives such as the Baker and Brady Plans directly through ODA or JEXIM loans, as well as indirect assistance through IFIs. The 1985 Baker Plan, which focused on new money from private banks, targeted the fifteen most heavily indebted countries, ten of which were in Latin America. The Japanese government committed billions of dollars in financial contributions to IFIs. It also committed itself to using JEXIM's bilateral untied loans to promote public and private capital flows to middle-income indebted countries, though actions by commercial banks were minimal. The 1989 Brady Plan, which was based on the Japan-initiated Miyazawa Plan, was the debt and interest rate reduction scheme. Before the July 1989 Arche Summit, the Japanese government expanded its "Capital Recycling Plan" of May of 1987, which aimed to promote private and official flows to developing countries, from the original amount of US$30 billion to US$65 billion, and pledged that this expanded program would support the Brady Plan. Mexico, the first country that applied the Plan, in mid-1989, received US$4.1 billion from IFIs and an additional US$1.9 billion from JEXIM. Following the Mexican case, JEXIM made untied loan commitments to Venezuela (1990), Argentina (1993), Ecuador (1995), and Peru (1996) in the context of the Brady Plan.[7]

The Japanese government's response to the Latin American debt crisis can be explained by its relationship with the United States and with Japanese commercial banks. U.S. pressure on Japan seems to have been a vital reason why Japan has gone along with U.S. strategy.[8] In the 1980s, tension between the two countries mounted because of their trade imbalances. The Latin American economic crisis was allegedly responsible for 25 percent of the drop in the total U.S. trade balance in the 1980s, and in order to improve their balance of payments and to service their debt, Latin American debtors cut their imports and adopted aggressive export-oriented strategies that contributed to the decrease in U.S. exports and imports in the region. In view of U.S. budget difficulties in the mid-1980s, Japan was seen as the only possible alternative provider of significant financial resources to the heavily indebted region. The Japanese government appears to have used its enhanced financial commitment to Latin America as a foreign policy tool to maintain good relations with the United States and other creditor countries.

Meanwhile, through their syndicated loans of the 1970s, Japanese commercial banks had heavy lending exposure to developing countries at the onset of the 1982 debt crisis. In subsequent years, Japanese banks put pressure on the government to secure their exit from Latin America and to provide them with a better environment for absorbing such debt without excessively impairing their business performance. As a result, the role of Japan's government in protecting banks from failure became prominent in the 1980s. In other words, this degree of mutual dependence, together with the government's commitment to protecting the Japanese banking sector, led the Japanese government to react to the demands of private banks.[9]

Foreign Direct Investment (FDI)

Against the backdrop of the yen's appreciation in the latter half of 1980s, Japanese firms ambitiously expanded production capacity in North America, Western Europe, Southeast Asia, and other parts of the world.[10] As a result, in 1989, Japan became the world's largest FDI supplier, recording an annual outflow of $US44 billion. With the collapse of the asset bubble, Japanese firms have had to face higher capital costs, a slowdown in domestic demand, and increasing competition from other production networks in Asia. Consequently, Japan's outward FDI flows decreased from 1990 to 1993. However, the second *endaka* (strong revaluation of the yen against the U.S. dollar), in the early 1990s, set the stage for a surge of Japanese activities in Asia. FDI bottomed out in 1993 and, despite the overall sluggishness of the economy, it has continued to recover since then (except in 1998 and 2000, when FDI to the United States almost halved compared to previous years).

The most striking change in the composition of Japanese outward FDI by host region (country) is that, after declining sharply, Europe's share increased rapidly during the second half of the 1990s, and the region replaced the United States as the largest destination of Japanese FDI (see table 2.4). This

TABLE 2.4
Japan's Outward Investment by Country and Region, FY1990–2000 (100 million yen)

	1990	*1991*	*1992*	*1993*	*1994*	*1995*	*1996*	*1997*	*1998*	*1999*	*2000*
North America:	39,958	25,763	18,972	17,591	18,525	22,394	25,933	26,247	14,011	27,629	13,562
United States	38,402	24,671	17,993	16,936	18,016	21,845	24,789	25,486	13,207	24,868	13,413
Canada	1,557	1,093	978	656	509	549	1,144	761	803	2,760	149
Latin America:	5,289	4,547	3,525	3,889	5,499	3,741	5,008	7,775	8,274	8,295	5,783
Argentina	304	55	24	39	21	110	15	70	164	9	45
Brazil	892	235	606	492	1,308	287	993	1,451	597	730	249
Chile	43	102	35	4	14	136	2	28	15	15	31
Mexico	248	261	78	61	651	202	128	393	106	1,655	230
Venezuela	113	138	32	23	6	27	66	44	31	72	2
Offshore Centers	3,553	3,742	2,724	3,262	3,418	2,951	3,784	5,741	7,340	5,733	5,201
Other	136	14	26	8	8128	20	48	21	81	25	
Asia	10,343	8,107	8,316	7,672	10,084	11,921	13,083	14,948	8,357	7,988	6,555
Middle & Near East	39	123	896	251	303	148	268	578	187	126	21
Europe	20,975	12,832	9,176	9,204	6,525	8,281	8,305	13,749	17,937	28,782	26,974
Africa	804	1,014	308	630	366	367	485	407	569	574	59
Oceania	6,119	4,476	3,119	2,275	1,507	2,716	1,011	2,525	2,833	997	737
Totals	83,527	56,862	44,313	41,514	42,808	49,568	54,094	66,229	52,169	74,390	53,690

Source: Ministry of Finance.

was primarily because of a surge in investment in finance, insurance, and real estate in FY 1998, and in the food industry in FY 1999. Investment in finance and insurance in the EU was directed mainly at the UK, France, and the Netherlands, where Japanese firms were involved in a number of acquisitions to gain access to the asset securitization business. In these countries, the local affiliates of Japanese companies were also having greater difficulty obtaining capital financing because of the increase in the "Japan premium," i.e., what Japanese borrowers must pay over the market rate for short-term loans.

Within these global trends, FDI from Japan to Latin America has shown five key characteristics:

1. Japan's presence as a provider of FDI to Latin America declined rapidly. In the case of Brazil, for example, the share of Japanese FDI declined from 6.3 percent at the end of 1995 to 0.6 percent at the end of the first half of 2000.
2. Japanese FDI in Latin America has concentrated in the financial sectors of offshore centers because of tax incentives in such countries. In 1998 about 70 percent of Japanese investment in Latin America was directed to the Cayman Islands, owing to investment in special purpose companies (SPCs) established by large Japanese commercial banks in the islands in an effort to consolidate their capital base.
3. The transportation sector is another major destination of FDI among nonmanufacturing industries. This is mainly because of the investments in "flags of convenience" in Panama by Japanese maritime companies.
4. The largest portion of direct investment in manufacturing sectors went into the transportation equipment sector (i.e., the automotive industry), with the electronics and electrical sectors, food, and chemicals putting in a strong showing.
5. Looking at the composition of FDI from Japan by host country, apart from off-shore centers, Brazil and Mexico are major destinations of Japanese FDI in the region. These two countries also frequently appear among the most promising countries for FDI in the annual questionnaire survey conducted by the JBIC.[11]

The stagnation of Japanese FDI in the region (aside from off-shore centers), especially in the service sector, can be explained by the following factors:

1. According to the *World Investment Report 2000,* from the United Nations Conference on Trade and Development (UNCTAD), privatization has been an important means in recent years of attracting FDI to Latin America's nonmanufacturing sectors, such as telecommunications, electricity,

transportation, water, airports, and ports. These are sectors in which Japan is not internationally competitive because of tight regulation and protection by the government, and a lack of expertise and know-how. Japan's most internationally competitive sectors are still the manufacturing sectors, especially the automotive and electric/electronic sectors.

2. There is also a difference in the type of FDI that Latin America receives from Japan and from the rest of the developed countries. According to UNCTAD, like trends in global FDI, the growing cross-border mergers and acquisitions (M&As) have been the driving force for growth in FDI in Latin America by European and U.S. firms, particularly by Spanish firms in industries such as finance, telecommunications, utilities, oil, and retail. In contrast, the JBIC FY 1999 survey shows that nearly 60 percent of the respondents that are planning to invest in Latin America said they would invest in the form of 100 percent ownership. About 40 percent chose the joint venture option, and only 5 percent said that they plan investment by M&A.
3. Attributes peculiar to the Japanese firms include reliance on the lifetime employment system, seniority-based pay structures, the bottom-up decision-making mechanism, and so forth. These characteristics, and the collective memory of bitter experiences in Latin America in the 1980s, are believed to make the Japanese private sector very slow to respond to structural changes in the region.
4. Another factor that makes Japanese firms' movement slow, and thus makes many Japanese firms in the region unprofitable, is their policy of human resource allocation. In contrast to U.S. and European firms, which dispatch high-profile people with deep experience in the region, Japanese firms typically dispatch persons without much regional knowledge; they rarely recruit local executives; and they do not permit local managers to make commitments on investments because decision-making mechanisms are centered at the headquarters.

Portfolio Investment

Until the 1980s, Japanese institutional investors' portfolio investments were directed toward foreign currency-denominated bonds issued by OECD government entities. However, during the first half of the 1990s, because of the substantial exchange losses incurred by the outstanding balance of their foreign investment portfolios, Japanese investors shifted their investment from foreign currency-denominated securities to yen-denominated bonds. At the same time, Japanese investors showed new interest in investing in emerging markets. For developing countries, yen-denominated instruments have become attractive because of low interest rates (and low spreads) prevailing in Japan, because of deregulation of the international yen-denominated bond market, and because of the increasing accessibility of readily available risk hedge products, including currency risk (e.g., the deepening and widening of swap markets).[12] As a result, yen-denominated bond issues by developing countries—Euroyen issues or *Samurai* bonds issued in Japan—have become increasingly popular instruments for bond sales.[13] The *Samurai* bond market had been virtually closed to foreign bond sellers for about two years because of international financial turbulence originating in Asia, but it has recently been reactivated.

Portfolio investment in Latin America increased significantly during the late 1990s, supported by steady and strong acquisitions of bonds and notes by Japanese investors who invested in asset-backed securities (ABSs) issued by SPCs established by Japanese companies and financial institutions mainly in the Cayman Islands. They also invested in subordinated debt securities issued by large Japanese commercial banks in an effort to consolidate their capital base. Investment in money market instruments also expanded substantially because *samurai* commercial paper (CP)—issued by SPCs and established by Japanese financial institutions in order to liquidate their assets—was purchased continuously.

Other than investment in offshore financial centers, Latin American penetration in the *Samurai* bond market is noteworthy. In 1995 in particular, Latin American countries sharply increased *Samurai* bond issues, which amounted to $US5.2 billion, more than the amount issued by all Asian countries combined. Argentina and Mexico were major issuers, selling the equivalent of US$1.7 billion and $US1.6 billion, respectively, to Japanese investors. In 1996, yen-denominated bond issuances by Latin American countries surpassed those of 1995. The largest sovereign issuer was Mexico (US$2 billion), followed by Argentina (US$1.5 billion), Brazil (US$0.7 billion), and Colombia (US$0.4 billion). Latin American governments came back to the *Samurai* market in 1999. The total amount of *Samurai* bonds issued by Latin American governments reached US$3.5 billion as of the end of 2000.

Private Bank Lending

A need to strengthen balance sheets, boost core profitability, and meet rising supervisory standards has forced Japanese banks to substantially scale back their involvement in international activities. The 1997–1998 crisis in East Asia constituted another shock, which has further harmed banks' financial positions. Thus, according to the Bank of Japan, the number of internationally active banks fell from eighty (out of 145) in September 1997 to forty-five in March 1998. Japanese banks have also continued to lose their market share, mainly to European banks. Data for the exposure of developed country banks, according to the Bank for International Settlements (BIS), show that between 1995 and the first half of 2000, the cumulative loss on claims of Japanese banks within the BIS nonreporting area reached 12 percentage points (from 21.5 percent to 9.4 percent).

These declines have been occurring globally, but particularly in Asia, where loans from Japanese banks dropped by 47.5 percent from the end of 1997 to the end of 1999. Japanese banks now account for about a quarter of claims vis-à-vis Asia, down from a peak of 48 percent at the end of 1988. However, excluding claims on off-shore centers, which accounted for 66 percent of total claims outside the BIS reporting area as of the end of 2000 March, Asia remains the largest destination for Japanese banks' international lending.

With regard to Latin America, Japanese exposure declined slowly in the latter half of the 1980s as banks retreated from the region by swapping their debts for equity at a discounted rate and/or by writing them off. The 1989 "Brady Plan" came as a blessing for Japanese banks that wanted to exit Latin America. Following an agreement with Mexico in 1990, most Japanese commercial banks opted for the principal reduction option, converted principal to discount bonds, and almost immediately sold them on the secondary market, even at a loss. Since completing its disposal of restructured debt, Japan's banking sector has remained cautious about Latin America. Japanese banks have stronger reservations regarding the region's alleged recovery and economic boom because they were so badly burned by Latin America during the 1980s.

Challenges Ahead

As a prerequisite for maintaining its role as the largest provider of capital to developing countries, Japan must consolidate its own economic recovery, and restructuring its corporate and banking sectors is crucial in fulfilling this prerequisite. Avoiding a reduction in ODA volumes will also require reaching a national consensus on a medium-term fiscal strategy to restore the health of public finances, and will also require convincing Japanese citizens that the use of public funding is an effective means of fostering development in developing countries.

Once the Japanese economy returns to a course of self-sustained recovery, one can expect renewed interest in and expansion of business activities of Japanese firms and financial institutions in Latin America for a number of reasons. First of all, it is likely that Japan will continue to have a current account surplus and thus, Japan will continue to be a net capital exporter, at least for the medium term, because of reasons already explained. Part of these capital outflows will be directed not only to the offshore banking sector, but also to the real sector in Latin America in light of the region's importance as a market for Japanese manufacturing goods, and as a source of raw materials. As the potential growth rate of matured economies is said to be no more than 3 percent, it is imperative for private firms to secure their market in rapidly growing emerging economies. Latin America's attractiveness rests not only on economic reasons, such as macroeconomic stability (compared to the 1980s), progress in structural reforms, and a regional integration process, but also on other aspects such as the consolidation of democratization and the lack of ethnic conflict. Second, exploiting natural resources, which are exported mainly to Japan, has been and will remain one of the most common types of investment in Latin America by Japanese trading companies. This type of business is mostly uninfluenced by the Japanese and host countries' business cycles. In addition, Japanese trading companies usually have long-term contracts with state-owned Latin American companies. Third, there will be a substantial change in the Japanese corporate system and its decision-making mechanism. It will evolve into a more global system in the coming years as more and more FDI enters Japan from Europe and the U.S., facilitating quick decision-making, and the diversification and localization of the overseas operations of Japanese transnational corporations (TNCs).[14]

The Advantages of a Free Trade Agreement (FTA)

Japan is one of the few countries in the world that has not pursued bilateral trade arrangements because Japan's commercial policy has principally been based on the General Agreement on Tariffs and Trade/World Trade Organization (GATT/WTO) rules. By contrast, Latin American nations have aggressively promoted bilateral and subregional integration. Among them, Mexico and Chile are the most aggressive and have proposed starting FTA negotiations with Asian countries such as Japan, Korea, and Singapore. On Japan's part, there has been increasing interest in the issue and, in December 1999, Japan officially announced that it would start preparing for an FTA with Singapore (an agreement has since been concluded). With respect to an FTA with Latin American countries, the Japan Federation of Economic Organization (*Keidanren*) and the Japan External Trade Organization (JETRO) presented their reports on the possible effects of a Japan-Mexico FTA, both of which concluded that the FTA would help deepen economic interaction between the two countries.[15] In fact, the benefits of an FTA between Japan and Latin

American countries—and, conversely, the opportunity cost of not having such an arrangement—would be substantial.[16]

First, an FTA between Japan and Latin American countries would provide broader and more institutionalized access among Japan and the countries of Latin America and the Pacific Basin, especially at a time when multilateral arrangements such as the WTO and the Asia-Pacific Economic Cooperation (APEC) are experiencing difficulty. Second, an FTA would not only promote trade relations, but would help increase Japanese investment in Latin America. Japanese investors would benefit from the elimination of tariffs on imported parts and components for production. Also, the rules on investment promotion and protection would improve the investment environment. Third, if Japanese firms in Latin America receive disadvantageous treatment compared to local and Western firms because of the lack of an FTA or FTA-like arrangement, they will lose business opportunities, leading to a further decrease in Japan's economic presence in the region. Consequently, Japan's status is likely to decline overall because economic interactions underpin the exchange of cultural and human resources.

Dissemination of Information

As mentioned above, certain characteristics of the Latin American market make it attractive to Japanese firms. Moreover, the investment environment has improved in a number of ways. Nevertheless, it remains as difficult as ever to obtain information in Japan on investing in Latin America. Not only is there insufficient general information on the Latin American economy and market, but there is also a shortage of information on topics such as deregulation and other developments affecting the investment environment; potential partners in Latin America, such as firms seeking to merge or enter into joint ventures; possible local investment destinations; local government programs for attracting foreign firms; and government policies for promoting inward FDI, such as low-interest loans to foreign firms and tax incentives. Although information on Latin America is now easily accessible through the Internet, there are still difficulties in obtaining necessary information. In addition to the problems of information availability, the notion, stemming from past experience, that business in Latin America is not profitable makes Japanese firms reluctant to expand Latin American business. To solve these problems, effective use of services provided by various public and private channels such as JETRO, a government entity, and the Japan Institute for Overseas Investment (JOI, a nonprofit organization that assists potential Japanese investors with finding a desirable destination overseas), and by the bilateral Japan–Latin America Businessmen's Joint Committees, should be promoted.

Their services include providing up-to-date information on the FDI environment in Latin America; conducting programs, such as sending advisors and sponsoring exhibitions; helping countries develop their supporting industries; and the like.

Authorities in Latin American countries, in turn, should provide information that is more detailed and covers a wider scope. Greater emphasis will have to be placed on information of specific interest to Japanese firms mentioned above. Comprehensive information should be provided via channels such as electronic media.

In sum, this chapter sheds fresh light on recent developments in capital flows from Japan to Latin America. As this essay outlines, we see a clear regional bias of Japanese capital flows toward Asia among developing countries. Moreover, Japan recently scaled back its activities in Latin America because of a number of factors, both external and domestic. However, the development of Japan's relations with Latin America over the past four decades is noteworthy considering the region's geographical, historical, and cultural remoteness. Because Latin America is so richly endowed with natural resources, expanding financial and commercial ties would be mutually beneficial. Capital flows from Japan to Latin America will be reactivated in accordance with the acceleration of economic recovery in Japan and Asia, and through joint efforts to strengthen economic relations.

Notes

1. Japan Center for Economic Research, *Japan's Balance Sheet in 2025—Long-term Economic Projection* (February 26, 1998).
2. The IMF projected the current account surplus of US$100.2 billion (2.9 percent of GDP) for 2002 and $127.0 billion (3.4 percent of GDP) for 2003 in its *World Economic Outlook* (April 2002).
3. This paper does not analyze grants by nonprofit private agencies because of problems of data availability and their relatively minor importance.
4. There are several different types of ODA: (1) *Grant aid* is provided mainly to low-income countries and is channeled to support basic human needs (BHN) and human resources development; (2) *Technical cooperation* includes: a) the dispatch of experts, b) the acceptance of trainees, c) the provision of equipment and materials to facilitate technology transfers, d) project-type technical cooperation involving all of these, and e) the dispatch of the Japan Overseas Cooperation Volunteers; (3) *ODA loans* make funds available to developing countries at low interest rates and with long repayment periods to develop and improve economic and social infrastructure; and (4) *Contributions and subscriptions to multilateral institutions*, especially as Japan attaches growing importance to aid through multilateral institutions. Currently Japan is

the largest shareholder of the Asian Development Bank and the African Development Bank, and the second largest shareholder of a number of multilateral institutions including the International Monetary Fund, the World Bank, and the Inter-American Development Bank.

5. According to the Development Assistance Committee (DAC) of the OECD, Japan was the world's largest ODA donor throughout the 1990s. In the year 2000 it was surpassed by the United States, however, and it remained the world's second largest donor in 2001.

6. As part of the overall administrative reform, the former Overseas Economic Cooperation Fund (OECF) and the Export-Import Bank of Japan (JEXIM) were merged into the Japan Bank for International Cooperation (JBIC) as of October 1999.

7. During the 1990s, JEXIM also offered Argentina US$800 million in order to cope with the liquidity crisis in 1995. For the Brazilian rescue package in November 1998, the Bank of Japan provided $1.25 billion.

8. Barbara Stallings, "The Reluctant Giant: Japan and the Latin American Debt Crisis," *Journal of Latin American Studies*, 22, no. 1 (February 1990): 1–30.

9. The banks influence the government because of their economic and political importance and their symbiotic relationship with the Ministry of Finance (MOF). Until the autumn of 1997, when a number of major financial institutions collapsed, the government used the "convoy system," which implied that it would not allow any major financial institution to go into bankruptcy.

10. In Japan there are two kinds of FDI statistics. One is "inward/outward FDI statistics," based on the reports and notification submitted to the Ministry of Finance, and the other is the "balance of payments (BOP) statistics," compiled by the Bank of Japan in accordance with the manual issued by the IMF. The figures in this essay are the statistics provided by the MOF unless otherwise specified.

11. The purpose of this survey is to identify the current and future trends of FDI activities by Japanese manufacturing companies operating overseas. The survey covered 786 manufacturing companies that have three or more foreign affiliates, including at least one production base, as of the end of 1998.

12. Of particular importance is the January 1, 1994, elimination of the ninety-day lockup period before which sovereign yen-denominated Eurobonds could be sold to Japanese investors after initial placement, facilitating access by sovereign issuers to the domestic investor base. Other important deregulations were the January 1, 1996, elimination of the minimum credit rating requirement for *Samurai* bonds, and the elimination of the ninety-day lockup period on all other nonresident yen-denominated Eurobonds after August 2, 1995.

13. *Samurai* bonds are yen-denominated bonds issued by non-Japanese residents and sold to investors in Japan under Japanese regulations. This differentiates *Samurai* bonds from *Euroyen* bonds, which are issued in the international offshore market.

14. According to the Ministry of Finance, in 1999 FDI inflow in Japan grew for a second straight year, soaring 105.5 percent to US$21.51 billion, an all-time high. The major force behind this growth was the EU, particularly French firms, which made large acquisitions in Japan's automobile, auto parts, finance, and insurance industries, replacing U.S. firms as the leading foreign investors in Japan.

15. Working Group on Japan-Mexico Bilateral Treaties, Keidanren, *Report on the Possible Effects of a Japan-Mexico Free Trade Agreement on Japanese Industry* (April 20, 1999); and JETRO, *Nichiboku Keizai Kankei Kimmitsuka Iinkai Houkoku* (April 2000).

16. The premise of the discussion is that an FTA between the two countries should be a comprehensive one, which would include elimination of tariff and nontariff trade barriers as well as rules on investment, government procurement, antidumping, and intellectual property, together with effective dispute-settlement mechanisms.

3

Economic Relations between Korea and Latin America

Taik-Hwan Jyoung

IN MID-1997 A DEVASTATING FINANCIAL CRISIS struck the economies of East Asia and dealt crushing blows to Thailand, Indonesia, the Philippines, Malaysia—and South Korea. By the late 1990s its effects had spread to Mexico, Brazil, Argentina, and other parts of the world. At the time, it appeared that the "Asian crisis" might lead to downturns that could unravel the still-evolving global economy. While that prediction seems overly pessimistic in hindsight, it is clear that the crisis has had—and will continue to have—significant implications for the world economy. In order to identify and understand these long-term implications, we are greatly in need of empirical research about the crisis and its effects on transregional economic relations.

This chapter discusses and analyzes the effects of the financial crisis on the economic relationship between Korea and Latin America. Specifically, I address the following questions:

- What has been the effect of Korea's financial crisis on capital flows and on trade between Korea and Latin America?
- Does the East Asian–Latin American connection remain viable despite the adverse effects of the financial crisis?
- In what direction should the Asian–Latin American relationship move in the future?

To establish the appropriate context for these inquiries, we begin with a brief examination of Korean–Latin American relations from the 1960s through the 1980s.

Korea and Latin America: Historical Background

Latin America was long ignored by most Koreans. Until the 1980s, Korea's trade with Latin America had been modest, as was emigration to Latin American countries. The number of Koreans living in Latin America has increased in recent years, however, approaching one hundred thousand in 1999. Trade and investment between Korea and Latin America have also been increasing at a rapid pace (however, there has not been much research to identify the forces driving these trends). Asia and Latin America share a vast potential: They are emerging as two of the fastest-growing regions in the world. Closer cooperation between the two regions has only been given serious consideration in recent years. With the rapid development of regional and global economic integration since the early 1990s, the potential for transregional cooperation between Asia and Latin America has attracted growing interest. With this prospect in mind, let us turn to the recent economic histories of the two regions.

Asian countries achieved rapid economic growth in the latter half of the twentieth century. Japan has become the second largest economic power in the world. Singapore, Taiwan, Hong Kong, and Korea have emerged as the so-called Newly Industrializing Economies (the NIEs, also known as "the four dragons"), registering the fastest growth in the world in the 1980s. The Association of Southeast Asian Nations (ASEAN) countries are catching up with the NIEs. (ASEAN consists of ten countries including Thailand, Indonesia, Singapore, the Philippines, Malaysia, Brunei, Cambodia, Laos, Myanmar, and Vietnam.) If China maintains its present rate of growth, its GDP is expected to catch up to that of the United States some time in the first half of the twenty-first century. In fact, China's economy grew at an average of more than 10 percent a year from 1992 to 1995, and more than 8 percent from 1996 to 2000.

Latin America registered relatively low growth rates during the same period. During the 1960s and 1970s, many of the Latin American economies were fettered by import-substitution policies, which put up trade barriers to imported manufactured goods in an attempt to reserve national markets for local goods. Many of the Latin American economies suffered as a result of restrictive and protectionist policies imposed by military regimes. The 1980s were, in many ways, a lost decade for the economies of Latin America; burdened by heavy obligations arising from external debt, they experienced frequent crises and recessions.

Neoliberal reforms espoused by the International Monetary Fund (IMF) and other international agencies during the 1980s—according to the so-called Washington consensus—led to the liberalization of trade, the privatization of public enterprises, and the deregulation of private industry. A critical point was reached with the demise of the military government in Chile in the late 1980s. Its successor, the new civilian government, accepted and extended the reforms initiated under General Augusto Pinochet and Chile quickly emerged as a model for other countries of the region. Following this example, Latin American countries in general maintained stable growth in the 1990s, although some Latin American countries, including Argentina, Brazil, and Mexico, continued to experience recurrent economic crises.

According to calculations by the Wharton Econometric Forecasting Associates (WEFA), Asia's share of world GDP (not including Japan) reached 10.4 percent in 1999, up from 8.7 percent in 1995. This figure is expected to rise to 12.3 percent in 2005. Latin America's GDP share registered 5.1 percent of world GDP in 1999; though down from 5.9 percent in 1995, this percentage is projected to grow to 5.4 percent by 2005. Real GDP growth between 1996 and 2005 is projected to average 5.9 percent annually in Asia, and 3.8 percent in Latin America, according to WEFA's estimates. This level of growth in Asia (excluding Japan) is all the more impressive because Asia contained 54.4 percent of the world's population in 1999, while Latin America had only 8 percent.

Asia (not including Japan) controlled 17.9 percent of the world's trade in 1999. That figure is expected to grow to 19.7 percent in 2005. By comparison, Latin America was engaged in 3.6 percent of world trade, and is expected to maintain that level until 2005. Korea, Hong Kong, Taiwan, and Japan increased their shares of trade with Latin America between 1990 and 1994, while Malaysia, Singapore, and China stayed at the same level or decreased their shares. Such figures represent an impressive increase in trade volume between the two regions. Nevertheless, interregional trade between Asia and Latin America has been modest compared to the volume of their trade with other regions and the rapidity with which that volume increased, especially in their trade with the more advanced countries. For example, Asia's trade and investment in Europe and North America have grown rapidly and have brought about a higher level of interdependence between those regions, compared to Asia's trade relations with Latin America.

Why, then, are the economic ties between Asia and Latin America so underdeveloped? The answer lies in several causes—some representing the similarities between the two regions, others arising from their differences. First, both regions have, until recently, been motivated more by trade rivalry than by cooperation with one another. Second, until recent times, the two regions were not economically complementary because they had similar industrial structures that made trade between them redundant in many sectors. Third, there were important differences in trade policy. Asian countries were predominately outward-looking in their attitudes toward international trade;

that is, they tended to favor policies that encouraged trade—especially exports of their own goods. In contrast, Latin American countries tended to favor import-substitution policies, which limited trading opportunities by imposing protectionist barriers. In recent years, however, protectionist policies have been jettisoned in favor of "open regionalism" and transregional agreements. The Asia Pacific Economic Cooperation (APEC) forum, the Asia-Europe Summit Meeting (ASEM), and the EU–MERCOSUR (European Union–Southern Common Market) Free Trade Area are examples of this new trend. These new transregional coalitions burgeoned in order to avoid the familiar drawbacks associated with more traditional alliances of neighboring regimes bent on an inward-looking or exclusive worldview.

Now there is a growing prospect for the formation of a transregional alliance to foster economic ties between Asia and Latin America, as shown by inauguration of the Forum for East Asia–Latin American Cooperation (FEALAC, described in more detail in other chapters). As is true of other such cross-regional coalitions, it has the potential to benefit not only the parties concerned, but also to redound to the advantage of the global economy in general. Such efforts at transregional cooperation may eventually promote more balanced development in the world economy through increasing complementarity between remote or "peripheral" areas.

There are strong incentives for cooperation. For one thing, trading opportunities will arise naturally from the inherent differences in the two regions' present industrial structures. And the Latin American nations now seem to be evolving toward generally more open and liberal trade policies. But these new opportunities could be lessened or lost entirely unless the two regions make heartfelt efforts to promote greater mutual understanding. To this end, intensified cooperation in trade and investment and expansion in cultural exchange between Asia and Latin America would be highly useful.

Korea's Financial Crisis and Relations with Latin America

It is widely imagined that Korea's financial crisis in 1997 was triggered by a lack of foreign currency. In contrast, most financial experts believe that the crisis arose from structural weaknesses and from underlying attitudes and beliefs on the part of Korea's economic and political elites. In particular, analysts cite three factors in the etiology of the crisis: chronic governmental intervention, a widespread belief in the hypothesis of "too-big-to-fail," and a lack of transparency, or openness, in corporate governance.

Even worse, Korean firms tended to focus on strategies for maintaining their global market shares without adequate concern about the profitability and financial soundness of their investments. This modus operandi was made even riskier because of the heavy leveraging that made such enterprises possible. As a result, when corporate conglomerates laden with excessive debt failed, their demise usually precipitated extensive chains of bankruptcies.

Confronted with an unprecedented financial crisis in the mid-1990s, the Korean government initiated comprehensive reforms in the financial, corporate, labor, and public sectors. The first round of restructuring was implemented during the period from the second quarter of 1998 to the end of 1999. A second round of restructuring followed in 2000. A severe credit crunch and an overall contraction of the economy followed the financial crisis. In 1998, Korea's GDP contracted by 6.7 percent, the poorest result since the 1960s.

During the financial crisis, the financial vulnerability of Korean corporations became a major impediment to economic recovery. Many Korean firms went bankrupt because of a liquidity shortage and the concomitant contraction of profits. Ultimately, Korean firms had to revise their financial strategies merely in order to survive. They placed their first priority on securing liquidity. To this end, they instituted several measures: They forced cost reductions, including cuts in their work forces, they reoriented their operations to emphasize exports, and they canceled or delayed many of their domestic and overseas projects. Finally, in an effort to remain solvent, they sold assets.

The Korean *chaebols*, or large business groups, were forced by their creditor banks to reduce their debt-to-equity ratios to less than 200 percent by the end of 1999. They were also obliged to eliminate their cross-debt guarantees with affiliated companies by April 2000. Under such circumstances, Korean firms had to reexamine and revise their corporate strategies for trade and investment abroad.

For example, the Daewoo Group, the second largest *chaebol* in Korea, put into place a debt workout arrangement in August 1998. Subsequently, one of its major associates, Daewoo Motors Corporation, went into court receivership in November 2000. The fiasco of the Daewoo Group has become a benchmark of failure in business history—and it was a failure on a worldwide scale. By the end of 1998, the Daewoo group subsumed 253 overseas subsidiaries. At the time, that was the largest number of subsidiaries in any of Korea's five big *chaebols*. It took over a year of negotiations with overseas banks to arrive at a settlement, in the year 2000, of its overseas financing, amounting to some $4.8 billion U.S. dollars. As a consequence of their stipulation with Daewoo, most of these banks suffered major losses in 2000. Since then, most other Korean companies operating abroad have experienced difficulties in obtaining financing because the Daewoo fiasco diminished the credit reputations of Korean companies generally.

In the aftermath of the crisis, Korea's trade with Latin American countries declined drastically, with the import sector leading the spiral downward. Ironically, however, Korea's trade surplus grew larger than ever because the dramatic devaluation of the *won* enhanced the price competitiveness of Korean exports. This made Latin America a more attractive partner in the eyes of Korean trade strategists.

Korean Investment in Latin America after the Financial Crisis

In order to attract foreign currency to the Korean investment market, the government introduced a new, liberalized regime of foreign exchange transactions in general, and of foreign direct and portfolio investment practices in particular. These reforms were achieved by abolishing the existing Foreign Exchange Transaction Law and enacting a new law, effective in April 1999. It applies to virtually all capital account transactions, including overseas borrowing and investment by Korean investors, and portfolio investment in Korean securities by foreigners. As a result, Korea's capital market has been fully liberalized, and the new law can be said to have had a salutary effect. As of the end of 2000, foreigners held a 29.9 percent share of all investments in the Korean stock market—a substantial increase from their 14.6 percent share in 1997. Korea's inflow of capital from abroad now exceeds its outflow of both direct and portfolio investment.

Korea thus maintains its position as a net importer of capital. Since 1998, both foreign direct investment and foreign portfolio investment have increased rapidly. This has occurred thanks to the full liberalization of the Korean capital market and a revision of laws allowing hostile mergers and acquisitions by foreigners without reservation. Formerly, foreign investors needed to receive consent from directors representing more than 33 percent of the company's total shares in case of hostile mergers and acquisitions, which served as a major barrier to attracting foreign capital. Inward foreign direct investment for Korea increased from $7 billion in 1997 to $15.6 billion in 2000. Furthermore, the net inflow of foreign portfolio investment expanded more than tenfold in just three years, from $1.1 billion in 1997 to more than $11 billion in 2000.

Korea's outward direct investment (or overseas direct investment) experienced a significant fluctuation in the aftermath of the financial crisis. The annual number of new investment projects plummeted to 533 in 1998 and 998 in 1999, well below the four-year average of 1,320 for 1994–1997. Upward momentum returned in 2000, when the number of new projects climbed to more than 1,900. The financial volume of net overseas investment showed similar oscillations. After steady expansion to 1998 (exception a slight downturn in 1997), Korea's foreign investments dropped by almost 40 percent in 1999, from $3.7 billion in 1998 to $2.2 billion in 1999. This was a direct result of the contraction resulting from the country's financial crisis. The downward trend was evident again in 2001, when overseas investment slipped to less than $2 billion. (There appeared to be an exception in the year 2000, when investment rose to $3.7 billion—65 percent higher than in 1999—but this was partly due to large-scale offshore investments in Bermuda in that year.) In general, Korea's corporate community has yet to regain confidence in overseas investments and in the global economy at large.

How did the financial crisis affect Korea's overseas investment practices? Most of the large Korean conglomerates, the *chaebols*, suffered a diminished capacity for carrying out large-scale overseas investments because the business slowdown weakened the constituent firms' financial conditions. Their liquidity shortage was exacerbated by Korea's worsened overall credit. Cash-strapped enterprises were suddenly unable to obtain financing in countries targeted for investment projects. Ultimately, Korea's financial crisis and the subsequent economic recession slowed or reversed Korea's earlier momentum in overseas direct investment—around the world in general, and in Latin America as well.

Beginning in the early 1990s, large Korean companies, including the *chaebols* (most of which were multinational corporations), had come to favor global management strategies. With the support of heavy foreign financing, they vigorously expanded their overseas investments until the outbreak of the financial crisis forced them to retrench. Certainly, Korea's financial malaise played a strong role in reversing Korea's overseas expansion. But, in retrospect, we can now see that other etiological factors were extant in the business culture of Korea. Prominent among them were the all-too-prevalent "too-big-to-fail" hypothesis, as mentioned previously, and the problem of moral hazard within the banking and corporate sectors—which confidently expected governmental bail-outs in case of bankruptcy without any due accountability. After the financial crisis, Korean business groups could no longer expect financial support from banks for their overseas projects. As a result, many prospective investments in Latin America were cancelled, reduced in size, or postponed indefinitely. For example, Kia Motors' overseas projects in Indonesia and Brazil were abandoned when Kia became mired in financial difficulties in early 1997. Eventually, as a result of its difficulties, Kia was merged into Hyundai Motors in November of 1998.

Statistics compiled by the Korea Export and Import Bank reveal that Korean companies' annual investments abroad have declined substantially since 1999. Despite the severe credit crunch, in fact, net investment in 1998 increased by 11.3 percent over 1997, even in the midst of the crisis. This can be explained by the fact that the opportunity cost of the already-planned investment projects seemed to be greater than the costs incurred from canceling or delaying the project. Companies focusing more on export operations rather than domestic sales were less affected by the recession. What's more, they actually benefited from the sharp depreciation of the Korean currency. On average, small and medium-size firms specializing in exports were in a better financial position than many large conglomerates that were struggling to expand or even continue existing projects. As a result, the number of projects undertaken by small and medium-sized firms (rather than large conglomerates) increased sharply during the crisis period.

As of December 2001, Korea's overseas direct investments outstanding totaled $28.7 billion, equal to 6.8 percent of the country's GDP. Since the mid-1990s, the largest regional share has gone to Asia, with China showing an especially rapid increase. North America has the second largest share, but it is declining. Europe's share increased in the 1990s—possibly because Korean corporations responded to rulings in the European Union, where firms were required to meet local contents in order to be eligible for duty-free treatment. Latin America's effective share has been around 5 percent.[1]

Overall, the magnitude of Korean projects has been declining. The average investment went from $9.2 million per project in 1997 and $28 million in 1998 to just $3.9 million in 2002. This trend can be explained by the fact that many large overseas investment projects had to be reduced or modified because of the unfavorable financial situations of their parent companies. Their difficulties were exacerbated by their degraded credit standings in the international financial market. These changes in investment patterns favored small and medium-sized firms, and, as a result, the portion of investment projects undertaken by these firms has increased in Latin America.

Mexico, Brazil, Argentina, and Panama are the major Latin American beneficiaries of Korean investment in Latin America, together receiving 52.1 percent of the total of $1.4 billion invested in the region as of the end of 2001.[2] Mexico became a major recipient not only because of its strategic ties through the North American Free Trade Agreement (NAFTA) with the United States (and Canada), but also because of the potential of its domestic market. As a gateway for access to Latin American markets, Panama served as a major destination of Korean direct investment, especially for international trade purposes. Brazil and Argentina became important to Korea because of the potential of their domestic markets as well, and, in addition, because of their roles in MERCOSUR.

Manufacturing, fisheries, and international trade are the three major areas of Korean investment in Latin America. About half of all projects have been in the manufacturing sector, with the average investment reaching over $3 million per project at the end of 2001. As of the mid-1980s, the production bases of Korean labor-intensive light industry, including textiles and apparel, began moving to Caribbean countries to take advantage of two things: (1) the U.S.–initiated Caribbean Basin Initiative, which provided easier access to the U.S. market and tax incentives; and (2) inexpensive labor.

Official overseas investment statistics do not reflect Korean investments—even large ones—made through the agencies of foreign entities based in third countries. In the 1990s, for example, the largest Korean investments in Mexico were made through Korean subsidiaries based in the United States. Samsung Electronics Corporation's U.S. subsidiary set up an industrial complex in Tijuana, Mexico, investing about $420 million to manufacture home electronic appliances such as color televisions, refrigerators, and washing machines. This project was not included in Korean overseas investment statistics. Neither were projects by Daewoo and LG, which were also producing home electronic appliances in Mexico (in Sonora, Querétaro, and Mexicali). In Manaus, Brazil, Samsung is producing computer monitors and mobile phones. Its market share for computer monitors became the largest in Brazil in the second quarter of 2000. Other facilities to manufacture home electronics in Brazil are being planned. (Asia Motors Corporation's Bahia Automobile Project for manufacturing motor vehicles in Brazil is under way despite its merger with Hyundai Motors in 1999.)

There are many other examples of Korean direct investment in Latin America. To illustrate the point: In Guatemala, a Korean-owned garment company employed fourteen hundred Guatemalans and fourteen Koreans to manufacture five million shirts a year for export to the U.S. market; total investment in the project is $9.5 million. In Chile, Samsung Electronics Corporation invested $150 million to acquire 12 percent of the total equity in a joint venture with a Chilean telecommunications company. (Samsung has recently left the project. Likewise, LG divested its copper mining venture in 1996.) In Peru, a Korean consortium that consisted of Korea Petroleum Corporation, Daewoo, and SK has engaged in oil production, and another Korean consortium is involved in oil exploration. In the Dominican Republic, more than twenty-five small and medium-sized Korean-owned companies were fully localized and manufactured shirts, bags, tents, balls, and hats in 1999.

These investments reveal several important recent trends. First, the Korean *chaebols* have begun to extend their operations to Latin America. This signifies that they recognize that their growing partnership with Latin America is important, not only for the purpose of benefiting from its market potential but also because of Latin America's strategic access to the U.S. market. Second, large-scale Korean investments in Latin America have been on the rise. (Not surprisingly, this increase coincides with the consolidation of NAFTA). Third, the Korean investment community has switched its emphasis to automobiles and the technology sector, including electronic appliances, and information and telecommunication devices. Fourth, the economic impact of these investments can be expected to grow, yielding benefits for Latin America in terms of employment, the upgrading of industrial structure, and the acquisition of technology.

The motivation for Korean FDI in Latin America responds to push and pull factors. Key push factors are (1) high labor costs in Korea since the late 1980s; and (2) Korean multinational companies' growing need, since the early 1990s, to employ strategies devised to take full advantage of the movement toward economic globalization. The pull factors consist of (1) improving economic conditions in Latin America, including increased economic stability; (2) the growing market potential in Latin America due to the rise of a burgeoning middle class; (3) the ever-increasing complementarity between the industrial structures of Korea and Latin America; and (4) the need to respond to the growing trend toward regional integration. During the 1980s, Korea had essentially two main motivations for FDI in Latin America: cheaper labor costs and better access to lucrative markets in the West. Since the early 1990s, however, Korea's investments have been more closely related to the globalization strategies of its multinational companies. These strategies have been designed in response to the increasing regionalization of the world's markets, as represented by such economic integration schemes as NAFTA and MERCOSUR. Since the early 1990s, too, Latin American companies have become increasingly important partners of Korean firms.

The financial soundness of Korean investments abroad can be assessed through relevant surveys. A study by the Korea Institute for International Economic Policy (KIEP) in 1997 sampled financial data from 372 randomly chosen Korean overseas investment projects. The survey revealed that the financial performances of Korea's overseas direct investments, as of 1995, were, in general, inferior to those of domestic investments, mostly due to their relatively high debt ratios and lack of appropriate management. The survey further showed that Korean direct investments in Latin America earned net profits of 2.9 percent relative to the total assets, which is slightly higher than the average of 2.8 percent in the domestic manufacturing firms. But net earnings per sale were only 2.2 percent, lower than the average of 2.8 percent. This difference resulted from higher financing costs arising from higher debt-to-equity ratios (610 percent in 1995), compared to the average for Korean domestic firms (287 percent in 1995).

According to another study by the Korea Export and Import Bank, as of the end of 1998, there were seventeen large Korean investment projects in Latin America that were capitalized in excess of $10 million each. The total amount of capital injected by Korean investors for these projects amounted to $621 million, and total assets amounted to $4.3 billion. This showed that large-scale investments increased in the mid-1990s. But this trend may not continue, as Korean firms became more cautious and sensitive to leverage ratios in the wake of the financial crisis.

Korean–Latin American Trade after the Financial Crisis

From the mid-1980s until the outbreak of the crisis, Korea's exports to Latin America and its imports from Latin America both increased rapidly. In the three years from 1993 to 1996, the amount of total trade nearly doubled, growing from $7.3 billion in 1993 to reach its peak at $13.3 billion in 1996—when Korean exports to Latin America totaled $9 billion and imports from Latin America reached $4.4 billion.

The crisis of 1997 had a dramatic, depressing effect on trade. With a sharp contraction in its demand for imported raw materials and primary goods, Korea's total trade with Latin America declined for two consecutive years in 1998 and 1999. During 1998 alone, Korea's imports from Latin America decreased by 46 percent—from $4.07 billion in 1997 to $2.2 billion; at the same time, Korean exports to Latin America actually showed a slight increase of 2.3 percent. By 1999 two-way trade amounted to merely $11.5 billion dollars. In 2000 and 2001, Korea's trade with Latin America rebounded slightly, as exports increased by 8.4 percent and 3.9 percent, and imports by 13.9 percent and 5.6 percent respectively. As a result, the total amount of two-way trade in 2001 amounted to $13.2 billion—thus approaching the peak of 1996.

As of 2001, Latin America represented a 4.5 percent share of Korea's total trade. Latin American countries consumed 6.5 percent of Korea's exports and produced 2 percent of Korea's total imports. After the financial crisis, Latin America's share of Korean trade decreased in general, except for the case of Panama—whose share in exports increased from 1.42 percent in 1997 to 1.73 percent in 1999. Even though Latin America's share of Korea's trade declined after the crisis, however, its share was still among the highest when compared with other Asian countries. Despite the fallout from the crisis, Latin America has managed to maintain a strong trade relationship with Korea.

Historically, Korea's exports to Latin America have consisted mainly of manufactured goods: automobiles and parts; home electronic appliances, including color TVs, VCRs, and refrigerators; garments and textiles; ships; and mobile phones. In contrast, Korea's imports from Latin America are composed of raw materials and primary goods. These consist of mineral products, including iron ore, copper, crude oil, and steel; paper pulp; and agricultural products, such as fruit juice, soybeans, and coffee. From 1998 through 2001,

Korea's cumulative trade surplus with Latin America amounted to $24.8 billion, accounting for nearly one-third of Korea's total trade surplus ($84 billion) during this same period.

Latin America's importance as a major Korean trading partner has steadily grown. In the future, Korea's trade with Latin America will largely depend on trade relations with member countries of MERCOSUR and NAFTA. (Korea recently experienced a setback in exports to these countries as a result of their economic recessions and their subsequent austerity measures that resulted in a reduction in their demand for Korean consumer goods and capital.) Korea's active participation in the new areas such as construction, telecommunication, and privatization of public industry in Latin America will certainly create new opportunities for trade and investment. Korea's eventual accession to the Inter-American Development Bank, which is still uncertain, will accelerate trade and investment with Latin America.

A New Partnership between Asia and Latin America: A Practical Agenda for Closer Cooperation

After jettisoning import-substitution policies in the 1980s, Latin America finally joined the liberal track of free trade in the 1990s. In contrast, Asia has long pursued an outward-looking policy of free trade. Partly as a result of the divergence in their paths toward development, the two regions did not have a sufficiently strong impetus for a viable economic partnership until the late 1990s. But the fact that the two regions pursued historically different economic policies seems to have eventuated in an advantage to their prospective trading relationship; as a result, they have developed differences in their economic needs and capacities that are complementary, and, therefore, conducive to trade. This advantage, coupled with the economic dynamism of the two regions, bodes well for a closer partnership in the future.

At the same time, the possibility of more active cooperation between the two regions has been dampened by two factors: the persistent tendency toward cultural isolation and the language gap. But there is another side to that coin. According to an old Asian saying, those who suffer the same disease become friends easily. Asia and Latin America suffered the same illness in the form of the financial crises of the 1990s, and they can certainly use that experience as the basis for developing a common agenda.

I therefore propose that the two regions collaborate in devising common means to avert the recurrence of financial crises by strengthening transregional institutional cooperation in the international financial market. To advance this shared agenda, they might establish a consultative body in which participants could exchange information on strategies learned from the management of their respective financial crises.

A second proposal is to construct a network of cyber marketplaces for trade and investment among the countries concerned in order to provide easier access to information on trade and investment. A portal site for collective service should be created in advance and all information can be provided in English to overcome language differences. To give an example, Korea's Silkroad 21 site (www.silkroad21.com) provides a trade mart where sellers and buyers can meet in cyberspace and engage in negotiations. If sites of this kind in each country assemble in one portal site, this can serve as a practical e-marketplace. Such an idea could be realized without great difficulty or with little funding through an organization like FEALAC. Leading roles could be played by public trade- and investment-related organizations (Korea Trade and Investment Corporation in the case of Korea) in participating countries.

A third suggestion is to expand cultural programs and scholarly exchange. By engaging experts from academia, business, and government, such programs could enhance mutual understanding and help determine the shape and scope of transregional cooperation.

A fourth idea involves the development of free trade agreements on a bilateral basis, whether within or across geographical regions, which has gained momentum in recent years (see chapter 4 in this volume). Korea and Chile are working toward the completion of a historic free trade agreement. Korea has several reasons for pursuing an FTA with Chile at this time. They are to: (1) extend bilateral cooperation with Chile, even though Korean trade and investment with Chile are still relatively small (the trade volume between the two countries in 1999 accounted for less than 1 percent of Korean trade, but more than 4 percent of Chilean trade); (2) take advantage of the relative ease and political simplicity with which an FTA can be concluded due to Chile's liberal trade policy; and, mainly, (3) build a legal and political model of an FTA that can be applied in the future to relationships with other trading partners. The FTA between Korea and Chile will include provisions not only on trade and investment, but also on agriculture, services, and intellectual property. According to current estimates, the FTA between Korea and Chile is expected to increase Korea's trade by one billion dollars per year.

Studies are now under way to explore the feasibility and the economic effects of establishing further FTAs. For example, Korea, Japan, and China are currently engaged in such study. Conjoint efforts such as this can be helpful in creating an atmosphere of cooperation among prospective partners in regional or cross-regional trading alliances. Such collaborative efforts can serve as an example for the further development of transoceanic organizations such as APEC, which is seeking to regain its status as a major institutional player in the Pacific Rim. Or perhaps that player will arrive in the form of FEALAC, which might eventually sponsor an Asian and Latin American Summit Meeting.

In conclusion, as Asia and Latin America contribute increasingly to global growth, new approaches and decisive actions are urgently needed to foster closer cooperation between the two regions. This cooperation has vast potential for promoting prosperity and stability around the world. Asia and Latin America have many common tasks ahead.

Notes

1. There was a temporary spike up to 9 percent in 2000 and 2001, but this was a misleading statistic.
2. Not counting an erratic and unusual investment of $1.35 billion in Bermuda in 2000.

4

Modes of Economic Integration between East Asia And Latin America

Shoji Nishijima and Akio Hosono

REGIONAL ECONOMIC INTEGRATION BEGAN to flourish in earnest in the Western Hemisphere in the 1990s, with Latin America at the center of the action. Countries of the region worked to revitalize existing subregional schemes and also launch new arrangements aimed at expanding the scope of economic cooperation. Creating a dense network of multilateral and bilateral Free Trade Agreements (FTAs) among themselves, some Latin American countries have established formal arrangements with extraregional partners as well.

Regional integration in Latin America is not a new phenomenon. Latin American nations formed numerous regional pacts and trade frameworks in the 1960s, but these agreements were mostly limited to protecting native markets by substituting domestically produced goods for imported ones—a policy known as import substitution. In contrast, Latin America's movement toward regionalism in the 1990s arose primarily from the desire to relax trade barriers. Under the influence of "neoliberalism," Latin American countries enacted three major reforms: (1) abandonment of interventionist strategies that helped bring about serious economic crises in the 1980s, (2) liberalization of trade and capital flows, and (3) deepening of the privatization of state-owned enterprises. These reforms enabled Latin American countries to stimulate economic growth and to attract foreign direct investment (FDI). As we shall see, regional economic integration, both as a cause and a goal, played a central role in bringing about these policy changes.

Asian countries took a different course: They expanded their trade through "market-led integration" without formal agreements. The exceptions were the Association of Southeast Asian Nations (ASEAN) Free Trade Area (AFTA) and broad, more general forums such as the Asia-Pacific Economic Cooperation forum (APEC).[1] Recently, however, some East Asian countries have begun to show interest in forming bilateral FTAs within Asia and with Latin American partners.

The purposes of this chapter are to identify and analyze the driving forces behind the proliferation of intraregional and interregional FTAs among Latin American countries, and to assess the prospects for bilateral FTAs between Latin America and Asia. We examine these topics in five stages. We begin by discussing theoretical and practical issues affecting bilateral FTAs in general, and FTAs in Latin America, in particular. We review the process of regional integration in Latin America in the 1990s, and then move on to examine the current state of economic relations between Latin America and East Asia. We analyze the prospects for FTAs between Japan and Mexico, and between Japan and Chile. Finally, we describe a new approach to cooperation between East Asia and Latin America, the Forum for East Asia–Latin American Cooperation (FEALAC).

Pros and Cons of Bilateral Frameworks

What accounts for the drive toward bilateral FTAs? This question is especially pertinent to Latin America, which has historically favored multilateral rather than bilateral forms of negotiation. There are essentially three reasons for the new trend: (1) some Latin American countries have been using bilateral FTAs as a means to boost the prospects of their domestic policy reforms, (2) some countries lost confidence in the prospects for multilateral cooperation after the 1999 meeting of the World Trade Organization (WTO) failed to launch a new global trade round, and (3) APEC has essentially ceased to be an active player in promoting regional economic cooperation around the Pacific Rim. Indeed, APEC has been at a virtual standstill since the Asian financial crisis of 1997–1998, and seems, for the time being, unable to provide much impetus for further liberalization.

Aside from these conjunctural factors, however, there are deep-seated elements that help explain, at least from a theoretical viewpoint, why these countries have turned toward bilateral agreements:

- Compared with multilateral FTAs, which tend to cover a range of complex issues, bilateral agreements tend to contain fewer sensitive issues; thus, negotiating these types of agreements is likely to be simpler.
- In contrast to the predetermined roster of members included in a typical multinational FTA, the bilateral strategy allows a country to select an individual partner—which may provide it with significant gains from trade, while presenting fewer difficulties at the negotiation table than forging a multilateral agreement.

- Bilateral agreements may allow a country to avoid the liberalization of some sensitive sectors, which would have to open under multilateral agreements, such as those negotiated in the WTO framework.
- Being a member of numerous bilateral FTAs would provide a country with bargaining power in subsequent negotiations for a regional bloc that included its FTA partners.
- Agreements such as ECAs (Economic Complementarity Agreements) and CFAs (Cooperation Framework Agreements) allow the member countries to make incremental progress toward fuller cooperation through initial accords that cover largely noncontroversial issues. ECAs and CFAs can thus play an important role as stepping-stones toward comprehensive FTAs.
- If a multilateral FTA forms a bilateral FTA with an outsider country, the outsider might be able to pressure the multilateral grouping not to engage in protectionist or exclusionary policies against other outsider countries. Such a bilateral FTA could, then, pave the way for further increases in the membership of the multilateral FTA, and, consequently, guarantee "open regionalism."[2]

In sum, the negotiation of a bilateral agreement tends to be faster and less contentious than forging an agreement with multiple partners.

At the same time, bilateral FTAs have risks and limitations. In general they result in less liberalization of trade than do multilateral agreements. Some of the specific shortcomings of bilateral FTAs are as follows:

- Bilateral agreements may provide long phase-out periods for the more sensitive sectors, or exclude these sectors altogether from their coverage.
- If a bilateral FTA adopts restrictive rules of origin, it will, in effect, maintain barriers against nonmembers.
- Differences in the rules of origin among various FTAs could result in a complex web of discrimination, which would impede unfettered trade flows and complicate subsequent efforts to merge the bilateral FTAs into a multilateral FTA (such as the proposed Free Trade Area of the Americas, FTAA).
- A bilateral FTA of the "hub-and-spoke" variety could encounter difficulties owing to the differences in trade policies between the hub and the spokes.[3] If trade among spoke countries has not been previously liberalized, they have free access only to the hub, while the hub continues to benefit from the preferential access it enjoys to the markets of each of the spoke countries. The hub is therefore likely to reap greater economic benefits from the FTA than any of the spokes. As a result, the hub may oppose the formation of separate FTAs among the spoke countries.

- If the bilateral agreements in the hub-and-spoke model are based on divergent rules, the degree of access to the hub market is likely to vary across the different spokes, which could be a source of friction between the competing spokes, or between the less-favored spokes and the hub.
- Unlike a member of a multilateral FTA, a spoke country cannot usually launch negotiations for a new bilateral FTA with the hub country. Thus, the spoke is likely to oppose the formation of a new bilateral FTA between the hub and another spoke.
- The liberalization process in the hub-and-spoke arrangement might be biased in favor of a hub country with a particularly strong negotiating position.

Theoretically, then, bilateral FTAs can present numerous obstacles to multilateral liberalization (or to open regionalism). On balance, however, we believe that bilateral agreements in Latin America have offered a pragmatic way to accelerate trade liberalization.

Three Phases of FTA Formation in Latin America

This section analyzes driving forces behind the proliferation of intraregional and interregional bilateral FTAs in Latin America in the 1990s. Scholars of international economics have paid increasing attention to FTAs as highly effective instruments for pursuing trade policy reforms in today's world.[4] However, only a handful of studies addresses the theoretical issues discussed in the previous section, especially in reference to Latin America.

What are, then, the forces behind the spree of FTA formation in Latin America since the early 1990s? As shown in table 4.1, two countries, Chile and Mexico, have been particularly active in pursuing bilateral agreements with countries throughout Latin America. Their combined experience allows us to identify three distinct phases in this evolution of free trade agreements—from limited FTAs to comprehensive FTAs to interregional arrangements.

Phase I: Recognition of FTAs as Effective Policy Instruments

After the debt crisis of the 1980s, Mexico set out on the path of extensive trade policy reform. Mexico's first important step was to join the General Agreement on Tariffs and Trade (GATT) in 1986. The second step came in June 1990, when President Carlos Salinas de Gortari joined President George Bush in announcing that the United States and Mexico would launch negotiations for a bilateral free trade agreement. This declaration sent a clear signal

TABLE 4.1
Regional Arrangements of Chile, Mexico, and MERCOSUR

	(As of end 2002)		
	Participant Country or Region	*Type*	*Inception*
Chile	Bolivia	ECA	July 1993
	Venezuela	ECA	July 1993
	Colombia	ECA	January 1994
	Ecuador	ECA	January 1995
	MERCOSUR	ECA	October 1996
	Canada	FTA	July 1997
	Peru	ECA	July 1998
	European Union	CFA	April 1999
	Mexico	FTA	August 1999
	Korea	FTA	Negotiated October 2002
	United States	FTA	Negotiated December 2002
	Central American countries	FTA	Under Negotiation
	Cuba	FTA	Under Negotiation
Mexico	U.S., Canada (NAFTA)	FTA	January 1994
	Colombia	FTA	January 1995
	Bolivia	FTA	January 1995
	Costa Rica	FTA	January 1995
	Nicaragua	FTA	July 1998
	European Union	FTA	July 2000
	Chile	FTA	August 1999
	Israel	FTA	July 2000
	Guatemala, Honduras, El Salvador	FTA	January 2001
	EFTA	FTA	July 2001
	Uruguay	ECA	Effective
	Peru	ECA	Effective
	Argentina	ECA	Effective
	Brazil	ECA	Effective
	Ecuador	FTA	Under Negotiation
	Peru	FTA	Under Negotiation
	Panama	FTA	Under Negotiation
	Trinidad and Tobago	FTA	Under Negotiation
	Japan	FTA	Under Negotiation
MERCOSUR	European Union	CFA (FTA 2005)	December 1995
	Bolivia	ECA	January 1996
	Chile	ECA	October 1996
	CACM	CFA	April 1998
	Andes	CFA	April 1998
	South Africa	FTA	Under Negotiation

Notes: FTA: Free Trade Agreement; ECA: Economic Complementarity Agreement; and: CFA: Cooperation Framework Agreement.
Sources: Mexico: Secretaría de Economía; Chile: DIRECON; and Mercosur: Mercosur Committee in Uruguay.

that the Mexican government was determined to make the liberalization process irreversible. Mexico confirmed this message by reaching FTAs with several Latin America countries in the early 1990s.[5]

Chile's efforts to extend FTAs to a number of countries in the region began also in the early 1990s. However, the Chilean motives differed from those of Mexico. First, Chile was hoping to emerge from the prolonged diplomatic isolation resulting from the seventeen-year dictatorship of General Augusto Pinochet. Second, after almost fifteen years of unilateral liberalization, Chile had come to realize that its policy had not necessarily improved access to other countries' markets. In reaction, Chilean leaders now sought "preferential, assured, and predictable" market access through reciprocal reductions of tariffs with other countries.[6] Chile also worked for the reduction of nontariff barriers and the adoption of rules that would curtail discretionary and arbitrary forms of protectionism.

Mexico and Chile had thus divergent interests in pursuing the new, liberal trade policies, but they clearly agreed on one thing: the idea that FTA formation was one of the most effective policy instruments to advance the overarching goal of trade liberalization. Not surprisingly, the two countries subsequently entered into one of the earliest bilateral agreements—an Economic Complementarity Agreement, or ECA—in January 1992, almost two years before the North American Free Trade Agreement (NAFTA) went into effect. (Even before the Mexico-Chile ECA was ratified, an ECA between Argentina and Chile took force).

Under ECAs, the trade of goods is liberalized, either partially or fully, in keeping with provisions of the Latin American Integration Association (LAIA, known from its Spanish initials as ALADI). ECAs under the ALADI framework can be regarded, in many cases, as types of FTAs, but they can also be more limited; indeed, ECAs typically address only the exchange of goods. In contrast, a comprehensive FTA, such as NAFTA, has detailed rules of origin and well-formulated provisions covering services, dispute settlement, intellectual property, investment, and government procurement. Such FTAs are both broader and deeper than standard ECAs.[7]

Phase II: Deepening and Widening of FTAs

The transformation of simple FTAs into comprehensive FTAs comprised the second phase in the evolution of economic cooperation within the Americas. As reported above, Mexico and the United States initiated talks on a comprehensive bilateral trade agreement in mid-1990, soon after the Canada–United States Free Trade Agreement (CUSFTA) went into effect in

1989. Canada became concerned that the proposed Mexico–U.S. FTA could jeopardize the advantages that Canada had gained through CUSFTA. So, in efforts to protect its interests, Canada decided to participate in the negotiations for NAFTA. The trilateral NAFTA talks began in 1991.

All three countries had their own special, and very different, reasons for joining NAFTA. They nonetheless opted for a mutual trading relationship—NAFTA—that was novel in its comprehensiveness. NAFTA was hardly the first attempt to foster economic ties in North America. Throughout the long and varied histories of Canadian–U.S. and Mexican–U.S. economic relations, attempts had been made to establish cooperative trading arrangements. However, these agreements proved unsatisfactory in two ways: they were unable to overcome impediments to the liberalization of investment and trade, particularly trade in services; and they had inadequate mechanisms to resolve commercial disputes such as those related to automobile trade between Canada and the United States, or to the rules governing the maquiladoras in the U.S.–Mexican border zone.

Mexico had its own special reasons to favor comprehensive FTAs. In the case of NAFTA, Mexico's motivations were as follows:

(a) Since Mexico was already engaged in efforts to liberalize its own trade and investment policies, its government sought to draw the greatest benefits from the situation by seeking concessions through a trade agreement with the United States, Mexico's largest trading partner.

(b) Petroleum had been declining rapidly as a component of Mexico's total exports. In response, Mexico sought better access to as many foreign markets as possible through more comprehensive bilateral, regional, and multilateral trade agreements. NAFTA was one such agreement.

(c) The Salinas administration considered it very important to ensure the continuity of its economic policies, including the lowering of trade barriers. Mexican policy makers regarded NAFTA as a means to prevent future Mexican governments from deviating from the liberal trade policies (the tactic has been referred to as the "locking-in" effect).[8]

After NAFTA was established, Mexico sought bilateral FTAs with several Latin American countries. In 1995, a trilateral FTA with Colombia and Venezuela was developed into the G3 (*Grupo de los Tres*). FTAs with Costa Rica and Bolivia followed soon thereafter. In 1998, Mexico concluded an FTA with Nicaragua and initiated negotiations on FTAs with three other Central American countries: El Salvador, Guatemala, and Honduras. It then turned to negotiations with Panama, Ecuador, Peru, Belize, Trinidad and Tobago, and the Dominican Republic.[9] Finally, Chile and Mexico agreed to upgrade their simple ECA to a comprehensive, NAFTA-type FTA; the new treaty took effect in July of 1999.

Chilean leaders considered bilateral FTAs to be especially effective policy instruments for liberalizing trade. According to Sebastián Sáez, former director of trade negotiations of the Chilean Foreign Ministry, the rules governing negotiations on the multilateral level tend to diminish the bargaining power of small countries. Deliberations on given products are usually carried out between the principal exporters and importers, and then extended to other GATT members. Since small countries are not likely to be the principal suppliers of specific products (much less the foremost importers), their room for maneuver is limited.[10]

Chile's first comprehensive FTA was the Canada-Chile FTA, which went into force in 1997. Since the negotiation of this FTA, according to Sáez, Chile has turned toward increasingly comprehensive agreements. In its more recent FTAs, Chile has favored the inclusion of terms covering investment, trade in services, and the resolution of disputes.[11]

Following its initial ECAs with Argentina and Mexico, Chile entered into several free trade agreements under the ALADI framework: with Venezuela and Bolivia in 1993, Colombia in 1994, Ecuador in 1995, MERCOSUR in 1996, and Peru in 1998. Chile also initiated bilateral negotiations with Canada in 1996 and with the Central American Common Market in 1999.

In short, Mexico and Chile have, since the mid-1990s, been transforming themselves into hubs of various FTAs in Latin America. At the same time, they have worked to broaden the scope of their FTAs, moving from relatively simple arrangements to fully comprehensive and liberalized treaty agreements on economic cooperation.

Phase III: The Pursuit of Interregional FTAs

In the late 1990s, Mexico and Chile turned their attention toward countries outside the Americas. This trend is quite recent and has yet to be analyzed in depth. But one thing seems clear: The trend signals a major shift in the two countries' trade policies. And it seems likely that, as this new trend evolves, Mexico and Chile will become FTA hubs in trade accords, not only within Latin America, but also in interregional FTAs connecting existing or developing treaty organizations in Europe, in Asia, and in the Western Hemisphere (beyond Latin America).

Let us first consider Mexico's motives. After the advent of NAFTA, Mexican exports increased dramatically, from \$51.9 billion in 1993 to \$136.9 billion in 1999. At the same time, Mexico's dependency on the U.S. market also increased. By 1999, 88 percent of Mexican exports went to the United States (while only 3.3 percent of Mexican exports went to the EU). And even though the expansion of trade with the United States was viewed favorably in Mexico, there were concerns that too much reliance on the U.S. market might make Mexico vulnerable to downturns in the U.S. economy. What's more, there were political reasons for Mexico to show reserve in its dealings with its neighbor to the north. Mexico worried that a manifestly close relationship with the United States might weaken Mexico's political standing in Central and South America. Not surprisingly, starting in the mid-1990s, Mexico pursued bilateral negotiations with countries outside the Western Hemisphere. As a case in point, Mexico concluded free trade negotiations with the European Union (EU) in December 1999. The EU–Mexico FTA became effective in July 2000.

Chile's motives in seeking expanded trade agreements outside of the Americas were somewhat different. By the end of the twentieth century, Chile already had one of the most liberalized economies in the world. Since 1999, Chilean tariffs have been reduced by one percentage point every year, with the rate scheduled to reach just 6 percent by 2003. Moreover, Chile has adopted uniform tariffs. Under this system, no sector of the Chilean economy is granted preferential treatment or protection. Therefore no domestic industry or sector will be regarded as "sensitive" or deserving of special treatment.

Given its own remarkably open economy, Chile's principal interest in expanded trade agreements has been to accelerate trade liberalization in partner countries. Specifically, Chile has sought to improve its access to export markets by negotiating a series of regional accords in the form of FTAs, ECAs, and AIPs (Agreements for Investment Protection) with hemispheric and nonhemispheric trading partners alike. Notwithstanding the differences in motivation between Chile and Mexico, their policies have frequently taken the same direction. Like Mexico, for example, Chile negotiated an interregional accord with the EU in 1999. (That agreement is expected eventually to become an FTA.) Chile also attaches great importance to the resumption of free-trade negotiations with the United States.

At the same time, Latin American countries have demonstrated increasing interest in bilateral FTAs with Asian countries. Once again taking the lead, Mexico and Chile have explored the possibility of agreements with Japan, Korea, and Singapore. The prospect of FTAs between Japan and Mexico and between Japan and Chile has already been the subject of several formal studies and preliminary consultations. The trend toward bilateral free trade agreements within Latin America is giving rise to growing interest in Asia.

MERCOSUR has pursued various bilateral schemes. In 1995 it signed a CFA with the EU that is scheduled to become an FTA by 2005. In 1996, Bolivia and Chile joined MERCOSUR as associate members. MERCOSUR subsequently formed framework agreements with Central America and with the Andean Community. Very recently, MERCOSUR began FTA negotiations with South Africa.

Economic Relations between Asia and Latin America

This section presents an overview of the current state of economic relations between Latin America and East Asia. We concentrate on two main areas: trade and foreign direct investment.

Intra-Regional and Interregional Trade

Trading patterns changed dramatically during the 1990s: The countries within NAFTA, Latin America, and East Asia greatly increased their shares of trade within their own regions as a percentage of their total foreign trade. As table 4.2 shows, the NAFTA countries increased intraregional trade shares from 41.4 percent in 1990 to 51 percent in 1998. Latin American countries (not counting Mexico) increased the proportion of their trade with Latin American partners from 13.7 percent to 31.4 percent in the same period. In East Asia, intraregional trade as a share of total trade climbed from 35.7 percent in 1990 to 43.4 percent in 1997 (but then decreased slightly in 1998 as a result of the currency crisis). As mentioned above, the increase in intraregional trade within Latin America can largely be attributed to institutional integration in the form of multilateral and bilateral FTAs. The story has been somewhat different in East Asia, where the increase in intraregional trade is mainly due to de facto regional integration led by market forces rather than by formal agreements.

The share of East Asian exports to Latin America has been stable, around 2–3 percent; Latin America has been only a moderately important market for East Asia. (Japan's exports to Latin America are included in this figure; other East Asian countries have an even smaller export share with Latin America.) In contrast, East Asia was the recipient of about 10 percent of all Latin American exports. Clearly, East Asia has been a very important export region for Latin America. And, just as clearly, there is an apparent asymmetry in the respective importance of these two regions as export markets for one another.

The two regions have similar "comparative advantages," to use a concept from the theory of international trade, which means that their principal exporting industries and their dominant importing sectors have been more competitive with one another than complementary. However, changes in the industries of both regions, particularly in their manufacturing sectors, may

TABLE 4.2
Intra- and Inter-Regional Trade Share by Region

		(Proportions)								
Exporting Region	*Importing Region*	*1970*	*1975*	*1980*	*1985*	*1990*	*1995*	*1996*	*1997*	*1998*
NAFTA	NAFTA	.360	.346	.336	.439	.414	.462	.476	.491	.510
	Latin America	.081	.089	.086	.056	.048	.067	.067	.071	.073
	East Asia	.176	.152	.168	.147	.187	.202	.200	.181	.152
	European Union	.233	.195	.216	.170	.196	.162	.181	.154	.164
	Oceania	.022	.017	.018	.021	.019	.016	.016	.015	.015
Latin America	Latin America	.112	.119	.169	.119	.152	.261	.274	.284	.314
	NAFTA	.322	.338	.287	.332	.350	.270	.289	.292	.283
	East Asia	.054	.048	.063	.065	.088	.115	.109	.099	.083
	European Union	.332	.268	.214	.257	.241	.231	.211	.193	.194
	Oceania	.001	.001	.002	.005	.004	.004	.003	.003	.002
East Asia	East Asia	.287	.286	.327	.318	.357	.390	.435	.434	.384
	NAFTA	.325	.235	.235	.334	.280	.240	.233	.238	.263
	Latin America	.037	.060	.047	.028	.018	.026	.025	.028	.027
	European Union	.135	.134	.144	.114	.162	.137	.121	.135	.140
	Oceania	.034	.034	.028	.070	.022	.016	.018	.020	.027
European Union	NAFTA	.097	.069	.067	.112	.082	.077	.079	.086	.096
	Latin America	.031	.035	.033	.018	.012	.023	.023	.022	.023
	East Asia	.033	.029	.031	.041	.051	.072	.073	.007	.110
	European Union	.487	.484	.509	.503	.550	.624	.614	.558	.561
	Oceania	.016	.012	.028	.010	.008	.008	.008	.008	.008
Oceania	NAFTA	.169	.134	.144	.128	.135	.089	.088	.097	.118
	Latin America	.007	.019	.012	.010	.009	.013	.017	.014	.016
	East Asia	.326	.391	.385	.408	.443	.509	.456	.482	.431
	European Union	.247	.173	.141	.131	.121	.117	.115	.102	.132
	Oceania	.061	.061	.064	.070	.076	.099	.097	.095	.083

Notes: NAFTA (U.S., Canada, Mexico), Latin America (Mexico not included), East Asia (Japan, China, Hong Kong, Indonesia, Korea, Malaysia, Philippines, Singapore, Thailand; Taiwan not included), and Oceania (Australia, New Zealand).
Source: Department of Transportation/IMF

offer new opportunities for intraindustrial trade between the regions. And even though the structure of trade between the two regions may not change in the short run, economic liberalization can lead to changes in the variety and quality of traded products. Such differentiation, in turn, can pave the way to expanding trade between Asia and Latin America. Institutionalized regional cooperation could, thus, serve to accelerate the expansion of interregional trade between Asia and Latin America.

Foreign Direct Investment

Asian countries received FDI at an increasing rate up to 1997, but investment declined somewhat in 1998 and 1999 because of the regional currency crisis. In contrast, FDI to Latin America continued to increase despite the Brazilian crisis of 1999. During that year, $90 billion of FDI from all outside investors flowed into Latin America while about $62 billion went to Asia.

The main reasons for these different levels of FDI flow are as follows: (1) privatization in Latin America created new opportunities for FDI (accounting for about 30 percent of FDI in the region); (2) the Japanese recession induced Japanese investors to pull back their FDI in Asia; (3) the currency crisis seems to have affected Asia more than Latin America; and (4) U.S. and European multinationals invested enthusiastically in M&As (mergers and acquisitions) in Latin America, envisioning the region as an important future market endowed with an expanding network of viable trading partners. Spanish multinationals, such as Telefónica de España, Endesa-España, Banco Santander, and Banco Bilbao Vizcaya, have been conspicuously active. The total of Spanish FDI in Latin America more than tripled in two years, going from $4 billion in 1996 to $12.6 billion in 1998.

Japan increased its FDI in Asia through 1997, and then scaled back in 1998 and 1999 as a consequence of the region's financial crisis in general and Japan's domestic financial instability in particular. The share of Japanese FDI apportioned to Latin America appeared, for a time, to have increased slightly. Yet a closer examination reveals that a major part of Japanese FDI in Latin America went to the Cayman Islands, Bermuda, and Panama as havens from taxes and shipping registration ("flag") convenience. In fact, Japanese FDI in Latin American manufacturing and service sectors is very small—only about 2.2 percent of total Japanese FDI in 1998 and 5.5 percent in 1999. (By comparison, U.S. FDI in Latin America has been very stable; in 1999 it amounted to 14.1 percent of total American FDI.)

Japanese investment in Latin America has been declining recently. The main reason is that the greatest opportunities for FDI in Latin America have been in areas such as telecommunications, electricity, energy, and the like. These are fields in which Japan does not compete well. Moreover, a good deal of FDI has recently started to take the form of M&A, and Japanese firms lack the experience to compete with investors from other countries that are better versed in this special field. This fact, among others, suggests that Japan is losing its competitiveness in the world economic theater and should proceed promptly and forcefully to bring about meaningful internal structural reforms.

Prospects for Japan-Mexico and Japan-Chile FTAs

Here we focus on new initiatives to strengthen economic cooperation between East Asia and Latin America, with emphasis on plans to establish bilateral FTAs both between Japan and Mexico and between Japan and Chile. In preceding sections, we examined the motivations of certain Latin American countries to strengthen their external economic ties through FTAs, and we touched briefly on their burgeoning interest in FTAs with counterparts beyond their own regions—for example, the EU and Japan. Now we consider the other side of the equation: What factors motivate East Asian countries, especially Japan, to seek stronger ties with Latin American countries through FTAs?

Goals and Motivations

Japan, Korea, and other East Asian countries have long valued trade with Latin America because of the continent's abundant resources of minerals and foodstuffs. But in recent years, East Asian countries have taken a new interest in developing more comprehensive economic relations with their Latin American counterparts.

Although the exact nature of this interest varies from nation to nation in East Asia, the case of Japan is largely typical. We can identify at least two major reasons for Japan's growing interest in FTAs with Latin America. One is Japan's recognition of the importance of FTAs in general; the other is Japan's concern that it will be excluded from Latin America, an outcome that would provide a further competitive advantage to the United States and the European Union.

In recent years, Japan, Korea, and Singapore have developed a more positive view of FTAs, including bilateral or regional agreements and various forms of subregional cooperation. Indeed, Japan and Korea (the only two significant GATT/WTO members never to have taken part in any formal FTA or other form of regional institutional integration) have recently abandoned their objection that FTAs are antithetical to multilateralism. Trade authorities at the ministerial level in the Japanese government signaled this change in the *White Paper* of 1999 issued by the Ministry of International Trade and Industry (MITI).

> Japan, convinced of the importance of consistency with the principles of GATT, and considering the possible negative effects of regional integration on regional and extra-regional countries, has thus far adopted a very different position from that of most other countries of the world, which have promoted regional integration (FTAs and customs unions) in addition to the multilateral trading system. . . . Nevertheless, there is a growing need to address this issue in a more flexible and constructive manner, since the following positive effects of regional integration are evident and they could help to strengthen the multilateral trading system. First, there has been a net growth of trade and investment in the specific cases of NAFTA and MERCOSUR. Second, in the context of globalization, some rules of the international economy have been fixed by means of the harmonization of many national circumstances. It should therefore be easier to establish rules (such as TRIMs, TRIPs, dispute settlement, government procurement etc.) among countries with similar socio-economic conditions. Third, in negotiating the multilateral system of international trade, a greater role is now played by groups of countries engaged in regional integration or cooperation. . . . Japan should assume a more active posture towards regional integration and cooperation initiatives, and should propose a model that will help strengthen the multilateral system.[12]

Less than a year later, the Trade and Investment Committee of Keidanren (The Federation of Economic Organizations of Japan) published a report titled *Free Trade Agreements Should be Strongly Promoted: Towards a New Approach to Trade Policy*, and presented it to the Japanese government in July 2000. The document presented a comprehensive analysis of the need for Japan to join FTAs. It also described the scope and contents of the proposed FTAs by reviewing such issues as trade in services, rules of origin, antidumping measures, liberalization and protection of foreign direct investment, standards and certification, intellectual property rights, government procurement, competition policy, electronic commerce, and dispute settlement.

Japan began negotiations with Singapore in early 2001 for a "New Age FTA." Here the parties are considering some novel issues relating to electronic commerce and information technology, in addition to the more traditional areas regarding comprehensive trade and investment. Japan is also considering a new bilateral treaty with Korea. The two governments have agreed to set up study committees, each entrusted with developing measures to strengthen the links between their two economies. A further effort was made by Keizo Obuchi, then prime minister of Japan, during his visit to Korea in March

1999, when he presented the "Agenda 21 of the Japan-Korea Economy: Towards Stronger Japanese-Korean Economic Relations in the Twenty-First Century."

Japan, Korea, and other East Asian countries are becoming increasingly concerned about falling further behind the North American and European countries in the competition for trade relations with Latin America. East Asian countries already lag substantially behind the United States, Canada, and Europe in trade and in foreign direct investment in Latin America. There are various explanations, of course, but the key fact is this: In comparison with the United States (which has taken a leadership role in the FTAA discussions) and the EU (which concluded an FTA with Mexico in 2000 and is negotiating FTAs with MERCOSUR and Chile under existing framework agreements), there have been no similar initiatives to date between Latin American and East Asian countries, including Japan. Moreover, Japan has a special reason for developing institutional links with outside partners: Membership in a comprehensive FTA could have the effect of accelerating badly needed structural reforms in the Japanese economy, which has languished for a decade in the backwash of a serious recession.

Purposes and Prospects for a Japan-Mexico FTA

During a visit to Japan in November 1998, then-president Ernesto Zedillo proposed that Mexico and Japan consider measures to strengthen their economic relations. In response, the Japan External Trade Organization (JETRO) established a commission to study the idea. In April 2000, JETRO and the Secretariat of Trade and Industrial Development (SECOFI) of the Mexican government both presented reports. JETRO summarized its conclusion as follows:

> An FTA would be an effective means of strengthening economic ties between Japan and Mexico. . . . The promotion of a Japan-Mexico FTA would not only contribute to the establishment of trade and investment rules in multilateral negotiations at the WTO, for instance, but also play a major role in diversifying Japan's trade policy options and in preventing the formation of regional economic blocs in North America, Europe and Asia. . . . In promoting a Japan-Mexico FTA, an initiative should be taken also to seek a more comprehensive, higher-level agreement that will cover not only trade and investment liberalization but also intellectual property rights, standards certification, government procurement, and dispute settlement mechanisms. At the same time, even while giving adequate consideration to possible effects on domestic industries, every effort should be made to create a basic framework to realize an FTA at the earliest date possible.[13]

The JETRO report emphasized three central points: (a) a Japan-Mexico FTA should be comprehensive; (b) its effects on domestic industries, especially agriculture, should be taken into consideration; and (c) interregional FTAs, like the eventual Japan-Mexico FTA, can help avert the creation of exclusive intraregional blocs in the world economy.

The Japan-Mexico Economic Committee of Keidanren has been even more specific in its advocacy of an FTA between Japan and Mexico. Citing a recent survey by the Japan-Mexico Chamber of Commerce (in Mexico), Keidanren leaders have noted that about 80 percent of Japanese firms operating in Mexico criticized the Japanese government for not forming an FTA with Mexico. Among the reasons for their concern: (1) Mexican tariffs have increased by about 3 percent for imports from non-FTA countries since January 1999; (2) the special advantages for in-bond maquiladora industries and for products under the PITEX program[14] would be abolished by the end of 2000; and (3) compared with FTA members, Japanese firms are at a disadvantage in competing for local government procurement contracts and for privatized infraprojects (i.e., infrastructure construction projects that are "concessioned" to the private sector) due to the tariffs levied on imports from Japan. In light of these concerns, most Japanese companies doing business in Mexico favor a comprehensive FTA with Mexico.

Of the Japanese firms surveyed, electronic and transportation firms expressed the greatest interest in such an FTA. And most of the firms in the study, in fact an overwhelming 72 percent, expressed concern that the recently concluded EU–Mexico FTA would have a negative effect on their businesses. In response, Keidanren has become decidedly circumspect in its consideration of possible Japanese countermeasures aimed at allaying exclusionary tactics against Japan by NAFTA and the EU–Mexico FTA.[15]

Japan and Mexico have already undertaken some positive steps. During President Fox's visit to Japan in June 2001, the two governments agreed to establish an official joint committee to study means of achieving a bilateral FTA. Furthermore, President Fox expressed his hope to sign the FTA by 2003.

Prospects for a Japan-Chile FTA

In November 1999, Gabriel Valdés, the minister of foreign relations of Chile, suggested to the president of JETRO the idea of a feasibility study for a possible Japan-Chile FTA. Three months later, Chile's undersecretary for foreign relations followed up by proposing an official start to the study. In response, JETRO established a study committee on a Japan-Chile Free Trade

Agreement in May 2000. The committee published its report in mid-2001, reaching the conclusion that:

> Having duly considered the advantages and disadvantages of a free trade agreement between Japan and Chile, and having adequately considered the potential impact on Japan's specific domestic industries, the multifaceted role of agriculture, and the need to secure a stable supply of natural resources, we conclude that the maximum effort should be made to conclude a free trade agreement between Japan and Chile as soon as possible. . . . For all of these reasons, the free trade agreement to be concluded between Japan and Chile should be comprehensive, addressing not only market access but also investments, services, government procurement, standards and certification, and competition policies. In this way, it will not only promote bilateral trade but also promote mutual investment flows and encourage businesses from the two nations to cooperate in developing markets in third countries. In addition, as a result of the agreement's motivational effect, Japan and Chile will enter into a closer and more multilevel economic relationship. Not only that, by concluding a forward-looking free-trade agreement demonstrating that both nations regard free trade as a matter of national policy, Japan and Chile will be contributing to the liberalization of trade and investment throughout the world.[16]

Although the impetus for the projected Japan-Chile FTA is generally similar to that of the Japan-Mexico FTA, there are some differences. First, there was a very real prospect that Japan might have been excluded from preferential trade relations with Chile. This is all the more urgent in light of Chile's negotiations with the United States (and NAFTA) and the EU. Second, the volume of trade and investment between Japan and Chile is less than the amount of trade and investment between Japan and Mexico. Nonetheless, the JETRO report points to several reasons for seeking an FTA with Chile: (a) Chile has been a model of economic development, (b) Japan has come to admire Chile's free trade policy, (c) Chile is well advanced in information technology (IT) compared to other Latin American countries, and (d) Chile is in a position to serve as a "gateway" for trade between Asia and Latin America, especially MERCOSUR. With these advantages in mind, JETRO emphasizes that Chile is important to Japan as a potential FTA partner.

The Potential Significance of Japan-Mexico and Japan-Chile FTAs

Because the initiatives toward developing FTAs between Japan and Mexico and between Japan and Chile are still in their early stages, we are not yet able to offer an in-depth analysis of the ramifications of these agreements. Instead, we shall cite the following factors as crucial to the success of their negotiation:

(a) Japan is highly motivated because it is worried about being left out of new frameworks for institutional cooperation in the Latin American theater. This is particularly so because the United States, Canada, and the EU have already concluded comprehensive trade accords with the Latin American countries. Japan is very concerned about losing further ground in Latin America, especially in the lucrative Mexican and Chilean markets.

(b) Japan will seek to minimize or prevent any potentially damaging effects of these FTAs on certain of its domestic industries—especially agriculture, livestock ranching, and fisheries. Japan can be expected to adopt domestic policy measures and to push for special terms in order to shield these native industries from harm. Precedents for such terms already exist in the EU–Mexico FTA, and they are considered to be consistent with GATT/WTO.[17] Such accommodations would blunt political pressures against FTAs from sensitive sectors of the Japanese economic community.

(c) Prospects for these FTAs depend on the progress of WTO negotiations on agriculture and on the stance of Japanese government regarding further liberalization in this sector. It should be noted that there are strong political pressures against liberalization in Japan, due to the multifaceted and traditional roles of agriculture in Japanese economic and political life.

(d) In all likelihood, Japan will be influenced by the outcome of the prospective Japan-Singapore FTA as well as by other initiatives in Asia currently under negotiation.

(e) Similarly, Japan will be influenced by the course of negotiations and the final details of interregional FTAs between other East Asian countries and Latin America, such as the Chile-Korea FTA and the Singapore-Mexico FTA.

(f) Japan will be keenly interested in the progress of two proposed FTAs currently under negotiation: (i) the campaign to establish the FTAA in the Western Hemisphere, and (ii) the effort to institute the EU–MERCOSUR FTA. A crucial matter in the progress toward an FTAA is whether the George W. Bush administration will be able to obtain congressional authorization for fast-track negotiations.

Bilateral FTAs between Japan and Mexico and between Japan and Chile may prove useful as stepping-stones for expanding the relationship between Japan and Latin America. For instance, Japan would like to reverse the recent downward trend of its FDI flows to Latin America. Bilateral FTAs should enable Japan to promote its FDI, not only in its partner countries, but also in other Latin American countries that are connected to partners by treaty.

Japan's discussions with Mexico and Chile will themselves have a further influence on initiatives for other bilateral FTAs within Asia and on the APEC liberalization process. (Mexico and Chile are APEC members.) Of course, such FTAs must guarantee that they will promote multilateral liberalization—or at least not hinder it. And such FTAs should not exclude third countries; indeed, they should have unambiguous qualifications for accession.

New Initiatives for Cooperation between East Asia and Latin America

In addition to the movement toward bilateral FTAs, Asian and Latin American countries have embarked on a new framework for bi-regionalism. To initiate this new approach, Singapore Prime Minister Goh Chok Tong proposed in October 1998 a meeting to bring together the leaders of Asian countries, including Japan, and Latin American countries. It was called the East Asia–Latin America Forum (EALAF, or in Spanish, FALAE). A preparatory meeting was held in September 1999 in Singapore, and the inaugural ministerial meeting was held in Santiago, Chile, in March 2001. At that meeting, the participants agreed that the organization's official name would become the Forum for East Asia–Latin America Cooperation (FEALAC).

The participating countries at the Singapore meeting were China, South Korea, Japan, the ten countries of ASEAN (Brunei, Cambodia, Indonesia, Laos, Malaysia, Myanmar, the Philippines, Singapore, Thailand, and Vietnam), Australia, New Zealand, and twelve countries from Latin America (Argentina, Bolivia, Brazil, Chile, Colombia, Ecuador, Mexico, Panama, Paraguay, Peru, Uruguay, and Venezuela). At the FEALAC meeting, El Salvador, Costa Rica, and Cuba were added as members. Thus, one of the salient features of this forum lies in the fact that almost all of the Latin American countries have joined. In comparison, only three countries from Latin America have so far been admitted to APEC.

According to a communiqué issued at the Santiago meeting, FEALAC marked the beginning of an unprecedented dialogue and the opening of a new era of cooperation between the two regions. FEALAC announced that its goals were to find common ground on political, cultural, social, economic, and international issues. To advance these objectives, the members would seek to strengthen the ties between their two regions vis-à-vis the challenges and opportunities of an ever more interdependent and globalized world. The ministers approved frameworks establishing the principles, objectives, and methods to guide the forum's future work. FEALAC declared its intention to employ a multidisciplinary approach in order to achieve its objectives and involve both the public and private sectors in efforts to realize its agenda.

FEALAC established working groups in three broad areas: (1) political/cultural affairs, (2) economic/social policy, and (3) education/science and technology. According to a statement by the cochairs of the Santiago meeting, the working groups are to follow important guidelines:

(a) Forum-wide projects should comply in all of their aspects with detailed formulae for cooperation between the two regions;
(b) Where possible, the working groups should endeavor to coordinate and harmonize already existing national projects with proposed forum-wide projects; and
(c) The working groups should consider suggestions from all member states. At the same time, they should ensure that any such suggestions avoid duplication with the existing work of other regional and international forums, groups, and institutions.

FEALAC intends to address two potentially trying issues in the near future: (1) its relationship with the United States, which is, so far, a nonmember; and (2) its relationship with APEC. At the time of this writing, we do not have any information regarding the U.S. official stance on FEALAC. With regard to APEC, tensions could arise from the fact that FEALAC has similar objectives and overlapping membership. But according to a high Chilean official, "APEC has nothing to do with this forum [FEALAC]. It's an economic and commercial forum. We [in FEALAC] will take up social, cultural and political issues. Political issues are very important to us."

If the FEALAC concept becomes a reality, Asia and Latin America—with a combined population of 2.3 billion people—will, for the first time, have an institutional framework for economic interchange that will surely play an important role in the relationship between the regions well into the future.

Conclusion

East Asian countries, including Japan, have pursued multilateralism under the auspices of GATT/WTO, and, in a less formal way, have achieved some measure of "market oriented" regional integration. Now it is becoming apparent that formal regional integration need not conflict with multilateralism. Rather, it can be seen as an effective means to accelerate the liberalization of trade and investment. But East Asian countries have fallen into a disadvantageous position in the competition for foreign markets in countries that have already joined trade agreements. In an effort to regain lost ground, East Asian nations are no longer reluctant or slow to join the ranks of countries pursuing trade advantages through regional cooperation. In fact, East Asian countries have themselves recently initiated negotiations with several countries about forming FTAs. And bilateral FTAs with Latin American countries have lately become especially attractive.

Several Latin American countries, particularly Mexico and Chile, have had rich experience with bilateral FTAs, although they have voiced strong reservations in the past about FTAs with countries in East Asia. But now they appear to be ready to undertake new initiatives in East Asia. As shown by recent developments in the Mexico–EU FTA, Mexico is already looking for new FTAs with extraregional partners. Mexico and Chile seem to be well aware of the merits of bilateral FTAs, and their strong interest in forming new FTAs appears to be at the forefront of a growing international movement. In this new political climate, the outlook seems to be increasingly favorable for building transregional FTAs between Latin American and Asian countries.

Extrapolating from these trends, we venture to conclude with two predictions: (1) Asian and Latin American countries will employ bilateral FTAs initially as leverage to promote the liberalization of trade and investment. It is likely that the two regions will then abandon their FTA ties in favor of even more comprehensive forms of trade cooperation. (2) Japan will use FTAs not only as a means to strengthen its connections with Latin America, but also—and just as importantly to the Japanese economy—as a stimulus to bring about its own internal structural reforms. Because of these two compelling needs, one from within and one from without, Japan, in particular, can be expected to assume a leadership role and pursue aggressively the creation of FTAs with Latin American countries. These FTAs should ultimately be congruent with the ideals of the multilateral free trade system.

Notes

1. See Akio Hosono, "Investment Opportunities in Latin America and Asia and the Pacific," in *Inter-regional Cooperation in Trade and Investment: Asia and Latin America*, UN-ESCAP (2000); and Akio Hosono, "Economic Integration in Asia and Pacific: Experiences and New Initiatives," *Integration and Trade*, No. 12, Vol. 4, IDB/INTAL (December 2000).

2. See Shoji Nishijima and Peter H. Smith, eds., *Cooperation or Rivalry? Regional Integration in the Americas and the Pacific Rim* (Boulder, Colo.: Westview Press, 1996), 269–274.

3. See Christopher Findley, "Old Issues in New Regionalism" (paper presented at the ANU-Kobe conference held at RIEB, Kobe University, February 2001).

4. See, for example, MITI, *White Paper on International Trade* (Tokyo, 1999).

5. Beatriz Leycegui, "¿Socios naturales?: Una visión general," in Beatriz Leycegui and Rafael Fernández de Castro, eds., *¿Socios Naturales?: Cinco años del tratado de libre comercio de América de Norte* (Mexico City: ITAM, 2000), 30; and Maureen A. Molot, "¿NAFTA: Resultado de decisiones políticas o inducido por la inversión?," *NAFTA y MERCOSUR: Un diálogo Canadiense-Latinoamericano,* eds. Richard C. Lipsey and Patricio Meller (Santiago: CIEPLAN, 1996), 310.

6. Sebastian Sáez, *Estrategia y negociación en el sistema multilateral de comercio* (Santiago: Dolmen Ediciones, 1999), 166.

7. Some authors refer to the comprehensive FTAs à la NAFTA as "third-generation" or "last-generation" FTAs. See Sáez, *Estrategia,* 164.

8. See Leycegui, "Socios," 31–32.

9. Mexico also signed an FTA with Israel in 2000.

10. See Sáez, *Estrategia,* 166–67.

11. Sáez, *Estrategia,* 173–74.

12. See *White Paper,* 1999, 37–38. The Ministry of International Trade and Industry, MITI, was reorganized in the process of administrative reform and it is now known as the Ministry of Economy, Trade and Industry, or METI.

13. JETRO, *Report on Closer Economic Relations between Japan and Mexico* (Tokyo: JETRO, 2000), 45.

14. In May 1990, the president of Mexico enacted the "Decree Establishing Temporary Import Programs to Produce Export Articles (PITEX)." The purposes of PITEX are to promote exports of nonpetroleum products, advance vertical integration, and encourage sales of export-quality products in the Mexican domestic market. A company seeking to operate under the auspices of PITEX must obtain authorization from the Secretariat for Trade and Industrial Development (SECOFI).

15. See *Keidanren* (October, 2000), in Japanese.

16. JETRO, *Study Report on the Japan-Chile Free Trade Agreement* (Tokyo: JETRO, May 2001), 16.

17. In the case of the EU–Mexico FTA, about 25 percent of agricultural products are included in a "waiting list" that does not fix a deadline for liberalization. The adoption of such pragmatic compromises facilitated the negotiation of this treaty.

5

Agents of Interaction: The Changing Roles of Business Firms

Kotaro Horisaka

The economy of Latin America has changed dramatically in the last ten years. From the 1930s through the 1970s, the era of Import Substituting Industrialization (ISI), the leading protagonist in the business arena was always the government—including its administrative apparatus, state-owned corporations (SOCs), and national banks. The state also played a predominant role in the 1980s, the "lost decade" of the debt crisis. At that time the main questions for every nation in Latin America were how to escape the indebtedness trap and subsequently how to put its economic house in order. Governmental leadership was overwhelmingly the key factor at that stage.

With the lifting of state controls and the consequent opening of the economy, however, the players began to change roles. State-owned corporations and banks no longer have leading parts. Government left center stage, seemingly in recognition of its new role as a regulator of economic activity rather than as principal protagonist. The tripodal model comprising state, transnational corporations (TNCs), and local capital—which was considered peculiar to the industrialization of Latin America, most notably Brazil—has been relegated to the past.[1]

Concurrently, private transnational firms working behind the scenes have taken center stage in Latin America. Spanish, Portuguese, Korean, and Chinese companies have taken advantage of business opportunities, adding their investments to domestic capital and existing foreign capital from the United States, England, Germany, Japan, and elsewhere. New ventures such as resale of electricity and highway building and management concessions have been launched. Moreover, the resumption of foreign direct investment (FDI) has introduced new technologies and management know-how to the region. As a result, business communities in Latin America now include broad arrays of firms with distinct national and corporate cultures. Local critics sometimes disparage this trend as a form of denationalization or transnationalization of the economy. From my viewpoint, though, the coexistence of companies from different nations, including other countries of Latin America, has begun to create complex and "cosmopolitan" business communities.

This chapter focuses on the importance of business firms in Latin America's changing economic environment and its relations with East Asia. There are, of course, extensive volumes of literature on economic relations within and between regions—mostly dealing with such matters as trade, capital flows, technology transfer, and labor migration. Only recently can one begin to find serious studies of business firms in Latin America.

The first two sections of this essay examine the roles of private corporations in the process of economic integration in Latin America, using the East Asian situation as a reference point. A third section identifies driving forces connecting Latin America and East Asia, with special emphasis on business firms as agents of interaction.

Business Firms and Regional Integration

One question frequently raised in the 1980s among Japanese scholars was why it was apparently so difficult for Latin America to achieve an integrated market. Countries of the region generally share a common history and culture of Iberian origin, a similarity of language, and religious and Roman law backgrounds, and yet integration remained elusive. East Asia, by contrast, readily attained an integrated market despite significant historical, cultural, linguistic, religious, and legal differences between nations.

This question led us to consider the role of business firms in regional integration. The explanation commonly accepted in Japan regarding East Asia is that this region has developed de facto integration through market mechanisms that are in accordance with the business interests of private firms. It was business interests that integrated the East Asian economies, rather than a widely proclaimed strategic framework or an official free-trade scheme.

Consequently, East Asia conformed to a pattern of regional development that came to be known as the "flying wild geese formation," or inter-economy sequencing of the industrialization process. This entailed the diffusion of internationally competitive, manufacturing-based economies from Japan to the Asian NIEs (Newly Industrializing Economies), then to the Association of Southeast Asian Nations (ASEAN), and now to China and Indochina. Today,

East Asia itself has become the largest export market for East Asian manufactured goods, and local markets are attracting additional FDI into the manufacturing sector. Still, the principal incentive for companies in Japan (and NIEs and ASEAN nations) to invest in neighboring countries has been and remains the wage differentials in labor markets.

Regional economic integration in East Asia is, thus, de facto, and represents a market-led (i.e., business-led) unification. In contrast, Latin American integration can best be described as a "system-preceding" unification. This characterization especially holds true for the 1960s and the early 1970s. Intraregional trade and investment within Latin America were limited despite strong efforts by diplomats and politicians to integrate regional or subregional markets through free trade agreements (FTAs) or customs unions. Business firms, safely protected by policies of ISI, did not follow up on the idea of internationalizing their activities. Their attitude was in complete contrast to that of East Asian business firms, which were very keen on internationalizing their activities.

At that time, Latin American business leaders were concentrating their efforts on their respective domestic markets and, to a lesser extent, on markets in developed countries—if, of course, they had any interest in exports. For transnational corporations, too, their concern was mainly the specific country in which they invested, not a larger region encompassing several countries.

It is clear that business firms—both exporters and importers—can promote regional economic integration without a formal framework. It is also true that, without the active participation of private enterprise, the grand design of a regional framework would be nothing but pie-in-the-sky. This does not, however, mean that the political and diplomatic initiatives and efforts to institutionalize these systems have been unimportant. In recognition of this fact the Japanese government, which has traditionally been a strong advocate of multilateral trade rules, has finally started to consider negotiation of bilateral free trade agreements, as discussed in chapters 4 and 13 of this volume. China, too, has proposed a formal FTA with neighboring ASEAN countries.

Internationalization of Latin American Firms

Since the early 1990s, newspapers and magazines in Latin America have been increasing their coverage of local and transnational companies throughout the region. This serves as an indication of the growing importance of business firms as economic agents. Within this context, internationalization has been rapidly gathering momentum, as if corporate management had suddenly been cured of its "obsession" with the protective industrialization policy of import substitution.

For these reasons a group of Japanese scholars, including myself, decided to explore changes of attitude within the Latin American business community. Keeping the East Asian case in mind, the group gathered data from newspaper accounts, in order to be able to quantitatively identify and plot trends in the internationalization of Latin American companies. Data compiled during the first half of the 1990s had already corroborated the new role of business firms as agents of economic or business connections in the region. The study reached the following conclusions, among others:

1. "Outwardly-oriented internationalization" of business activities has occurred since at least 1990 in the four major Latin American economies: Argentina, Brazil, Chile, and Mexico. As a result, certain "multinational corporations, speaking broadly, have emerged and are noted for conducting business beyond any one country's borders, having one or more production bases abroad."
2. In internationalizing their corporate management practices, these companies tend to acquire other companies instead of forming alliances, establishing subsidiaries, or arranging joint ventures. For these firms, the main purpose of internationalization is to get a footing in new "markets." Other objectives, such as securing cheap labor or production/export bases for supplying third countries—especially markets of developed countries, a common goal for East Asian firms—are minor considerations.
3. The process of internationalization follows in the footsteps of the North American Free Trade Agreement (NAFTA) and the Common Market of the South (MERCOSUR), and the internationalization of Latin American firms has helped to advance "market integration" in the area. These firms are currently regarded as "local multinationals," which, while internationalizing their management practices, make the integration of local markets their first priority.[2]

Accordingly, the business community that we see today in Latin America is completely different from what we saw before. Firms are now the major agents of interaction in regional economic or business interactions. Indeed, shared business interests have helped avoid a rupture of MERCOSUR during periodic trade conflicts, especially between its two leading members, Argentina and Brazil, and also during their moments of economic crisis.

Several characteristic aspects of development can be observed in Latin America with regard to regional business connections. In other words, private firms have different reasons and modes for the pursuit of internationalization.

Development through Market Opening

It cannot be emphasized enough that open-market policies implemented since the late 1980s by Latin American nations have formed the most important and fundamental basis for business connections. With the democratization of politics and the termination of ISI policies, Latin American nations have lowered tax barriers and non-tax barriers between them more rapidly than Asian nations.

The business relationship between Argentina and Chile—which once was so overwhelmingly hostile that military conflict was a real threat—is the most telling example of this change. Chile was the first Latin American country to actually put into effect its economic restructuring, and its relatively strong financing capacity transformed it into an "investment-oriented country." Chilean firms looked first toward Argentina to tap opportunities outside of the country. They have since expanded their activities—given increased momentum by their operations in Argentina—into surrounding countries such as Brazil, Peru, Bolivia, and Colombia, and even into Costa Rica and Mexico. Stimulated and challenged by the arrival of Chilean capital, Argentine corporations also began to invest in neighboring markets. It should be remembered that Chilean participation in MERCOSUR as an associate member came in the wake of its increasing involvement with other countries of the Southern Cone.

As mentioned above, the various nations in Latin America share many cultural, religious, linguistic, and other characteristics. As a result, once political and economic conflicts and trade barriers are removed, and firms start to become interested in internationalization, corporate activities readily expand into neighboring regions. The situation now allows a greater number of companies, including small- and medium-sized companies, to more easily conduct business abroad. The spread of Mexican food manufacturer Grupo Bimbo throughout the Americas and of Brazilian paint manufacturer Tintas Renner into neighboring markets are good examples.

Regionalization of TNC Interests

Transnational corporations (TNCs) are also becoming important in the conduct of cross-border business among Latin American countries. Take, for example, the automobile and auto parts industries. They were formerly set up in individual countries and did not typically target groups of countries as markets. This situation arose because of the protective ISI policies strictly imposed throughout Latin America. Today, TNCs active in the automobile industry are exchanging models and/or types of cars assembled by their respective subsidiaries in Argentina and Brazil. Increasingly, their auto parts come from suppliers in both countries. This is in line with the realization that what is needed nowadays is not a strategy for individual nations, but a strategy for an entire region as an integrated market. An example of this is the influence of transnationals' interests upon government negotiations involving agreements such as the Common MERCOSUR Automotive Regimen.

With the structural changes taking place in Latin American economies, the interest of TNCs in investment has proven to be contagious, spreading from one country to another. The best example is investment in telecommunications, energy, and the financial sector, especially by Spanish firms, including Telefonica, Endesa, Repsol, Banco Santander, and Banco Bilbao Vizcaya Argentaria. For Spanish firms, the outcome of regional integration in Latin America is becoming a decisive factor in their global presence.

Alliances in the Face of Competition

Bitter competition with the market heavyweights has induced Latin American firms to form cross-border alliances. This was clearly exemplified by the privatization of Somisa and Sidor, the state-owned steelworks of Argentina and Venezuela, respectively. Three steelworks from Argentina, Brazil, and Chile jointly acquired Somisa, and steelworks from Venezuela, Mexico, Brazil, and Argentina formed a group to acquire Sidor.

The recent networking or linkage of gas and oil pipelines and transmission lines for electricity across South American borders is another attempt to strengthen the overall economic and business competitiveness using regional resources widely and effectively. Such efforts to enhance infrastructure are important to the physical consolidation of such regional integration schemes as MERCOSUR.

Interaction between Latin American and East Asian Firms

What might we say about the business relationships of firms in Latin America and East Asia under the new paradigm of globalization? Data on FDI show that the relationships between these two regions are not very encouraging. Both regions are keen to internationalize their activities, but not in relation to one another. This lacuna is sometimes called the "missing link." Japan is no longer the major investor in Latin America, and its name is rapidly disappearing from the top-ten list of foreign direct investors at a time when Latin American countries are experiencing a historically high level of FDI.

Under these circumstances, governments in both regions are trying to encourage their respective business communities to wake up and take the opportunity to foster their interest in one another. One recent diplomatic effort involves the formation of the Forum for East Asia–Latin America Cooperation, FEALAC (the former East Asia–Latin America Forum, EALAF), first proposed by Goh Chok Tong, the prime minister of Singapore. A question arises in this context as to whether the two regions have any binding factors to attract the interest of business firms. Without enthusiastic follow-up by business firms, even the best-laid plans of the diplomatic corps will be in vain.

Taking recent business trends into account, the following perspectives deserve careful consideration. Changes are not yet pronounced, but they nonetheless have begun.

Size of Prospective Markets

It is my view that East Asia and Latin America could make a good start toward enhancing their mutual interests by recognizing the size of one another's markets. The trade structure between these two regions has been quite uneven for many years now, consisting largely of exports of raw materials from Latin America to East Asia on the one hand, and exports of capital goods, parts, and intermediate materials for manufacture from East Asia to Latin America on the other. This trade has resulted in both regions' maintaining a traditional and stereotyped image of the other's market.

Once business firms start to take note of the size of the markets involved, however, this situation might begin to change. One good example is Cemex, Mexico's cement company. After expansion of subsidiaries into Europe and the neighboring Americas—including the United States—the company launched production in Southeast Asia by acquiring local companies in the Philippines, Indonesia, and Thailand. It then launched sales operations in Japan. Recognizing that weighty raw materials such as cement were not and are not tradable transoceanic goods, Cemex forged a strategy to conquer a new consumer market through merger and acquisition. For Cemex, Asia represented an essential market because of the magnitude of its demand. Today, Cemex is the third-largest cement company in the world.

Another example made possible by changes in the traditional views of the nations involved is the participation of Kawasaki Heavy Industries, one of the leading Japanese manufacturing companies, as a supplier of wings to the Brazilian aircraft maker Embraer. This came about thanks to the Japanese firm's simple recognition of Embraer's high production capacity, regardless of the fact that the latter company is based in a developing country.

Japanese and Korean investments in the electronics industry in Mexico's maquiladora sector and Korean and Taiwanese investments in the textile and apparel industries in Central America and the Caribbean are also market-oriented. They seek to take advantage of preferential access to the United States market under the NAFTA and Caribbean Basin Initiative (CBI) or other special arrangements.

Critical Needs for East Asia

Latin America continues to supply both raw materials and foodstuffs worldwide. This was one reason why, prior to the debt crisis of the 1980s, Japan had made heavy direct investments in the production of iron pellets, aluminum, pulp, salt, soybeans, and the like. The subsequent availability of these commodities through trade markets in the United States and Europe made it less attractive for Japan to continue to expand this direct source of supply. A further influential factor was the substantial burden of past investments and loans.

The rapid expansion of the East Asian economy has renewed interest in Latin American raw materials and foodstuffs. In 1992, when the Peruvian government privatized its state-owned iron ore mines, Hierro Peru—the largest in the country—one of the buyers was a Chinese state-run company, Shougang. For China, the stable supply of raw materials is becoming crucial to its industry. Likewise, negotiations between Companhia de Vale do Rio Doce (CVRD), Brazil's privatized state-owned iron ore company, and China's flagship steel maker, Shanghai Baosteel, were slated for mid-2001 in an effort to extend Shanghai Baosteel's holdings of overseas resources.

It is not surprising that Korea too is once again planning to participate in exploration for natural resources in Latin America as soon as the East Asian economy stabilizes. The Korean company Daewoo and the Korean Oil Developing Corporation obtained the concession rights for a Peruvian oil field with Argentinean and Canadian companies in the late 1990s. Likewise, the Korean conglomerate SK acquired development rights for oil and natural gas in southern Peru.

To a lesser extent, the Southeast Asian countries are also looking to establish a closer business connection with Latin America in order to secure reliable supply sources. An example of this is that NatSteel of Singapore in 1997 joined with Brazilian private partners to purchase a stake in the Brazilian former state-owned steel mill Açominas; as a result, NatSteel holds now 21.4 percent of Açominas capital.

Global Strategies of TNCs

Although there is usually no direct motivation to connect East Asia and Latin America, the global strategy of transnational corporations can help forge links between the two regions. The most striking case of this is Nissan Motor, Japan's second biggest carmaker. Nissan recovered quickly in 2000 (its consolidated profit posted a record high of 331.1 billion yen, i.e., about $2.7 billion U.S.) from its devastating financial situation in 1999 (when it sustained a total loss of 684.8 billion yen). It achieved this through plant closures, supplier cuts, management changes, and debt reduction in Japan. Now the company plans to boost production in Aguascalientes, Mexico, by 30 percent, and to start assembling pickup trucks in Curitiba, in the Brazilian state of Paraná, as a part of its post-revival plan. It also expects to begin production in Argentina in the near future, targeting the MERCOSUR market as a whole.

This is all occurring under the strict management control of the French automobile company Renault, Nissan's 36.8 percent shareholder. Nissan will assemble Renault's minivan together with its own models in Mexico, and will use the Renault plant in Brazil as a production starter. As a byproduct of its global strategy, in other words, the Renault/Nissan group will strengthen the relationship between East Asia and Latin America. It will also consolidate intraregional ties within East Asia, as Nissan has forged joint ventures in both Thailand and Indonesia.

Implementation of these global strategies set out by TNCs, however, is not always reflected in statistics on bilateral FDI and trade, such as between Japan and Brazil. TNCs' investment and trade behavior is much more complex than that of traditional corporate bodies. Hence, it is often misleading to discuss the economic and business relationships between two nations on a merely bilateral basis.

Patterns of Industrial Reorganization

Another trend that warrants careful scrutiny is the global reorganization of industries. In today's economic environment it is not unusual (1) for reorganization of an industry to be caused by severe sales competition for major products in the buyer's industry, (2) for reorganization of industry in leading nations to engender reorganization in other countries, and (3) for reorganization of a core industry to have a ripple effect on related industries.

One example is the steel industry. In January 2001, Nippon Steel and France's Usinor announced a strategic alliance to exchange know-how for steel sheets used in cars. The following month Usinor reached an agreement to merge with Arbed of Luxembourg and Aceralia of Spain. In April, Kawasaki Steel and NKK, Japan's second and third largest steelworks, announced the creation of a joint holding company to integrate their activities.

In the specific case of the steel industry, it is the intense competition in sales to the automobile industry that led to the trend toward mergers and acquisitions. Nissan, for instance, concentrated its purchase of steel sheets in few companies such as Nippon Steel and Usinor in order to cut purchasing costs. This decision also changes totally the outlook for other firms facing severe competition.

Local steel companies in Latin America cannot remain unaffected by the reorganization of the steel industry in Japan and Europe. They are inextricably linked to the major steel groups through either capital sharing or business association, and through technology linkage. Good examples of this are Brazil's Usiminas with Japan's Nippon Steel, Acesita with France's Usinor, Gelvasud with Germany's Thyssen, and Argentina's Techint with Japan's NKK. At the same time, the reorganization of the steel industry affects the capital holding of iron ore ventures. A desperate fight broke out between two world giants, BHP of Australia and CVRD of Brazil, both of which hoped to acquire Brazil's second, third, and fourth largest companies in the sector.

Thus, reorganization of industry can be another source of business connection between two regions, although this may not be directly targeted. Similar situations of global reorganization can be found in the automotive and electronic industries, telecommunications services, and the financial sector.

Human Dimensions and Personal Contacts

Last, human contacts are also worth mentioning as a time-honored source of business connections—although they tend to be more sporadic and less systematic than other factors. One new aspect to be reckoned with in Japan is a phenomenon called *dekasegi* (temporary migrant laborers). More than 250,000 *Nikkeijin*, Japanese descendants from Brazil, are living in Japan in order to work, mostly in the unskilled job sectors. The sudden influx of *Nikkeijin*, an immigration novelty, started in the late 1980s when the economy of Brazil was deep in crisis, and Japan was enjoying a full economic boom. In spite of the subsequent upswing in the Brazilian economy and a Japanese downswing, the number of *Nikkeijin* continues to be high. Brazilian communities have formed in certain areas of Japan. Many microbusinesses involving Brazil and Brazilians living in Japan flourish in these towns. They are becoming new points for business encounters.

These modest activities, of course, are not comparable to those of TNCs. Nevertheless, they could conceivably constitute the basis for increased mutual understanding and confidence, from the bottom up. Local chambers of commerce and industry have started to pay attention not only to local *Nikkeijin* businesses but also to Brazil itself as a business opportunity. As a case in point, the Brazilian Chamber of Commerce in Japan (Câmara de Comércio do Brasil no Japão, CCBJ) was inaugurated in November 2001 as a forum for networking and exchange of information; its membership is composed of Brazilian companies in Japan, Japanese companies interested in Brazil, and newly created local *Nikkeijin* firms.

Likewise, those overseas Chinese who travel widely can frequently play an important role by using their own family networks as a bridge, not only between Latin America and mainland China or Taiwan, but also between Latin America and Chinese communities spread throughout Southeast Asia.

Another suggestive phenomenon is the emergence of global business figures with experience in both Latin America and Asia. The heads of three (out of the total of eight) Japanese carmakers have had hands-on experience working in South America: the COO (Chief Operating Officer) of Nissan, Carlos Ghosn, is a Brazilian who ran French tire-maker Michelin's Brazilian operations; the COO of Mitsubishi Motors, Rolf Eckrodt from DaimlerChrysler, is a German who was the president of Mercedes Benz do Brasil; and the President of Mazda, Mark Fields, is an American who was the president of Ford Argentina.

Transnational corporations, such as Carrefour, a French supermarket chain, and Parmalat, an Italian food-processing company, sent their person in command in Brazil to China when they opened their first operations in that country. It was said that the experience of running firms in a large and diverse country like Brazil would be helpful in business management activities in China.

It is not always true that these global business entities work to connect countries where they have experience doing business. What should be noted here, however, is that they tend to put East Asia and Latin America in the same global panoramic context.

Conclusion

As we have seen, business firms are major agents of interaction both within a region and between regions. Keep in mind, however, that they could also cause a great deal of trouble if they were to come into and leave host countries based solely on their own interests. Even private firms have to act responsibly within the communities where they run their business, no matter where the capital originated.

In other words, corporations have a fundamental obligation to society, as does the state. Moreover, governments do not gain immunity from responsibility regarding business activities merely by adopting market-oriented and business-friendly policies. Argentina's economic crisis and political turmoil of 2001–2002 provide ample testimony of this fact.

In this context, national governments must confront four prime challenges: (1) strengthening regulatory oversight bodies, (2) strictly enforcing rules for corporate governance and accountability, (3) encouraging firms to list (at least part of) their stocks in host-nation capital markets, and (4) making every effort to oblige foreign firms to open information to public scrutiny. All of these matters must also be discussed at inter- and intraregional meetings of government officials, diplomats, and businesspeople. To ensure a sound and open field of activities is the prerequisite for the development of business interactions.

Notes

1. Robert N. Gwynne, *Industrialization and Urbanization in Latin America* (London: Croom Helm, 1985), 49; and Peter Evans, *Dependent Development: The Alliance of Multinational, State, and Local Capital in Brazil* (Princeton: Princeton University Press, 1979), 11 and passim.
2. Kotaro Horisaka, Akio Hosono, et al., *Latin America's New Multinationals* with Japanese title *Latin America Kigyouron* (Tokyo: Nihon Hyouronsha, 1996.)

PART II

DEVELOPMENTAL STRATEGIES COMPARED

CHAPTERS IN THIS SECTION offer long-term assessments of developmental strategies in East Asia and Latin America, with particular emphasis on the economic role of the state. Why and how have Asian and Latin American development strategies diverged? What lessons might emerge as a result?

Gilmar Masiero maintains that, in comparison with stop-go planning in Brazil, the "strategic pragmatism" adopted by East Asian states has met with substantial success. Especially in Korea and Japan, models of export-led growth have benefited from prompt and opportunistic adaptation of industrial production and from close collaboration between public and private sectors. Long-term economic planning has not only produced high levels of growth, but has also yielded other positive developments—formation of a meritocracy based on educational attainment, allocation of expenditures to productive infrastructure, and high savings rates. For its part, the Brazilian state also engaged in economic planning as it pursued import-substitution industrialization strategy from the 1950s through the 1970s. Since then, however, the gradual transformation toward a more liberal model has been constrained by Brazil's fragmented political party system. Persistent unemployment and modest growth lead Masiero to question the effectiveness of neoliberal reform as espoused by the "Washington consensus." Instead of reducing the economic role of the state, Latin American leaders might be well-advised to examine the policy trajectories of East Asian nations.

Through a rigorous comparison of Korea and Mexico, José Luis León further demonstrates the effectiveness of the Asia-based "developmental state" model. In contrast to Mexico, Korea managed to achieve economic growth with equitable income distribution from the 1950s through the 1990s. Classifying states according to two criteria—capacity and autonomy—León finds a strong correlation between economic development and bureaucratic efficiency. In both Korea and Mexico, years of high growth and equitable distribution coincide with high levels of state autonomy and capacity. Yet León expresses apprehension about the future, since the Korean state has been losing capacity and the Mexican state has been losing autonomy. Despite the Asian economic crisis of 1997–1998, it is too early to conclude that the region's "economic miracle" has come to a final end.

In a similar vein, José Luis Estrada-López compares poverty rates and poverty policies in three key countries and observes that, through this lens, Korea has been the most successful, Mexico the least successful, with Chile in the middle. Korean economic policies led to steady demand for labor, while in Mexico, by contrast, sluggish and uneven growth has resulted in persisting unemployment and expansion of the informal sector. Chile's neoliberal reforms have led to impressive and sustained growth but have not diminished inequality. Key differences between Korea, on the one hand, and Mexico and Chile, are the pace and sequence of reforms: While Korea followed a gradual, sequential, and selective course, Mexico and Chile adopted rapid, comprehensive reforms. Of course Korea had the advantage of a more propitious starting point in the 1950s—with lower levels of inequality, and with a major land reform in place.

As volume editors, we find it striking that, at a time when governmental intervention in economic matters has come under criticism throughout much of East Asia, all of these essays—all from Latin America—offer positive assessments of Asian policies. We see at least two reasons for this apparent anomaly: One is that these chapters analyze long-term change over decades, rather than short-term interruptions; another is that, from the Latin American standpoint, the eruption of one single crisis does not discredit an entire economic strategy. As a whole, these chapters vividly reveal the eagerness of Latin American experts and policy makers to derive meaningful lessons from the Asian experience.

6

Pragmatism and Planning in East Asia and Brazil

Gilmar Masiero

IT IS WIDELY AGREED THAT ECONOMIC GROWTH results from three factors: (1) the accumulation of factors of production, including human and physical capital; (2) the efficient allocation of resources; and (3) improvements in technology. Policies aimed at achieving macroeconomic stability, high employment, and an equilibrated external trade balance have been identified as key. Long-term strategic planning models provide a framework for ensuring that a clearly defined goal—a vision for the achievement of economic growth—is broken down into steps, a process for moving from each step to the next, and the articulation of the expected consequences.

By putting forward a set of prescriptive policy guidelines, the "Washington consensus" aspired to provide a long-term strategic vision for developing countries seeking to stabilize their economies.[1] As first articulated in the late 1980s, the Washington consensus urged the adoption of certain reforms: fiscal discipline, proper priorities for public expenditure, tax reform, financial liberalization, stabilization of exchange rates, trade liberalization, encouragement of foreign direct investments, privatization of state-owned enterprise, deregulation of markets, and property rights protection. Two items were added by the mid-1990s: (a) creation and development of key national institutions such as independent central banks, effective governmental budget offices, independent and incorruptible judiciaries, and agencies to sponsor productivity missions; and (b) increasing resources for education and channeling funds toward the primary and secondary levels.[2]

These economic reforms were extensively applied in Latin American countries, small and large alike, from Chile in the 1970s to Brazil the 1990s. Similar reforms were implemented in Argentina beginning in 1989, in Peru under Alberto Fujimori starting in 1991, in Venezuela with the arrival of Carlos Andrés Pérez in 1989, and in Bolivia after 1985. Through the early 1990s, Mexico was a leading exemplar of neoliberal reform; after the peso crisis of 1994–1995, however, the country's underlying problems became painfully apparent, as low economic growth and sharp income inequalities provoked social disturbances and destabilized the government by challenging the ruling party.

The Washington consensus had one fault in common with other formulas attempted in the Americas in the 1990s: It did not deal explicitly and effectively with such core issues as unemployment and long-term national development. Nowhere, in its prescriptions, did the consensus encourage governments to develop a coherent vision and a clear set of goals; instead, it focused attention on short-term adjustment and stabilization. To put it more simply, it did not directly confront the critical question of how to accelerate economic growth. The Latin American economies grew, but slowly and unevenly; with the single exception of Chile, countries of the region have failed to sustain high rates of growth. The persistence of this failure raises serious questions about the efficacy of the remedial measures administered thus far. How can the Latin American economies move beyond the modest gains achieved through policies that have brought stabilization and liberalization, but little more? Should they emulate the East Asian economies, as proposed by some analysts, or should they devise their own model for development?[3] Is the Washington consensus outright wrong, or are its prescriptions merely insufficient?

This chapter analyzes a variety of models for development. We will examine the pragmatic style of East Asian long-term national economic planning and compare it with Brazilian economic policy during the latter part of the twentieth century. As a result of these case studies, I conclude that long-term planning is much better for the industrialization process and is more likely to bring about economic growth than the policies nowadays employed in most Latin American countries. I intend to conduct this analysis without falling into ideological argumentations about the relative merits of state intervention versus market forces in promoting economic growth.

Both state and market were, and still are, important in the development of the less-industrialized economies. On this point I take a nonideological course: Interventions by governments and by multilateral organizations should be guided by long-term plans that emphasize the reduction of poverty, illiteracy, famine, unemployment, and economic inequalities between developed countries, on the one hand, and developing countries, on the other. At the same time, I do not claim that the East Asian experience should be unthinkingly emulated by developing countries in other regions. Instead, I simply identify some strategies that have been usefully employed in East Asia, but not in Latin America. As we shall see, these strategies—rather than historical, institutional, and cultural conditions—have proven to be the most decisive elements in promoting economic growth and development.

Pragmatism in East Asia

Generally speaking, Asia has been more successful than Latin America in adapting its production in response to variations in global demand. Perhaps this is due to the special collaboration between government and industry in Asia. Japan, for example, has adopted a dual tactic of market responsiveness and public-private cooperation successfully since World War II. Thomas Huber describes this system as a "strategic economy." As he has written, "a consensus has begun to take shape . . . that although Japan enjoys a vigorous private commerce, at the same time, the Japanese government is somehow a participant in Japan's techno-industrial system. The system seems to have the benefit of some kind of business-government partnership."[4]

Strategic pragmatism comprised a key element in Asia's rapid economic growth. Michèle and Henrik Schmiegelow have described how Japan, in less than a half century, rose from the devastation of World War II to become the world's second greatest economic power. "There is no denying that Japan's private and public economic policy-makers stand out for their always-maintained sense of direction. In that sense, their policy-making can be called strategic. But their strategy is different from the conspiratorial ones suspected by the Japan, Inc. paradigm. As true pragmatists, they have been deriving their sense of direction from the nature of the changing problems to be solved. If there is need for a label on such policy-making, we can think of nothing better than 'strategic pragmatism'."[5]

This strategic pragmatism is based on policies that are rational and market-oriented. Guidance from the public sector is welcomed by the private sectors, which frequently need it in order to share the burden of risk that entrepreneurs and even the most financially sound asset holders are unable to bear alone. This policy of sharing economic burdens reflects a consensus in modern social sciences: The essence of strategic organization is unity of ends and plurality of means. In other words, the system coordinates the efforts of diverse agencies for one common purpose. Any such system must have both appropriate institutional structures for the coordination of policy and a coherent vision of the purposes for which such facilities are being employed.

This approach has produced remarkable dividends for the Japanese economy since the mid-1950s. As a coda to its well-known national goal of "doubling the national economy," Japan doubled its GNP in less than a decade and again in the following decade. In this same era, per capita income and social indexes such as life expectancy, literacy, per capita consumption of calories, and the like improved faster than ever.

One of the most significant factors in Japan's postwar development was macroeconomic stability. This is essential for encouraging savings and funds for long-term investment. Of special importance in Japan was the growth of "postal savings" (that is, time savings, nursing care, collection, housing, education, and other popular savings collected by post offices and administered by the government). The main objective was to amass funds from small savers for the purpose of investing in social infrastructure. By competing with commercial banks, the postal savings system mitigated the inflationary effects of the otherwise high interest rates that would have been charged by private financial institutions. The maintenance of modest interest rates was a crucial element in Japan's postwar success, along with the country's emphasis on the export sector and its special public-private partnerships.

Six large trading companies, called *sogososha,* dominate Japanese industry. They represent, respectively, the six leading conglomerates or *keiretsu.* These companies deal with a wide range of products, from raw materials to finished products, and operate in many countries. They have performed the export functions for many Japanese companies that are too small by themselves to reach out to overseas markets, and they have provided credit to small and medium-sized companies. In this capacity they serve as "quasi-banks"—they borrow from banks and lend to companies inside their *keiretsu.* They also function as general contractors for overseas development construction projects, and are engaged in third-country trade where both buyers and sellers are non-Japanese.

As a consequence of Japan's emphasis on exports, companies were compelled to attain high levels of efficiency in order to be internationally competitive. The close relations between the government and large Japanese enterprises provided objective criteria for measuring the performance of a company's operations and assessing the effectiveness of its credit and financial support. Similar opportunities were perhaps lost in many other countries, where import-substitution policies and the presence of monopolies by public companies mitigated the need for domestic firms to improve their competitiveness in the international arena. But in Japan, product market competition and the link between market performance and access to credit limited the government's financial risks in allocating its resources. In fact, governmental management of its credit-based financial systems played a key role in Japan's industrialization process. Noting the implication of high debt-to-equity ratios in the corporate sector, the political economist John Zysman has concluded, "selective credit allocation is the single discretion necessary to all state-led industrial strategies."[6]

Through effective policy coordination, the Japanese government was able to promote flexible adjustments of the private sector and effective responses to economic trends. Its credit policy goals were narrowly focused and well coordinated with other policies. They were also oriented toward promoting industrialization and exportation. Foreign exchange, fiscal policies, and the tax system were likewise directed toward these same goals. The allocation of foreign exchange was coordinated with domestic credit policies to effectively support the industrial policy goals—which were extensively discussed with the large Japanese industrial groups and, through consensus, formalized in the National Economic Development plans.

Along with these cooperative structures and the competitive strategies of the business sector, Japan's development strategy was characterized by a credible and consistent vision (rather than detailed quantitative plans) that gave higher priority to industrialization and economic development than to organization of the financial sector.[7] Administrative guidance discouraged consumer credit and financing housing, and encouraged the continuous growth of large industrial groups.

Industrial strategy in Japan has been changing in response to international, as well national, economic pressures. During the postwar recovery period, the emphasis focused on the rationalization and modernization of equipment in heavy industries, as well as the development of the machine-tool industry. The central goal was the promotion of industrial organization. In subsequent years, there was a need to restructure industrial sectors suffering from overcapacity and to provide smooth adjustments for other sectors that were in decline. In the 1980s, a new industrial policy sought to promote technology, energy conservation, and information networks. Accelerated depreciation allowances and tax-free incentives were given to profitable target companies to reinvest their profits. As a result, these companies grew more rapidly than firms in the nontargeted sectors.

Despite periodic fluctuations, the postwar Japanese economy has been vibrant and dynamic. Growth-oriented targets for output, inflation, and the balance of payments were monitored constantly by the Economic Planning Agency in order to better guide social and economic development. Japan's economic plans were indicative in nature and provided desirable targets and projections for areas of the economy that were consistent with state priorities and with economic capacities.

Japan's national economic plans were broad in design. In the process of planning, extensive participation and consultation took place in order to form a consensus within the government and to coordinate the policies of various ministries. For this reason, the majority of officials in the Economic Planning Agency was and still is on leave from other government agencies, particularly from the Ministry of Finance (MOF) and the Ministry of International Trade and Industry (MITI).

The Economic Planning Agency serves as the secretariat of a top advisory committee to the prime minister's Economic Council, which is to deliberate on important economic policies and formulate long-term economic planning. The agency assists the council with the technical tasks of making projections and estimates in line with the major goals of the plan put forward by the prime minister. Once the council has debated the various policy aspects of these goals, the agency works on the policy implications in close consultation with other ministries. After the plan is completed, it is submitted to the cabinet for approval. Once approved, it becomes the official National Economic Plan (NEP).

At this point all other governmental ministries and programs—in such areas as land use, regional development, and public investment—are expected to support the NEP. In addition, because all government ministries and agencies and public enterprises have to submit budget requests to the Ministry of Finance (MOF), the ministry makes sure that the approved budget is consistent with the NEP. The plan subsequently enters the government budgeting process for implementation. Thus, Japanese economic policy encompasses both macroeconomic and sector-specific policies: The planning process establishes macroeconomic guidelines, which are then followed in order to integrate individual sector policies.

In this fashion the Japanese state has guided both the direction and the pace of the country's industrialization. It has acted by setting ends instead of dictating means. Companies have been free to implement policies as they wished. Government actions were related to restructuring industries in order to guarantee that there would be a half-dozen viable companies competing in any given area of economic activity. Establishing goals at the top but having the means accomplished through competition at the bottom of the system fully preserves the benefits of freedom at the bottom while retaining the advantages of coordination and united purpose at the top.

Within this scheme, as Miguel Urrutia has observed, "the Japanese experience is instructive because it points towards the useful role that long-range planning can play. By creating a consensus of what major problems an economy must overcome, the planning process can organize the inevitable negotiations between the different economic agents by forcing them to accept certain basic premises. This limits the degree of conflict between them and makes economic policy decision-making more rapid and more consistent."[8]

Since January 2000 the Economic Council has been considering new ways to stimulate "economic revival" for Japan. The 1990s proved to be a decade of recession and stagnation. And in the aftermath of decades of growth, the inertia of traditional systems has led to major misalignments between economic trends and productive capacity. Despite this setback, the Japanese model of "strategic economy" remains the benchmark for other countries in East Asia.

One beneficiary of the Japanese example of "strategic pragmatism" was the city-state of Singapore.[9] Another was South Korea. As Leroy Jones and Il Sakong have noted, "the 'Korean miracle' is not a triumph of laissez-faire, but a pragmatic non-ideological mixture of market and non-market forces. Where the market works, fine; where it doesn't, the government shows no hesitation in intervening by means that range from a friendly phone call to public ownership."[10] Performing in this way and often placing economic growth above most other concerns, the Korean state has kept economic development as its principal focus since the end of World War II. This trend has only intensified since the early 1960s.

South Korea did not have a national plan during the 1940s and '50s. It was the military government that took charge not only of designing plans but also of implementing them. Throughout almost the entire period of President Park's regime (1961–1979), Korea was characterized by direct state involvement in all sectors of the economy. The Economic Planning Board (EPB) and related semi-governmental organizations, essentially drawn from the Japanese model, appear to have spearheaded the formulation and, to some degree, the implementation of Korea's National Economic Plans. Through these plans and a strong emphasis on education, the Korean government built a society with one of the lowest income inequalities in the world. An increase in the number of educated individuals in the job market leads to a decrease in the relative income that can be retained by elite groups.

The Korean state and business conglomerates (such *chaebols* as Samsung and Hyundai) produced rapid growth through a combination of sound public policies and high rates of investment. The average rate of capital formation in the heavy industry and chemicals sector was similar to that of the traditional labor-intensive light industries during the 1960s; in the 1970s, it was nearly twice as high. Since this rate of capital formation was supported in part by rapid growth in the money supply, inflation accelerated and the government, in order to minimize the pressure on prices, held the nominal exchange rate of the *won* constant.

The early 1980s brought a shift in policy. Structural and macroeconomic imbalances created by the heavy and chemical industrialization drive were aggravated by the second oil crisis (1979–1983). After the assassination of

President Park, a new government, which took office in 1980, sought to stabilize the economy and solve financial problems in major industries. Classical adjustment policies were put in place with assistance from IMF and the World Bank. Preferential tax concessions were reduced in order to limit the expansion of credit and to reduce the budget deficit. Government actions thus became more general and less industry or firm specific.

In the 1990s, the process of globalization and the creation of the World Trade Organization, as well as South Korea's entry into the OECD (Organization for Economic Cooperation and Development), provided yet another impetus for change. The new times and events demanded that Korea alter its national economic strategy, and it consequently transformed its administrative style and introduced reforms in its industrial and financial structures. For some Korean analysts, the rapid change in economic behavior and reforms was one of the main causes of the financial crisis in 1997.

In the South Korean elections of 1992, Kim Young Sam was chosen president. Soon after taking office, he launched a vigorous campaign against corruption (arresting more than five thousand individuals, including the two preceding presidents) and demanding the release of public information about properties owned by political and military figures. In the economic realm, Kim Young Sam promoted the *segyehwa* movement, designed to improve the international competitiveness of Korean companies. In 1998, Kim Dae Jung became president and continued promoting the development model based on democracy and market economics.

What have been the key elements in Korea's long-term success? The World Bank's famous 1993 study, *The East Asian Miracle,* depicted the developmental process as resulting from "a winner group of fundamentals and intervention." Others describe the Asian model as "market conforming," "market friendly," "embedded capitalism, " or "market augmenting." In my own view, Korea's process of rapid industrialization resulted from a more complex array of factors.[11]

The geopolitical context of the postwar era proved to be a major impetus. During a period of military occupation, U.S. forces dismantled power structures linked to traditional Japanese interests; in particular, sweeping programs for agrarian reform and compulsory education helped create the basis for a more egalitarian society. As the Cold War intensified (and led to warfare on the Korean peninsula), the United States bestowed massive amounts of economic and military aid on South Korea; and during the Vietnam War, Washington boosted economic growth by its large-scale acquisition of Korean products. (In fact, cultivation of the U.S. market lasted throughout the entire industrialization process, while Japan emerged as the principal source of industrial know-how, equipment, and technology.) In addition, the persistence of political tensions with North Korea and the unyielding stance of organized labor—which was generally met with repression—helped legitimize governmental demands for public sacrifice in order to safeguard national sovereignty and to promote economic growth.

Within this context, economic policy and planning acquired a crucial role. Starting in 1961 the Korean state emphasized exports without abandoning import substitution policies, and also developed a government-led system of resource allocation. Economic activity was organized on the basis of five-year development plans that favored light industries in the 1960s and chemical and heavy industries in the 1970s, followed during the 1980s and '90s by their internationalization and the development of intensive knowledge-based industries. Government policy placed little emphasis on foreign direct investment. State-directed credit programs and the acquisition and/or transfer of mature technologies were controlled by a bureaucratic elite that, through the process of public bidding for government contracts, boosted its power, authority, and discretion (rather than promoting the structure of the legal system).

Moreover, cooperation between the government and large companies lasted throughout business cycles—cycles involving intense competition, declines in production, and the liquidation of problematic companies, followed by new industrial promotion policies, intensive support for the largest and most efficient companies, the achievement of economies of scale, and the expansion of exports. Moving beyond exports, the construction of infrastructure in the Middle East and in neighboring countries (as well as within Korea) played a decisive role in terms of obtaining foreign reserves and providing the economic resilience required to overcome the oil crises of the 1970s.

Korea's export strategy was designed with forethought and care. Labor-intensive industries were encouraged to prioritize product lines that did not require after-sale service. Production scale and turnaround were more important than quality. The rates of technological innovation were high, which served as an impetus for the construction of factories in short time. The existence of general trading companies—firms in charge of connecting local producers with the international market—enabled the development of a network of information inside the *chaebols* that leveraged their presence in the international markets, while pressing the government to maintain the control of the exchange rates in their favor. The Federation of Industries, the Chamber of Commerce, and the Association of Exporters helped top-level firms and executives to obtain special treatment with regard to licenses and loans in order to support the expansion and diversification of their activities. These firms also hired retired officials from the government in order to take advantage of expeditious access to privileged information.

Following South Korea's accession to the OECD in 1996, and the deep financial crisis that erupted in 1997, the government initiated significant transformations in the public, corporate, financial, and labor sectors in order to meet the challenges of a commercially integrated world and to promote a new cycle of economic expansion. (See chapter 11 in this volume.) This new cycle has been guided by the Five-Year Economic Plan on Innovation in Science and Technology (1997–2002), which encompasses the Highly Advanced National Project, or "HAN Project" (for the development of strategic areas such as biotechnology, software, aerospace, nuclear energy, and oceanography); the Creative Research Promotion Project; the Strategic National R&D Projects; and Telecommunications Technology Development, among others.

Common Features of East Asian Development

A focus on human resources has played a central role in East Asia's pragmatic development experience. Comprehensive land reform, universal basic education, promotion of labor-intensive production, a shift to light manufactured exports in the face of heavy import substitution, and performance-based incentives to industry are the core of the policy on human capital. According to James W. McGuire, the "approach holds that government policies aimed at redistributing land, skills, and jobs, as well as at guiding and sometimes overriding market forces, are crucial to growth, equity and poverty reduction, and that the volition of political actors, shaped and constrained (but never fully determined) by historical legacies and social-structural conditions, decide whether or not such policies will be implemented."[12]

Correcting market failures through industrial policies, cooperation and competition, equality, and export-led growth are key features of the East Asian miracle. According to Joseph Stiglitz, former chief economist at the World Bank and recent Nobel laureate, "East Asia's success was based on a combination of factors, particularly the high savings rates interacting with high levels of human capital accumulation, in a stable, market-oriented environment—but one with active government intervention that was conducive to the transfer of technology."[13]

Technology transfer is another crucial element. It is associated with the shift to new export-generating activities as income levels of the country rise and comparative advantages change. Cotton textile was the first industrial sector in which Japan achieved large-scale export success in the years following World War II, but export competitiveness in this industry shifted within the East Asian region from Japan to the NIEs (Newly Industrializing Economies) during the 1960s and 1970s. As a consequence, cotton production declined in

Japan and other activities replaced it as the major export sector. Currently, cotton is declining in the NIEs but it expanding in other countries, such as China.

East Asian countries have consistently managed to correct and adapt their policies in light of actual outcomes and economic trends. It is difficult to describe some of these corrections and adaptations as having been inspired by conscious, critical rationalism of the economic agents involved. Instead, they seem to result from the continuously changing political and economic struggles for self-sustained development. Some of these changes may come too late and cost more than necessary. Even so, the Japanese Economic Planning Agency (EPA) and the Korean Economic Planning Board (EPB) have been conducting serious studies and developing thoughtful contingency plans ever since the 1950s and '60s, respectively. Despite growing criticism of these agencies and of economic planning in general, they have continued to provide long- and short-term plans to better guide their countries' economies.[14]

East Asian countries differ widely in colonial heritage, geopolitical situation, and development process. The divergences in economic development are so huge between Japan, the NIEs, and the developing countries that it is difficult to think in terms of an "Asian model," as specialists frequently do. In general, the Asian development experience was considered a great success up until the "Asian crisis" of 1997—and ever since then, the model has attracted widespread skepticism. But in spite of this short-term criticism and the vast cultural and historical differences among East Asian countries, they share broad similarities in their industrialization processes. Indeed, these common experiences yield ten key lessons for development:

1. Build a more egalitarian society. It is difficult to build an industrial society in a country dominated by large landowners. Land reforms in Japan, Korea, and Taiwan, for example, destroyed the old, rigid social power structures and paved the way for future development.
2. Pursue political stability and economic growth. Development is a long-term process that requires some sacrifices in the present to have some benefits in the future. A strong and active state is required in order to build a national consensus for development.
3. Emphasize education and technical skills. No country can move toward industrialization if it has an illiterate population lacking rudimentary technical skills.
4. Respect and institutionalize the principle of reciprocity. The government supports business, when necessary, but never gives businesses anything for free without a concrete performance. A close relationship between the public and private sectors was necessary for establishing

and implementing policy priorities in a coherent manner in the countries of East Asia.

5. Recognize the government's central role in setting the goals and the framework for development. In East Asian countries, the government has protected and monitored public and private enterprises, and when selective industrial intervention has conflicted seriously with prudent macroeconomic policy, the intervention has been abandoned.
6. Expand investment in all aspects of development. Most countries of East Asia have increased human and physical capital formation from 10 percent of GNP to 40 percent or more.
7. Subcontracting, outsourcing, and original equipment manufacturing. Concentrate on a few industrial sectors in which the country could attain a comparative advantage, and shift quickly to sectors exhibiting forward and backward linkages.
8. Increase investments in R&D. Emphasize technology rather than science, with very limited reliance on foreign capital for purposes other than the transfer and development of technology.
9. Seek out a favorable international economic environment at the beginning of the industrialization process. Korea received large amounts of aid and preferential access for its products in developed country markets. Maintain macroeconomic balances in domestic and external accounts. Give priority to labor-intensive exports and encourage imports to industries rather than to consumers.
10. Build strong, but not large, bureaucracies. Recruit civil servants from state-run universities who have international training and experience, as these aspects will likely bring pragmatism and rationality to public affairs. When such civil servants are insulated from political pressures and private lobbying, they can adjust development targets through quick and flexible actions, in line with changes in domestic and external spheres.

Through various economic and institutional arrangements, the Japanese and the Korean governments have been encouraging private agents to foster economic growth. In addition to extensive consultations and the creation of effective monitoring systems, these governments have designed and propagated credible long-term visions. All economic activities were intensively discussed and formalized in national economic plans; macroeconomic stability, export orientation, domestic competition, and financial as well as industrial policies were taken into account. Policies related to infrastructure, housing, and education were also incorporated in the plans in ways that supported the industrialization process. Moreover, the Japanese and Korean strategies emphasized dynamic comparative advantage rather than static cost considerations. In the past, state policies directly supported the creation of industries; nowadays they indirectly support research and development activities. The idea has been to explore complementarities in production for both domestic and export markets where elasticity of demand is high, technological progress is rapid, and labor productivity is able to rise.

Development Planning in Brazil

Strategic state development plans were first utilized in Brazil in the 1950s. Although various plans were adopted in subsequent decades, Brazil's principal goal was to promote economic growth on the basis of state-led industrialization and import substitution. During the periods when Brazil guided its economy with national plans, as in Asia, it achieved high rates of economic growth; when it departed from this strategy, the results were disappointing.

After the Revolution of 1930, when the idea of a nation-state was redefined and reinforced by new political leaders, industrialization became a central goal for Brazil. The Great Depression of the 1930s and World War II in the 1940s revealed the economic vulnerability and precariousness of a development strategy based on raw materials and agricultural products. The collapse of world markets forced the state to promote economic diversification, especially into manufacturing. The state also restricted imports through tariffs, currency reevaluations, and other measures designed to protect and nurture domestic industry. The emphasis on the production of durable consumer products and capital goods was the core of the 1956–1960 plan adopted by the government of Juscelino Kubitschek.

The formulation and implementation of this plan was preceded by prominent efforts to understand the workings of the Brazilian economy. The Simonsen Report, the Cooke Mission, the Salte Plan, and the Abbink Mission in the 1940s and the Brazil–USA Commission in the early 1950s were the most important.[15] The Brazil–USA study identified bottlenecks in the economy and the need to upgrade infrastructure. It suggested the development of some industrial sectors through foreign direct investment, which would bring in financial and technological resources to foster the industrialization of the country. All of these ideas were incorporated in Kubitschek's *Metas* Plan (hereinafter referred to as the "Plan").

The Plan was implemented through such new arrangements as the Development Council and Executive Groups. Other government agencies like the BNDES (National Economic Development Bank), and divisions of the Bank of Brazil—mainly the CACEX (Foreign Trade Department) and the SUMOC

(Superintendency of Currency and Credit)—were also part of the state apparatus that designed and implemented the Plan. According to J. L. Mattos Dias, the components of the Plan were divided along two broad lines: "First, [it] aligned the government's investments in infrastructure and energy, directly carried out by the federal government or by state companies. Second, an extensive group of projects were designed and implemented in order to broaden and modernize the industrial sector that had available various kinds of credit and exchanges rate incentives."[16]

The result of the Plan was an economy that grew an average of 8.1 percent a year during the 1956–1960 period, reaching a peak of 10.8 percent in 1958. The structural transformation of the economy was seen not only in the growing participation of the industrial sector (20.4 percent of GNP in 1955 and 25.6 percent in the last year of the Kubitschek administration), but also in its diversification. In qualitative terms, the leading industries of 1950—food products and textiles—grew at an annual average of 6 percent between 1956 and 1960, while the manufacture of automobile and electrical components, initiated under the Plan, grew by 25 percent per year.[17]

The Plan's main drawback was its means of financing economic growth. Since tax reforms were not implemented, an excessive expansion in money and credit by the government led to an acceleration of inflation. Public deficits appeared and external debt increased. Also resulting from the Plan was concentration of wealth, primarily because income was transferred from the agricultural sector to investments in capital-intensive industries.

In the early 1960s, amid economic and political instability, a Three-Year Plan was adopted. It was not as successful as the *Metas* Plan, and the military, fearful of growing leftist influence in the government and the threat of radical reforms, seized power through a coup d'état. Authoritarian generals started ruling the country and imposing their will in both the political and economic arenas. In 1964, another plan—the PAEG, the Governmental Plan for Economic Action—was implemented to control inflation and to rebuild mechanisms intended to foster industrialization and economic growth. The main goals of the plan were to reduce the public deficit through tax reforms, increased tariffs, credit restrictions, and a slowdown of salary increases. Within three years inflation was reduced from 65 percent to around 20 percent per year, although economic growth did not return to the levels of the 1950s.

During the mid-1960s some important reforms took place. Financial institutions began to support the acquisition of durable consumer goods; commercial banks offered short-term loans, the stock market provided funds for investments, and a National Housing Bank (BNH) was established. In addition, there were corrections on the monetary front, such as the selling of government bonds in order to stimulate savings and buttress public finances. On the external front, Brazil was able to obtain substantial economic assistance under a U.S. foreign policy program known as the *Aliança para o Progresso* (Alliance for Progress).

The period between 1968 and 1973 was guided by two other plans—the Strategic Development Program for 1968–1970 and the First National Plan for 1972–1974. At this time growth rates were the highest in recent Brazilian history—averaging more than 10 percent a year and climbing to 14 percent in 1973, with inflation stabilized around 15 percent. While the country's economy was performing better than ever before, the political arena was suffering from systematic repression by the ruling military government.

The main sources of growth were government investment in infrastructure (resulting from previous fiscal reform and new financial mechanisms created to improve savings), the growing investments of state-owned companies, and credit expansion to end-consumers of durable goods. The finished consumer goods sector grew more than 20 percent a year, and housing construction, another sector benefiting from credit expansion, grew at an average of 15 percent a year. As world trade increased, Brazil more than doubled the value of its exports.

The Brazilian industrialization process followed the import substitution strategy from the 1940s to the late 1980s. Until the 1950s, Brazilian industry was oriented to the production of consumer goods; from the *Metas* Plan to the years of the "economic miracle" (1969–73), a focus on durable consumer goods sector was added. Capital goods (such as paper, steel products, and chemicals) and intermediate goods required further development in order for Brazil's industrial structure to advance. This was accomplished in the second half of the 1970s. These two sectors received special attention in the Second Brazilian Development Plan ("PND II") in 1974–1979.

To implement PND II, the state took the leadership in productive investments and sustained an average economic growth rate of around 7 percent. Foreign investment became the main financial source of development. Later, when interest rates increased, the ability of the state to continue investing and paying its external debts deteriorated. In 1979, Brazil's external debt was around $50 billion and interest rates began to climb. Meanwhile, inflation soared to 77 percent. The second oil crisis, commercial deficits, and unfavorable balance of payments left the country in severe financial crisis.

In retrospect, it should be noted that the formulation of an industrial strategy through the national economic development plan was an important, if not central, component of Brazil's political economy for more than four decades. According to Wilson Suzigan and Anibal Villela, "past experience provides some important examples of this practice, like the *Metas* Plan

(1956–61) and PND II (1974–79). Under strong political command (democratic in the case of the *Metas* Plan, even though there was a 'parallel administration' for the implementation of industrial policy, and authoritarian in the case of PND II), in both cases there was a political option for industrial development and a preponderant role of the President of the Republic."[18]

Both plans reflected the will of the government and defined formal mechanisms to coordinate the instruments and the auxiliary policies between each other and with the macroeconomic policy. Both plans targeted specific industries and clearly established sectoral goals. The instruments and policies were reasonably articulated and synchronized. Institutional organizations were created in order to improve specialization, together with a functional division to implement policy. Guided by these plans, the Brazilian economy grew as fast as that of other newly industrialized countries up to the 1980s, when the country suffered the most serious economic crisis in its history.

Political and economic changes in the United States exerted major effects upon Brazil. In 1979 the U.S. Federal Reserve adopted a restrictive monetary policy to deal with the increasing devaluation of the dollar that had been occurring ever since Richard Nixon's abandonment of the gold standard in 1973. This policy restricted credit and made it difficult for the U.S. Treasury to make economic adjustments. When the Reagan administration took office in 1981 and began to implement "Reaganomics" or "supply-side economics," the situation worsened. In order to attract foreign capital within a context of restricted credit, the American government raised interest rates. International investors transferred their capital to the United States in order to benefit from these rates, and some countries, like Brazil, began to experience a severe financial crisis as a result.[19]

To deal with this situation, the Third Brazilian Development Plan ("PND III") was formulated for 1980–1985. Its goals were completely different from previous targets. Controlling the external accounts and inflation were emphasized. The then–economy minister, Delfim Netto, had already taken steps in this direction in 1979. His developmental and monetarist program devaluated the currency by 30 percent, fixed the exchange rate, controlled interest rates, expanded credit to the agriculture sector, and created a special agency to control state companies (SEST).

Unlike PND II, PND III was not implemented as designed. Faced by increasing instability of the economy, governmental authorities struggled to reinvigorate growth. In 1984–1985, after years of gradual transition, the military government was replaced by an elected civilian president. The transition was not smooth and the two main political parties—one pro-government, the other opposed—were fragmented into many smaller parties. Traditional leftist politicians, as well as unions and new political parties supported by them, reappeared on the political scene. The diversification of interests and the fragile structure of the political party system were, and still is, one of the major political problems in Brazil. There could be no consensus on national development strategies. Long-term economic plans were not designed and, from 1980 onward, the economy was (mis)managed by a dozen short-term stabilization programs.[20]

After numerous efforts to control inflation, the government finally succeeded through a very innovative scheme known as the *Real Plan*, which was implemented in three stages. The first phase involved fiscal adjustment, achieved through the creation of a new tax on the financial sector (IPMF) and a new social emergency fund that reduced the transfer of federal funds to the states. Every effort was made to balance the national budgets of 1994 and 1995. The second phase involved the introduction of a new unit of currency value called the URV (*Unidade Real de Valor*, Real Unit of Value). All prices were indexed in this new quasi–currency unit. Three months later, the third phase began with the replacement of the URV by a new currency, the *real*. Credit was restricted and interest rates kept high in order to constrain demand. With the slowdown of inflation, the demand for durable consumer goods increased greatly in spite of high interest rates. People were generally more worried about being able to obtain goods than about their final prices or prevailing interest rates.

During the first year of the plan, inflation declined from 50 percent a month to 30 percent a year. The economy grew by 5.7 percent in 1994 by 4.2 percent in 1995. Fernando Henrique Cardoso, the finance minister who devised the plan, won the presidential elections of 1994 and took office in January 1995. In addition to controlling inflation, Cardoso has implemented a number of constitutional reforms aimed at liberalizing the economy and fostering development. The Real Plan has succeeded in containing inflation, but economic growth has been relatively slow. Moreover, an overvalued currency has undermined all public accounts while the country's external and internal debts have sharply increased. The trade and current account balances have been negative as well: This situation was a principal cause of Brazil's financial crisis in January 1999.

Another key issue has been stagnation in the levels of investment. Over the long term, according to Armando C. Pinheiro, "the average rate of investment, expressed in 1980 prices, dropped from 23.3 percent of GNP in the 1970s to 18.2 percent in the 1980s, and to 14.6 percent between 1990 and 1992. Public investment, in particular, was strongly affected, dropping from an annual average of 7.4 percent of GNP in 1980–1982 to a meager 5.5 percent in 1991–1993."[21] Economic growth will require major investments in infrastructure. Current price stability partially depends on the growth of capital formation in transportation, telecommunications, electric power, and so on. This is clearly stated in the Cardoso administration's new Multiyear Plan of Investments, which states "stabilization not only requires a well-managed short-term economic policy. It is necessary to create conditions for more investment and to increase competition between domestically-produced goods and services." The plan also claims that the reduction in infrastructure investment over the last fifteen years has led to "a deterioration of transportation systems, the obsolescence of ports, the prospect of energy blackouts, and a technological lag already accumulated in the telecommunications sector."[22]

The era during which Brazilian development was based on a combination of state companies, multinationals, and domestic capital seems to be definitely over. The country's financial crisis has yet to be overcome, and the capacity of the state to invest, or to finance investments, is very low. Even though the government's latest stabilization plan seems to be successful, growth cycles have been very short. By studying the successful economic development plans of the past, one may reasonably conclude that the government should design new development plans to guide the economy toward growth and to improve the living conditions of Brazil's 170 million inhabitants.

Conclusion

In key East Asian countries, U.S. occupation forces abolished the political and cultural power of landlords as a class, and dismantled the concentrated power of a small group of families. The situation in Latin America is the opposite. The elites of Latin America retain tremendous judicial, political, and economic power. They hold extensive landholdings, great political influence, and enormous informal influence in the countryside. In addition, large multinationals and strong unions exert major impacts on the policymaking processes of Latin American countries. Neither the "Washington consensus" nor liberal theories of development have any clear or meaningful recommendations as to how to reconcile all these divergent interests.

After more than a decade of compliance with the Washington consensus, Latin American countries appear to be suffering from "stabilization fatigue." Even though most of the formula's recommendations have been implemented in most countries, economic growth has not materialized. Most of the proposals concern the role of the state in governing the economy and do not address economic growth. The Washington consensus tends to emphasize short-term, not long-term, economic development. It assumes that market forces alone are enough to build markets and improve the welfare of the population. The recent inclusion of two more factors—institutional building and education—has not done enough to stimulate the growth process.

Government policies formulated and implemented with respect to the long term in Japan and South Korea, as well as in Brazil up to the 1980s, have resulted in relatively rapid economic growth. Strategic pragmatism guided by national economic plans was at the core of the industrialization processes of these countries. The *Metas* and PND II Plans in Brazil were two such successful plans (one carried out by a democratic government, the other by an authoritarian regime). They were used to build a broad consensus about national goals, and economic growth was achieved. During the 1980s and 1990s, disagreements between the public and private sectors intensified in Brazil, and long-term national plans were either not designed or not implemented.

The economic success of Japan and Korea has derived primarily from their long-term strategies. The plans and policies in these high-growth economies have established some standards that are reproducible elsewhere. These standards include land reform, government-guided free enterprise emphasizing labor-intensive and export-oriented industries, high rates of savings, emphasis on meritocracy based on education, control of population growth, acceptance of foreign technology and ideas, political stability, and expenditures for a productive infrastructure. Ever since the Meiji Restoration, Japan has been emulating the most advantageous Western practices and technologies. "From imitation to innovation" was the central idea in the South Korean industrialization process. Because East Asian countries were able to benefit from other experiences, they developed with impressive speed. Why have Latin American countries not been able to do the same?

Evidence presented in this chapter suggests that if determined leaders in Brazil and Latin America want to go beyond the Washington consensus, they should pay careful attention to East Asian practices and long-term strategies. Looking through the lens of static economic models, it is not difficult to see shortcomings and negative aspects in the East Asian development experience. But besides building consensus, the significance of planning is to maintain policy coherence. Discontinuities, rather than continuity of government policies, are the common feature of Latin American economies, and this is one of the main obstacles to sustained economic growth.

Brazil and other Latin American countries need to grow rapidly in order to reduce their serious social inequalities. To date, neither the free play of market forces nor the development strategies implemented by some Latin American governments have been able to reduce traditional social inequalities caused by unemployment, informal employment, poverty, illiteracy, and social exclusion. To achieve more encompassing and sustained development, economic growth should not only be planned in keeping with national interests, but also include all social agents, as has been the practice in East Asia.

Notes

1. John Williamson, ed., *The Political Economy of Policy Reform* (Washington: Institute for International Economics, 1994).
2. John Williamson, "The Washington Consensus Revisited," *Inter-American Development Bank Conference on Development Thinking and Practice* (Washington: September 1996).
3. Mitsuhiro Kagami, *The Voice of East Asia: Development Implications for Latin America* (Tokyo: Institute of Developing Economies, 1995).
4. Thomas Huber, *Strategic Economy in Japan* (Boulder: Westview Press, 1994), 1.
5. Michèle and Henrik Schmiegelow, *Strategic Pragmatism: Japanese Lessons in the Use of Economic Theory* (New York: Praeger, 1989), 12.
6. John Zysman, *Government, Markets, and Growth: Financial Systems and Politics of Industrial Change* (Ithaca: Cornell University Press, 1983), 76.
7. Mark Fruim, *The Japanese Enterprise System: Competitive Strategies and Cooperative Structures* (Oxford: The Clarendon Press, 1992).
8. Miguel Urrutia, "New Approaches to Development Planning," in *Development Planning in Mixed Economies,* eds. Urrutia and Setsuko Yokata (Tokyo: The United Nations University, 1988), 11.
9. See Edgar Shein, *Strategic Pragmatism: The Culture of Singapore's Economic Development Board* (Cambridge: MIT Press, 1996).
10. Leroy P. Jones and Il Sakong, *Government, Business, and Entrepreneurship in Economic Development: The Korean Case* (Cambridge: Council on East Asian Studies, Harvard University, 1980), 3.
11. Gilmar Maseiro, "A economia coreana: Características estruturais" (paper presented at Seminário Sobre a Coréia, Instituto de Relações Internacionais—IPRI, Rio de Janeiro, October 2000).
12. James W. McGuire, "Development Policy and Its Determinants in East Asia and Latin America," *Journal of Public Policy,* 14, no. 2 (April 1995): 205–242.
13. Joseph E. Stiglitz, "Some Lessons from the East Asian Miracle," *The World Bank Research Observer,* 11, no. 2 (August 1996).
14. Functions of the Korean EPB were taken over by the Ministry of Finance and Economy in 1993.
15. Celso Lafer, "The Planning Process and the Political System in Brazil: A Study of Kubitscheck's Target Plan 1956–1961," (Ph.D. dissertation, Cornell University, 1970).
16. J. L. Mattos Dias, *O BNDES e o Plano de Metas 1956/61* (Rio de Janeiro: BNDES, 1996), 49.

17. Clóvis Faro and Salomão Quadros, "A década de 50 e o programa de *Metas*," in Angela Gomes, ed., *O Brasil de* JK (Rio de Janeiro: Editora da FGV, 1991), 63–65.

18. Wilson Suzigan and Anibal B. Villela, *Elementos para discussão de uma política industrial para o Brasil*, IPEA Working Paper 421 (Brasilia: IPEA, 1996), 15.

19. Monica A. Baer, *O rumo perdido: a crise fiscal e financeira do Estado Brasileiro* (Rio de Janeiro: Paz e Terra, 1993).

20. L. C. Bresser Pereira, "The Failure to Stabilise," in *Brasil: the Struggle for Modernization.* (London: University of London, 1993), and "Attempts to Stabilise," in *Economic Crisis and State Reform in Brazil* (Boulder: Lynne Rienner, 1996).

21. Armando C. Pinheiro, "O setor privado na infra-estrutura brasileira" (paper presented at III Encontro Anual da SOBEET—Sociedade Brasileira de Estudos de Empresas Transnacionais e da Globalização da Economia, São Paulo, November 1996).

22. *Plano Plurianual 1996–1999* (Brasilia: Ministério do Planejamento e Orçamento, 1995).

7

The Role of the State in Economic Development: Korea and Mexico

José Luis León

IF DEVELOPMENT CAN BE DEFINED as economic growth with equity, South Korea has over the past half-century posted a truly impressive performance. In turn, Mexico has undergone, at least since the early 1980s, a process of relative stagnation. To explain the difference, this chapter examines the role of the bureaucracy in economic development. My underlying purpose is not to provide a detailed empirical analysis of economic indicators, but to broaden the conceptual debate about the intervention of the state in developing economies.

The essay begins by comparing the economic performance of South Korea and Mexico from 1950 to 2000. A second section provides a theoretical exploration of the role of state in economic development, with special attention to two characteristics—autonomy and capacity. Taking these elements as a basis for comparison, I discuss the trajectory of the Mexican state from 1950 to the present, and then examine the evolution of the Korean state during this same period.

Clearly, the intention of comparing Korea with Mexico is to analyze different trajectories of development, assuming that there are lessons to draw from the East Asian experience. But is it still accurate to consider East Asian economic performance a "miracle"? As of the early 1990s, a number of analysts argued that Asian growth would inevitably come to a halt.[1] Their forecasts seemed to fit reality in light of the Asian financial crisis that erupted in mid-1997. For many Western observers, the crisis meant not only the interruption of an impressive process of growth, but also the end of a model of development. I would counsel caution in this regard. Inasmuch as economic development is a long-term process, the performance of East Asia should be analyzed in a historical perspective. Between 1950 and 2000, most indicators were undeniably healthy. In this sense, it seems too early to conclude that the East Asian miracle is over.

Growth and Distribution in Korea and Mexico

It is commonplace to point out that East Asian countries have achieved, since 1950, an impressive record of economic development—that is, growth with a reasonable distribution of income. I will briefly analyze GDP and GDP per capita as indicators of economic growth, and income distribution and the human development index as measurements of social development.

Table 7.1 evaluates GDP growth in Mexico and Korea using a cross-time and cross-region comparison. Clearly, Mexico has undergone two stages: Between 1950 and 1979, its rates of GDP growth were higher than both the world economy and all of the regions included in the sample (with the exception of South Korea). In the 1980s, however, Mexico experienced a collapse of economic growth, ranking below most countries in its comparison group. In the 1990s, the Mexican economy recovered somewhat, but its overall performance was still less dynamic than most countries, including those in the sample. In other words, Mexico has regressed: The so-called lost decade of the

TABLE 7.1
Growth in Mexico and Korea: A Comparative Perspective, 1950–1999

	(% Growth of GDP)					
	*1950–1959**	*1960–1969*	*1970–1979*	*1980–1989*	*1990–1999†*	*1950–1999†*
Mexico	6.31	6.65	6.44	2.23	2.80	4.80
South Korea	4.33	7.69	8.82	7.86	5.97	7.00
Western Europe	4.70	5.09	3.38	2.29	2.04	3.50
Australia and New Zealand	3.53	4.41	3.22	2.74	2.31	3.23
United States and Canada	3.62	4.46	3.09	2.96	2.08	3.24
Eastern Europe	4.65	4.82	3.34	1.46	−4.29	2.00
Latin America	4.86	5.13	5.63	1.84	3.29	4.15
Asia	5.97	5.62	5.61	5.45	6.63	5.76
Africa	4.21	4.66	4.08	2.60	2.56	3.62
World Economy	4.60	4.96	4.05	3.23	3.04	3.98

*Some entries refer to time spans within the decade.
†With estimates for 1999.
Source: Author's calculations.

1980s meant, among other things, a collapse in economic growth, thus widening the gap between it and East Asian countries. Korea, in turn, has experienced significant economic growth. While in the 1950s it grew at a rather mediocre pace, between 1960 and 1999 South Korea surpassed all of the countries and regions included in the sample. Despite the recent Asian crisis, the GDP of South Korea grew at a sustained average of 7 percent per year over five decades.

The comparative evolution of GDP per capita in Mexico, Korea, and other countries can be seen in table 7.2. In 1970, the Mexican GDP per capita was almost double that of Korea and Taiwan, and about 40 percent of Japan. By 2000, Mexico's GDP per capita was about one-third of Taiwan's, one-half of South Korea's, and one-seventh of Japan's. In the years of the sample, GDP per capita increased five-fold in Argentina and Guatemala. It increased by six-fold in Mexico and eleven-fold in Brazil, two of the Latin American economies widely heralded as "miracles." Meanwhile, the Japanese GDP per capita grew by eighteen times, the Taiwanese by thirty-three times, and Korea's by thirty-six times.

It is clear that Korea has given a virtuoso economic performance in the last fifty years. The country has advanced from being an agricultural nation, which in the 1960s was considered a basket case, to becoming a prominent member of the world economy. At the dawn of the twenty-first century, South Korea ranked twelfth in the world economy in terms of GDP, slightly behind Russia and ahead of Mexico, Australia, India, the Netherlands, Argentina, Switzerland, Belgium, Sweden, and Indonesia.[2]

As to distribution of income and quality of life, Latin America is one of the richest areas of the world in terms of natural endowment. It is, however, one of the most socially unequal as well. The late economist Fernando Fajnzylber showed that between 1965 and 1986 none of the Latin American countries managed to achieve balanced levels of income and growth. Some grew faster

TABLE 7.2
GDP per Capita in Selected East Asian and Latin American Countries, 1970–2000

	(In U.S. dollars, current prices)						
	1970	*1975*	*1980*	*1985*	*1990*	*1995*	*2000*
Argentina	1,334	2,096	7,478	2,906	4,369	7,501	8,028
Brazil	366	766	1,228	1,617	4,318	4,290	3,912
Mexico	790	1,615	2,899	2,344	3,049	3,169	5,175
Guatemala	361	584	1,139	1,405	827	1,469	1,587
Taiwan	426	961	2,326	3,224	7,881	12,134	13,980
South Korea	275	599	1,632	2,290	5,893	10,873	9,882
Japan	1,967	4,482	9,071	11,120	24,061	41,016	36,464

Source: International Monetary Fund, *World Economic Outlook Database* (Washington, D.C.: IMF, 2000).

than the industrial economies, but did not distribute income evenly (Mexico, Brazil, Colombia); others achieved an acceptable distribution, but with slower rates of growth (Uruguay, Argentina); the rest had unfair income distribution and remained stagnant (most of Central America, Bolivia, Peru). Missing from Latin America is even a single case of growth and equity at the same time.[3] Recent trends have only confirmed Fajnzylber's argument; in fact, income distribution in Latin America is now more skewed than ever.

The Korean story clearly contradicts the notion that growth comes first and distribution later. To substantiate this point, let us review the evolution of the Gini index (a summary measure of inequality) in East Asia and Latin America between 1965 and 1990. This index diminished from 0.34 to 0.33 in South Korea, from 0.32 to 0.30 in Taiwan, and from 0.50 to 0.41 in Singapore. In Argentina, by contrast, it stayed at 0.43 during this period; in Brazil, it grew from 0.57 to 0.60, and in Chile from 0.50 to 0.53. In Mexico this indicator declined from 0.58 to 0.53—still a high level by any standard. These findings are consistent with the fact that Korea ranks above Latin America in practically all available indicators of social development, such as adult literacy, employment, population per telephone, percentage of roads paved, equity between urban areas and the countryside, and life expectancy.[4]

The State and Economic Development: A Theoretical Exploration

The study of economic development is a demanding exercise. To explain the unequal performance of peripheral areas in the world economy, scholars have presented a variety of competing hypotheses—relating to such factors as policy choice, regime type, international conditions, and ideologies of development. While I would not deny the explanatory power of any of these variables, none of them seems sufficient, by itself, to account for economic development.

Here I explore the role of the state as an intervening variable. In fact, state intervention in the economy is a given everywhere, regardless of the ideological preferences of economists and political scientists. Hence, the accurate real-world debate is not about intervention versus nonintervention, but about the manner in which the state intervenes. Thus, it is a fallacy to think that reducing the size of the state will automatically augment its efficacy. It is a fallacy, too, to think that a bigger state apparatus is conducive to economic growth. Both extremes can mislead. One confuses quantity with quality. The other takes for granted the quality of the state and ignores institutional weaknesses, information failures, or deficient policy analysis.[5]

State quality matters. Indeed, it is key to understanding why similar policies lead to different outcomes in different countries. What are the elements of a successful state intervention? The answer I posit is that the combination of state autonomy and state capacity has a crucial effect on the process of economic development.[6] These two elements act as fundamental filters for other contributing variables. To elaborate this argument I will now present operational definitions of autonomy and capacity and propose a typology of intervention styles.

Autonomy and Embeddedness

In order to carry out successful interventions, the state must be relatively autonomous from other domestic actors (the civil society) and from other members of the international system. This condition has been extensively discussed in the literature on political economy. Indeed, most analyses of industrial policy depict the insulation of a technocratic core as a critical factor for successful state intervention, on the ground that institutional insulation detaches economic decision-makers from the particularistic pressures of society and political leaders.[7]

Autonomy is always relational. In the international realm, autonomy does not mean that a given state can act freely in world politics; in fact, autonomy is contingent upon national power. In the domestic arena, autonomy does not mean that all initiatives come from the government. It means that the state has enough room for maneuver to design and pursue developmental goals in most areas—never in all of them. Perhaps the critical proof of an autonomous state comes from instances of conflict. If a state is able to pronounce the last word on a given issue, we can regard it as having relative autonomy.

But if it lacks channels of communication with society, an autonomous state easily turns into an autistic creature. As Peter Evans has convincingly pointed out, "embeddedness" becomes a crucial condition for effective state intervention.[8] This is important because, however coherent and efficient the state, economic transformation cannot be undertaken without the vigorous participation of civil society—particularly the private sector. Unrestrained and unilateral action of the state in economic affairs cannot long endure. While businesses might reluctantly accept some arbitrary governmental measures in the short run, they can in the long run take away their capital, thus reducing investment, employment, and output. The mechanisms for achieving embeddedness are likely to vary from time to time and place to place. Principal strategies include (1) periodic meetings between top businessmen and high-level bureaucrats, (2) formal or informal deliberation councils, and (3) mobility of personnel between the public and the private sector.

State autonomy seems to be a *necessary* condition for economic development, but is not *sufficient* by itself. On the one hand, the creation of autonomy is path-dependent. Autonomous states tend to be the byproduct of social cataclysms, such as foreign interventions, civil wars, coups d'état, massive migrations, and revolutions.[9] As long as these historic changes are more the exception than the rule, autonomy, the first condition of state strength, is difficult to find—let alone create. On the other hand, if autonomy is employed for the rulers' personal profit, state intervention may be unsuccessful or even disastrous. At this point, state capacity becomes a crucial factor.

State Capacities

The other leg of the developmental state is capacity, which can be defined as the ability of a government to perform institutional, technical, administrative, and political functions with a high level of efficiency and responsiveness.[10] Well-organized and efficient bureaucracies are likely to produce better interventions than inefficient and disorganized administrative apparatuses. While an autonomous state might have the will to lead the process of economic development, a capable state has the skill to carry out such an endeavor. A capable state must possess at least three qualities: (1) well-organized public agencies and efficient institutions; (2) administrative resolution, decisional efficacy, and the ability to implement coherent policies over time; and (3) low levels of systemic and administrative corruption.

Regarding the organization of the state, it seems impossible to achieve noteworthy economic performance without a public administration that works with a fair degree of quality, efficiency, and stability. An efficiently organized state should be able to formulate coherent and far-sighted policies that are conducive to economic development. To be efficient, the agencies of the state must have a high degree of specialization and organizational coherence, continuity in the corps of public administrators, clearly established functional divisions, universalistic rather than particularistic criteria, and, no less important, esprit de corps. Moreover, the recruitment and promotion of officials should take place via open and competitive examinations administered by neutral bodies.[11]

Another crucial point is "hardness," defined as the ability to translate state decisions into action. Economic development requires institutions with enough strength and continuity to implement a given policy over time. Experience shows, however, that some states design ambitious plans that, after a while, succumb to the erosion of the original goals. Gunnar Myrdal labeled such entities as "soft states," which are reactive and vulnerable to pressures and manipulation from external sources. As a result, policies of "soft states" are implemented weakly, if at all.[12] Such authors as Joel Migdal and Douglas Chalmers identify the source of the problem in struggles between governments and societal organizations and the consequent politicization of key decisions. Powerless to resist pressures, weak states allow vested interests to influence, if not shape, crucial economic strategies.[13] The transformational breadth of public initiatives is neutralized by the very milieu that they seek to transform. The final outcome is starkly different from the goals of the original plans.

Hardness, then, is an essential quality of state capacity. One must be careful, however, to avoid conceptual confusion between administrative and political hardness.[14] An authoritarian state is not necessarily a hard state, as frequently shown by tyrannies in underdeveloped countries. Conversely, a democratic state is not necessarily a soft state, as shown by the experience of France, Scandinavia, and Japan.[15]

Due to its illegal character, corruption, defined as the use of public resources for private purposes, is extremely difficult to measure. Yet there is little doubt that corruption weakens state capacity. Decades ago, functional approaches of the 1950s and '60s argued that corruption may ease the workings of the bureaucratic machine and facilitate political stability, hence contributing to institutionalization. However repulsive it seemed, corruption came to be seen as a positive influence (a "functional dysfunction") in political and economic development.[16] More recent literature on the subject usually emphasizes the negative consequences of corruption. For instance, Martin McGuire and Mancur Olson posit that a "stationary bandit" (a state led by rational autocrats) is less detrimental to economic growth than a "roving bandit" (engaging in petty and decentralized exploitation).[17] Others have suggested that corruption that is centralized and organized as a monopoly is better than those institutional arrangements in which a businessman has to bribe several public officers ("independent monopolists") to get and implement a contract.[18]

Corruption is a universal fact that occurs even in the most developed countries, so the key question is not whether corruption exists. It is whether the corruption is serious enough to deter economic development. My point is that, in weak and incapable states, corruption is likely to have a negative impact on economic development.[19]

A Typology of States

Most theories of political economy are based on two ideal types of state: the predatory and the developmental. At one extreme, some analysts see the state as a basically predatory entity, with low autonomy and capacity. At the other, advocates of industrial policy usually focus on the East Asian developmental states, which are endowed with high degrees of capacity and autonomy. Although some observers acknowledge that most states are located somewhere between these two extremes, most studies have not devoted much attention to this fact.[20] The category of "intermediate states" is a grab bag into which most states would fall, but which has been underexplored from an empirical standpoint. Given that there are a number of differences among intermediate states, I would propose refining the existing typologies through the addition of two additional categories. The first would include those states with a high level of autonomy and a low level of capacity (protodevelopmental). The second would be comprised of states with limited autonomy but considerable capacity (administrative/postdevelopmental). According to this classification, which is visually depicted in figure 7.1, there are four types of states.

Predatory states have low levels of autonomy and capacity. These states are the quintessential examples of "crony capitalism." They have weak and inefficient institutions, poorly staffed bureaucracies, clientelistic arrangements, zero accountability, and widespread corruption. At the very least, these states can be defined as paternalistic. In most cases, however, they become outright kleptocracies, where specific groups monopolize the state. This would be the case of Anastasio Somoza's Nicaragua, the Dominican Republic under Rafael L. Trujillo, the Philippines under Ferdinand Marcos, ex-Zaire under Mobutu, or present-day Russia. It is this kind of state that often provokes skepticism about the merits of state intervention. Most, if not all, of the states in developing areas are assumed to exhibit the negative qualities of predatory states.[21]

Protodevelopmental states have high autonomy and low capacity. Some of the most conspicuous cases of accelerated (but not sustainable) growth occur

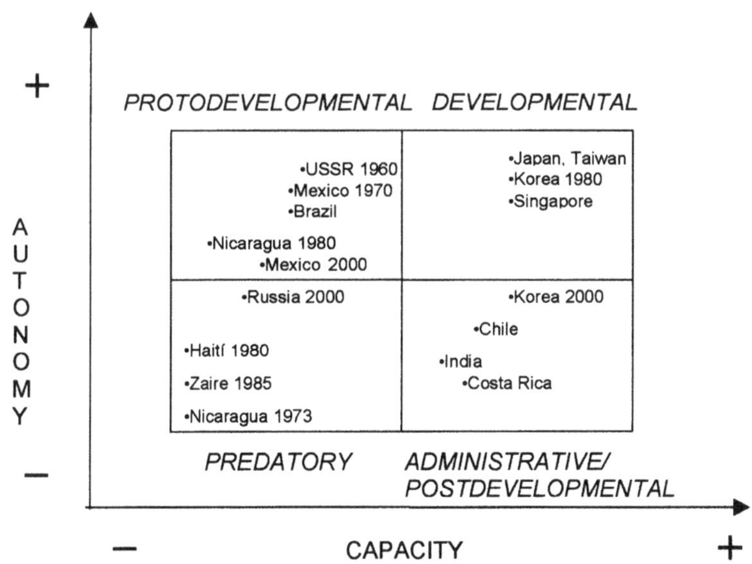

FIGURE 7.1
State Intervention in Economics: A Typology

in this kind of state. Although protodevelopmental states have some room for maneuver in relation to societal actors, their overall capacities do not enable them to become developmental. More often than not, these states create a dual administrative structure in which "pockets of efficiency" coexist with a pervasive spoils system in which paternalism, clientelism, and high turnover rates are the order of the day. With disappointing frequency, the logic of unprofessional state agencies taints the islands of efficiency, thus disabling and even dismantling the overall capacities of the state. Examples of protodevelopmental states include Brazil in the 1960s, Mexico from the 1940s through the 1980s, North Korea, Cuba, Vietnam, and the now-extinct USSR.[22]

Administrative/postdevelopmental states have low autonomy and high capacity. This situation can be the result of two different trajectories. In the *administrative* case, the state is not autonomous, but public policies work fairly well, thanks to capable institutions. This is the case of India, many former British colonies, Chile, and Costa Rica. These states usually have a well-trained civil service, either formal or informal. In the *postdevelopmental* state, economic success can undermine the state's autonomy and its ability to continue policies that lead to accumulation and distribution, while at the same time civil society becomes stronger. In such a case, the capacities of the state remain constant. Postdevelopmental states emphasize regulation and administration over promotion. Although developed economies are beyond the scope of this work, I would place the United States and most Western European countries in the postdevelopmental category. Korea is a newcomer to this group.

Developmental states are characterized by high autonomy and high capacity. These states are Weberian in organization and Schumpeterian in goals. They are relatively independent from social groups, and have efficient institutions with highly qualified employees. In this case, the state is able to lead a process of selective targeting, strategic investment, rapid growth, expedient collaboration with business, and a fair income distribution that can be sustained over time. Developmental states can take the lead in the risky and almost impossible journey from the periphery to the core of the world economic system. Contemporary examples of developmental states are Japan, Taiwan, Singapore, and Korea up to the early 1990s. Some observers would include France, Israel, and China on this short list.

Mexico: A Failed Developmental State

This section traces the evolution of state strength in Mexico over the last half-century. As figure 7.2 shows, Mexico was a rather autonomous state during most of the period. However, it was unable to create capacity. Indeed, at some

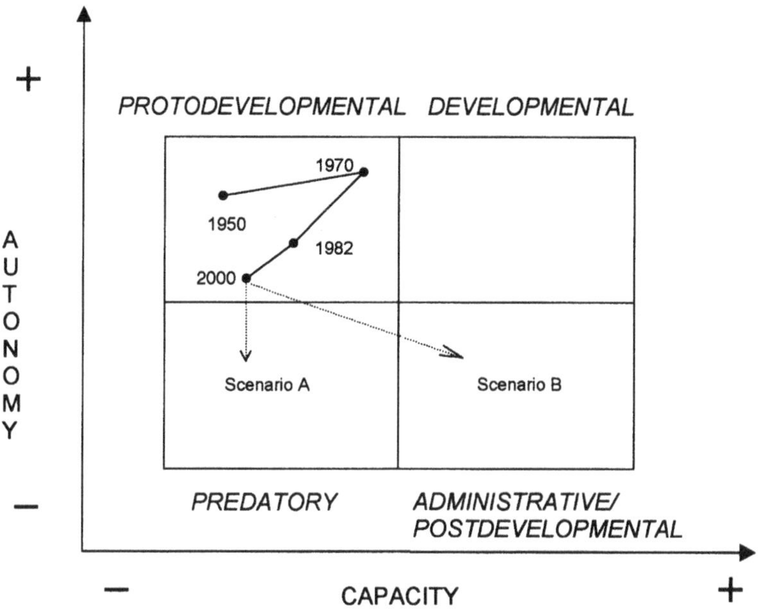

FIGURE 7.2
State Autonomy and State Capacity in Mexico, 1950–2000

point in the late 1960s, it seemed possible that Mexico would turn into a developmental state, but the process was aborted due to the nature of the political system and to presidential strategies that undermined the ministerial core of the Mexican bureaucracy.

Autonomy of the Mexican State

After the Mexican Revolution (1910–1920), the state became powerful enough to impose its will on most social groups. Throughout the 1920s, however, the hegemony of the state was called into question by the remaining agrarian oligarchy, by the United States, by the interests of foreign companies, and by a fragmented political class, integrated by a set of local bosses (*caciques*). The key episode in achievement of political stability was the foundation in 1929 of a state-affiliated dominant party known since 1946 as the Institutional Revolutionary Party or PRI (*Partido Revolucionario Institucional*). The presidency of Lázaro Cárdenas (1934–1940) provided a leap forward in the construction of an autonomous Mexican state and a political system that was legendary for its longevity, its inclusiveness, and its meager checks and balances. The main components of the Mexican political system under the PRI were the presidency, the bureaucracy, and the party itself. Although all of these pieces were strongly intertwined, there was an unambiguous hierarchy within the system: The presidency was at the apex. In turn, the PRI was an instrument for controlling social groups; in fact, the official party was an intermediary between the bureaucracy and the citizens, and served to mobilize the electorate in election times.[23]

How embedded was the Mexican state with regard to business? Several authors point out that the Mexican postrevolutionary elite was detached from the economic elite, especially regarding recruitment channels. Yet there was almost always fluid communication between the private and public sectors. Unlike East Asia, where there was a well-defined institutional framework that favored embeddedness, the efficiency of private-public communication in Mexico depended more on the market-friendliness of economic policies than on formal linkages.

It was natural that the leverage of business would increase as the nation's economy became more complex. Economic growth and industrialization in the 1950s and 1960s strengthened the structural power of business in relation to the state. Over time, business developed a veto power, particularly regarding taxation issues. The conflict between the state and the private sector became a hallmark of the administration of Luis Echeverría (1970–1976). His successor, José López Portillo, initially tried to alleviate the acute polarization between the state and business but eventually ended up by nationalizing the banking system in September 1, 1982. Inheriting a disastrous economic situation, President Miguel de la Madrid (1982–1988) had to invest a good portion of his political capital into restoring the confidence of domestic and international business interests. Carlos Salinas de Gortari (1988–1994) maintained the policy of courting business via the privatization of state-owned companies. From a marriage where the state had the upper hand, the relationship was transformed into a "marriage of convenience," where business has increasing veto power and can blackmail the state with the threat of capital flight. Throughout the 1990s, business (specifically financial capital) gained the power to take the initiative. In fact, the triumph of Vicente Fox in the presidential elections of July 2000 could mean a step forward in the direct participation of business in power.

The deterioration of the autonomy of the Mexican state with regard to other social groups and foreign actors has been more gradual. On the domestic front, since the 1970s there have been signs of increasing participation of unions, some independence of the press, and the marginal advancement of opposition parties. On the foreign front, imprudent economic management, compounded by the deterioration of state capacities, has led to foreign indebtedness, inflation, and a lack of fiscal discipline. The autonomy of the state in external economic affairs began weakening as a result of negotiations undertaken with international financial institutions (IFIs), and the rapid economic changes advocated by Carlos Salinas and his collaborators required the creation of new political arrangements. Given the uncertainty of his legitimacy (in the wake of the bitterly contested election of 1988), Salinas had to employ the traditional control apparatus of the PRI, but also needed to garner the support of crucial interest groups—such as business, the Catholic Church, foreign investors, and the United States. The strategy was rather successful in terms of Salinas' political objectives, but was quite detrimental to state autonomy. Although the state is still autonomous from such groups as the peasantry and intellectuals, it has lost the initiative vis-à-vis many other social and political actors.

Capacity of the Mexican State

In terms of state organization, Mexico does not have a uniform civil service. Instead, there exists a dual structure where a small number of meritocratic agencies ("pockets of efficiency") coexist with a vast majority of dependencies where patronage, personal loyalties, and unwritten rules are the order of the day. In fact, the operation of a formal civil service has been limited to certain areas—namely the armed forces, the diplomatic service within the Ministry of Foreign Affairs, and, more recently, the Federal Electoral Institute. This duality tends to undermine, in the long run, the functional efficiency of public policy as a whole.[24]

From top to bottom, the public administration of Mexico features a complex system of patron-client networks in which jobs become rewards offered by the patrons in exchange for unconditional loyalty and (sometimes) hard work from the clients.[25] This system of recruitment and mobility leads to the creation of *camarillas* (cliques) or *grupos políticos* in which confidence is valued over competency, and loyalty is valued over skill. In Martin Greenberg's words, "Who you know regularly makes more difference than what you know."[26] The consequences of this system are factionalism, personalism, and a lack of commitment to organizational goals. In the absence of tenured posts, it is absolutely rational for public servants to have more loyalty to the boss/clique than to the country/state.

Some observers of Mexican politics have seen the long tenure of the PRI as conducive to administrative continuity.[27] The entrenchment of the PRI notwithstanding, the combination of a strong executive office and a spoils system has produced high turnover levels and the continuous reshuffling of personnel. The beginning of any six-year presidential term (*sexenio*) has typically been accompanied by the massive replacement or redeployment of bureaucrats, directors of state enterprises, governors, members of parliament, PRI officials, and municipal mayors. Frank Brandenburg calculated that at the beginning of every *sexenio*, turnover affects 18,000 elective offices and 25,000 appointive posts.[28] This figure is striking in light of the fact that only about 1,000 bureaucrats change between presidential administrations in the United States. In Japan, the prime minister appoints around 20 ministers (and occasionally some vice-ministers) while the rest of the administrative structure remains basically unchanged.[29]

The Mexican system is efficient in the sense that it maintains political control by reinforcing political legitimacy and fueling the hopes of vertical mobility within the political class. There seems to be, however, a trade-off between political stability and economic performance. It does not take a Nobel laureate to realize that the mix of turnover and patronage politics hinders the continuity of public policies; leads to diseconomies of scale in the public sector; contributes to inefficient policy making; and devalues specialization, expertise, and planning skills.[30]

Could a developmental Mexican state have flourished under such circumstances? The answer lies in the realm of *institutions*. According to Miguel Centeno, up to the 1970s Mexico had a virtual "double vice presidency" in which the Ministry of Government (*Secretaría de Gobernación*, Segob) managed political affairs, and the Ministry of the Treasury (*Secretaría de Hacienda y Crédito Público*, SHCP) coordinated economic policy.[31] The financial wing of the administration was well insulated from political strife. The SHCP headed a guidance cluster whose other members were the Bank of Mexico (*Banco de México*, Banxico), and the development bank known as *Nacional Financiera* (Nafinsa). This institutional troika fulfilled the role of a core bureaucracy that undertook informal planning, policy coordination, and the design of long-term economic plans.[32] With time, bureaucrats trained within this institutional triangle "colonized" such ministries as Trade and Industry, expanding the logic of the islands of efficiency to other agencies.[33] This kind of institution could have been the nucleus of a developmental state. Unfortunately, such was not the case. On the contrary, during the 1970s these institutions succumbed to the "politics of survival," a process by which political leaders impair state agencies perceived as potential rivals.[34]

Presidents Echeverría and López Portillo systematically sapped the ministerial core of the Mexican bureaucracy in order to concentrate power in the presidency. Why did they do so? Their motives were clearly political. The massive antigovernment demonstrations of students, members of the middle class, and workers and peasants in 1968 inflicted profound trauma on Mexico's ruling class. In order to heal the wounds left by the bloody repression of October 2, 1968, Echeverría had to distance himself from the previous administration. The president saw SCHP and its ministerial allies as elitist and conservative agencies, alien to Mexico's political and social problems. In fact, they were clearly ill-suited to the expansionary, distributive, state-led economic policy that Echeverría had in mind. In August 1970, Echeverría took economic policy into his own hands: as he grew accustomed to saying, "economic policy is made at *Los Pinos*" (the name of the Mexican presidential residence).[35] The president appointed his close friend López Portillo as head of the SHCP, and in 1976 he anointed López Portillo as his successor in the presidency. (Interestingly, this was the first time that a Treasury minister had become president of Mexico since the 1860s.)

Once he became president, José López Portillo undertook an ambitious reform of the state apparatus, the cornerstone of which was the creation of the Ministry of Programming and Budget (*Secretaría de Programación y Presupuesto,* SPP).[36] Together with the functions of planning, statistics elaboration, budgeting, control of expenditure, and allocation of federal resources to the states, this new ministry wielded an eminently political function taken from the Ministry of the Interior. The most important innovation was the pairing of planning and budgeting, two areas of traditional bureaucratic contention. Clearly, López Portillo conceived the SPP as a pilot agency, similar to the Japanese Ministry of Industry and Technology (MITI) or the South Korean Economic Planning Board (EPB). What he created, however, was a Frankenstein too powerful and politicized to be controlled. Indeed, the "double vice presidency" of the 1950s and 1960s disappeared, and a good deal of its power was concentrated in the SPP. As long as the SPP retained its power, there were overwhelming incentives for its ministers to seek the PRI's nomination for president. Not surprisingly, Miguel de la Madrid, Carlos Salinas, and Ernesto Zedillo—successive presidents between 1982 and 2000—had been ministers at SPP.

Parenthetically, López Portillo, who also distrusted the Treasury Ministry, expected that the SPP would further undermine the influence of the old ministry. What resulted, however, was a structural stalemate between SCHP and SPP. The story of economic policymaking in Mexico between 1976 and 1992 is, to a great extent, the story of fierce interbureaucratic battles between these two ministries.[37] Unfortunately, the ministerial war between the SPP and SHCP occurred in an era of continuous international shocks—during which oil prices were on a roller coaster ride, the foreign debt became a crippling problem, interest rates climbed steadily, and the volatility of international financial markets made national economies extremely vulnerable. Precisely at a time when the Mexican economy demanded more planning and coordination, ministerial frictions were reducing the capacity of the state to offer creative responses to international and domestic challenges.

In sum, the organizational reforms undertaken after 1970 led to the eventual demise of a nascent developmental state in Mexico. This outcome led to inefficient implementation of public policies. To be sure, it has been commonplace for Mexican governments to unveil elaborate plans for economic development. Rather than being comprehensive and integral, however, they have generally been decorative, strong on rhetoric, and cobbled together from assorted pieces of disparate policies. In addition, formal planning institutions in Mexico have traditionally been weak. Mexican economic history is plagued with frustrating examples of plans and powerless planning institutions. From 1928 to 1962 there were at least fifteen successive, short-lived agencies for economic planning and at least four full-fledged economic plans.[38] Even during administrations prone to state intervention in the economy, no economic planning entity has performed particularly well in Mexico.

As to corruption in Mexico, the political system has not been immune to frequent self-aggrandizing behaviors. For a long time after the Revolution, the Mexican state, controlled by what has been called the "Revolutionary Family," had "a virtual monopoly over opportunities for wealth and mobility."[39] The political system has created, of course, a strong structural incentive for corruption in Mexico. As long as political careers at the top level last, at most, two or three *sexenios*, job insecurity encourages quests for illicit personal gain, and public officials frequently prepare themselves for the future by building their own, illegal, retirement system.[40] An additional form of corruption comes from the private sector, which has tended to regard the government as a source of privileges. Instead of deploying their entrepreneurial capacities and deriving profits from innovation or productivity, many businessmen have sought the protection and favoritism of the state.[41] The implicit pact of reciprocal corruption between the state and business in Mexico has created what in other contexts has been labeled "political capitalism" or, more bluntly, "pseudocapitalism."[42]

One has to wonder, of course, just how pervasive, systemic, and decentralized corruption has become in Mexico. The answer is necessarily tentative, but the spread of corruption is unquestionably serious. Transparency International has classified Mexico as one of the world's most corrupt countries in 1995–2000.[43] Indeed, the "Revolutionary Family" of Frank Brandenburg appears to have turned into the "*Cosa Nuestra*" that Roger Hansen foresaw in his classic work.[44] If this is true, systemic corruption will become a source of further deterioration of state capacities.

This analysis suggests that, at least since the 1970s, there has been a sustained erosion of state autonomy and capacity. And if these trends continue, the Mexican state could move from the "protodevelopmental" category to the "predatory" group. (See Scenario A of figure 7.2). There is, however, a tenuous light of hope. Although nothing can be guaranteed, the transition to democracy and the defeat of the PRI in the presidential elections of July 2000 could lead to the reinvigoration of state capacities. On the one hand, democracy and the increasing participation of civil society in politics should be an incentive for improving governance. On the other hand, democracy is not enough for solving long-standing administrative and organizational problems. If the democratic transition is accompanied by a thorough reorganization of bureaucracy, the establishment of a full-fledged civil service, the creation of strong institutions, and an efficient struggle against systemic corruption, Mexico could turn into an administrative state (Scenario B of figure 7.2). But if the new government fails to modify the politico-administrative system, if it trades governance for an agreement with organized crime, and if it gives priority to vested interests, the Mexican state could continue its slide into the predatory category.

South Korea: The Evolution of a Developmental State

The workings of the Korean state offer arguments for thinking about state efficiency not only as a problem of size, but above all of quality. This section examines the relationship between the state and civil society (especially business and unions) and emphasizes the levels of autonomy and capacity achieved by the Korean state during the second half of the twentieth century. I also analyze the transformation of South Korea from a developmental to a postdevelopmental state, as depicted in figure 7.3.

Autonomy of the South Korean State

It is widely agreed that the Korean state has enjoyed a high level of autonomy. The agrarian reform, which was undertaken in the 1950s as part of the social restructuring spurred by the Korean War, allowed the political neutralization of the landholding elites. Due to their conservatism, these groups frequently oppose industrialization and economic growth coupled with income distribution.[45] The state also enjoyed considerable autonomy with regard to unions. In fact, as Frederic Deyo points out, part of the success of this model of development was based on the lack of political clout of South Korean workers, whose leverage was notably inferior to that of unions under Juan D. Perón in Argentina or Lázaro Cárdenas in Mexico.[46]

Moreover, the Korean state maintained great autonomy in its relations with business. At many points, the relationship between the bureaucracy and business was far from harmonious. A few months after his rise to power in 1961, President Park Chung Hee nationalized the banks and imprisoned various owners of *chaebols*, the South Korean economic conglomerates. After this

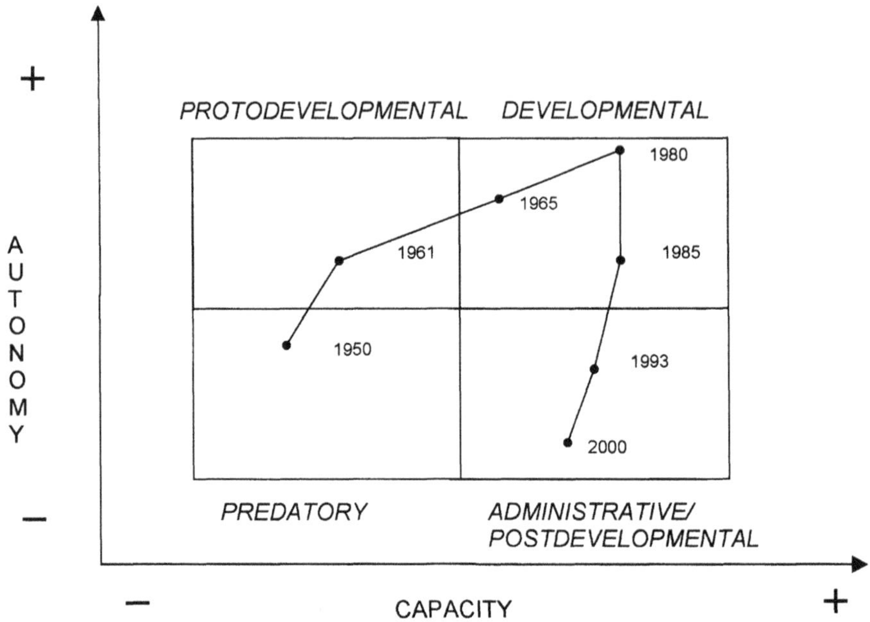

FIGURE 7.3
State Autonomy and State Capacity in South Korea, 1950–2000

initial clash, the state and *chaebols* began to act concurrently in affairs related to industrialization and the promotion of exports. Subsequently, the government's strategy toward business was a well-tempered mixture of carrots and sticks, in which the state maintained control of the relationship through an assortment of incentives, but could also implement punishments against businessmen who refused to obey the developmental directives of the administrative apparatus. Under these conditions, the presidency and the bureaucracy emerged as the strongest actors in Korea, with remarkable capacities for shaping the behavior of capital and labor.[47] At the same time, the executive managed to insulate and depoliticize the strategic agencies of the cabinet, a deed that allowed bureaucrats to concentrate on their institutional duties.

It would be a mistake to think that the autonomy of the state was indiscriminate or that the bureaucracy was autistic and alien to the needs of capital. Rather, the Korean experience has closely corresponded to the concept of "embedded autonomy." The communication channels between the state and business were multiple and crossed through various levels. For the manufacturing sector in general the most important institution for dialogue was the Federation of Korean Industries (FKI), designed to be similar to the *Keidanren* in Japan. Individual firms were compelled to join one of the 62 chambers that operated as intermediaries between the Ministry of Trade and Industry (MTI) and the business sector. At a less formal but equally important level, the government established numerous deliberation councils that facilitated meetings between bureaucrats, businessmen, and scholars. These groups monitored the implementation of policies, screened national and worldwide economic trends, and proposed functional and sectoral strategies to increase the competitiveness of the Korean economy.[48]

Capacity of the Korean State

In the realm of bureaucratic organization, the South Korean developmental state relied chiefly on a merit-based system, as well as on the establishment of clear rules, transparent mechanisms for recruitment and promotion, and a widely shared sense of purpose and mission. The civil service in Korea has deep historical roots extending over centuries.

After seizing power through a coup d'état in 1961, Park Chung Hee began an ambitious program for the modernization of bureaucracy. Under this program, the compulsory retirement of the old guard of public employees was enforced, civil service examinations were reinstated, and a system for promotion based on achievement (and not only on seniority) was designed. All ministries were required to create internal offices for planning and control, and to outline long-term goals in their planning. Park frequently dismissed ministers who did not fulfill at least 80 percent of the outlined objectives. His successor, Chun Doo Hwan, who took power ten months after Park, but was assassinated in 1979, continued this kind of practice.[49] Nowadays, recruitment and promotion of South Korean bureaucrats (*kwanri*) is via open competitive examinations. Entrance examinations are extremely selective: Less than 2 percent of candidates manage to pass. The integrity of the civil service is maintained in all of the ministries and levels of public administration.[50]

With regard to institutions, the Park regime created or restructured a group of organizations for the promotion of economic growth. The most notable among them include the Presidential Economic Secretariat, the Ministry of Trade and Industry (MTI), The Ministry of Finance (MOF), the Ministry of Science and Technology (MST), the Ministry of Construction (MOC), the Bank of Korea (BOK), and the Korea Development Bank (KDB). Without doubt, the paragon of institutional efficiency was the Economic Planning Board (EPB), founded in July 1961. The EPB was created from the fusion of the Ministry of Reconstruction (MOR), which undertook planning tasks, the Statistics Office of the MOF, and the Budgeting Office of the Ministry of Internal Affairs (MIA). The EPB eventually assumed key roles in the elaboration of Five Year Plans (FYPs). It also gained control over subsidies, foreign trade, import licenses, and pricing policies; it prepared governmental budgets, established competition policies, and managed the census and national accounts; and it was responsible for the coordination and evaluation of economic policies.[51]

The head of this pilot agency enjoyed strong presidential support. As a matter of fact, from December 1963 onward, the Minister of the EPB was also the Deputy Prime Minister. This move dispelled any doubts about who held the decision-making power in economic policy. The concentration of planning, budgeting, and evaluation in a single organization increased the coherence of economic policy, and helped avoid coordination problems. Over time, the EPB "colonized" other ministries, thus creating informal networks of officers with shared experiences and common points of view.[52] In short, Korea's EPB bore an unmistakable resemblance to MITI.

In Korea, thus, an ambitious reform of the public sector preceded any attempt by the state to lead the economy. Before "governing the market," the Korean bureaucracy learned to govern itself. This institutional innovation seems to have been a key prerequisite for development, insofar as the public administration was capable of forming a long-term vision for the country's economic transformation. In addition, merit incentives favored the continuity of public policies and helped protect the bureaucracy from particularistic, short-term demands of social groups.

Like many other countries, Korea designed an array of development plans (or FYPs). With encouragement from the United States, the seeds of the planning effort sprouted timidly during the Syngman Rhee administration (1948–1961). It was not until the 1960s, when the planning effort was put into practice, that its first fruits were harvested. Aside from establishing specific goals in terms of macroeconomic indicators, the various FYPs emphasized the development of specific industrial sectors as well as strategies for social improvement. Unlike the bulk of Third World countries, most of development plans in South Korea have surpassed their original goals. For instance, six out of the eight FYPs implemented between 1962 and 1997 surpassed their targeted GDP growth rate.

As to corruption, Western observers tend to characterize the countries of East Asia as areas with relatively little dishonesty.[53] South Korean analysts usually express less optimism on this subject. They indicate, for example, that the nation's modern history has been plagued with episodes of corruption, and that the close relationship between the government and the *chaebols* has not been exempt from illegal agreements. As an example of corruption, South Korean analysts mention the frequent purges that have had to be implemented, particularly those put into action by Park in 1961 and 1975–1977 and by Chun in 1979–1981.[54] The Kim Young Sam administration launched a spectacular anticorruption campaign in 1993–1996. As a result, three ministers and five vice-ministers were fired. The climax of this campaign was the so-called trial of the century, which culminated in 1995 and 1996 in the arrest and sentencing of ex-presidents Chun and Roh.[55]

It is not easy to take a firm position on this issue. Nonetheless, Transparency International reports that the levels of corruption in East Asia and South Korea are perceived to be among the lowest in the developing world.[56] One thing is evident: Whatever the level and the nature of corruption in Korea, it has not prevented the country from achieving outstanding economic performance. The facts show (certainly in an ex post facto fashion) that Korea's developmental state generally administered its promotional tools without paralyzing the economic growth of the country as a whole.

Since the early 1980s, however, Korea's institutional arrangements have shown symptoms of exhaustion. Under the democratic governments of Kim Young Sam (1993–1998) and of his successor Kim Dae Jung (1998–2003) the Korean developmental state has further declined. The state has been losing autonomy and, by maintaining only its capacity, it is converting itself into a postdevelopmental state. The loss of state autonomy appears to be taking place with respect to the private sector, the IFIs, and the unions. The bureaucracy itself is showing signs of losing its ability to design and execute coherent public policies with the same efficiency as in the past.

With regard to the *chaebols*, the state has been largely a victim of its own success. The strategies for industrialization that the bureaucracy supported in decades past required the emergence of strong businesses. But the stronger *chaebols* are in the national and international arenas, the more independent they become in relation to the state. Additionally, the state has been discarding many of the mechanisms that permitted it to shape the behavior of the private sector—namely, the control of credit. Meanwhile, financial globalization has increased the opportunities for businesses to obtain credit from foreign sources. This correlation of forces has led to increasing tensions and bitter relations between the state and *chaebols*, formerly close partners in the "Korea Inc." project.

The same is true regarding IFIs. During the 1980s South Korea became the Asian country with the greatest foreign debt, both in absolute and relative terms. Although in the 1990s the external debt ceased to be a critical problem, its financing has implied the acceptance, in greater or lesser measure, of the policies suggested by the IFIs. The crises of 1980 and 1997, which led South Korea to sign various stabilization and structural adjustment agreements with the International Monetary Fund (IMF), also weakened state autonomy. In the last few years, Korea has enthusiastically adopted orthodox policies, such as the liberalization of foreign trade, fiscal discipline, privatization, and deregulation. It is likely that one of the main consequences of this policy shift will be a further reduction of state autonomy.

Labor unions have been showing a renewed activism since the late 1980s. The Federation of Korean Trade Unions (FKTU), usually a close ally of government and business, has not been able to control social unrest. Strikes have mushroomed since 1987 and union activism has been successful in raising real wages. Thus, the subordination of labor, taken for granted by the developmental state, seems to be disappearing. Ultimately, this trend will weaken the state.

Another challenge to state autonomy comes from pressures to restructure the bureaucracy itself. South Korean public opinion has been seduced by the idea that the country's public administration has become costly and inefficient. Analysts and politicians denounce the bureaucracy's close association with the authoritarian regimes of the past, while critics demand a change from the rule of men into the rule of law.[57] Ironically, some support for reducing the role of the state has emerged within the economic bureaucracy itself. During the 1980s the dominant wing of the EPB embraced liberal ideologies and trade liberalization. As has occurred almost everywhere, the preoccupation with price stability has replaced the emphasis on growth as a central objective of economic policy.[58] In the 1990s, the downsizing of the state apparatus, formerly used as a tool in political purges, acquired a more systematic character and a rationale of efficiency and austerity. The most relevant change has been the disappearance of the EPB and the consequent dispersion of economic policy-making responsibilities among various ministries. In 1994, the EPB and the MOF were melted into the Ministry of Finance and Economics (MOFE), from which were removed the tasks of coordination and evaluation of public policy. In February 1998, Kim Dae Jung reduced the cabinet from 21 to 17 ministries, decreed a freezing of all bureaucratic posts, launched a plan for reducing the payroll of employees in the public sector by 10.9 percent by the year 2001, and announced a scheme for subcontracting some governmental activities.[59]

All of these changes are having a strong psychological, political, and institutional impact on the Korean bureaucracy. An evident risk of the ministerial fragmentation is the loss of coherence in economic policy-making. Moreover, these reforms are generating a considerable loss of motivation within the bureaucratic ranks.[60] The crisis of Korea's developmental state could imply not only the ongoing loss of state autonomy, but also a growing deterioration of the civil service and, hence, of state capacities.[61] In this sense, the most important challenge of the transition toward a postdevelopmental state will be to avoid an institutional vacuum. This could occur if the demolition of the developmental state goes faster than the construction of new administrative structures.

Concluding Remarks

In contrast to Mexico, Korea managed to achieve economic growth with equitable distribution from 1950 through the 1990s. Despite the contemporary Asian crisis, the Korea still offers one of the most compelling illustrations of economic development in recent history.

In this chapter I have taken the position that state autonomy and state capacity are crucial intervening variables in the process of economic development. In order to support this argument, I have compared the evolution of state autonomy and state capacity in Mexico and South Korea. Certainly, my initial findings are more descriptive than deductive. I have perceived, however, a close correlation between economic development and bureaucratic efficiency. The years of higher growth and distribution in Mexico coincide with high levels of state autonomy and capacity; the same can be said about South Korea.

It is foreseeable that, at least in the near future, the Mexican state will not be able to regain its lost autonomy and channel it toward developmental purposes. Although the democratic transition could bring plenty of benefits to Mexico, it will most likely hinder the reconstruction of state autonomy. And if the transition to democracy is not matched by increasing state capacity, the Russia-like scenario of a predatory state cannot be dismissed out of hand. In the best-case scenario, the weakening autonomy of the state would be offset by an improvement of state capacities. In such a case, Mexico could become an administrative state.

As to Korea, maturation of the private sector, as well as the strengthening of unions and other social actors, has led to the reduction of state autonomy, especially in the 1990s. Thus, South Korea has become a postdevelopmental state, similar to state apparatuses in developed countries. While the developmental state sets a premium on the promotion of industry, the postdevelopmental state focuses its efforts on regulation and setting the rules of the game. Clearly, the outstanding achievements of South Korean industrialization from the early 1960s to the mid-1990s were boosted by the strong and efficient intervention of the state. The state's role has been weakening, however, and it remains to be seen whether Korea can avoid the dangers of an institutional vacuum.

Notes

1. Paul Krugman, "The Myth of Asia's Miracle," *Foreign Affairs* 73, no. 6 (November-December 1994); Walden Bello and Stephanie Rosenfeld, *Dragons in Distress: Asia's Miracle Economies in Crisis* (San Francisco: The Institute for Food and

Development Policy, 1990); William Easterly, "Explaining Miracles: Growth Regressions Meet the Gang of Four," in *Growth Theories in the Light of Asian Experience*, eds. Takatoshi Ito and Anne O. Krueger (Chicago: University of Chicago Press, 1995).

2. World Bank, *1999 World Development Indicators* CD-ROM, (Washington, D.C.: The World Bank, 1999).

3. Fernando Fajnzylber, *Unavoidable Industrial Restructuring in Latin America* (London: Duke University Press, 1990), 3–5.

4. Fajnzylber, *Unavoidable Industrial Restructuring*, 3–5; José Edgardo Campos and Hilton L. Root, *The Key to the Asian Miracle: Making Shared Growth Credible* (Washington, D.C.: The Brookings Institution, 1996), 20–26, 220.

5. See Merilee Grindle, "The New Political Economy: Positive Economics and Negative Politics," in *Politics and Policy Making in Developing Countries: Perspectives on the New Political Economy*, ed. Gerald M. Meier (San Francisco: International Center for Economic Growth, 1991).

6. See Theda Skocpol, "Bringing the State Back In: Strategies of Analysis in Current Research," in *Bringing the State Back In*, eds. Peter Evans, Dietrich Rueschemeyer, and Theda Skocpol (Cambridge, Mass.: Cambridge University Press, 1985), 17–18; Byung-kook Kim, *Bringing and Managing Socioeconomic Change: The State in Korea and Mexico*, Ph.D. dissertation (Harvard University, 1987), 6–7; Iyanatul Islam and Anis Chowdhury, *Asia-Pacific Economies: A Survey* (London and New York: Routledge, 1997), 29. Notwithstanding these contributions, empirical studies on the economic effects of state capacity and autonomy are still scarce.

7. See Dietrich Rueschemeyer and Peter Evans, "The State and Economic Transformation: Toward an Analysis of the Conditions Underlying Effective Intervention," in *Bringing the State Back In*, 49; Stephan Haggard and Tun-jen Cheng, "State and Foreign Capital in the East Asian NICs," in *The Political Economy of the New Asian Industrialism*, ed. Frederic Deyo (Ithaca: Cornell University Press, 1987), 101; Barbara Geddes, *Politician's Dilemma: Building State Capacity in Latin America* (Los Angeles: University of California Press, 1994), 49–50; Adam Przeworski and Fernando Limongi, "Political Regimes and Economic Growth," *Journal of Economic Perspectives* 7, no. 3, (Summer 1993), 55–56, 65; World Bank, *The East Asian Miracle* (New York: Oxford University Press, 1993), ch. 4; Thomas M. Callaghy, "Political Passions and Economic Interests: Economic Reform and Political Structure in Africa," in *Hemmed In: Responses to Africa's Economic Decline*, eds. Thomas M. Callaghy and John Ravenhill (New York: Columbia University Press, 1993), 467; Pranab Bardhan, "The Political Economy of Development Policy: An Asian Perspective," in *Economic and Social Development into the 21st Century*, ed. Louis Emmerij (Washington, D.C.: Inter-American Development Bank, 1997), 279.

8. Peter Evans, *Embedded Autonomy* (Princeton: Princeton University Press, 1995), 12.

9. See Theda Skocpol, *States and Social Revolutions: A Comparative Analysis of France, Russia, and China* (New York: Cambridge University Press, 1979), 29–30; Joel Migdal, *Strong Societies and Weak States: State-Society Relations and State Capabilities in the Third World* (Princeton: Princeton University Press 1988), ch. 8; Minxin Pei, "Constructing the Political Foundations of an Economic Miracle," in *Behind East*

Asian Growth: The Political and Social Foundations of Prosperity, ed. Henry S. Rowen (London: Routledge, 1998), 45.

10. Merilee Grindle, *Challenging the State: Crisis and Innovation in Latin America and Africa* (Cambridge, UK: Cambridge University Press, 1996), 3–8.

11. See Chalmers Johnson, *MITI and the Japanese Miracle: The Growth of Industrial Policy, 1925–1975* (Stanford: Stanford University Press, 1982), 78; Evelyne Huber, "Assessments of State Strength," in *Latin America in Comparative Perspective: New Approaches to Methods and Analysis,* ed. Peter H. Smith (Boulder, Colo.: Westview Press, 1995), 169; Campos and Root, *The Key to the Asian Miracle,* 139; Geddes, *Politician's Dilemma,* 49.

12. See Gunnar Myrdal, *Asian Drama: An Inquiry into the Poverty of Nations* (New York: Pantheon, 1968); Naomi Caiden and Aaron Wildavsky, *Planning and Budgeting in Poor Countries* (New Brunswick and London: Transaction Books, 1985); Pranab Bardhan, "The Political Economy of Development Policy: An Asian Perspective."

13. Douglas Chalmers, "The Politicized State in Latin America," in *Authoritarianism and Corporatism in Latin America,* ed. James Malloy (Pittsburgh: University of Pittsburgh Press, 1977), 24–26; Migdal, *Strong Societies and Weak States,* 31.

14. See Wade, *Governing the Market,* 29; Ronald Findlay, "The New Political Economy: Its Explanatory Power for LDCs," in *Politics and Policy Making in Developing Countries,* 19–21.

15. See Myrdal, *Asian Drama,* 898; Stephen D. Krasner, *Defending the National Interest: Raw Materials Investments and U.S. Foreign Policy* (Princeton: Princeton University Press, 1978), 69; Leroy P. Jones and Il Sakong, *Government, Business, and Entrepreneurship in Economic Development: The Korean Case* (Cambridge: Harvard University Press, 1980), 308; Hilton L. Root, *Small Countries, Big Lessons: Governance and the Rise of East Asia* (New York: Oxford University Press, 1996), 170.

16. Joseph S. Nye, "Corruption and Political Development: A Cost-Benefit Analysis," *American Political Science Review* 61 (June 1967); Samuel P. Huntington, *Political Order in Changing Societies* (New Haven: Yale University Press, 1968).

17. Martin C. McGuire and Mancur Olson, "The Economics of Autocracy and Majority Rule: The Invisible Hand and the Use of Force," *Journal of Economic Literature* 34, no. 1 (March 1996).

18. Andrei Schleifer and Robert W. Vishny, "Corruption," *The Quarterly Journal of Economics* (August 1993).

19. The rankings of Transparency International show a robust correlation between high levels of corruption and low levels of economic welfare. For the outcome and evolution of these rankings in 1995–2000, see the Internet site www.gwdg.de/~uwvw.

20. Tony Smith, "The Underdevelopment of Development Literature: The Case of Dependency Theory," *World Politics* 31, no. 2 (January, 1979), 279–280; Migdal, *Strong Societies,* 241; Krasner, *Defending the National Interest,* 56; Evans, *Embedded Autonomy,* 60–73.

21. Deepak Lall, *The Poverty of Development Economics* (London: Institute for Economic Affairs, 1983), 108.

22. In *Strong Societies and Weak States,* 269, Migdal considers North Korea, Cuba, and Vietnam to be "strong states." In my typology, however, these countries are not

included in the developmental cluster. From my viewpoint, they have not been able to combine their undeniable autonomy with increasing capacities. This would contribute to the explanation of their poor economic performance in the 1990s.

23. See Richard Fagen and William Tuohy, *Politics and Privilege in a Mexican City* (Stanford: Stanford University Press, 1973), 29–33; Pablo González Casanova, *El estado y los partidos políticos en México* (México: Ediciones Era, 1981), 183–186; Miguel Angel Centeno, *Democracy within Reason: Technocratic Revolution in Mexico* (University Park, Penn.: Pennsylvania State University Press, 1994), 51–59.

24. Peter H. Smith, "The Rise and Fall of the Developmental State in Latin America," in *The Changing Role of the State in Latin America*, ed. Menno Vellinga (Boulder: Westview Press, 1998), p. 63.

25. See Merilee S. Grindle, *Bureaucrats, Politicians and Peasants in Mexico: A Case Study in Public Policy* (Los Angeles: University of California Press, 1977), chs. 2 and 3; Roderic Ai Camp, *Politics in Mexico* (New York: Oxford University Press, 1996), ch. 5.

26. Martin H. Greenberg, *Bureaucracy and Development: A Mexican Case Study* (Lexington, Mass.: D.C. Heath and Company, 1970), 3.

27. William Glade, "Mexico: Party-Led Development," in *Politics, Policies, and Economic Development in Latin America*, ed. Robert Wesson (Stanford: Hoover Institution Press, 1984).

28. Frank Brandenburg, *The Making of Modern Mexico* (Englewood Cliffs, N.J.: Prentice Hall, 1964), 157; Lorenzo Meyer, "La encrucijada," in *Historia General de México*, ed. Daniel Cosío Villegas, vol. 2. (México: El Colegio de México, 1976), 1321. Lorenzo Meyer's figures differ slightly from Brandenburg in terms of appointive posts (20,000) and radically with respect to elective posts (6,000). Despite the divergent data, the differences are not enough to dismiss the characterization of the Mexican administration as a spoils system.

29. Johnson, *MITI and the Japanese Miracle*, 52.

30. Several authors have pointed out this fact, although there are few in-depth quantitative studies about the economic consequences of the Mexican political system. See Grindle, *Bureaucrats, Politicians, and Peasants in Mexico*; Peter H. Smith, *Los laberintos del poder: El reclutamiento de las élites políticas en México, 1900–1971* (México: El Colegio de México, 1981); John J. Bailey, *Governing Mexico: The Statecraft of Crisis Management* (New York: St. Martin's Press, 1988); María del Carmen Pardo, "Neutralidad o compromiso de los funcionarios públicos," in *Tendencias contemporáneas de la administración pública*, ed. Víctor Bravo Ahuja (Mexico: Editorial Diana, 1989).

31. Centeno, *Democracy within Reason*, 77.

32. See B. K. Kim, *Bringing and Managing Socioeconomic Change*, 300; Robert J. Shafer, *Mexico: Mutual Adjustment Planning* (Syracuse: Syracuse University Press, 1966), 105–109; Rainer Godau, *Estado y acero: Historia política de las truchas* (Mexico: El Colegio de México, 1982), 155–171; Antonio Ortiz Mena, *El desarrollo estabilizador: Reflexiones sobre una época* (Mexico: El Colegio de Mexico and Fondo de Cultura Económica, 1998),45–49.

33. Centeno, *Democracy within Reason*, 78, 135; Bertram M. Gross, "A Prefatory Comment," in Shafer, *Mexico: Mutual Adjustment Planning*, xvi.

34. Migdal employs this term in *Strong Societies and Weak States.*

35. Gabriel Zaid, *La economía presidencial* (Mexico: Editorial Vuelta, 1987), 11.

36. See B. K. Kim, *Bringing and Managing Socioeconomic Change,* 157; Centeno, *Democracy within Reason,* 89; María del Carmen Pardo, *La modernización administrativa en México* (Mexico: El Colegio de México, 1991), 102–104; Mercedes Blanco, *Empleo público en la administración central mexicana: Evolución y tendencias (1920–1988)* (México: Centro de Investigaciones y Estudios Superiores en Antropología Social, 1995), 85.

37. See Jorge G. Castañeda, *La herencia: Arqueología de la sucesión presidencial en México* (Mexico: Extra Alfaguara, 1999).

38. Gross, "A Prefatory Comment," xii.

39. Stephen D. Morris, *Corruption and Politics in Contemporary Mexico* (Tuscaloosa: University of Alabama Press, 1991), 42.

40. Smith, *Los laberintos del poder,* 193.

41. Raymond Vernon, *The Dilemma of Mexico's Development: The Roles of the Private and Public Sectors* (Cambridge: Harvard University Press, 1963), 152; Menno Vellinga, "The Changing Role of the State in Latin America," in *The Changing Role of the State in Latin America,* 13.

42. See Ben Ross Schneider, "Partly for Sale: Privatization and State Strength in Brazil and Mexico," *Journal of Interamerican Studies and World Affairs* 30, no. 4 (1988); Alice H. Amsden, Jacek Kochanowicz, and Lance Taylor, *The Market Meets Its Match: Restructuring the Economies of Eastern Europe* (Cambridge: Harvard University Press, 1994).

43. See Transparency International, *Corruption Perception Indexes,* 1995–2000, at www.gwdg.de/~uwvw.

44. Roger D. Hansen, *The Politics of Mexican Development* (Baltimore: Johns Hopkins University Press, 1971).

45. See Stephan Haggard, *Pathways from the Periphery: The Politics of Growth in the Newly Industrialized Countries* (Ithaca: Cornell University Press, 1990), 35–37.

46. Frederic C. Deyo, "State and Labor: Modes of Political Exclusion in East Asian Development," in *The Political Economy of the New Asian Industrialism.*

47. Sung Deuk Hahm and L. Christopher Plein, *After Development: The Transformation of the Korean Presidency and Bureaucracy* (Washington, D.C.: Georgetown University Press, 1997), 41–42. The authors indicate that the executive maintained the upper hand in his relationship with the bureaucracy.

48. Roy Hofheinz, Jr. and Kent E. Calder, *The Eastasia Edge* (New York: Basic Books, 1982), 80–81; Gerald Caiden and Jung Duck Jung, "The Political Economy of Korean Development Under the Park Government," in *Administrative Dynamics and Development: The Korean Experience,* eds. Bun Woong Kim, David S. Bell, Jr., and Chong Bum Lee (Seoul: Kyobo Publishing, 1985), 25–26; Martin Hart-Landsberg, *The Rush to Development: Economic Change and Political Struggle in South Korea* (New York: Monthly Review Press, 1993), 51; World Bank, *The East Asian Miracle,* 181–189; Campos and Root, *The Key to the Asian Miracle,* 89–91, 164–167.

49. See Hahn-Been Lee, *Korea: Time, Change, and Administration* (Honolulu: East-West Center, University of Hawaii, 1968), 123; Jon Woronoff, *Asia's "Miracle"*

Economies (Armonk, N.Y., and London: M. E. Sharpe, 1986), 96; Hart-Landsberg, *The Rush to Development*, 55; Campos and Root, *The Key to the Asian Miracle*, 140; Clifford, *Troubled Tiger*, 47.

50. See B. K. Kim, *Bringing and Managing Socioeconomic Change*, 41; and Kim and Leipziger, *Korea: A Case of Government-Led Development* (Washington, D.C.: The World Bank), 41.

51. L. L. Wade and Bong Sik Kim, *The Political Economy of Success: Public Policy and Economic Development in the Republic of Korea* (Seoul: Kyung Hee University Press, 1977), 227–228; Byung-Sun Choi, "The Structure of the Economic Policy-Making Institutions in Korea and the Strategic Role of the Economic Planning Board (EPB)," *The Korean Journal of Policy Studies*, 2 (1987): 1–23; Woronoff, *Asia's Miracle Economies*, 97; Wade, *Governing the Market*, 224; Kim and Leipziger, *Korea: A Case of Government-Led Development*, 29; Root, *Small Countries, Big Lessons*, 20; Clifford, *Troubled Tiger*, 47–48.

52. B. K. Kim, *Bringing and Managing Socioeconomic Change*, 42.

53. Hofheinz and Calder, *The Eastasia Edge*, 45; Wade, *Governing the Market*, 286–289; Ronald Dore, "Reflections on Culture and Social Change," in *Manufacturing Miracles: Paths of Industrialization in Latin America and East Asia*, eds. Gary Gereffi and Donald Wyman (Princeton: Princeton University Press, 1990), 360; Ugo Pipitone, *Tres ensayos sobre desarrollo y frustración: Asia Oriental y América Latina* (Mexico: CIDE-Miguel Angel Porrúa, 1997), 75.

54. Suek Hong Oh, "The Counter-Corruption Campaign of the Korean Government (1975–1977)," in *Korean Public Bureaucracy*, 322–344; Jong Sup Jun, "The Paradoxes of Development: Problems of Korea's Transformation," in *Administrative Dynamics and Development*, 61–70; Young Jong Kim, *Korean Public Administration and Corruption Studies* (Seoul, Hak Mun Publishing, 1996).

55. See *Korea Annual*, 1994 (Seoul: Yonhap News Agency, 1994), 56–57; Clifford, *Troubled Tiger*, 12, 132.

56. Transparency International, *Corruption Perception Indexes*, 1995–2000, at www.gwdg.de/~uwvw.

57. See Bun Woong Kim and David S. Bell. Jr., "Bureaucratic Elitism and Democratic Development in Korea?" in *Administrative Dynamics and Development*, 19; and Ro, *Public Administration and the Korean Transformation*, 1993, 12–16.

58. See Choi, "Economic Policy-Making Institutions in Korea," 11–13.

59. See OECD (Organization for Economic Cooperation and Development), "1998 Country Report: Korea," Internet site www.oecd.org/puma/gvrnance/surveys/pubs/report98/surv98ko.htm.

60. Ro, *Public Administration and the Korean Transformation*, 149, 156.

61. Evans, *Embedded Autonomy*, 233.

8

Economic Reform and Poverty in Korea, Chile, and Mexico

José Luis Estrada-López

POVERTY IS A PERVASIVE FACT OF MODERN LIFE. While capitalism has brought many benefits over the past several centuries, it has failed to eliminate this moral and social blight. Economic innovations and technological advance have led to widespread improvements in health, wealth, and well-being, but inequality and deprivation continue to persist. In a world of rapid globalization, trade, and opportunity, the majority of people live under conditions of poverty and powerlessness. This phenomenon is particularly acute in so-called developing areas—such as Africa—but it is present in advanced societies as well. Why is this so?

Latin America and East Asia offer promising laboratories for exploration of this issue. First, both the Americas and East Asia were affected by the expansion of Western powers and, with the exception of Japan, transformed as a result of colonization. This process began in the Americas in the fifteenth century and accelerated in East Asia during the nineteenth century. While the Native American civilizations were decimated by Spanish (and to a lesser extent Portuguese) rule and evolved into ethnically hybrid societies, Asian cultures were for the most part able to retain their integrity and self-identity. This was the case of the Meiji restoration in Japan, which managed to negotiate with Western powers and assimilate technology to become an economic power in the Far East. In the case of Korea, however, the native Choson dynasty did not survive the pressures of outside powers. Following an isolationist strategy, the dominant neo-Confucianist elite succumbed to annexation by Japan in the early twentieth century. From 1910 to 1945 the country underwent radical transformations in order to meet the needs of Japanese expansionist policy.

Second, economic development over the past half-century in Asia and Latin America has led to sharply contrasting outcomes. Several East Asian countries have achieved remarkable success through unusual combinations of state-led developmental policies and reliance upon market forces. In Latin America, by contrast, disappointment has been commonplace. Although the region's economic outlook appeared promising at the end of World War II, Latin American economies have suffered major crises and prolonged bouts of stagnation, particularly during the 1980s. More recently, radical reform programs have led to substantial transformation, as countries of the region have become more open to trade and capital flows. Many have also joined regional free-trade blocs (such as the North American Free Trade Agreement [NAFTA] and the Southern Common Market [MERCOSUR]). Whereas more leverage has been given to market forces and less to state intervention, the results remain unsatisfactory: Growth has been uneven, while poverty and inequity continue to persist. Aside from differences in overall growth performance, one of the principal contrasts between Latin American and Caribbean (LAC) economies and East Asia lies precisely in the patterns of poverty and income distribution.

The purpose of this chapter is to analyze the relationship between poverty and economic reform in three key countries: South Korea (henceforth Korea), Chile, and Mexico. As demonstrated elsewhere in this volume, Korea sustained an impressively high rate of growth from the early 1960s through the mid-1990s (and has rapidly recuperated from the financial crisis of 1997–1998). For most of this period, the country's economic performance led to low unemployment and to steady demand for labor. This experience contrasts sharply with Mexico, where sluggish and uneven growth has produced high chronic unemployment and large informal sectors. Chile's economy also suffered from crisis and stagnation, culminating in the financial crisis of 1982–1983, but the country has since then reaped the benefits of the neoliberal reform: There has been high and sustained growth, but only moderate reduction in poverty and hardly any progress against inequality. The three countries also vary in regard to trade patterns and policy. In the case of Chile, the trade liberalization strategy followed since the mid-1970s has confirmed the country's pursuit of comparative advantage through the exports of natural resource products (such as copper and lumber). Korea, on the other hand, is not well endowed in natural resources, and has consequently specialized in the export of manufactured products (such as electrical appliances and automobiles). As will be shown below, Mexico's pattern of exports has been quite diversified.

Key questions addressed by this chapter concern the impacts that economic reforms have had on poverty on Korea, Chile, and Mexico: (1) What are the short- and long-term effects of trade liberalization on poverty? (2) What are the corresponding effects of export promotion? To establish background and context, I first analyze conceptual and empirical dimensions of poverty, and survey the extent of poverty around the world and in East Asia and Latin America. The following section assesses the impact that economic reform, especially trade liberalization, can have on poverty in developing economies. A final section explores the processes of economic reform and social policy within the countries under consideration.

Concepts and Measurements of Poverty

In the most general sense, poverty refers to the lack of opportunity for an individual or a family to have a decent life. There are various forms of poverty: extreme poverty, in which individuals cannot satisfy basic nutritional requirements for reproduction; structural poverty arising from the marginalization of families, or entire communities, in both rural and urban settings; and moderate poverty, in which individual may meet some basic requirements but not all that are considered socially necessary.[1] In this chapter I use the conventional concept that relates poverty to the satisfaction of minimum needs. Thus, a poverty line is defined as a critical consumption threshold of essential goods and services, below which individuals cannot satisfy basic needs. Given the quality of data available for crossregional comparisons, it is most feasible and reasonable to rely on poverty lines that are based on income and consumption criteria. It should be remembered, however, that these concepts and measurements provide only a gross approximation of socioeconomic realities.

The problem of poverty is complex and there are many factors that determine its magnitude, forms, and incidence. To a considerable extent, poverty and inequality are long-term problems that depend on enduring features of the socioeconomic structure—urban-rural disparities, the relative importance of traditional and modern activities, and inequality in the distribution of assets and opportunities.[2] But as debt and currency crises in Latin America and Asia have shown, poverty can also be critically affected by short-term factors.

Long-term structural determinants of rural poverty can be related to asset ownership, as well as to unemployment and migration. In rural areas, the lack of sufficient land for peasants to cultivate is one of the major determinants of poverty. This combines with insufficient access to adequately remunerated employment in rural enterprises. Poverty, especially extreme poverty, affects the work capacity of individuals and thus limits their participation in labor markets. Conversely, the inability of an economy to provide sufficient jobs for its labor force affects the income of the temporarily unemployed (or underemployed), and may push them into poverty traps—since poverty leads to malnutrition, which affects capacity to work, which thus leads to poverty.[3]

Research and analysis during the 1990s has led to the recognition that poverty alleviation is more complex than previously thought. Indeed, the World Bank has come to recognize a variety of features about contemporary poverty. First, market reforms do not necessarily lead to sustained growth and poverty reduction; their economic and social effects depend on the nature of institutions as well as political and social structures. "Market reforms can indeed boost growth and help poor people, but they can also be a source of dislocation."[4] Second, technological change during the past decade has led to a bias in favor of skills; instances of successful growth in developing countries have not provided much support or relief for unskilled labor, which means that they have not done much to alleviate poverty. Third, the expansion of social services has been insufficient and inefficient.

In this analysis, I assume that economic growth is a necessary condition for reducing the incidence of poverty. As growth generates employment opportunities and incomes, investment in human capital tends to raise future incomes. Economic growth needs to be fast enough to satisfy the demand for jobs resulting from the growth of the labor force, however, while reducing the size of the informal economy. Second, how fast economic growth translates into reduced poverty depends on the pattern of income distribution. Even in the event that growth is accompanied by a worsening of income distribution, it is nonetheless possible that growth may have reduced the degree of worsening. Third, a variety of other factors can be identified in the circumstances of specific countries or regions that determine their poverty situation, such as marginalization of groups or communities. Thus, the question is what combination of pro-growth policies and social policies provides the most appropriate mix for any particular economy.

There are two widely used measures of poverty. One is known as the Head Count Ratio (HCR), and is defined as the proportion of people in a given population who live below the poverty line. The other is the Poverty Gap Ratio (PGR), which is defined as the additional per capita income that would be needed to raise all poor people just above the poverty line, divided by the average income within the society. The PGR has been introduced to overcome limitations of the HCR, which counts only the number of poor persons—without regard to how poor they are. The HCR also ignores the facts that individual and household needs vary considerably among various groups of people, and that, within limits, poor families manage to survive with very little monetary income.[5]

Poverty: Some Basic Facts

Poverty is a worldwide phenomenon with huge contrasts between the underdeveloped and the advanced industrial economies. Extreme poverty has reached stratospheric levels: At present over one billion people are deprived of basic needs such as food, adequate health services, housing, and sanitation.[6] The vast majority of the world's poor live in underdeveloped or developing economies. Poverty, however, is also a real and serious problem within the most advanced industrial countries such as the United States, although it differs from the type of poverty that affects most of the underdeveloped world.[7]

Using World Bank data, we first compare the situation and trends in poverty during the 1990s. In 1998, the number of poor people—those living on less than two dollars a day—was higher in East Asia and the Pacific (EAP, with 885 million) than in Latin America and the Caribbean (LAC, with 159 million). Even excluding China, the World Bank estimates that there are 252 million poor people in EAP. But the trends are more favorable for EAP, with a substantial decline in the HCR from 67 percent in 1987 to 49 percent in 1998; in LAC the absolute number of poor people has actually increased, although there was a slight decline in the regional HCR from 35 percent to 32 percent.

Table 8.1 presents social and poverty indicators for Mexico, Chile, and Korea. According to conventional criteria, poverty exists in all these countries, although to a much lesser extent in Korea. The data reveal high levels of extreme and moderate poverty in Mexico and intermediate levels in Chile. The infant mortality rate indicator is very high for Mexico, while Chile and Korea both register fairly low levels. Illiteracy rates in Mexico are also higher than in the other two countries.

One poverty-related issue that reflects a marked contrast between the East Asian and Latin American countries is income distribution. Latin America has had a very unequal distribution of income, both in absolute terms and relative to other regions. As one recent study has shown, the average Gini coefficient for LAC since the 1960s is over .50, while the corresponding average for EAP is just over .36, with very little change over time.[8] Based on income shares, we see a very unequal distribution of income in both regions but much more in LAC: The lowest quintile in Latin America receives much smaller share of income (3.42 percent in the 1960s, 3.69 percent in the 1970s, 3.67 percent in the 1980s, and 4.52 percent in the 1990s) than in East Asia (6.44 percent in the 1960s, 6.00 percent in the 1970s, 6.27 percent in the 1980s, and 6.84 percent in the 1990s). Moreover, the top quintile in EAP countries has lower income share (45.9 percent in the 1960s, 46.5 percent in the 1970s, 45.51 percent in the 1980s, and 44.33 percent in the 1990s) than in LAC (61.6 percent in the 1960s, 54.18 percent in the 1970s, 54.86 percent in the 1980s, and 52.94 percent in the 1990s).

TABLE 8.1
Poverty and Socioeconomic Indicators: Mexico, Chile, Korea

	Mexico	Chile	Korea
Population below $1 per day (as % total)	12.2	<2.0	<2.0[a]
Poverty Gap Ratio (as %)[b]	3.5	<0.5	<0.5[a]
Population below $2 per day (as % total)	34.8	18.4	<2.0[a]
Poverty Gap Ratio (as %)[b]	13.2	16.0	<0.5[a]
Infant mortality rate[c]	35.0	4.8	9.0
Female illiteracy rate (as %)[d]	10.6	4.6	3.6
Male illiteracy rate (as %)[d]	3.7	4.2	0.9
Total population[e]	98.0	15.2	47.3
Gross national income[f]	497.0	69.9	421.1
Income per capita[g]	8,790	9,100	17,300

[a]Data refer to 1993.
[b]PGR as defined in text.
[c]Mortality rate per thousand children age 0–5, as of 1998.
[d]Percentage of population age 15 and above, as of 1999.
[e]Millions of inhabitants, as of 2000.
[f]Billions of U.S. dollars, Atlas Method, 2000.
[g]U.S. dollars as of 2000, Purchasing Power Parity Method.
Source: World Bank, *World Development Indicators.*

Most Latin American countries have also shared a similar evolution of poverty and unequal distribution of income over time. One comprehensive study found that poverty and income distribution improved during the growth phase of the 1970s, worsened during the stabilization period of the 1980s, and did not improve significantly during the recovery of the 1990s. Using the income share of the upper quintile as an indicator of income concentration in the region, a small two-point reduction is observed (from 55.3 percent to 53.3 percent) to the benefit of the lower quintiles between 1970 and 1982. During the 1980s there is an opposite trend. The income share rises from 53.3 percent in 1981 to 55.7 percent in 1990, and remains about the same thereafter, reaching 58.3 percent in 1994 and falling to 57.7 percent the year after.[9]

Poverty and Reform

This section assesses the impact that economic reform policies can have on social conditions in a technologically backward economy. Liberalization means opening an economy to the free flow of goods and services as well as to the free flow of capital, in the form of both foreign direct investment (FDI) and financial (portfolio) investment. To date liberal reforms have not extended to the flow of human resources, which remains highly restricted. While there is a substantial body of theoretical work on specialization and trade in goods and services, there has been much less work on the consequences of financial liberalization. In contrast to the benefits of FDI, portfolio investment can have serious destabilizing effects—which result from the combination of very high volatility with inadequate domestic institutions and regulatory mechanisms. This was the case during the financial and banking crisis in Chile in 1982, the debt crisis of 1982 and the financial crisis of 1994–1995 in Mexico, and the financial contagion in Korea and other Asian countries in 1997–1998.

How does trade liberalization affect poverty? Trade liberalization consists of dismantling most protective barriers in order to open up economies to worldwide market opportunities and competition, so countries can specialize according to comparative advantage and worldwide prices. As a consequence, a process of relocation takes place in which some business sectors will expand—those associated with export opportunities (the winners)—and other sectors will contract or disappear altogether (the losers). This process may or may not result in a new situation with full employment of labor, although it is usually assumed that it will.

According to conventional trade theory, liberalization of trade brings benefits to the general population even in a relatively backward and low-wage economy. Newly established relative prices will improve allocative efficiency and foreign competitive pressures will tend to reduce technical inefficiencies—either by forcing domestic producers to restructure or simply because the less efficient will disappear. How these static gains will be distributed remains open to question and depends on premises. If export growth increases demand in an industrial sector where low-skill workers are already employed, this should push up wages in relation to returns on capital. And since poor people are mostly unskilled, then the opening-up of trade and the resulting specialization of labor-intensive exports will contribute directly to reducing poverty. But returns on capital will be greater in a more advanced, high-wage economy with a skilled labor force. It has been argued that this is a principal reason why East Asian nations fared better than Latin American economies that continued with import-substitution policies.[10] It is from this perspective that inward-oriented industrialization is criticized, since it tends to prevent labor-intensive specialization in favor of more capital-intensive specialization in countries with capital scarcity and labor abundance.

Let us extend the analysis and consider two types of workers: unskilled and skilled. It is possible that the opening-up of trade and specialization in labor-intensive goods can lead to an increase in the wages of relatively skilled labor, compared to less-skilled and unskilled workers. Although this argument was initially used to explain the relative decline of wages for low-skilled labor in advanced industrial economies, it can also apply to developing economies.[11]

Take another case. The principle of comparative advantage assumes that trade liberalization and specialization takes place in a context that assures the maintenance of full employment and equilibrium in bilateral trade. There are reasons to doubt that this has to be the only, or even the most likely outcome for developing economies. According to standard theory, unemployment equilibrium can result from rigidities in labor markets that do not allow the wage rate to fall sufficiently so as to allow a rapid shift from declining industries toward expanding export sectors. From this perspective the problem lies in the need to reform the labor market—to make it sufficiently flexible—and not in the opening-up of trade. There are several objections to this argument. First, it presumes that the countries involved are in roughly similar stages of development, and that their economic agents have equal access to technological and organizational knowledge; if this is not the case, the absolute disadvantage may result in long-term unemployment and a trade deficit.[12] Second, the problem may lie in insufficient effective demand in the economy, as argued by Keynes. Finally, reform of the labor market and achievement of labor flexibility might take extended periods of time. Under such conditions, the persistence of unemployment or underemployment will negatively affect the poor, and will call for the implementation of substantial compensatory policies.

By providing economies with new markets, trade can have positive effects on countries with excess capacity. To take advantage of this opportunity might require governmental subsidies to compensate for competitive disadvantage in relation to foreign producers of comparable goods. This seems to have been the case of Korea's textile exports during the 1960s.

Consider a country with a considerable disadvantage in relation to major manufacturing exporters in world markets. Such was the case of Korea at the beginning of the 1960s. According to the principle of comparative advantage, the disparity in productivity would have to be adjusted in order for bilateral trade to be possible. And if a fixed exchange rate is assumed, this adjustment will take place through a general fall in the average wage rate. This will give the technologically backward country competitiveness in the most labor-intensive tradable-good sector, but will produce a negative effect on poverty. In the case of Mexico, after liberalization took place (1985–1987) the real wage rate fell considerably, with only small upsurges in the average manufacturing rate for short periods of time.

In general, it is impossible to establish the net effect of links between trade liberalization and poverty in developing countries with great precision. This is the conclusion of an extensive analysis that starts with the well-known Stolper-Samuelson theorem and develops a variety of economic and institutional scenarios. What can be said is that, the greater the effect of demand for unskilled labor-intensive goods and services, the stronger will be the impact of trade liberalization on poverty. In the case of agricultural liberalization, this should result in high demand for construction, domestic service, and simple manufacturing, thus producing favorable benefits for the rural poor.[13]

Analysis of investment flows adds considerable complication to traditional trade theory, which does not account for the movement of factors across international boundaries. Ricardo himself acknowledged—when proposing his theory of comparative advantage between Portugal and England—that if capital were internationally mobile, the optimal situation would be for capital to move from less-productive England to more-productive Portugal. This is what is happening in the current stage of global development. Multinational corporations (MNCs) have a predominant role in the conduct of foreign trade by means of intra-firm and intra-industry trade.

There is not necessarily an inherent contradiction between the specialization models for trade and FDI by MNCs. In most cases, foreign corporations locate their subsidiaries in accordance with the factor endowment of the host country, as in the case of labor-intensive maquiladora-type operations now present in many developing countries. In some cases, however, relocation of production by multinational corporations can involve the establishment of plants that are not labor-intensive, as in the case of auto production in the NAFTA countries. Although this pattern of exports of capital-intensive and high-tech products started prior to Mexico's liberalizing reforms, it has deepened with NAFTA.

Even if trade liberalization tends to worsen poverty conditions in a low-wage developing economy, foreign direct investment may offset some negative effects. It can do so by means of the additional demand for and provision of investment resources, through technology transfers and learning, and through the spillover effects that subsidiaries might have on domestic production. But there can be costs as well, particularly in terms of (1) loss of sovereignty in host countries, (2) dependence on foreign institutions and agencies, and (3) FDI-induced economic distortions, especially when capital inflows alter equilibrium exchange-rate levels that are compatible with trade.

In summary, we can weigh the positive and negative effects of trade liberalization on poverty conditions of a developing economy. Positive effects arise from the increased efficiency that is expected to take place in some sectors of the economy. If full employment is maintained when an economy opens up to free trade, possible negative effects on the poor will likely arise precisely because of their lack of skills and knowledge required to take advantage of newer and better opportunities. Those in extreme poverty will be at an even greater disadvantage due to their reduced work capacity derived from malnutrition. The overall effect of trade liberalization will be better or worse depending on the degree of employment attained after trade liberalization.

The likelihood that free trade will have negative effects on a backward economy does not imply that a more autarkic strategy will render better results. In a world of dynamic technological innovation, mostly at the industrialized center of the world economy, the main benefits of partial or all-out trade liberalization reside in the nation's access to foreign knowledge. Trade specialization of an underdeveloped economy is determined by its competitive advantage and trade regime. Once specialization is attained, perhaps the most important growth effect of trade liberalization lies in technical progress.

The connection between income distribution and economic growth is complex. The common starting point is the inverted-U-shape relationship postulated by Simon Kuznetz, in which income distribution deteriorates at initial stages of development and improves at later stages. In the Latin American context, some analysts have argued that inequality can have a positive impact on growth by increasing the saving and investment rates of upper-income sectors.[14] Others have identified a negative association between income distribution and economic growth, since inequality limits aggregate demand and thus inhibits long-term economic growth. As to magnitude, it has been asserted that a reduction of one standard deviation in inequality—as measured by the Gini coefficient—will raise the annual growth rate of GDP per capita by 0.5 to 0.8 percentage points. Although this finding is highly significant, it does not account for most of the difference in economic performance between East Asia and Latin America—or between Asian countries like Korea and the Philippines. Moreover, the specification of causal relationships among these and other factors has been problematic.[15]

Economic Reforms in Korea, Chile, and Mexico

Within this theoretical context, we now turn to empirical studies of economic orientation and social policy and their impact on poverty alleviation. We begin with Korea and then focus on Chile and Mexico.

Korea

Contrasting with centuries of inward orientation, Korea engaged in rapid capitalist change after liberation from the Japanese occupation at the end of World War II. The import-substitution strategy applied during the 1950s was followed by a major but selective economic reform during the 1960s. With the takeover by General Park in 1961, the government shifted toward export-oriented industrialization with the goal of strengthening the nation's capacity to remain independent and avoiding the type of hardships suffered under colonization. The government followed a pragmatic international policy and entered into a long-term alliance with the United States, which in turn supported Korea's industrialization strategy. Relations with Japan were normalized and exchanges of technical knowledge were resumed. Domestically, the Park regime established what can be seen as a social contract between the government and the burgeoning business class, which clearly delineated the roles of the state and of the *chaebols.* The Korean state firmly established its leading role in the newly conceived exporting economy, and assured its preeminence through its ownership and management of banks. Businesses, especially the *chaebols,* acquired the task of constructing an efficient exporting industrial sector—with government support in the form of subsidized credit, allowance of required imports, and temporary import protection.

As a consequence of long-term, market-oriented reforms and state guidance, Korea established an evolving pattern of industrial specialization. The initial stage was based on exports of labor-intensive products (cotton textiles, apparel, plywood) that corresponded to the factor-endowment trade theory, but which required government subsidies to partly compensate for cost disadvantages. A second stage of heavy industrialization was promoted by the government in collaboration with the already prosperous *chaebols* during the 1970s.[16] During the 1980s, liberal reforms were undertaken that radically changed the Korean economy. A new wave of exports developed as a consequence of the productive capacity built during the previous decade.

Economic reform under General Park's regime sought to impose order and to set the basic conditions for future industrial plans. The strategy was implemented in combination with state intervention and selective protectionism to support the export-oriented strategy.[17] Reforms were limited to an exchange rate reform and partial trade liberalization. The *won* was devalued to correct for distortions and a unified flexible exchange rate was established. Import substitution policies continued to be applied on a selective basis to promote new industries

From the 1960s to the 1990s Korea had one of the fastest-growing economies in East Asia. Between 1965 and 1975, for example, Korean output grew at an average yearly rate of over 10 percent, while manufacturing grew at nearly 20 percent per year. This led to a rapid structural transformation. While in 1961 agricultural output was near 40 percent of total output, by the middle of the 1970s this share had fallen to 25 percent. At the same time, the share of manufacturing output rose from around 14 percent to 26 percent. At the beginning of the 1960s, about 16 percent of the urban labor force was reported to be unemployed or underemployed, while for rural areas the unemployment rate was only 3 percent. By 1976, these rates had dropped to 6.3 percent and 1 percent respectively.[18]

Aside from economic growth, other factors have contributed to the well-being of Korean society since the 1960s—among them, relatively low population growth and a relatively even distribution of income. Average population growth rates in Korea declined from 1.79 percent in the 1970s to just 1 percent in the 1990s. Mexico experienced very rapid population growth during the 1970s, by contrast, and reduced its pace to 1.85 percent only in the last decade; Chile's population growth remained at around 1.6 percent for the whole period. The Korean economy has also benefited from its demographic transition, as shown by evolution of the dependency ratio. The proportion of the working age population to total population has been considerably higher in Korea than in Mexico and Chile, increasing from .38 in the 1970s to .47 in the 1990s. Recent studies highlight the demographic factor as one of the principal explanations for the growth performance of East Asian economies.[19]

One special condition that deserves attention in relation to Korea's income distribution is land tenure. As mentioned above, Korea was able to provide its population with a system largely free of the extreme poverty that is found in many other developing countries. One of the main reasons for this achievement lies in land tenure. After the country was liberated from the Japanese in 1945, Korea underwent a radical and swift agrarian reform from 1949 to 1952. The political climate was conducive to radical policy, since a great deal of land was owned by Japanese and by local landlords who had closely collaborated with them.[20] There were three redistribution schemes: (1) land previously owned by the Japanese was transferred to the original Korean tenants under a government contract (this amounted to 240,000 hectares), (2) large landholdings were transferred to tenants on a small-scale basis (up to three hectares per family) through the government (a total of 330,000 hectares were redistributed under this scheme), and (3) other land was directly sold to tenants by landlords at low prices (550,000 hectares).[21] Since the agrarian reform did not break up the actual plots, reform also had a positive impact on agricultural productivity. This process created a more egalitarian distribution of land that had a strong positive effect on the future of the economy. Korean farmers took advantage of their land ownership and with government support were able to increase farm productivity.

A second stage of liberal economic reforms took place after the political and economic crisis that was aggravated as a consequence of President Park's assassination in 1979. Major reforms included bank privatization and trade liberalization, although these were still undertaken in a selective way. Since Korea had already developed a strong export position in foreign markets, trade reforms at the beginning of the 1980s were directed at correcting the imbalances and distortions that had been created by the heavy industrialization program. In contrast to Mexico, the reforms did not aim to shift the economy toward an outward-oriented strategy. Moreover, since the economy had already achieved high productivity growth rates, trade liberalization was not primarily seen as a way to improve efficiency. To a certain extent, liberalization was promoted to help stimulate light industry; and to an even greater extent, import liberalization was adopted in response to protectionism in developed countries and to external pressures to reduce Korean trade surpluses, especially in its commercial accounts with the United States.[22]

A third stage of market reforms began prior to the 1997 Asian financial crisis, but gained momentum as a consequence of the crisis. As Jaebong Ro shows in chapter 11, the crisis revealed deep structural problems in the Korean economy. In fact the government had begun to address three fundamental areas even prior to the crisis: (1) corporate governance, (2) finance, and (3) labor relations. And while the conglomerates *(chaebols)* had helped promote industrial competitiveness during previous phases of economic development, their structures and modes of operation came to be recognized as an obstacle to further progress.

As might have been expected, this crisis aggravated poverty in Korea. Based on national poverty lines, the Korea Statistical Office estimated a substantial increase in the proportion of poor families, from 1.9 percent in 1997 to 4.9 percent in 1998. World Bank data also indicate a sharp increase, from 8.5 percent to 22.9 percent. Although the absolute levels depend on the concepts and levels for poverty lines, the direction of the variation is clearly established.[23] This increase in poverty was clearly associated with the downturn in macroeconomic activity, which raised unemployment rates from 2.2 percent in July 1997 to 7.4 percent in July 1998 (and has since been reversed by the rapid recovery of the Korean economy).[24] The long-term structural poverty may be solved by a more active social policy on the part of the Korean government.

In conclusion, we can make several interrelated observations: (1) Korea's long and sequential process of liberalization has allowed the country to develop a strong industrial exporting sector; (2) since the country has developed a very concentrated economic structure, led by the *chaebols*, trade liberalization during the 1980s actually favored increasing economic concentration;[25] and (3) the economy's export potential played a part in shortening the periods of adjustment after the economic crises of 1972 and 1979, and in successfully reducing its debt burden during the latter episode. A new wave of major reforms that affect traditional *chaebol* interests is still underway, and aims to transform the economy to meet the new requirements of the information age.

Chile

After the military coup of 1973, General Pinochet established a radical "free to choose" growth strategy. Since then, there have been several policy stages.

From 1974 to 1983, a sweeping liberal reform was implemented at the same time that stabilization programs were pursued to control inflation. During this ten-year period, economic reforms were largely unsuccessful in terms of stabilizing the economy and achieving sustained growth. The serious banking and financial crisis that Chile suffered from 1981 to 1983 revealed fundamental flaws in the original plan, which adhered to laissez-faire ideology. After weathering economic crisis and social unrest in the early 1980s, the trade and market reforms were fundamentally maintained, but in combination with a more pragmatic approach to financial matters—strict controls on capital flows were established together with other mechanisms for mitigating external and/or trade shocks. During the last five years of the military regime, from 1984 to 1989, the economy rebounded and per capita GDP grew at an average yearly rate of 5.5 percent. During the 1990s, successive democratic governments maintained neoliberal policies while forging new instruments to address the pervasive problems of poverty and unemployment.

As a consequence of trade liberalization and other property reforms, a new pattern of specialization was established. Traditional mineral exports continued growing but nontraditional exports became more dynamic, based primarily on the country's agricultural, sea, and forest resources. While the government maintained state ownership of copper corporations like Codelco, private investment in the mining sector was allowed. This has led to massive investments in mining by foreign and local businesses, which have expanded mineral output and exports considerably. In 1997, the value of exports reached almost $17 billion (three-fourths in primary products and foodstuffs). Manufacturing exports accounted for the remaining fourth, including cellulose, paper, and printing. Mining still accounted for almost 50 percent of total exports.

A radical agrarian policy helped the expansion of the newly exporting sector. After a series of redistributive agrarian reforms by previous governments, the military regime decided to permit private corporations to own unlimited amounts of farmland. Thus, "the spectrum of land holdings goes from traditional crop producers and small holders to large commercial ventures with an export orientation."[26]

Social gains proved to be selective. The business community took advantage of opportunities to increase exports. And while the population and the labor force grew at modest rates, a number of social problems became acutely manifest during the Pinochet years: Poverty and extreme poverty became aggravated, and unemployment rates remained very high in urban and rural areas. In 1987, before the political transition, 45 percent of households were reported to be in poverty while 17.4 percent were below the line of extreme poverty. Contrary to what happened in Mexico during its reform period, there was no decline in real wages, but Chile's adjustment policies led to increasing unemployment. The open unemployment rate was 15 percent in 1975 and more than 10 percent in 1981, and then jumped to nearly 20 percent during the 1982 crisis. Eventually, unemployment declined only as economic growth progressed from 1986 onward.[27]

Chile's strategy involved simultaneous reform of all markets. Since the country was at the time of the coup suffering from a severe macroeconomic disequilibrium with an acute foreign exchange shortage, a high fiscal deficit and high inflation, stabilization policies and all-encompassing structural liberal reforms were implemented early and at the same time. Reforms included domestic market liberalization (removal of price controls) and unilateral trade liberalization (removal of quantitative import restrictions and lowering of trade tariffs). State-owned enterprises were privatized (except the copper parastatals). Financial reform included liberalization of interest rates and deregulation of financial intermediation. Labor markets were also significantly affected, especially by legislation that prohibited labor union activity.[28]

Success was not immediate. Two phases can be identified in the attempts to tackle hyperinflation and the balance-of-payments crisis. In the first phase, orthodox contractionary policies were applied. Anti-inflationary policy was based on major reductions in monetary growth and fiscal deficits. These anti-inflationary measures were seen as insufficient to eliminate the balance-of-payments crisis, and therefore "major expenditure-switching" measures were also taken, mainly through currency devaluations. In addition, a passive, crawling-peg exchange-rate system was established with a view to maintaining purchasing-power parity. During the second phase, the persistence of inflation motivated a major shift in stabilization policies. The idea was to use the exchange rate as an anti-inflationary tool. An "active" crawling-peg system was established, which consisted of pre-announced exchange-rate targets (up to six months in advance). The rate of devaluation was set by a pre-announced schedule (the *tablita*) at a rate lower than the existing difference between domestic and worldwide inflation.

As in Mexico, stabilization and liberal reform policies applied in Chile (1974–1978) were not completely successful in bringing down inflation (the average annual growth of the CPI was 79 percent for 1977 and 1978), in spite of success in reducing the fiscal deficit to 1.3 percent of GDP. In Chile there was a persistent problem with very high real interest rates that could not be easily explained. The next steps were managing the exchange rate to reduce inflation, and opening up to foreign capital.[29] The combination of large inflows of foreign capital, especially during 1978–1981, led to an economic boom and to currency overvaluation.[30] As has happened during times of crisis elsewhere, firms that were allowed to engage in risky financial operations ended by provoking widespread banking crises.[31]

In evaluating the impact of the liberal economic reforms in Chile during the period from 1974 to 1982, it is not easy to pinpoint the causes of the failure. Although trade unions became weak after the military takeover, and "mobility was increased by the new labor laws of late 1979 and the social security reform of 1981, Chilean wages were fully indexed to the consumer price index for the private and public sector."[32] This might have undermined the stabilization program. Although it is possible that, as Sebastián Edwards argued, the 1982 crisis cannot be directly ascribed to the basic economic reforms (fiscal reform, trade liberalization, and social security), but rather to the financial reform that was carried out without sufficient supervision. A more serious mistake was the government's reliance on "automatic monetary adjustment" when the crisis started to develop.[33]

The shift from the authoritarian military regime to democratic government brought about significant changes in social and political matters. Politically, the shift toward democracy reduced uncertainty as to the stability of the rules established during the military government. The success of the government coalition in consolidating democracy, in continuing with the liberal and export-oriented economic strategy, and in addressing pressing social issues greatly increased confidence in the country's new democracy. This was reflected in economic matters. In the years that followed democratization (1990–1998), the country maintained its growth record: GDP per capita grew by an annual average of more than 5 percent, while real wages increased by an average of 3.7 percent. Thus, the combination of rapid growth and social policy reduced the head count of people living in poverty from 5 million persons in 1990 to 3.3 million in 1996. Patricio Meller has also analyzed the key question of how the social policies of Chile's democratic governments have contributed to the reduction of poverty, and calculates that economic growth reduced poverty by 60 percent—while social policy contributed 40 percent to the overall reduction.[34]

Chile entered a period of economic slowdown in 1998, and progress in alleviating poverty has ground to a virtual halt. One recent study has found that the pace of relative poverty reduction was slower in 1997–2000 than before, and that the absolute number of person actually living in extreme poverty has increased—largely as a result of disparities in regional development and urban-rural differences.[35]

Mexico

Mexico's inward-oriented and government-led strategy went to the extreme of carrying its economy to a grave situation of instability (exchange rate volatility, high foreign indebtedness, a very high fiscal deficit, and excessive trade and current account deficits). After two decades of strong and stable growth during the 1950s and 1960s, state policy during the 1970s pursued high economic growth but failed to maintain macroeconomic stability. During the 1980s, the Mexican economy stagnated amidst recurrent crises due to external shocks as well as to failures in economic policy. As the price of Mexican oil climbed to more than $30 per barrel, the administration of José López Portillo followed an irresponsible policy of high deficit expenditure and overvalued currency. The economy became extremely dependent on oil revenues, inflation accelerated, the peso became overvalued, and exports lost competitiveness. In August 1982 the government announced it would no longer be able to service its foreign debt, and a decade of crisis ensued. Miguel de la Madrid took office in December 1982 with inflation running over 50 percent, a foreign debt of $90 billion, and no access to foreign credit.

Under these inauspicious circumstances, the process of trade liberalization in Mexico followed a radical and mostly unilateral approach. By the end of 1982, in response to the balance of payment crisis, the government established import licenses for all products. Later, during the first phase of reform (1983–1985) there was a partial process of liberalization by lifting license requirements for a small proportion of imports. Radical steps to liberalize trade were taken in 1985, when new legislation lifted quantitative restrictions and established a tariff system for most import categories. The following year the country entered the General Agreement on Tariffs and Trade (GATT), and by 1987 almost 75 percent of imports were subject to tariffs. The proportion of imports subject to import licenses decreased from 92 percent in June 1985 to 47 percent by the end of the year and to 25 percent by the end of 1987. In some industries, such as textiles and clothing, liberalization was more radical than in others, like automobile production. However, this swift liberalization was initially compensated by the increased protection allowed by an undervalued peso and the low import demand generated by sluggish economic growth.

Between 1983 and 1989, GDP per capita fell by 2.97 percent and real incomes deteriorated through a sharp reduction in real wages. Since the minimum wage was used as an anchor to contain inflation, the reduction was very sharp (−46.8 percent between 1982 and 1988); the reduction in the average wage was slightly lower for the same period (−40.8 percent). Social expenditure was also sharply reduced. Expenditure in education fell by 57.3 percent for the primary level and by 35.6 percent for the secondary level. This period of "export-led stagnation" was driven mainly by the debt burden that Mexico incurred during the oil boom episode, the deterioration in terms of trade, and the rising cost of money.

Unemployment increased in Mexico as a result of sluggish economic growth, while the informal sector expanded. Unemployment levels had been relatively high during the 1970s, but declined along with the economic expansion of the oil boom, to a low of 4.2 percent just before the debt crisis of 1982. It then increased to nearly 7 percent in 1983, followed by a downward trend until the 1994–1995 crisis, when it again increased to over 6 percent. Compared with Chile, where unemployment at time approached 20 percent, adjustment policies in Mexico affected incomes more heavily than they did employment levels. However, due to serious problems with unemployment statistics, this statement should be taken only as an approximation of the comparative labor situations in the two economies.

In response to unfavorable prospects for formal employment, Mexican workers utilized various strategies: (1) migration abroad increased during the adjustment years from 1981 to 1993, when 240,000 Mexicans were admitted as permanent residents of the United States;[36] (2) occupation in informal activities increased to nearly 39 percent of the economically active population in urban centers;[37] and (3) acceptance of non-wage occupations expanded.

The Brady debt-relief plan helped the Mexican economy renew growth and continue its wave of neoliberal reforms (privatization, financial liberalization, and deregulation). In sharp contrast with the previous period, GDP per capita recorded a small increase of 5.95 percent from 1989 to 1994, amidst nation- and worldwide optimism about the administration of Carlos Salinas de Gortari. Also, there was a substantial recovery in social expenditure: From 1988 to 1994, expenditure on primary and secondary education went up by 140 percent and 122 percent respectively. These increases compensated the previous reductions such that, for the whole period (1982–1994), expenditure per student in primary education registered a small increase of about 7 percent, while it increased for secondary education by nearly 14 percent.[38]

Private incomes did not register sustained increases. From 1988 to 1994, the real minimum wage fell by as much as 27 percent, although the average real wage showed a modest increase of 14 percent. For a longer period, from 1982 to 1994, the minimum wage had lost over 60 percent of its purchasing power, and the average wage only 22 percent.[39]

The financial crisis that erupted in December 1994 and lasted throughout 1995 revealed the fictitious nature of Mexico's recovery. To a considerable extent, it resembled the short economic boom that Chile experienced from 1978 to 1982. Basic aspects they had in common were (1) a fixed exchange rate system that led to overvaluation of the currency, (2) high inflows of foreign capital that contributed to increased demand, and (3) increasing foreign current account deficits financed by those capital inflows. One significant difference, however, was that the type of wage-indexation system used in Chile at that time did not exist in Mexico during the 1994–1995 crisis.

One of the main goals of the Mexican reforms was to transform the previous repressed financial system into a modern one based on free-market institutions. Toward this end, the government took several steps: (1) reserve requirements were rapidly reduced and eliminated by 1992, (2) interest rate controls were eliminated, and (3) banks were privatized. In this highly unregulated financial context between 1989 and 1994, the new financial institutions and bankers led the system to a very unstable situation. It is especially noteworthy that, given the high price paid for the banks by private groups, there was a rush to increase lending, which increased their portfolios of nonperforming loans. When capital account liberalization took place, massive flows foreign funds entered the country, in a fashion similar to what would happen later in East Asia.[40]

NAFTA, which went into effect on January 1, 1994, represented for Mexico a continuation and consolidation of ongoing economic reforms—and a break with its long-term stance toward the United States. From an economic viewpoint, opening up to free trade with its main trading partner was a natural extension of the previous liberalization processes, and the signing of the accord signaled a commitment on the part of the Mexican government to continue its reforms. NAFTA benefits Mexico by guaranteeing access to the U.S. market, and by increasing and sustaining the inflow of U.S. investment in the country. This reinforces what has been a long-term tendency manifested in the relocation of industrial plants from the U.S. to Mexico's northern states, including labor-intensive facilities as well as other capital-intensive and high-tech industries. For the United States, there were compelling reasons to bring Mexico into the trade agreement—because of the opportunity to strengthen the U.S. position vis-à-vis Europe and Japan, because of Mexico's oil resources and its cheap labor, and because of the security issues stemming from their long common border.[41]

From a political perspective, the move represented a sharp departure from the postrevolutionary nationalist stand that was based on fear of the historical U.S. tendency toward expansionism. Internally, the trade agreement favors the forces of modernization, thereby transforming traditional political and economic alliances, and helps to strengthen the democratization process and weaken traditional authoritarian practices.

One of the main failures of Mexico's past economic strategy was its inability to eradicate poverty and to achieve a more equal distribution of income. This was true in spite of the implementation of land reform in the wake of the Mexican Revolution. As in Korea, the Mexican reform consisted of redistributing land from large units to poor peasants in small units. The Mexican policy did not grant the peasants ownership, however, but instead gave them rights to use the land, in most cases collectively under the *ejido* or communal systems, while the state maintained ultimate ownership. This process of agrarian redistribution stretched over decades, from the 1920s through the 1960s, while the lack of direct peasant ownership gave rise to an entire system of commercialization and credit under the management of public enterprises. This system proved compatible with industrialization during the 1950s and 1960s, but subsequently the rural sector entered a long-lasting crisis that has not yet been solved. Gross agricultural output expanded fairly rapidly during the 1940s and '50s, decelerated during the 1960s and '80s, and dropped to less than 3 percent per year in the early 1980s.[42] This declining trend in output, combined with an acceleration in population growth, reduced the agricultural surplus that had helped to support the process of industrialization. Stagnation and instability in output worked to discourage private investment in agriculture, while the distribution of low-quality land in later phases of the reform actually led to an increase in the number of poor rural families. The Mexican experience thus stands in sharp contrast to Korea, where agrarian reform took place within a compressed period of time and where rules of land tenure were clearly established.[43]

Table 8.2 shows the evolution of moderate and extreme poverty from 1960 to 1988. In 1963 almost 25 million people (around two-thirds of the population) were extremely poor, and nearly 6 million fell within the moderately poor category. Only slightly over 8 million (22 percent) escaped poverty at that time. By 1981, extreme poverty had been reduced to 15.5 million, but the number of poor people had grown to 17 million. People living under normal conditions amounted to nearly 39 million (over half the population). It should be acknowledged that national population grew by almost 33 million between 1963 and 1981, making it difficult to satisfy the basic needs of all.

TABLE 8.2
Poverty in Mexico, 1963–1996

	Extreme Poverty		*Moderate Poverty*	
	Millions	*%*	*Millions*	*%*
1963	24.4	63.3	5.7	14.8
1968	24.3	53.8	8.0	17.7
1977	19.1	30.2	18.4	29.1
1981	15.5	21.7	17.1	24.0
1984	18.1	23.8	27.5	36.1
1989	17.9	21.6	31.9	38.6
1996	22.7	24.5	26.2	28.3

Source: Enrique Hernández Laos, *Crecimiento económico y pobreza en México* (Mexico City: UNAM, 1982), 9; Enrique Hernández Laos and Alejandro Toledo Ocampo, *Escenarios económicos de largo plazo y efectos sobre la utilización de los recursos naturales* (unpublished, 1999).

During the period of stabilization and reform (1982–1996) poverty and extreme poverty increased—thus reversing previous trends. The number of people in extreme poverty returned to the levels of the 1960s (over 20 million), while poor people have declined from a peak number of nearly 30 million in 1989 to over 26 million in 1996. In proportion to the total population, the number of people free from poverty conditions shows an increase from around 40 percent during the 1980s to over 47 percent in 1996.

Obviously poverty did not originate with Mexico's neoliberal reforms, but it was certainly aggravated by them. Since poverty was considerably reduced but not eradicated during the years of high economic growth, we can consider two hypotheses. One idea emphasizes the role of such structural factors as (1) the permanence of a large indigenous population that is marginalized from the national economy and suffers extreme forms of nutritional, health, and educational deprivation; (2) the contradictions of production in rural areas where natural resources are not sufficient to sustain family life; and (3) the formation of marginalized urban areas filled with migrants from rural areas in search of better opportunities in urban centers, but who cannot find regular jobs because of inadequate economic growth. A second hypothesis focuses on the choice of growth strategy—in the case of Mexico, a succession of stages of import substitution—which discriminated against specialization based on labor-intensive activities.

Conclusion

I have compared episodes of economic reform in three semi-industrialized countries that have had contrasting results in terms of economic performance and poverty reduction. At different times, the three countries have followed an outward orientation with various economic strategies in terms of the combination of state policy and reliance on markets. They also had variations of authoritarian regimes throughout most of the period under study and have turned toward democratic paths in recent years.

Effects of trade liberalization on poverty in developing economies were analyzed from a number of theoretical perspectives. There are no clear-cut results. But the analysis points to the conclusion that the sectors of society that benefit the most are those that are well endowed to compete in open markets and take advantage of trade and technical progress. The poorest sectors are less likely to reap the benefits of trade reforms and market-oriented strategies. Moreover, the skill-bias embodied in recent technical progress tends to aggravate the negative effects that trade liberalization can have on these sectors. For developing economies in general, the increased vulnerability that results from trade and financial liberalization tends to counteract the potential benefits that liberalization can bring in terms of the inflow of direct investment, technology, learning, and market opportunities. This generalized vulnerability negatively affects the economic opportunities of poor social strata and further aggravates their situation.

Two strategies of market reforms were analyzed. Both Latin American countries applied rapid, radical, and all-encompassing pro-market reforms—Chile since 1973 and Mexico since 1985. By contrast, Korea followed a much more gradual, sequential, and selective reform process. Korea began its takeoff in the 1960s as a poor country, still recovering from the devastation of war, but with a relatively equal distribution of income. Of the three cases analyzed here, it has been the most successful in eradicating poverty and increasing the well-being of its population. The economic reforms and the outward orientation of the Korean economy began by the middle of the 1960s, underwent drastic changes in the 1980s, and have continued with recent reforms in the labor and financial sectors in the wake of the 1997 Asian financial crisis. Well-known vices of the Korean development strategy are found in the high economic concentration and discretionary management of the all-powerful *chaebols* together with a lack of transparency and other imperfections in financial markets.

Chile suffered increasing poverty and unemployment during its decade of adjustment and reform (1973–1984). Thereafter, it has been successful in achieving high economic growth, based on a primary-goods specialization, but has not yet eradicated poverty and continues to have one of the worst income distributions in the world. While macroeconomic indicators and business activity have improved considerably, the social problems of poverty and unequal income distribution have been aggravated. The transition in 1990 from the military regime to democratic coalition governments has helped Chile to consolidate economic reform and to address social issues, which has consequently led to a faster reduction in the incidence of poverty.

Mexico, the largest, most populated, and diversified of the three countries compared, has had the worst economic and social results with its free-market reforms. There the structural determinants of poverty (especially in rural areas) were manifested in the persistence of this evil even during the decades of high economic growth. Economic reform policies have not dealt with the most deep-rooted causes of poverty, namely: a highly unequal distribution of assets, an unsolved long-term agrarian crisis, and the structural diversity of Mexican society. During the period of adjustment and reform, poverty expanded in the informal sectors of urban centers. The eradication of poverty has become ever more elusive with the passage of time. The challenge has now been made even more difficult by prospects of further social disintegration, increasing lack of confidence in the reform program, and threats to government authority and stability. Due to recent emphases on export promotion, foreign participation and concentration of assets continue to characterize the nation's economic performance. Fragile as it is, Mexico's new democratic government faces a daunting array of challenges.

Notes

1. Amartya Sen's definition of well-being refers to a set of variables that vary from such elementary things as being adequately nourished, being in good health, and avoiding escapable morbidity and premature death, to more complex achievements such as being happy, having self-respect, taking part in the life of the community, and so on. According to this integral concept of poverty, the number of people counted as living in poverty would greatly expand. Amartya Sen, *Inequality Reexamined* (Cambridge: Harvard University Press, 1992).

2. Dagmar Raczynski and Pilar Romaguera, "Chile: Poverty, Adjustment, and Social Policies in the 1980s," in *Coping with Austerity: Poverty and Inequality in Latin America,* ed. Nora Lustig (Washington, D.C.: The Brookings Institution, 1995), 275.

3. Debraj Ray, *Development Economics* (Princeton: Princeton University Press, 1998), 267.

4. World Bank, *World Development Report* (New York: Oxford University Press, 2001), 32.

5. Sen, *Inequality,* 113.

6. United Nations Development Programme, *Human Development Report* (New York: Oxford University Press, 1998), 2.

7. Martin Feldstein, *Income Inequality and Poverty,* National Bureau of Economic Research Working Paper 6770 (1998), 5.

8. Klaus Deininger and Lyn Squire, "A New Data Set Measuring Income Inequality," *The World Bank Economic Review* 10, no. 3 (1996): 565–91.

9. Juan Luis Londoño and Miguel Székely, *Persistent Poverty and Excess Inequality: Latin America, 1970–1995,* Inter-American Development Bank, Working Paper #357, 1997.

10. Nancy Birdsall and Richard Sabot, "Inequality, Savings, and Growth in East Asia and Latin America" in *Rethinking Development in East Asia and Latin America* ed. James W. McGuire (Los Angeles: Pacific Council on International Policy, 1997).

11. Dani Rodrik, *Has Globalization Gone Too Far?* (Washington, D.C.: Institute for International Economics, 1997).

12. Anwar Shaikh, "Foreign Trade and the Law of Value," *Science and Society* 43, no. 3 (1979): 281–302.

13. L. Alan Winters, "Trade Policy and Poverty: What Àre the Links?" (background paper World Bank study on Trade Technology and Poverty, February 2000).

14. Nora Lustig, "Equity and Development" in *Development from Within: Toward a Neostructuralist Approach for Latin America,* ed. Osvaldo Sunkel (Boulder, Colo.: Lynne Rienner, 1993).

15. Roland Benabou, *Inequality and Growth*, National Bureau of Economic Research Working Paper 5658 (1997), 2–3.

16. R. M. Auty, "The Macro Impacts of Korea's Heavy Industry Drive Reevaluated," *Journal of Development Studies* 29, no. 1 (1992): 24–48.

17. Edward Mason, et al., *The Economic and Social Modernization of the Republic of Korea* (Cambridge: Harvard University Press, 1980), 127–132.

18. Mason, *The Economic and Social Modernization*, 126.

19. David Bloom, David Canning, and Pia Malaney, *Demographic Change and Economic Growth in Asia*, Center for International Development at Harvard University, Working Paper No. 15 (1999).

20. Mason, *Economic and Social Modernization*, 237–243.

21. J. P. Powelson and R. Stock, *The Peasant Betrayed: Agriculture and Land Reform in the Third World* (Boston: Oelgeschlager, Gunn, and Hain, 1987).

22. Alice A. Amsden, *Asia's Next Giant: South Korea and Late Industrialization* (New York: Oxford University Press, 1989); and C. Kim, "Republic of Korea," in Asian Development Bank, *Foreign Trade Barriers and Export Growth* (Manila: Asian Development Bank, 1988), 128–181.

23. Jong-Il You and Ju-Ho Lee, *Economic and Social Consequences of Globalization: The Case of South Korea*, Center for Economic Policy Analysis, Working Paper No. 17 (2000), 19.

24. International Monetary Fund, *International Financial Statistics*, various issues.

25. Amsden, *Asia's Next Giant*, 176.

26. The Economist Intelligence Unit, *Chile: Country Report* (London: The Economist, 1987/1988).

27. Raczynski and Romaguera, *Chile*, 284.

28. Vittorio Corbo, Jaime de Melo, and James Tybout, "What Went Wrong with the Recent Reforms in the Southern Cone?" *Economic Development and Cultural Change* 34, no. 3 (1986): 607–640, esp. 609.

29. The domestic capital market was reformed in early 1975 while foreign capital flows were strictly controlled until mid-1979. Afterward, restrictions on medium- and long-term capital were lifted but not so for short-term capital. Sebastian Edwards, "Monetarism in Chile, 1973–1983: Some Economic Puzzles?" *Economic Development and Cultural Change* 34 (1986): 535–59, esp. 538.

30. Edwards, *Monetarism*, 539.

31. Corbo, "What Went Wrong?," 637.

32. Corbo, "What Went Wrong?," 613.

33. Alejandro Foxley, "La transición económica en Chile: El gobierno de Aylwin," in *Chile-México: Dos Transiciones Frente a Frente*, eds. Carlos Elizondo and Luis Maira (Mexico City: Grijalvo, 2000), 232.

34. Patricio Meller, "Pobreza y distribución del ingreso en Chile (Década del 90)," in *El modelo chileno: Democracia y desarrollo en los noventa*, eds. Paul W. Drake and Iván Jaksic (Santiago de Chile: LOM Ediciones, 1999), 41–64.

35. Juan Carlos Feres, *La pobreza en Chile en el año 2000*, Serie de Estudios Estadísticos y Prospectivos de la CEPAL, No. 14 (2001).

36. OECD, *Estudios Económicos de la OCDE: México* (Paris: Organización para la Cooperación y Desarrollo Económico, 1997), 89.

37. Clara Judisman, *Tendencias de la estructura económica y el sector informal en México (1988–1993)* (Mexico City: Secretaría del Trabajo y Previsión Social, 1995).

38. Secretaría de Educación Pública, *Estadística del Sistema Educativo Nacional*, various issues.

39. Instituto Nacional de Estadística, Geografía e Informática, *Sistema de cuentas nacionales*, various years; and Banco de México, *Indicadores económicos y financieros*, various years.

40. Peter H. Smith, "Strategic Options for Latin America," in *Latin America in the New International System*, eds. Joseph S. Tulchin and Ralph Espach (Boulder, Colo.: Lynne Rienner, 2001), 35–72.

41. On the distributional effects of the reforms, see Miguel Székely, *The Economics of Poverty, Inequality, and Wealth Accumulation in Mexico* (London: Macmillan, 1998).

42. Angus Maddison, *The Political Economy of Poverty, Equity, and Growth* (New York and Washington: Oxford University Press, 1993), 174.

43. Powelson and Stock, *Peasant Betrayed*, 37.

PART III

CONFRONTING ECONOMIC CRISES

KEY COUNTRIES IN BOTH ASIA AND LATIN AMERICA were engulfed by sudden and devastating financial crises in the 1990s. What were the reasons for these crises? Can they be explained by the same factors in the two regions—or did they result from differing causes?

Peter H. Smith begins with an account of the Mexican peso crisis of 1994–1995 and stresses the role of political factors in shaping economic policy. He describes the background and incipient disintegration of Mexico's authoritarian political system, which confronted serious challenges in the early 1990s—assassinations of political figures, impunity of drug traffickers, and a popular uprising in the southernmost state of Chiapas. The resulting need to offer reassurance to foreign investors was exacerbated, and distorted, by the exigencies of presidential succession. As a result, the government resisted pressure to devalue the peso and instead drained the country's hard-currency reserves and issued dollar-denominated short-term debt. As portfolio investment left Mexico, the strategy became unsustainable and the peso promptly collapsed. Economic vulnerabilities and political crises conspired to produce a massive financial crises and recession, which required a major bailout package from the United States. Mexico's peso crisis had important political consequences as well as causes.

Nualnoi Treerat provides an in-depth description of the outbreak and consequences of the "Asian crisis" in the country where it all started, Thailand. In contrast to Mexico, the crisis in Thailand was unexpected: key economic indicators appeared to be sound, and total factor productivity had grown impressively as a result of FDI inflows and technology transfer. Yet these developments masked serious problems in the financial and banking sector, while political uncertainty hampered the effectiveness of public authorities. Such factors impeded effective management of the economic downturn of 1996–1997. Investors became particularly alarmed when export growth fell to zero, and subjected the *baht* to a speculative attack. The social costs of the resulting crisis were vivid and profound. The subsequent stabilization and structural reform program pursued with the International Monetary Fund (IMF) helped jumpstart the economy. Accompanying the economic reforms was further political opening and decentralization aimed at empowering Thai citizens, and, as such, breaking the political logjams between the rural and urban areas and between poor and wealthy voters.

Jaebong Ro follows up with an evaluation of governmental recovery policies in one of the countries hardest hit by the Asian contagion, South Korea. He argues that the economic turnaround in motion since late 1998 has been significant but incomplete. Financial and foreign exchange markets have stabilized, but unemployment has not been cut to the pre-crisis levels and imports remain depressed, which bodes ill for an economy reliant on imported raw materials and capital goods. However, forceful policy reforms have sought to mitigate distortions engendered by inappropriate practices during the era of high growth. Ultimately, the effectiveness of most reforms can be properly gauged only in the long run. Ro suggests that the Korean government should pursue a comprehensive reform package—one that combines change in the corporate and financial sectors with labor market flexibility.

Shoji Nishijima offers an analytical comparison of the origins of and responses to currency crises in the five countries most directly affected by the crises of the 1990s—Mexico, Brazil, Thailand, Korea, and Indonesia. Common threads are difficult to find. The five economies were marked by divergent current account deficits, levels of foreign reserves, types of investors (domestic or foreign) responsible for the capital flight, types of economic booms preceding the crises (consumption or investment) fiscal positions, and the timing of the IMF's rescue packages. Nonetheless, Nishijima concludes that a key facet in each crisis case was careless and precipitous economic liberalization, which, despite its manifold fruits, has produced deepening inequality and financial instability. Another finding stresses the importance of a healthy banking sector. The crises have shown that more thorough institutional reforms are required for pursuing social equality, higher employment rates, and accountability by both public officials and private sector leaders.

Adding a Latin American perspective, Gilson Schwartz concludes with a trenchant commentary on post-crisis policies in both Asia and Latin America. Recovery has to a great extent been attributable to favorable external conditions; however, external risks are still present, as manifested by the renewed pressures on Asian and Latin American currencies and the precariousness of these region's economies to U.S. economic trends. No simple solutions exist for Latin America, especially in view of Mexico's heavy dependence on the U.S. market and Argentina's massive economic crisis. In Asia, the future is perhaps more certain should domestic institutions be effectively reformed and intraregional trade receive a stimulus.

The overall implication of this section is somewhat discomfiting. In both regions, public authorities have been willing to settle for halfway measures instead of seeking genuine structural reform. Once superficial indicators of recovery appeared, the sense of urgency was lost—and with it the opportunity to bring about long-term improvements in economic prospects. In-depth structural reforms have not been undertaken and, in the long run, this may diminish the prospects for sustainable, long-term growth and development.

9

The Mexican Peso Crisis

Peter H. Smith

IT SEEMED LIKE SUCH A PROMISING AFFAIR. Laden with pageantry, the inauguration of Ernesto Zedillo Ponce de León as president of Mexico on December 1, 1994, attracted throngs of dignitaries from home and abroad. Outgoing President Carlos Salinas de Gortari received a thunderous ovation in honor of his remarkable *sexenio*, and in transferring the sash he conferred upon his hand-picked successor not only a symbol of the nation's highest office but also a public gesture of political endorsement. A sympathetic audience listened to the earnest but untested new president offer pledges of honesty, reform, and expanded political opening. Observers noted the conspicuous absence from the incoming cabinet of Pedro Aspe Armella, the much-admired secretary of the treasury under Salinas, but they found consolation in the presence of several holdovers. At luncheon the following day, a glittering assemblage of businesspeople took additional heart from Zedillo's repeated insistence that the economic watchword of his new administration would be "stability, stability, stability."

The chorus of praise then moved to Miami, where U.S. President Bill Clinton hosted on December 9–11 a resplendent gathering of hemispheric heads of state (except Fidel Castro) known as the "Summit of the Americas." Characteristically effusive about prospects for democracy and prosperity throughout Latin America, Clinton repeatedly extolled NAFTA as an exemplary case of economic integration and praised Mexico for its performance as a strong and dependable partner. There could be no doubt about it: Mexico was on a roll.

Suddenly the wheels came off. On December 19, as foreign reserves were rapidly dwindling, the Zedillo administration unexpectedly widened the band for trading pesos with dollars from 3.47 to 4.00—in effect, permitting a 15 percent devaluation of the peso—violating Zedillo's heartfelt December 2 pledge. This prompted a speculative run against the peso; within two days the government was obliged to abandon its position, letting the peso float freely against the dollar. Unable to persuade foreign investors of Mexico's trustworthiness, the newly installed secretary of the treasury—Jaime Serra Puche, the secretary of commerce under Salinas who had played a key role in the NAFTA negotiations—submitted his resignation after merely three weeks on the job. By late January the Clinton administration managed to put together a multilateral package of nearly $50 billion, including $20 billion from the U.S. government, but the peso continued to slide. One of the most judicious and knowledgeable U.S. experts on Mexico, Sidney Weintraub, arrived at a gloomy conclusion: "Ernesto Zedillo is off to a horrible start as president of Mexico."[1]

What could have gone wrong? Calamity struck unexpectedly in a country that in recent years had undertaken major economic reform, entered the North American Free Trade Agreement (NAFTA) with Canada and the United States, acceded to the prestigious forum for Asia-Pacific Economic Cooperation (APEC), and gained full membership in the Organization for Economic Cooperation and Development (OECD). Moreover, the nation could boast exceptionally talented, energetic, and intelligent leadership, as symbolized by the transmission of presidential power from one accomplished student of economic policy (Ph.D., Harvard University) to another (Ph.D., Yale University.) As Moisés Naím would later ask of the December debacle, "How can such smart guys make such dumb mistakes?"[2]

The purpose of this chapter is to describe the Mexican peso crisis of 1994–1995 and, in particular, to examine its political dimensions. First, I establish the long-term political context for the peso crisis. Second, I trace specific events and decisions leading up to the peso debacle, with special emphasis on the period from mid-1993 to end-1994. Instead of arguing that key actors in Mexico were making stupid decisions for irrational reasons, as a rigid application of economic criteria might suggest, I maintain that they were responding in rational and self-interested ways to existing political incentives and constraints (as will be shown, however, they could also make mistakes within this context). In other words, political logic prevailed over economic logic throughout this period.

Third, I analyze the consequences of the peso crisis for the Mexican political system and its subsequent transition toward democracy. Finally, I conclude with modest observations about the relationship between political change and economic reform and, in particular, on ways that the international community might absorb the lessons of the Mexican experience. It is telling and distressing, for example, that policy makers in Asia paid such scant attention to Mexico's misfortune. And as this chapter indicates, political factors are more than just unwelcome "nuisances" that stand in the way of coherent policy-making. Ultimately, political change must become part and parcel of successful economic reform.

Political Context for Crisis

The framework for the 1994–1995 crisis derives not from short-term events but from the long-term evolution of the Mexican political system. From the late 1920s to the 1980s, an authoritarian regime marked by a close alliance between technocrats, politicians, and leaders of key groups—especially labor and the peasantry—successfully imposed social and political stability. These coalitions were frequently sealed in explicit compacts, or *pactos*, that achieved and implemented consensus on economic policy. Key decisions were made at the top, behind closed doors, as an official party (the *Partido Revolucionario Institucional*, or PRI) routinely and regularly triumphed in not-very-contested elections. Opposition voices were muted, the media conspired openly with the ruling establishment, rebellions and protests were sparse. From the 1940s onward, even the armed forces accepted a civilian monopoly on the presidential office. Turbulent Mexico, land of the first major social revolution in the twentieth century, thus succumbed to forces of political domination. With traces of envy and admiration, the Peruvian novelist-politician Mario Vargas Llosa once christened Mexico's system as "the perfect dictatorship."

A defining feature of the regime derived from its tradition of presidential succession. In keeping with a key tenet of the Revolution, reelection to high office was strictly prohibited. Within the course of each *sexenio* (six-year term), however, the ruling president exerted supreme control over the nation's political life. Effective power flowed directly from the executive office and, as part of this arrangement, the outgoing president exercised a time-honored right to select his own successor. Indeed, this process of *dedazo*, or *destape*, was the culminating expression of presidential power. The inevitable triumph of this "chosen one" in the subsequent election constituted not a competitive victory but a ritual of confirmation, an acceptance by a pliant people of decisions from above.

Hyper-presidentialism permeated the Mexican system with an exaggerated form of what has come to be known as "temporal rigidity," or inflexibility in the transmission of political power. The outgoing president exercised supreme authority right up to the final moment of the *sexenio*, at which point the successor instantly assumed full command. Traditionally, too, relatively high rates of turnover in top-level positions heightened both the level and the perception of change.[3] The presidential inauguration thus signified an instantaneous, complete, and profound interruption and transfer of power. In Mexico, the process of executive transition was as brittle in substance as it was smooth in appearance.

Institutional Transformation

Starting as far back as the 1970s, the dominant-party system began to undergo fundamental rearrangements in its power structure. First, the historic coalition started to weaken: The peasantry no longer represented a significant resource; organized labor lost authority; and while small and medium business remained a fragile sector, large-scale business was accumulating power and independence from the government. Second, the party system shifted: Though still strong, the PRI came to stand at the center of a three-party system, with the *Partido Revolucionario Democrático* (PRD) on the left and the *Partido de Acción Nacional* (PAN) on the right, both of which were attracting considerable support from the urban middle class. At the same time, traditional fiefdoms reemerged: Old-time politicians (*dinosaurios*) found refuge in state governorships, for instance, and in niches within the party apparatus of the PRI.

During the 1980s and '90s, international drug cartels began to pose a serious challenge to legal authority. Soon after taking office, President Zedillo received an official report warning that "the power of the drug-trafficking organizations could lead to situations of ungovernability." The most dangerous of these cartels were involved not so much in marijuana or heroin, traditional products of Mexico, but in the transshipment of cocaine from Colombia. With an estimated $7 billion in annual profits, these groups could spend as much as $500 million per year on bribery—more than twice the total budget of the attorney general's office. By the mid 1990s Mexico had a half-dozen drug organizations of truly international scope (in Tijuana, Sinaloa, Ciudad Juárez, Guadalajara, and in the state of Tamaulipas, where traffickers operated a flourishing cocaine pipeline along the Gulf of Mexico). Drug cartels were implicated in a wave of violence that swept through Mexico, including the assassination of a Roman Catholic cardinal in 1993. Former prosecutor Eduardo Valle Espinosa proclaimed that the country had fallen under the heel of drug traffickers and, like Colombia, had become a "narco-democracy."[4] Whether or not this was true, there could be little doubt that violence and disorder were climbing to unprecedented levels.

In summary, Mexico was undergoing a significant erosion of institutional authority. There was less power at the center, even in the presidency, than there used to be. To be sure, Salinas was able to exert authority in an exceptional way, partly through personal guile and partly as a result of his lifelong immersion in the system, but Zedillo had neither the resources nor the opportunity to demonstrate such strength. Power was no longer as concentrated or extensive as it had been for many years: Forever resistant to facile nomenclature, Mexico's political regime in the mid-1990s might be thought of as "neo-authoritarian."[5]

One corollary of institutional deterioration was the increasing prominence of individual actors. It was Carlos Salinas, not the PRI, who represented and personified the regime as a whole. And it was Pedro Aspe, not the government or the economic team, who came to be seen as the guarantor of macroeconomic stability. Throughout 1994, foreign and local investors became increasingly preoccupied, and sometimes obsessed, by speculation over whether or not Aspe would remain as secretary of the treasury in the post-Salinas administration. Such fixation upon one individual should have been a warning in itself.

The Familial Crisis

Adding to this dissipation of institutional power was what might be called a "familial" crisis—the emergence of profound schisms within Mexico's political elite, once regarded as the "revolutionary family." For decades, the coherence (and internal discipline) of this ruling elite had comprised a central foundation for the persistence of political stability.[6] While there had been stresses and strains from the 1940s through the 1980s, and occasional cracks in the edifice of power (including the split-off of the *corriente democrática* against the PRI in 1986), there had been nothing that would compare to the fissures of the 1990s. Overt symptoms of these new tensions would not appear until 1994, but they pointed clearly to subterranean pressures and trends that were unfolding throughout the Salinas *sexenio.*

A central and spectacular scene in this drama revolved around two pairs of brothers: Carlos Salinas de Gortari and his older brother, Raúl; and José Francisco Ruiz Massieu and his younger brother, Mario. Both families had long been pillars of the Mexican establishment. José Francisco had also married (and divorced) a sister of the Salinas brothers, and was serving as secretary general of the PRI in late 1994. As he left a political gathering, José Francisco Ruiz Massieu was assassinated in downtown Mexico City on September 28, 1994.[7] His brother Mario, the assistant attorney general, was placed in charge of the investigation. Within a month Mario issued a statement suggesting that drug traffickers might have ordered the murder, and that high-level politicians were in league with *narcotraficantes.* In late November, about a week before

Salinas was to step down from the presidency, Mario publicly resigned from both his position and the PRI, accusing party leaders (but not Salinas) of conspiring to cover up the assassination.

On February 28, 1995, governmental authorities (presumably with Zedillo's permission) arrested Raúl Salinas de Gortari in connection with the Ruiz Massieu assassination. Rumors immediately began to whisper that Carlos Salinas must have been involved in the plot, on the ground that Raúl would never have undertaken such a brazen scheme without his brother's approval. On March 1 the deputy attorney general accused Mario Ruiz Massieu of obstructing justice during the investigation of his brother's assassination. The next day, Carlos Salinas de Gortari began a hunger strike in order to clear his reputation; Mario Ruiz Massieu left Mexico for the United States, where he was soon arrested (for carrying large amounts of undisclosed cash) while boarding a plane for Madrid. Carlos Salinas ended his hunger strike on March 4, after the Zedillo government released a mollifying statement, but soon left the country in disgrace.

The Salinas–Ruiz Massieu intrigues evoked images of sixteenth-century Italy under the Borgias, rather than a modernizing country of the late twentieth century, but they also contained profound political significance. First, they revealed a split within the ruling elite that had become more public and irreversible than at any time since the mid-1930s. Second, they indicated a breakdown in rules of civility that had long prevailed within the national elite. Even at the highest levels of the political establishment, violence and murder were coming to replace the once-prized arts of bargaining, negotiation, and cooptation.

Moreover, these developments left Ernesto Zedillo with an ambiguous claim to political legitimacy. It is to be remembered that Zedillo, the substitute candidate who was *destapado* by Salinas after the assassination of PRI nominee Luis Donaldo Colosio in March 1994, had a minuscule political base of his own. He ran for president on a platform stressing continuity with Salinas and his policies. To a very considerable extent, people who voted for him in August 1994 were voting for Salinas. The public rupture with Salinas in early 1995 thus left Zedillo to his own devices. While many angry Mexicans applauded Zedillo's actions, including his approval for the arrest of Raúl Salinas, the Salinas issue was far from resolved. In the meantime, the new president was struggling to develop his own political base.

Another stunning indication of intra-elite discord emerged in December 1995, when Carlos Salinas dispatched a late-night fax from Canada to Mexico City newspapers in which he denounced "the political offensive against me" by Luis Echeverría (president of Mexico in 1970–1976). In a system where former presidents were accustomed to maintaining complete solidarity (and a good deal of silence), this was an extraordinary breach of political etiquette.

To be sure, Echeverría had criticized Salinas' management of the economy policy in prior months, but he stoutly denied participation in any kind of coordinated campaign.[8] Even so, the *salinista* broadside offered stunning confirmation of the depth and rancor of cleavages within the national ruling elite.

In effect, Mexico was witnessing political disintegration at two distinct levels—among its uppermost institutions and within the political class. These developments intersected with each other and multiplied their mutual effects. Together, they set the stage for economic crisis.

Presidential Succession and the Peso Crisis

The peso crisis of December 1994 resulted from a series of decisions and events that unfolded over the course of more than a year. The central question is: What political factors prevented Mexican authorities from implementing orthodox economic policy? What prevented them from responding effectively to market signals and repeated warnings?

Vulnerabilities in the Mexican economic strategy were self-evident, especially in retrospect. The country was running a massive current-account deficit, as imports steadily exceeded exports; during the early 1990s, the deficit was being covered by inflows of foreign capital. The problem was that most of this capital came in the form of short-term portfolio investment, rather than longer-term foreign direct investment (FDI), with the result that it could be withdrawn from the country at the touch of an electronic button. As shown in table 9.1, portfolio investment vastly exceeded FDI from 1991 through 1993, by which time the ratio had climbed to more than 6:1. And just as quickly, the inflow of portfolio capital dropped to $8.2 billion in 1994. Here was one key to the crisis.

Confronted by this situation, Mexico's economic managers pinned their hopes on two predictions. First, that improvements in productivity would increase export competitiveness and close the trade gap. Second, that the implementation of NAFTA would attract capital, especially FDI, and thus provide

TABLE 9.1
Capital Flows into Mexico, 1991–94

	US$ Billions (Year-End)			
	1991	*1992*	*1993*	*1994*
Portfolio	12.1	18.0	28.4	8.2
Direct	4.7	4.4	4.9	8.0

Source: Adapted from data in *Lessons of the Mexican Peso Crisis: Report from an Independent Task Force* (New York: Council on Foreign Relations, 1995), 9.

some breathing room. These were, however, long-term aspirations. In the meantime, short-term pressures were evident and mounting.

The reaction of the Salinas team was to finance the current-account deficit by draining the country's international reserves, which dropped from around $30 billion in February 1994 to $5 billion by late December. The government thus squandered the nation's resources in an ultimately unsuccessful effort to sustain the value of the currency.

Why Not Devalue?

One of the most nagging questions is why the Mexican government did not devalue the peso sometime during the second or third quarter of 1994. This was a subject of public debate at the time, and most experts agreed that this would be an appropriate course. Why did Salinas resist?

The key political fact was that, throughout 1994, Carlos Salinas de Gortari was in the final year of his *sexenio*. To enshrine his place in history, and to promote his candidacy for the directorship of the World Trade Organization, he no doubt was eager to finish his term in a blaze of glory. This was not as simple as it might seem: As Jorge Castañeda once wrote, "Few things in the world are as persistent and disheartening as the impossibility for presidential terms to end well in Mexico."[9] With the partial exception of Miguel de la Madrid (1982–1988), every president over the previous quarter-century had left office in disrepute and/or disgrace. All had been relegated to ignominious retirement or to minor positions in the bureaucracy. Still young and ambitious, Salinas was determined to challenge this trend.

For symbolic, political, and economic reasons, devaluation of the peso had pealed a death knell for outgoing presidents. As José López Portillo (1976–1982) observed from his own bitter experience, "The president who devalues is himself devalued." As long as he could forestall it, Salinas was not going to take that step. This meant that he would have to court additional foreign investment, whatever the cost; and this, in turn, required maintenance of a stable currency. Ironically enough, his efforts brought about precisely the result that he was seeking to avoid. Like his predecessors, Salinas would discover the fateful rhythm of presidential politics to be unsparing and merciless.

It was not only a question of personal ambition. As of late 1993, Mexico was anxiously awaiting U.S. ratification of the North American Free Trade Agreement (NAFTA). As Congress prepared to cast its vote, pro-NAFTA forces persistently argued that the treaty would stimulate American exports and create new jobs. This scenario presumed a strong peso. For precisely this reason opponents of NAFTA, like Representative John LaFalce of New York, held hearings on the parity of the peso and accused the Mexican government of withholding its intention to devalue. Since Salinas had bound his political destiny so closely to NAFTA, he had no choice in the matter. As a result there could be no possibility of devaluation before, during, or just after ratification.

Implementation of NAFTA commenced on January 1, 1994, the same day that rebellion unexpectedly erupted in the southernmost state of Chiapas. Under the colorful leadership of *Subcomandante* Marcos, the *Ejército Zapatista de Liberación Nacional* (EZLN) rose up to challenge institutional authority, demand political reform, denounce NAFTA—and, for a time, capture popular imagination throughout Mexico. Although the Chiapas rebellion never posed a serious threat to political or economic stability, the Salinas government needed to allay anxieties of foreign investors. The administration thus sought to minimize the importance of the EZLN, cast doubt upon its authenticity, mobilize the military, and sustain peso-dollar parity. Apparently mollified, investors continued to pour capital into the country during January–February 1994. Ultimately, the Zapatista uprising contributed to the debilitation of Mexico's political system not by its military might or by the possibility that it might succeed. Rather, it was the prolongation of the conflict that accentuated a sense of uncertainty and erosion of power. The much-vaunted regime, and the president, began to look helpless and hapless in the face of what would otherwise have been a minor regional rebellion.

Why the *Tesobonos*?

In April 1994 the Salinas administration began issuing a series of dollar-indexed bonds known as *tesobonos*. The goal was to attract foreign capital, of course, and in this sense the idea paid off: Before the end of the year, the Mexican government issued approximately $30 billion worth of *tesobonos*. Because of its reliance on exchange rate stability, this strategy incurred monumental risk—and it would help precipitate disaster in December.

The immediate political rationale for the *tesobonos* derived from the assassination of *priísta* presidential candidate Luis Donaldo Colosio on March 23, 1994, after a political rally in the northern-border city of Tijuana. This was an utterly shocking event. It unleashed political uncertainty in Mexico, raised doubts about stability, and, within days, led Salinas to designate Ernesto Zedillo as the substitute PRI candidate for the presidency.

The Colosio murder frightened investors as well. Within hours, according to one report, a youthful fund manager from Fidelity Investments was on the telephone, seeking assurances from central bank officials that the peso would hold within its trading band. He was certainly not the only one. Within a couple of weeks, in fact, a consortium known as the Weston Forum approached the Salinas government with a series of "suggestions": that Mexico curb the speed of the peso's daily devaluation, insure foreign investors against currency-exchange losses on peso-denominated securities, issue long-term *tesobonos*, and, perhaps most important, back all these measures with central-bank peso purchases to bolster the currency.[10] Confronted by this ultimatum, the Salinas government responded with a multipart strategy: hiking interest rates, lifting the exchange rate to the top of the peso-dollar band (without changing the band itself), buying up pesos on the international market, and offering $10 billion worth of *tesobonos*. The effort was not entirely successful, as investors withdrew $10 billion from Mexico within six weeks of the Colosio assassination, but it may well have prevented even more capital flight.

It is difficult to measure the impact of the Weston Forum threats. "We have to listen to these guys," acknowledged Guillermo Ortiz Martínez, then undersecretary of the treasury. "But one thing is to listen and the other is to follow their policy recommendations. It is pretty obvious that we would be in deep trouble if we were to be following the advice of investors" about how to run the economy. But as the *Wall Street Journal* observed in June 1994,

> So far, the fund managers have reason to be pleased with Mexico's response. Soon after the Weston Forum meeting, Mexican officials launched a peso rescue operation. They issued longer-term *tesobonos* as the investor group asked, and cut back on the auctions of Mexican treasury bills, or *cetes*, to reduce short-term rates. Then, senior Mexican finance officials flew to Washington to announce a trilateral currency support program among the U.S., Canada, and Mexico. After these meetings, Mr. Aspe, the finance minister, visited with Fidelity's fund managers.[11]

Whether or not as a result of their efforts, foreign investors appeared to be getting their way.

Additional international influence came from a rise in U.S. interest rates, also beginning in April 1994. This had two consequences for Mexico: First, and most important, it attracted capital away from Mexico (and other emerging markets); second, it exerted upward pressure on interest rates in Mexico. When U.S. Federal Reserve Chairman Alan Greenspan began lifting interest rates in early 1994, Mexico would feel direct effects. As Moisés Naím later observed: "The hike in U.S. interest rates to curb inflationary pressures in the United States caused the Mexican markets to drop much more than did the news of a revolt in Chiapas."[12]

Why Expand the Money Supply?

Instead of raising interest rates in Mexico, the Salinas administration began easing restrictions on credit. Interest rates on 28-day *cetes* dropped from a peak of 18 percent in April to about 13.5 percent in November, even as the United States and other countries were raising interest rates. Although internal and external imbalances emerged, the government continued to run down reserves rather than raise interest rates. Autonomous in name but not in fact, the central bank expanded credit to the financial system by 400 percent from mid-1993 to mid-1994. During 1994, monetary expansion of more than 20 percent and lax credit policies added to the economic instability created by the decline in foreign investment.

The conventional explanation for this policy tends to focus on the electoral cycle (which is also viewed, by many, as the reason for the refusal to devalue). The basic idea is that the government was seeking to stimulate economic growth in order to earn the support of voters and thus secure a victory at the polls for the PRI and for Zedillo. This was especially necessary in 1994, it is often argued, since Zedillo was a second-choice candidate and an uncharismatic campaigner. By expanding the money supply, in other words, the Salinas administration was attempting to buy the election.

This interpretation contains a grain of truth, but tends toward exaggeration. It assumes that elections are competitive, that policy makers are shortsighted, and that voters are unable to ascertain chicanery (in effect, the model suggests that a handful of rogues are conspiring to deceive a populace of dupes). Elections did not affect political decisions the same way in Mexico as in many other countries. The PRI had won every national election since 1929. An opposition triumph in a presidential election remained unthinkable (and though this might have occurred in 1988, according to some accounts, the outcome was controlled by official fraud). Similarly, there was little genuine prospect that the opposition could win in 1994. It was not until early May that *panista* candidate Diego Fernández de Cevallos routed both Zedillo and *perredista* Cuauhtémoc Cárdenas in a television debate and posed, for the first time in living memory, the possibility of an opposition victory; and at precisely that point, Fernández suddenly and mysteriously stopped campaigning. When the ballots were counted in August, Zedillo emerged with a clear and decisive triumph.

In this setting, I would argue, the goal of economic policy toward the end of the *sexenio* was not to obtain an electoral victory for the incoming president, but to secure the legacy and popularity of the outgoing president. (And in this particular instance, as noted earlier, Salinas wanted to promote his candidacy for the WTO directorship.) An additional motivation was to maintain patronage and discipline within the PRI, among recalcitrant leaders as well as among the rank and file, and thus perpetuate the dominance of the nation's political machine. In all such respects, government decisions had more to do with the dynamics of presidential succession in an authoritarian system than with competitive prospects in the electoral arena.

Why the December Debacle?

In retrospect, it may appear that the period between the August elections and the December inauguration should have offered another opportunity for peso devaluation and macroeconomic readjustment. After all, there was historical precedent: Both Echeverría and López Portillo had devalued the peso shortly before leaving office. According to many sources, Zedillo requested that Salinas do the same—but Salinas firmly refused. Here is precisely the point: Salinas was determined to avoid the fate of his predecessors, who had suffered vilification over the years. To preserve his political stature, to enhance his international image, and to strengthen his campaign for the WTO, Salinas was insistent on leaving office with an untarnished record.[13]

Characteristics of the Mexican political system shed additional light on the unfolding of the crisis in December 1994, what ex-President Salinas would later refer to caustically as "the December mistake." As explained above, the process of presidential succession creates an extraordinary degree of uncertainty. Anxiety about the transmission of power and the incoming administration necessarily generate apprehension among investors, especially those who are knowledgeable about Mexico. (It is thus not coincidental that Mexican investors, not foreigners, were the first to begin removing funds from the country early in December). Temporal rigidity in politics tends to create problems for economics.

Moreover, the pattern of presidential succession made it difficult (if not impossible) for the Salinas team to devalue the peso during the month of November. As Pedro Aspe has maintained, it would have been necessary to embed a devaluation within an overall economic package—which could be assembled only by the incoming Zedillo team. So at a fateful meeting on November 20, 1994, there were six people present: Salinas, Aspe, the head of the central bank, two other cabinet ministers, and a top Zedillo representative. This group considered and rejected the possibility of devaluation.[14] Later in the day, spokesmen for the prevailing *pacto* expressed support for this decision.

Upon taking office, Zedillo continued efforts to sustain the peso, spending all but $3 billion of foreign reserves in the process. And when the government finally decided to devalue, the Zedillo team committed a number of blunders—attempting a mini-devaluation instead of overshooting expectations, inadequately informing the international community, and failing to support the devaluation with an overall economic package. Why did this young government make so many errors?

In part, it may have been a matter of inexperience. Jaime Serra Puche had been an outstanding secretary of commerce, but he had relatively little preparation for the Treasury. Bad luck (such as the rise in U.S. interest rates) may have played a role. Moreover, there was the built-in rigidity of the system, which meant that the Zedillo administration would start anew on December 1, thus raising the specter of potential change in policy and personnel.

Here occurred a failure of political analysis. Given the tradition of cabinet-level turnover, it was utterly in keeping with past political practice for Zedillo not to reappoint Pedro Aspe as secretary of the treasury (although there was precedent for doing so, as Antonio Ortiz Mena served two successive terms at this post from 1958 to 1970). The problem, apparently, was that Zedillo and his associates did not understand the extent to which the investment community identified macroeconomic stability not with the system but with Aspe himself. To emphasize the point, Mexico's *Bolsa* promptly reacted to the unveiling of Zedillo's cabinet, *sans* Aspe, by dropping fifty points. In other words, the Zedillo team failed to comprehend the degree to which the deterioration of longstanding institutions was leading to the personalization of politics and policy.[15] Although they were operating according to rules of Mexico's internal political logic, they made a serious miscalculation.

Political Consequences of Economic Crisis

Inevitably enough, the peso crisis of December 1994 had a painful aftermath. There were short-term and longer-term effects. Some of its eventual ramifications might still take shape in the future.

Mexico's *Annus Horribilis*

Nineteen-ninety-five proved to be a nightmare. The economic situation was desperate. Led by the Clinton administration and the International Monetary Fund, the international community put together a massive rescue package. For its part, Zedillo's economic team imposed a series of draconian measures. Seeking to bring the current-account deficit down to the equivalent of 1 percent of GDP, they increased the value-added-tax from 10 percent to 15 percent and slashed government expenditures (especially in the social arena). They undertook a number of initiatives to sustain the nation's tottering banking system—to relieve liquidity shortages, to strengthen banks' capital and reserves, and to give breathing space to hard-pressed debtors.[16] (Upholding the banks would eventually become a much more expensive proposition than anyone envisaged at the time).[17] Taken together, these severe adjustment measures led to steep rises in interest rates (and in inflation), to the liquidation of hundreds of small and medium-sized businesses, to sharp declines in purchasing power, to the loss of perhaps one million jobs, and to a contraction in economic output for the year that was estimated to be minus 7 percent (−10.4 percent for the first six months). The peso crisis of late 1994 precipitated a profound economic crisis that lasted throughout 1995.

In the political realm, public reaction to the crisis exacerbated the nation's ongoing crisis of institutional authority. For the first time in decades, rumors began circulating that an elected PRI president might not be able to finish his term. One public opinion poll in early 1995 showed that 48 percent of the respondents believed a military coup was possible.[18] Voters in the state of Jalisco, long a bastion of the PRI, elected an opposition-party PAN candidate as governor. Even where the PRI claimed outright victories, as in Tabasco and Yucatán, the results were sharply contested.

The fallout was far-reaching. One immediate consequence of the peso/economic crisis was, of course, the utter ruination of Salinas and his reputation. In late 1993, as president, Carlos Salinas had enjoyed approval ratings of higher than 60 percent, and he had been widely revered as a national leader of historic proportions.[19] By early 1995, in the early months of the crisis, he was thoroughly reviled: A March survey showed that 83 percent of the Mexican people held "no confidence" in Salinas (compared with a 54 percent confidence rating for the still-struggling Zedillo). At this same time, nearly two-thirds of the populace (64 percent) expressed the conviction that Carlos Salinas was somehow "implicated" in the assassination of José Francisco Ruiz Massieu.[20] Pundits routinely observed that Salinas had become so unpopular, and so widely detested, that it would be unsafe for him to appear in the streets of Mexico City. Forced to withdraw his candidacy for the directorship of the WTO, Salinas found his political fortune in tatters.

Second, the economic costs of the crisis produced popular backlash against NAFTA and, by implication, against the neoliberal model of economic reform. Early in 1995, 36 percent of respondents in a national survey declared the effects of NAFTA to be "bad" or "very bad," especially in view of its apparent impact on unemployment, while 30 percent judged it to be "good" or "very good."[21] The country was becoming polarized around this issue. Even more remarkably, barely one-third of business and finance executives (34 percent) agreed that the "neoliberal" economic model should stay in place as it was; another third (32 percent) believed that it should stay intact, but with substantial modification; and nearly as many (29 percent) wanted it to be discarded altogether.[22] Clearly, whatever consensus had existed in Mexico was pulling apart at the seams.

Pessimism prevailed. A questionnaire in March 1995 sought to explore popular perceptions of national well-being over the previous year, and in anticipation of the year to come. As reported in table 9.2, the results reveal a widespread picture of deterioration: 89 percent said that economic conditions were worse, 52 percent thought political conditions were worse, 48 percent reported social conditions were worse. Expectations for the future were a bit less gloomy (perhaps because some believed that conditions could only get better), but about one-third of the population expressed the view that conditions would continue get worse on all three dimensions.

In effect, Mexican citizens were beginning to see themselves as engaged in a zero-sum game: If total resources were stagnating, one person's gain could come only at someone else's loss. In stark contrast to the optimism of the early 1990s, this must have been eerily (and sadly) reminiscent of the despair that gripped the country in the 1980s. It was an ominous trend, and it may well have contributed to the palpable rise in crime and violence that the country endured for the remainder of the decade.

Finally, the economic crisis led to disappointment with Ernesto Zedillo as president. While many people appreciated his personal honesty and modesty and admired his willingness to stand up to the Salinas family, they did not regard him as an effective leader. As displayed in table 9.3, his approval ratings dropped from 53 percent in March 1995 (after the arrest of Raúl Salinas) to just 31 percent in June (as inflation and unemployment were on the rise); similarly, his disapproval ratings jumped from 34 percent in March to 61 percent

TABLE 9.2
Perceptions of National Well-being, March 1995

	A. Reflections on Past Year Responses (in %)			
Situation	*Better*	*Same*	*Worse*	*Don't Know*
Economic	1	9	89	1
Political	16	26	52	6
Social	9	34	48	9

Text of question: "¿Cómo siente las siguientes situaciones comparadas con hace un año?"

	B. Expectations for Coming Year Responses (in %)			
Situation	*Better*	*Same*	*Worse*	*Don't Know*
Economic	35	23	29	13
Political	37	27	21	15
Social	35	29	21	15

Text of question: "¿Cómo cree que serán las siguientes situaciones para el próximo año?"
Source: *Reforma,* March 10, 1995.

in June, and remained around that level through November.[23] Mexicans were becoming disenchanted with the nation's entire political elite, including (and especially) its technocratic cadres. There were no good guys anymore.

As Zedillo completed his first year in office, Miguel Pérez offered a retrospective assessment in the respected newspaper *Reforma*:

> With an unprecedented economic crisis, with inflation about to surpass official estimates, with a high rate of unemployment, without any progress [*claridad*] on investigations of the assassinations of Luis Donaldo Colosio and José Francisco Ruiz Massieu, and with the sewer of official corruption wide open, President Ernesto Zedillo today completes one year at the head of the government of Mexico.
>
> In merely 365 days, the country's GDP fell by more than 7 percent; inflation rose from 7 to 49 percent; and the rate of [open] unemployment climbed to more than 6 percent, which means that there are 2.5 million people without work.[24]

It was a devastating summation of a devastating year.

Aftermath—and Turnaround?

Things could only get better from here. And indeed, the Mexican economy showed impressive signs of recovery. According to table 9.4, the GDP expanded by 5.1 percent in 1996—and maintained strong growth rates for the remainder of the Zedillo *sexenio,* reaching 6.9 percent in 2000. Inflation came under control and dropped to single digits by the year 2000. Open unemployment and interest rates declined. Boosted by NAFTA, rising petroleum prices, and the weakness of the peso, Mexico's exports skyrocketed—so it took a surge of imports to produce negative trade balances in 1998–2000. The external debt was massive and growth remained uneven, but, in general, the economy seemed to be back on track.[25]

TABLE 9.3
Approval/Disapproval Ratings for Ernesto Zedillo, 1995

	Responses (in %)			
	March	*June*	*August*	*November*
Approve	53	31	34	31
Disapprove	34	61	56	60
Don't Know	13	8	10	9

Text of question: "¿Aprueba o desaprueba la forma como el Presidente Ernesto Zedillo está manejando el país?"
Sources: *Reforma,* March 10, June 11, September 1, and December 1, 1995.

TABLE 9.4
Economic Indicators for Mexico, 1996–2000

	1996	*1997*	*1998*	*1999*	*2000*
GDP change (%)	5.1	6.8	4.9	3.8	6.9
Unemployment (%)	4.1	2.8	2.6	2.0	1.9
Inflation (CPI as %)	27.7	15.7	18.6	12.3	9.0
Interest rates (28-day CETES)	27.3	19.0	31.2	16.3	17.6
Exchange rates (pesos/dollar)	7.85	8.08	9.87	9.50	9.65
Trade balance (US$ billions)	6.53	0.62	−7.9	−5.4	−8.0
External debt (US$ billions)	163.6	152.8	162.1	163.3	148.8

Source: *Latin Focus* at www.latin-focus.com/countries/mexico/mexindex.htm.

As economic growth continued, Ernesto Zedillo regained the support of the Mexican public. Presidential approval ratings climbed from just 31 percent at the end of 1995 to 45 percent by the end of 1996, 60 percent by 1997, 67 percent by 1999, and 69 percent throughout the year 2000.[26] This was a remarkable political achievement for a person once regarded as an inexperienced neophyte. Popular support was due in large part to the country's economic turnaround (such as it was), to his modest demeanor, to his rectitude, and to his unwavering support for major political reforms. Characteristics that were initially perceived to be liabilities—his lack of charisma and his tenuous ties to the long-ruling PRI—were turning out to be assets.

All of these factors came to a head during the presidential election of July 2000. Thanks mainly to extensive institutional reforms, this was perhaps the first such contest in Mexican history that was both free and fair, as opposition candidate Vicente Fox mounted a strong and credible campaign against the *priísta* Francisco Labastida. The election presented the outgoing president with a win-win situation: if Labastida triumphed, Zedillo would be credited with helping his party to another six-year term; if Fox won, Zedillo would be remembered as the leader who brought democracy to Mexico. (It was not always clear which outcome Zedillo truly preferred, which might explain the absence of any visible "coattail effect" in support of the PRI.) Fox emerged as the decisive victor in the July 2000 elections, and Mexico took a giant step in the direction of democracy.

The most important political consequence of the peso crisis was to generate uncertainty and to weaken Mexico's longstanding regime. Coming on the heels of the 1980s debt crisis, the debacle underscored the inability of PRI leadership to protect the economic well-being of Mexican citizens. Backbiting and finger-pointing over the crisis itself further unraveled the once-vaunted "revolutionary family." Continuing revelations of corruption added to popular distaste (providing Fox with a major issue in the presidential campaign), while millions of Mexicans struggled to survive the hardships imposed by the recovery package. Indeed, the Zedillo team seemed relatively impervious to the social costs of austerity policies: "Whereas Salinas over-politicized economic reform," in Denise Dresser's felicitous expression, "Zedillo sought to de-politicize it."[27] The result was to further fracture the regime's historic coalition—alienating much of organized labor and the peasantry, not to mention small business and the middle class.

The defeat of the PRI in 2000 did not guarantee inexorable progress toward complete democracy. Despite recent vicissitudes, effective power was overconcentrated in the presidency. Legislative representation was uncertain (ironically, the PRI held a congressional plurality and was in a position to curtail executive authority). The judiciary was weak, the police was largely ineffective, and citizens' rights were not always respected. Corruption remained a major problem at the state and local levels. One description of Mexico portrayed it as a "checkerboard democracy," with power residing in pockets—some democratic, others authoritarian. The promise of a democratic future was still hanging in the balance.

Lessons for Giving (and Taking) Lessons

Not surprisingly, the Mexican peso crisis precipitated a nearly instantaneous and multifaceted quest for "lessons" that it might convey. Journalists wrote widely on the subject. Academics offered sage advice.[28] Study groups delved into causes and cures. All these well-intentioned efforts sought to draw constructive lessons from the Mexican experience. When subjected to textual analysis, these multitudinous prescriptions inadvertently offered insight into the art of thinking about and learning from such episodes. At least five clear lessons (or meta-lessons) emerged.

1. Incorporate politics into explanations of causes for economic crisis.

In most analyses politics emerges as something of a nuisance, a series of unpredictable and unwelcome intrusions on the policy process. For example, an "independent task force" of the Council on Foreign Relations in New York observed that international confidence in the peso-dollar exchange rate was holding steady in the early 1990s: "However, political turmoil—events in Chiapas, the assassination of José Francisco Ruiz Massieu, and a series of political kidnappings—continued to erode confidence in Mexico's polity. The peso came under renewed pressure when the tensions between the government and the Zapatista insurgents intensified in December [1994]."[29] But for these unseemly intrusions, one is led to believe, economic rationality might well have prevailed.

But politics consists of more than random happenings and nettlesome events. Politics embraces the nature of the prevailing regime, rules for allocation of power, and incentives for political actors. It is impossible to understand the behavior of policy makers in Mexico, from Salinas to Zedillo, without comprehending the nature of the country's political system. As I have attempted to demonstrate throughout this chapter, these leaders were acting in accordance with a longstanding (if not especially laudable) political logic.

2. Recognize the political dimensions of economic reform.

In order to alter the behavior of key actors, especially policy makers, it is generally necessary to change the structure of incentives. In a country such as Mexico, this meant reshaping the political system as a whole. Piecemeal institutional reform had no hope of succeeding within the prevailing regime. It would have been impossible to achieve true autonomy for the central bank, as many have urged, so long as the president remained in near-total command of supreme power. It was senseless to insist on a transparent budgetary process with full legislative review, as others suggested, so long as the congress had no significant power or role of its own.[30] (Mexico has since made significant strides in these directions, but has not arrived there yet.)

What needs to be understood is that, despite their modest appearance, such institutional prescriptions required radical political surgery. They amounted to a call for nothing less than the full democratization of Mexico. There was no other way for economic reforms to acquire popular support.[31] There was no other way that government could be held accountable. There was no other way for public institutions and branches of government, including the central bank, to achieve genuine autonomy. It may well be that the ultimate lesson of the Mexican peso crisis is that authoritarianism might be effective for initiating economic reform, but only democracy can achieve consolidation and perpetuation.

3. Attack the problem of poverty.

Most analyses stress the importance of macroeconomic fundamentals and the restoration of investor confidence. Poverty does not receive the priority that it demands. It is usually mentioned in a tone of pious resignation and then dismissed as an unfortunate form of collateral damage: Get the policies right, according to conventional wisdom, and poverty will take care of itself. (It is not clear whether this means that poverty will disappear or that it will lose its political importance.)

This viewpoint is inadequate. First, it fails to acknowledge the magnitude of the problem. In the case of Mexico, for instance, the population share living below the national poverty line dropped from 77.5 percent in 1963 to 48.5 percent in 1981; but from 1982 to 1992, under pro-market reforms, it rose again to 66 percent. By 1995, according to international standards, 42.5

percent of the population was living on the equivalent of less than $2 per day; 17.9 percent was struggling to survive on less than $1 per day.[32] Second, large-scale poverty exerts an enormous drag on economic development. It reduces the size of national markets. It requires (or should require) social expenditures and income transfers. And third, poverty is a political time bomb, especially under conditions of increasing inequality. It can explode in a variety of ways—from armed rebellion to criminal activity to populist demogaguery—but it is bound to erupt at some point. Ultimately, poverty creates instability.

4. Take heed from advice intended for others.

We all have much to learn from one another's misfortune. It is impossible to say whether any of the damage from the "Asian crisis" of 1997–1998 might have been averted, or at least mitigated, if policy makers in Thailand or Korea had paid more attention to the dynamics of the Mexican crisis. Things would certainly not have gotten worse. By 1997, when crisis first appeared in Thailand, analysts had produced some excellent formulations of key lessons to be learned from the Mexican crisis.[33] These analyses may have been listened to in Mexico, well after the horse had escaped from the stable, but they were pretty much ignored elsewhere around the world.

This leads to a nontrivial piece of advice: Be careful of nomenclature. Reference to "the Mexican peso crisis" reinforced the idea that the problems of 1994–1995 were of Mexico's making and are therefore irrelevant to anyone else. Let us imagine that this episode had become known as "the NAFTA currency crisis" or "the 1994–95 portfolio investment crisis." Such labels would alter conceptual frameworks and perhaps shape different lines of inquiry. Putting names on things is not a neutral act; it can have significant (if unintended) consequences.

5. Be prepared for the worst.

Finally, the peso crisis of 1994–1995 suggests the need for preparedness, for a willingness to broaden horizons about the possible course of future events—in Mexico and elsewhere—and to tolerate the unexpected. Policy makers need to realize that Mexico has embarked on a path of irreversible transition, but setbacks and shifts in direction are almost certain to occur. There has been a tendency, in general, to place too much faith in the resolution of short-term financial crises—and then to assume that all will then be well.[34] This smacks of hubris and shortsightedness. In contrast, a more effective way to facilitate and foster orderly change in Mexico and other developing countries would be to make ample allowance for less-than-optimal scenarios. Paradoxically, the best way to avert future crisis may well be to expect it.

Notes

An earlier version of this paper appeared in *Mexico 1994: Anatomy of an Emerging-Market Crash,* Sebastian Edwards and Moisés Naím, eds. (Washington, D.C.: Carnegie Endowment for International Peace, 1997), ch. 1, 31–53. Reprinted by permission.

1. "Mexico: Honeymoon from Hell," *Hemisfile,* 6, no. 1 (January/February 1995), 1. For additional analysis see Nora Lustig, "Mexico y la crisis del peso: Lo previsible y la sorpresa," *Comercio Exterior* 45, 5 (Mayo de 1995): 374–382; Jaime Ros, "La crisis mexicana: Causas, perspectivas, lecciones," *Nexos* 209 (Mayo de 1995): 43–49; and Macario Schettino, *El costo del miedo: La devaluación de 1994/1995* (México: Grupo Editorial Iberoamérica, 1995).

2. "Mexico's Larger Story," *Foreign Policy* 99 (Summer 1995): 115.

3. Peter H. Smith, *Labyrinths of Power: Political Recruitment in Twentieth-Century Mexico* (Princeton: Princeton University Press, 1979), esp. ch. 6.

4. Eduardo Valle, *El segundo disparo: La narcodemocracia mexicana* (México: Oceano, 1995); and Silvana Paternostro, "Mexico as a Narco-Democracy," *World Policy Journal* (Spring 1995): 41–47.

5. See Denise Dresser, "Twilight of the Perfect Dictatorship: The Decline of Dominant-Party Rule in Mexico," paper presented at Latin American Studies Association, Washington, D.C., September 1995; Gabriel Zaid, *Adiós al PRI* (México: Oceano, 1995); and Juan Pablo González Sandoval and Jaime González Graf, eds., *Los límites rotos: Anuario político* (México: Oceano, 1995).

6. See Smith, *Labyrinths*; Miguel Angel Centeno, *Democracy within Reason: Technocratic Revolution in Mexico* (University Park: Pennsylvania State University Press, 1994); and Roderic Ai Camp, *Political Recruitment across Two Centuries: Mexico, 1884–1991* (Austin: University of Texas Press, 1995).

7. Eugenio Aguirre, et al., *Ruiz Massieu: El mejor enemigo* (México: Espasa-Hoy, 1995).

8. *Reforma*, December 4–5, 1995.

9. Jorge G. Castañeda, *The Mexican Shock: Its Meaning for the United States* (New York: The New Press, 1995), 65.

10. *Wall Street Journal*, June 14, 1994.

11. *Wall Street Journal*, June 14, 1994, A6.

12. Naím, "Mexico's Larger Story," 113.

13. See Rudiger Dornbush, "We Have Salinas to Thank for the Peso Debacle," *Business Week* (January 16, 1995), 20.

14. Accounts of this gathering appear in the *Wall Street Journal Americas,* July 6, 1995, with a response by Pedro Aspe in *Reforma,* July 14, 1995.

15. Reliable reports indicate that Zedillo offered Aspe any cabinet-level post he might want, with the sole exception of Treasury.

16. Claudio M. Loser and Ewart S. Williams, "The Mexican Crisis and Its Aftermath: An IMF Perspeactive," in Edwards and Naím, *Mexico 1994*, 259–273, especially 267–268.

17. See Rogelio Ramírez de la O, "The Mexican Economy under President Fox," *Enfoque* (Center for U.S.-Mexican Studies, University of California, San Diego) (Fall 2000/Winter 2001): 1–2, 10.

18. Encuesta Telefónica Nacional de MORI de México/*Este País*, March 1, 1995.

19. *Este País* (Septiembre 1994), 19.

20. *Reforma*, March 2, 1995.

21. *Reforma*, January 9, 1995.

22. *Reforma*, January 30, 1995.

23. As measured on a 10-point scale, Zedillo's ratings among the general public also dropped steadily throughout the year. See *Reforma*, March 10, April 27, June 11, July 11, September 1, and December 1, 1995.

24. Miguel Pérez, "El Presidente y sus 365 días," *Reforma*, December 1, 1995. The GDP contraction was later revised to –6.2 percent.

25. There would be a recession in 2001.

26. *Reforma*, November 27, 2000.

27. Dresser, "Falling from the Tightrope: The Political Economy of the Mexican Crisis," in Edwards and Naím, *Mexico 1994*, 70.

28. See Jeffrey Sachs, Aaron Tornell, and Andrés Velasco, "The Collapse of the Mexican Peso: What Have We Learned?" Center for International Affairs, Harvard University, Working Paper Series 95–7 (July 1995).

29. Council on Foreign Relations, *Lessons of the Mexican Peso Crisis: Report of an Independent Task Force* (New York: Council on Foreign Relations, 1996), 11.

30. These prescriptions appear in Sebastian Edwards, *Crisis and Reform in Latin America: From Despair to Hope* (New York: World Bank/Oxford University Press, 1995), 301–309.

31. See Stephan Haggard and Steven B. Webb, eds., *Voting for Reform: Democracy, Political Liberalization, and Economic Adjustment* (New York: World Bank/Oxford University Press, 1994).

32. World Bank, *World Development Report 2000/2001: Attacking Poverty* (New York: Oxford University Press,), Table 4, 280–281. See also chapter 8 in this volume.

33. See in particular Sebastian Edwards and Moisés Naím, introduction to *Mexico 1994*, esp. 18–28.

34. See, for example, the ebullient remarks about the Mexican rescue by Lawrence H. Summers, then Deputy Secretary of the U.S. Treasury, *New York Times*, June 19, 1996. For a more measured interpretation see Bradford De Long, Christopher De Long, and Sherman Robinson, "The Case for Mexico's Rescue," *Foreign Affairs* 75, no. 3 (May/June 1996), 8–14; and, for a skeptical view, Jorge G. Castañeda, "Mexico's Circle of Misery," *Foreign Affairs* 75, no. 4 (July/August 1996): 92–105.

10

Thailand's Unexpected Crisis

Nualnoi Treerat

NOBODY THOUGHT IT WOULD HAPPEN. Up to 1996 Thailand was widely admired for its rapid growth and macroeconomic stability. The country had managed to control inflation and unemployment, accumulate substantial foreign exchange reserves, and steadily reduce the incidence of absolute poverty. All that changed in 1997. Since then Thailand has undergone dramatic change, sinking deep into economic crisis and causing a contagion effect throughout Asia and the world. Confidence plummeted in the country's prospects and its financial institutions, most notably the Bank of Thailand. The International Monetary Fund formulated a rescue plan. Bangkok businessmen forced the government to resign; soon thereafter the governor and top officials of the Bank of Thailand also resigned under public criticism. The crisis had become much more serious than anyone ever expected.

Many have asked what went wrong with Thailand and Asia. Many interpretations about the Asian crisis have come forth. Financial liberalization and the movement of capital, especially short-term capital, have become central issues of discussion. And while the crisis imposed considerable costs, both economic and social, it also spurred much-needed reforms of economic, social, and political structures. Yet no one sees an easy way for Thailand to emerge from the crisis and achieve a stronger economy and society.

This chapter examines the fundamental problems of the Thai economy, the impacts of the crisis, and the challenges it poses to effective governance. My central argument is that, for Thailand to recover from its economic crisis, fundamental reforms must include not only the financial sector but also the "real" or productive sector. Moreover, the economic reforms must be accompanied by political and social reforms as well.

Thailand's Economy: Development, Structure, and Vulnerabilities

Ever since 1960, Thailand has followed the World Bank's recommendation that the government should encourage private enterprise for industrial development and devote its own energies to the provision of basic infrastructure. Thai industrial policy has been geared toward the coexistence of export promotion and import substitution. A fundamental challenge for this policy was how to combine import substitution with the growth of exports, which was considered since the 1970s to be essential to economic growth. Development planning thus focused on the expansion of international trade, with the role of the state limited to that of a facilitator. Citing national security, the government from time to time moved to monopolize several key industries—such as public utilities, telecommunications, and oil refineries. During the economic boom of the late 1980s, though, the inefficiency of state enterprises led the private sector to take an active role in providing public utilities and telecommunications through the granting of concessions.

From the 1960s through the late 1980s, Thailand implemented a capital-control policy to maintain economic stability through the use of interest rate ceilings, limits on the foreign exchange positions of commercial banks, and a withholding tax on foreign borrowing. Since 1988 the government has gradually allowed free capital movement. The first phase of liberalization was implemented by relaxing controls on interest rate ceilings and allowing more flexibility in capital accounts, and was further stimulated by the emergence of the capital market. Large capital inflows led to an economic boom and created financial bubbles. Household consumption rose while household savings went down, resulting in the deterioration of the current account deficit. The bubble first threatened to burst in 1991 during the Gulf War, and again during a period of political turmoil in 1992.

A second phase of financial liberalization began in 1993, with an effort to increase the flow of funds into Thailand through the Bangkok International Banking Facilities (BIBF). The central purpose of this policy was to convert Thailand into a regional financial center and to attract capital from abroad. A domestic interest rate above the world level, together with a fixed exchange rate regime, created incentives for the inflow of foreign capital. The excess supply of capital led to an excess supply of liquidity, and thus to a boom in the real estate and stock markets. Growth was rapid but unsustainable, as foreign debt further inflated the bubbles. Loans were mainly short-term and most were not hedged against currency fluctuation. The average debt/equity ratio of listed non-financial companies rose from 1.58 to 1.98 between 1994 and 1996.[1]

Consequently, the large inflow of foreign capital through the BIBF gave the property boom and the economic bubble a second wind. The high volume of foreign borrowing led to a rise in the real exchange rate. Terms-of-trade shifted in favor of non-tradable sectors such as real estate and durable consumer goods. The real exchange rate appreciated, thus exerting downward pressure on exports. Finally, the current account deficit soared to 8 percent of GDP.

Prior to 1996, growth in exports had ranged from 15 to 20 percent per annum. This expansion could accommodate an increase in indebtedness. A sign of trouble appeared in 1996, however, when export growth sank to zero percent. This phenomenon alerted foreign investors and speculators to look carefully at the Thai economy. By November of that year they began attacking the *baht* through massive sell-offs. The Bank of Thailand persisted in defending the *baht*, and the consequent depletion of reserves was hidden from the public by the forward sale of the dollar.[2] Reported foreign exchange reserves fell from US$40 billion at the beginning of 1997 to $33.8 billion at the end of June. However, the real foreign exchange position, net of forward commitment, went from $33 billion at the beginning of the year to around $2.5 billion at the end of June 1997. By the time the country adopted a floating exchange rate system on July 2, the Bank of Thailand almost ran out of foreign reserves.

The External Sector and Financial Liberalization

During the 1990s Thailand had large current account deficits. The deficits were financed by long- and short-term debts. Concern over the deficits, and over whether Thailand could accommodate its foreign debt, arose from the poor quality of investments, the overvalued real exchange rate, and the large decline of export growth in 1996.

With financial liberalization in 1988 and 1993, Thailand took several steps to attract investment funds from global capital markets. The main policies were (1) making it easier for foreign funds to flow into Thailand, (2) maintaining high domestic interest rates, and (3) keeping the *baht* fixed to the dollar. Taken together, these policies together left no room for the country to control monetary policy. Decisions were made by a very small number of persons who were not prepared to deal with the complexities of liberalization.[3] The large inflows, especially of short-term capital, combined with the policy environment, were the precursors of the 1997 collapse.

Peter Warr explains that an attempt by the Bank of Thailand to sterilize the impact of capital inflow on the domestic money supply resulted in high domestic interest rates, and thus increased levels of short-term foreign investment because of the increased rate of return:

> Now suppose an inflow of long-term foreign investment was occurring. If sterilisation was not occurring at all, the national prices of traded goods would not be affected, since they are determined (with lag) by international prices and the fixed exchange rate, but non-traded goods' nominal prices would be bid up by the increased domestic demand. That is, the capital inflow would produce a real appreciation—an increase in domestic non-traded goods' prices relative to domestic traded goods' prices—the phenomenon now known as the "Dutch Disease." . . . The current account deficit would increase, reducing the amount by which foreign exchange reserves would be increased by initial capital inflow.
>
> The outcome would be much the same if monetary authorities were attempting to sterilise but where the exchange rate was fixed, capital movements were unimpeded, and foreign and domestic assets were perfect substitutes. Any attempt to sterilise by raising domestic interest rates, through sale of bonds, would be defeated because it would produce an inflow of portfolio investment sufficient to drive the domestic interest rate down to its previous level. Demand would be increased by the monetary consequences of this inflow, producing the real appreciation described above.[4]

Capital inflows increased the level of foreign exchange reserves, while increases in current account deficits tended to lower the level of foreign exchange reserves. The conventional measure of reserve adequacy is based on the number of months of imports that reserves can finance. Available figures showed that reserves were sufficient to finance imports of more than six months in early 1997. At a time of financial panic, however, it does not matter how many months of imports reserves can finance. What matters is whether reserves can withstand capital flight. In early 1997, the stock of short-term, foreign-owned capital exceeded reserves by 80 percent, indicating Thailand's vulnerability to a financial crisis. The inflow of capital came to a halt when the external sector, especially export earnings, showed alarming signs of deterioration in 1996. This led to a large current account deficit and produced widespread expectations of devaluation. Once this expectation developed and portfolio capital headed for the exits, the process was unstoppable.[5]

The slowdown in exports was concentrated in manufactured goods from labor-intensive industries, and affected trade with Japan, the United States, and China. This could be explained by several economic factors. First, the appreciation of the *baht* arose from the demand effects of foreign capital inflow, as described above. Second, demand from importing countries declined. Third, China's competitiveness in international markets had increased sharply since the devaluation of its currency in 1994. Finally, real wages in Thailand steadily increased at around 9 percent per annum between 1990 and 1996, resulting in a decline in competitiveness.

The Real Sector

Thailand sustained spectacular rates of economic growth, nearly 10 percent per year, between 1987 and 1996. But the source of the boom did not lie in improvements in the quality of the labor force. By 1997 nearly 80 percent of Thai workers still had only a primary education. With the extension of compulsory schooling from six to nine years, the number of children attending secondary school had increased continuously since 1992. Even so, Thailand still had the lowest ratio of science and technology graduates in Asia.

Studies have shown that the growth of total factor productivity was less than one percent per annum before 1988. During 1989–1995, total factor productivity growth rose to 5 percent per annum because of technological know-how that accompanied foreign direct investment. During this boom, the foreign direct investment (FDI) inflow led to an increase in the ratio of foreign capital stock to total capital stock. Foreign and domestic capital stocks are differentiated; that is, they are imperfect substitutes for one another with an elasticity of substitution of 0.45. This indicator implies that the two are strongly complementary. This means that an increase in the stock of foreign capital will increase the productivity of domestic capital and also the level of domestic investment. Therefore, productivity growth has relied mainly on FDI.[6]

In effect, Thailand has a dualistic economy within and across sectors. The manufacturing sector has overtaken agriculture both in terms of export and production since the 1980s—but agriculture is still the major source of employment, accounting for more than 50 percent of all workers.

For Thailand's manufacturing sector, production for the domestic market and the export market has been separated in several major industries—such as automotive, electronics, leather products, and textile and garments. The production structure of these industries can be divided into upstream, midstream, and downstream. Many of the upstream and midstream firms developed as import-substitution industries whose products could be sold only on the domestic market because of their low quality. The downstream products for the export market mainly used imported materials. Clearly, the linkages among upstream, midstream, and downstream were not strong enough to benefit the industry's competitiveness. In many cases, the protection of upstream and midstream has added to the cost of downstream production.

Bubbles arise from excessive prices and result in excessive production in affected sectors. In Thailand, cheap funding for many years created an asset bubble. This funding was used to finance inefficient sectors and to speculate in the real estate market and on the stock exchange. The bubble's effect on income led to increased demand for commodities. Manufacturers expanded their investments to increase their production. Those industries turned toward the domestic market. As a result, overproduction and foreign debt both increased.

By early 1997 Thailand was showing very high levels of industrial oversupply. For example, the automotive industry had an estimated oversupply level of 192 percent; modern housing in Bangkok an oversupply of 200 percent; petrochemicals, an oversupply of 195 percent; steel bar production, an oversupply of 150 percent; and private hospital beds, an oversupply of 300 percent.[7] These industrial oversupplies mainly pertained to the domestic market. Even with a high growth rate, it still takes years for an economy to absorb an oversupply; with a contracting economy, it takes a much longer time. In 1998, total capacity utilization was around 52.2 percent. Transportation equipment utilized only 23.5 percent of its capacity, followed by iron and steel products at 33.3 percent and food at 33.7 percent.

Institutions and Politics

For many years economic technocrats, mainly at the Bank of Thailand, had a great deal of power and autonomy in the management of macroeconomic policy. This led to a stable economy. However, financial liberalization led to free capital mobility and thus inefficient monetary policy. At the same time, the political system moved toward democracy. And as a result, politicians wanted more control of economic policy.

The reputation of the Bank of Thailand was mainly established under the stewardship of Dr. Puey Ungphakorn, a prominent Thai technocrat and academic.

> The structure, organization and ethos of the Bank of Thailand was established during the 1950s and the 1960s, by then governor of the Bank, Dr. Puey Ungphakorn, a revered figure among the country's technocrats and academics. The institution that he led was imbued with a spirit of fierce integrity. In a country in which corruption is rife, the Bank of Thailand was considered to be the only institution where it was unthinkable that any corrupt practices could be found. This reputation of incorruptibility gave it considerable moral authority and prestige and allowed it to enjoy *de facto* autonomy, overriding its *de jure* subservience to the Minister of Finance.[8]

Eventually, the Bank of Thailand's management structure became outmoded. Power was concentrated in the hands of the governor. It has been observed that this kind of management was suitable when the objective was to shield the bank from the military, and when there was a clear gap in authority and seniority between upper and lower levels of the bank's hierarchy. As a result of extensive overseas training programs for new staff members at the bank, however, the governor—and the upper echelons—no longer monopolized expertise. Subsequent rivalries within the staff resulted in factionalism, a failure to make effective use of the bank's personnel, and a severe deterioration in the ethos of dedication to the public interest.[9]

The critical turning point for the Bank of Thailand was the appointment as governor of Vijit Supinit, a member of the first generation of scholars educated abroad. His tenure brought the first damage to the Bank of Thailand's reputation with the Bangkok Bank of Commerce (BBC) affair. The Bank of Thailand was criticized for providing a bailout of almost US$7 billion to prevent the BBC's collapse—to no avail, as the BBC was closed down in 1998. The BBC fiasco was followed by the failure of a criminal-action lawsuit against some of the BBC's former senior executives because the brief was submitted after expiration of the statute of limitations. In addition, the newspapers strongly criticized Governor Vijit's integrity.

The governor of the bank does not have a fixed-term appointment, but instead can be dismissed by the minister of finance. Early on that rarely happened. During the 1980s, however, two out of five governors were dismissed. These dismissals demonstrated the government's determination to intervene in the Bank. Some governors, therefore, tended to anticipate the minister's desires and followed the current political line. For example, when the time came early in 1997 to alter the pegged exchange rate, it appeared that the Bank of Thailand was reluctant to do so, partly for fear of political repercussions. Ammar Siamwala, appointed as member of a committee to investigate the work of the Bank of Thailand after the crisis, wrote:

> Combining my observations that the civil service section of the technocracy has declined and that the Bank of Thailand has severe internal tensions, I conclude that it is a dispirited and demoralized technocracy that confronted the economic crisis. Indeed it is doubtful even whether an autonomous technocracy exists any more. True, the Bank of Thailand is still very much in charge of monetary policy (including exchange rate policy) and of the supervision of financial institutions, but it has been so badly wounded by the BBC affair that it no longer has much authority with the public to obtain adequate support for its actions.[10]

A related factor concerned the prevalence of excessive guarantees and moral hazards. Thai policy was justified by the notion that financial institutions—especially the commercial banks—could never be bankrupted.[11] This belief was based on the fact that the commercial banks had been powerful for decades. Whenever financial institutions struggled to survive, authorities came to their rescue. Monetary authorities consistently based their actions on this belief during the crisis. But the policy was inconsistent with the environment of the world's financial markets, which are interdependent and linked through computer networks. Traditional practice went against the philosophy of competitiveness and against the idea that efficient management of financial markets was required for successful participation in the global economy. So long as bank liabilities were perceived to have an implicit government guarantee, but were essentially unregulated, they would therefore be subject to severe moral hazard problems. The government's Financial Institution Development Fund spent huge sums in financial loans to rescue the distressed nonbank financial companies as well as the commercial banks during the crisis. Those loans have since become a burden for all of Thai society.

Political uncertainty added further complications to this picture. Since 1992, the Thai political system has been moving toward democracy—more specifically, a parliamentary form of government. In the past, when the military controlled the government, economic policy was left in the hands of the technocrats. With the adoption of a parliamentary system, however, debates came to focus on the *allocation* of budget monies, rather than the overall *size* of the budget and related tax policy. One key consequence of this development has been an elevation in the expectations of constituents, particularly those in rural areas. Ambitious parliamentarians use pork-barrel tactics and vote-buying arrangements in order to bring home public works projects that generate side benefits for local politicians and rural elites (many of whom are quite active in the construction business). Despite the resulting prevalence of "money politics," constituents do not seem to care how projects are handled because they regard government money as a free resource for the community. It can even be claimed that they are happier the more corrupt their representatives are, because that means more money from Bangkok.[12] Besides, it seems that the role of politicians in formulating national economic policy is not of great concern to rural voters.

By contrast, voters in the Bangkok area pay considerable attention to their representatives' stance on national economic policy. For this reason, the minister of finance must usually be appointed from outside the parliament (unless the ruling party can put forth a well-known and widely respected candidate). Consequently, the Ministry of Finance, which is the central organ for the formulation of macroeconomic policy, tends to be occupied by former technocrats or bankers. However, elected politicians do not allow the minister to work independently on sensitive national issues. This makes it more difficult for the minister and top officials to respond to events or change policy at critical points.

As a result, public authorities often find themselves in disarray. In the face of crisis, when a strong and skilled finance minister was urgently needed, Thailand went through four finance ministers—most of them former technocrats and bankers—in the six-month period from May to November 1997. Naturally, it is relatively easy for the prime minister to dismiss a finance minister who is not an elected politician.

It was not surprising that when the Thai government sought help from the IMF in August 1997, leading businessmen and academics welcomed the news. The IMF was regarded favorably because many in Thailand reluctantly had come to the view that the country's institutional and political system was incapable of assembling a coalition to support measures needed to head off a catastrophic economic downturn.[13] But when the traditional rescue package was presented and the economy got worse, the public began to criticize the IMF and forced the prime minister to resign.

Economic and Social Impacts

Beginning with the collapse of the financial sector, Thailand's economic crisis led to the contraction of the real sector. Before the crisis, the annual GDP growth rate was remarkably strong (averaging 8.2 percent between 1990 and 1996). The rate plunged to –1.5 percent in 1997 and then –12.1 percent in 1998. This was the first time since 1960 that Thailand had experienced negative economic growth rates. The worst period occurred in the second and third quarters of 1998, with rates of –16.6 percent and –16.2 percent in comparison with 1997. The most severely affected sectors were construction and banking: During 1998 their outputs contracted by 63.8 percent and 42.0 percent, while education and public administration showed modest gains for the year. GDP growth finally became positive in 1999 with an increase of 4.1 percent (see figure 10.1).

On the expenditure side, total investment in physical capital declined significantly, by 82 percent in 1998, because of the reduction in private investment. This was followed by household consumption expenditure, which declined 13 percent. Although government expenditure dropped by 7 percent in the first half of 1998, it rose by 13 percent in the second half of the year. Overall, the government sector grew in 1998, and the Thai economy began to recover in 1999. Private consumption increased by 3.8 percent and government consumption rose by less than 1 percent. Investment expenditure nonetheless declined by 4 percent.

On the international side, the crisis caused a surplus in external trade and services. As a result of the *baht*'s depreciation, imports became much more

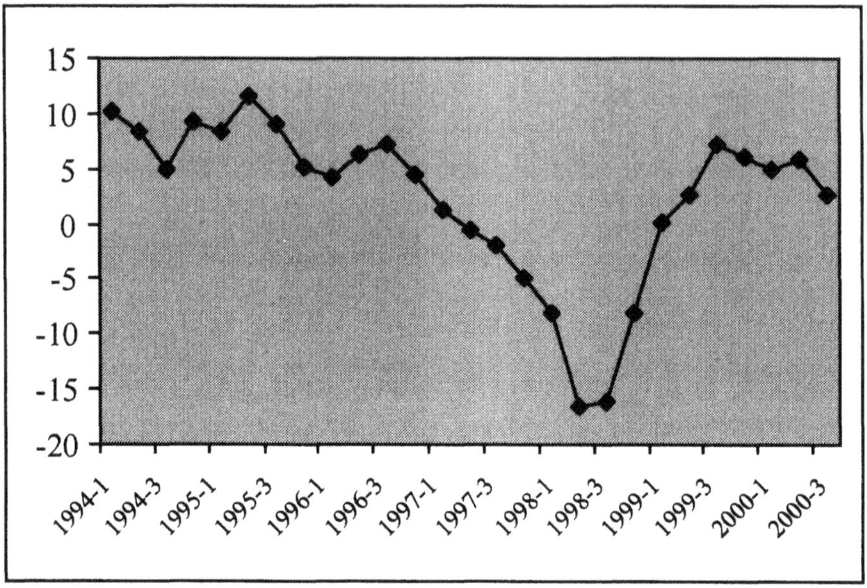

FIGURE 10.1
Thailand: Quarterly GDP Growth Rate, 1994–2000
Source: Ministry of Finance, Thailand.

expensive, and the demand for foreign goods dropped dramatically. It should be noted that the percentage change in quantity was larger than the percentage change in the currency. The cause of this disparity was a large economic contraction that resulted in a reduction in the real value of imports. Imports of goods and services in *baht* terms dropped by 11 percent in 1998. Exports in the first quarter of 1998 grew by 64 percent as a result of currency depreciation. However, because foreign demand for Thai exports dropped faster than the exchange rate in the fourth quarter of 1998, export growth in *baht* terms declined by 15 percent. The economic crisis led to a change in the external trade sector from deficit to surplus. The ratio of trade and service surplus to GDP was nearly 16 percent, the highest such ratio since 1960.

The social costs of the economic crisis became painfully apparent in 1998. The contraction of the real sector resulted in an increase in unemployment and the subsequent shrinking of incomes, which was exacerbated by the inflation that resulted from the *baht*'s depreciation. Here I describe these impacts in four areas: unemployment, the average standard of living, the incidence of poverty, and the education and health sectors.

1. Unemployment

In 1998 several organizations and groups—including the National Economic and Social Development Board (NESDB), the Ministry of the Interior, and private institutions and academics—attempted to estimate the impact of the economic crisis on unemployment. They came out with similar results, all showing that the unemployment rate for the total labor force was approximately 3.5 percent in 1997 and 5.6 percent in 1998—up from merely 1.5 percent in 1996. These figures were equivalent to 1.16 million people in 1997 and 1.85 million in 1998. These estimates include both laid-off and new entrant workers, and were made under the assumption that economic growth would slow by 3.5 percent in 1998. But because economic growth slowed by nearly 12 percent in 1998, almost three times the predicted rate, it was expected that unemployment would exceed these estimates.

One study of unemployment resulting from the economic crisis shows that persons unemployed as a result of the economic crisis numbered around 810,000 in the first quarter of 1998.[14] This figure does not include "natural"or structural unemployment. In fact, it is very hard to find accurate unemployment figures since the economic crisis contributed to a shift in employment patterns from the non-agricultural sector to the agricultural sector. People laid off in the non-agricultural sector returned to the agricultural sector as unpaid and self-employed workers. This shift led to a rise in underemployment. Other laid-off workers joined the informal sector.

2. Standard of Living

In the past, strong economic growth contributed to a substantial improvement in the standard of living, especially in rural areas. The economic crisis halted this improvement. Per capita real income dropped by 11.5 percent percent in the first quarter of 1998. Before the crisis, the long-term trend indices for per capita real income were 6.3 percent for the nation as a whole, 3.2 percent for urban areas, and 7.6 percent for rural areas. Then the crisis led to a sudden reduction in the standard of living in urban areas by 9.1 percent and in rural areas by 24.2 percent in the first quarter of 1998. The standard of living continued to decline in the subsequent period (table 10.1).

TABLE 10.1
Prior Trend and Crisis Indices for Change in per Capita Real Income in Thailand

		Crisis Index	
Areas	*Prior Long-Term Index (%)*	*Q1 1998*	*Q3 1998*
Urban areas	3.2	−9.1	−13.4
Sanitary districts*	5.2	−24.3	−31.0
Villages	7.6	−24.2	−31.3
Nation	6.3	−19.2	−24.8

*"Sanitary districts" are analogous to municipalities; as originally used, the term designated settlements that enjoyed sanitary amenities.

Source: National Economic and Social Development Board (NESDB), *Newsletter: Indicators of Well-being and Policy Analysis,* 2, no. 4 (1998): table 1.

Conducting an exhaustive socioeconomic survey, the National Economic and Social Development Board regularly estimates per capita welfare, which is defined as the ratio of a household's per capita income to that household's per capita poverty line. The index shows the percentage of excess income that a household has over its poverty line while taking into account the differences in needs and prices in areas of Thailand. The result shows that the economic crisis led to an overall reduction of 7.9 percent in per capita welfare in 1998.[15]

3. Poverty

The incidence of poverty was estimated to have risen from 11.4 percent in 1996 to 12.9 percent in 1998. Had the crisis not occurred, the "expected" number of poor in 1998—based on a linear extrapolation from previous years—would have been 6.4 million, whereas the actual number was 7.9 million (table 10.2). This implies that the crisis increased the number of poor people by 1.5 million. The Gini index—a summary measure of inequality that ranges from 0 toward 1.0—also shows an increase in inequality, rising from 0.477 in 1996 to 0.481 in 1998.

4. Education and Health

In general, it was widely assumed that the economic crisis would seriously affect both the education and health sectors. However, nationwide surveys in 1998 showed that the percentage of school-age people—those five to twenty-four years old—who were not attending school continued to decline. This unexpectedly positive trend resulted from the expansion of compulsory attendance from six to nine years and then to twelve years, new government loans for education, and delayed entrances into the labor market.

By contrast, the crisis severely affected the health sector, causing an enormous increase in the cost of medical treatment while consumers' incomes declined. This led to structural change. Private hospitals faced declining demand along with increasing costs of provisions. Public hospitals faced increasing

TABLE 10.2
Poverty in Thailand, 1988–1998

	Number of Poor (millions)	*% in Poverty*	*Poverty Gap Ratio (as %)*	*Gini Index*
1988	17.9	32.6	10.4	.481
1990	15.3	27.2	8.0	.481
1992	13.5	23.2	6.8	.499
1994	9.7	16.3	4.3	.486
1996	6.8	11.4	2.8	.477
1998	7.9	12.9	3.2	.481

Source: National Economic and Social Development Board (NESDB), *Newsletter: Indicators of Well-being and Policy Analysis,* 3, no. 1 (1999): tables 3, 6.

demand along with cashflow problems because the government cut its public health budget in 1998 and the poor could not pay full medical expenses. In 1999, however, the government increased its budget for public hospitals, especially those serving the poor.

The Policy Response

The combined currency and financial crisis of mid-1997 affected all segments of society. In resolving the crisis, the government has taken a systematic approach with the support of the IMF. The resultant policies were designed to achieve (1) stabilization, (2) stimulation, and (3) structural reform.

Stabilization

Immediately after the onset of the crisis, Thailand was faced with stabilization problems stemming from the large outflow of capital and the drastic depreciation of the *baht.* The government adopted tighter monetary and fiscal policies in an attempt to stabilize the economy by stopping the capital outflow. However, such policies resulted in high interest rates. High currency depreciation led to high inflation. The real sector faced a serious liquidity shortage. Domestic demand, both in consumption and investment, contracted more than expected, and the economy weakened more than anticipated. But the currency has now stabilized at around 40 *baht*/dollar after depreciating to as high as 53.7 *baht*/dollar in January 1998.

Stimulation

By the second half of 1998, the government and the IMF realized that, even with economic stability, a large contraction would only deepen the crisis. Subsequent measures aimed to stimulate the economy while maintaining stability. The government, rather than achieving its initial target of a surplus of 1 percent of GDP, increased the overall public deficit to 3 percent of GDP in fiscal year 1998. The budget deficit grew to around 5 percent of GDP in fiscal years 1999 and 2000. The government imposed an economic stimulus package, financed by loans from several sources, focusing on increasing government spending, private consumption, and private investment. The government also took measures to provide a social safety net to protect the most vulnerable elements of society. These policies succeeded in bringing down interest rates, and domestic demand began to rise again in the second quarter of 1999.

Structural Reform

The government's agenda included not only measures designed to address the current crisis, but also structural reforms to improve the foundation for long-term growth. These reforms aimed to increase overall economic efficiency. The government passed legislation to address debt restructuring, privatization, foreign business, and social security for the unemployed. However, these legal reforms have been criticized on the grounds that they favored foreign business interests.

In addition, the government has emphasized privatization as a way to increase the economy's efficiency, ensure the quality of goods and services, and reduce the government's fiscal burden. On September 1, 1998, the cabinet approved the Master Plan for the Reform of State-Owned Enterprises. The plan was meant to provide basic guidelines for the country's privatization program. State enterprises in Thailand are divided into five main sectors: energy, telecommunications, transport, water, and others. Under the 1999 Corporatization Act, almost all state enterprises were to be transformed into "limited companies" or "public companies." This would make it easy for government to sell its own shares to the private sector.

The government's principal focus was the restructuring of the financial sector. Large short-term capital inflows without adequate supervisory and regulatory capacity had caused the economic bubble and the subsequent crisis. To restructure the financial sector, the government undertook several measures to strengthen supervision, recapitalize financial institutions, and address the problem of nonperforming loans.

Long-Term Challenges

Despite these short-term achievements, Thailand continues to confront long-term challenges. It will be necessary to resolve these problems in order to assure the country's continued growth and development. Here I highlight three of these lingering issues.

1. Macroeconomic Management

Thailand's macroeconomic management was historically effective in that it brought about a balanced budget, low inflation, and high rates of savings and investment. Macroeconomic instability came from the external sector, especially from capital movement, and from mismanagement in the financial sector.

The most salient issue affecting the economic crisis was financial liberalization. The question was whether capital controls would make any difference. Thailand had imposed capital controls for many years until the late 1980s. The controls helped regulate speculative and destabilizing capital movements. As Peter Warr points out, however, capital controls do not seem to be the answer to preventing economic vulnerability.[16] If Thailand's capital controls had not been dismantled in the early 1990s, it seems likely that capital inflows would have been slower. But this alone would not have prevented the development of vulnerability. The most important task is to prevent the overexposure of domestic banks. When economies grow and become more complex, private financial intermediaries must direct resources to their most productive uses. To be efficient, the financial sector must be exposed to competition, both at home and from abroad.

In short, capital controls are no substitute for effective regulation of the financial sector. Indirect capital controls, through policies that increase the cost of short-term capital, such as withholding taxes, can help mitigate uncertainty from the external sector. However, the government must elevate its standards of supervision to improve the financial sector's efficiency. Regulation can be effective when regulators and inspectors are allowed to do their job independently, without political intervention. Therefore, macroeconomic policy makers must chart a course between stability and competitiveness.

2. Competition Policy

No matter how successful its reforms in the financial sector, Thailand will not be able to sustain economic growth in the long run if it ignores real sector upgrading.[17] Thailand experienced its first economic shock in 1996, when there was zero growth in the export sector. By the beginning of 1999, almost two years after the onset of the crisis, exports still had not grown as expected and the exchange rate had fallen by more than 20 percent.

Within the constraints of WTO rules and other trade agreements, the Thai government can promote industrial growth with fewer instruments of direct protection and subsidization. On the other hand, the private sector and officials must find means of handling the new instruments of international trade, such as the development of standards, antidumping measures, and so on.

Several manufacturing industries have been upgraded to medium-high technology through foreign direct investment. But the technological development, design, and brand name of these products are still predetermined in the country of origin. In the past, neither the government nor the private sector paid much attention to technological upgrading. Thailand's apparent comparative advantage in medium-high technology products was, therefore, based on low assembly costs or on cheap labor. However, this advantage vanished as wages increased continuously during the boom.

To increase and maintain competitiveness in the long run, therefore, government policy must help local firms succeed in real upgrading and in finding new market opportunities both regionally and globally. Technological upgrading requires human resource development. Education, training, and research development are the key issues that government policy must address to increase real sector competitiveness.

Agriculture, which is still an important sector in Thailand as a source of employment and of foreign currency, has been in crisis because of inefficient land and water management. The government should impose policies that lead to greater efficiency of land and water utilization.

3. Social Safety Net

In Thailand, the reliance on economic growth proved somewhat successful in reducing absolute poverty from the 1960s through the mid-1990s, but made no provision for the poor in times of uncertainty. Without any government-sponsored social safety net, the poor had to fend for themselves. During the crisis, they relied on personal relationships. Some laid-off workers, especially unskilled workers, returned to the rural areas where family relationships still existed.

At the same time, King Bhumibhol of Thailand attempted to assist the rural poor. In his birthday address on December 4, 1997, the monarch proclaimed: "To be a tiger is not that important, the most important thing is that we have sufficiently to meet our own need, and sufficient economy means sufficiency for self-supporting. Sufficient economy does not necessarily mean that every family must grow their own food, make their own clothes, but the village or the district must sufficiently produce to satisfy their own needs."[18] He then turned his attention to small farmers in Thailand, saying that if only one-fourth of them adopted more economical practices the country would survive future crises. The king's idea has been dubbed the "New Theory" of economic development.

Some economists have interpreted the king's suggestion as a way to immunize the economy against future crises. Many believe that such an immunization is crucial to survival in the emerging world of global competition.[19]

Although economic self-sufficiency has become a principal objective for the Interior Ministry, it is nonetheless regarded as a short-term policy. The government should implement a long-term policy to create a social safety net for the poor both in rural and urban areas to immunize the economy against future uncertainty.

State Adjustment under the Political Dilemma

Even though the crisis appeared first as an economic and financial crisis, it also exposed technocratic incompetence and failure. When Chuan replaced Chavalit as prime minister, Thailand appeared to gain several political advantages. First, the Chuan government had its base in the south and in Bangkok, areas where constituencies gave high priority to economic policy, whereas Chavalit had drawn most support from the poverty-stricken rural northeast. Second, partly as a result, Chuan's policy team displayed greater technical command of the issues at hand. And third, the new government could take office with a clean slate. The Chuan administration did not need to defend itself against blame for the crisis: This helped to calm the public's anger over previous policy errors. In turn, the patience of the Thai people helped the government concentrate on the work at hand without the distractions of protests or strikes. The public welcomed the Chuan government's finance minister and the new policy measures. Yet the process of implementation took a long time—while the economy, in contrast, went into a tailspin very quickly.

Meanwhile the bureaucracy under Chuan failed to perform efficiently. While the economy showed clear signs of recovery by mid-1999, its recovery was slower than expected. Nonperforming loans declined at a slower rate than in Korea and Malaysia, while the public debt rose dramatically. There was only a moderate expansion of credit. And while the financial sector underwent reform, the real sector—which had suffered a decline in competitiveness—continued to lag behind. In and of itself, financial reform could not achieve sustainable economic growth. The Chuan administration realized the importance of real sector reform; it was, however, too late. A dispirited public came to believe that Chuan's recovery policies were benefiting middle-class supporters and foreign investors more than Thailand's struggling masses. After three years in power, the Chuan government saw its popularity drop precipitously.

The political paradox of Thailand's democracy is that the rural majority chooses the government while the middle class retains the capability of ousting it.[20] Those who put the government into power are not the same as those who bring it down: There is a built-in veto mechanism. Moreover, these groups hold incompatible views of democracy.

For rural people, democracy is a means to bring greater benefits and official attention to themselves and their villages. Rural voters are not much concerned with political principles, policy issues, or perceptions of national interest. They vote on the basis of relationships between patrons and clients. For the educated middle class, however, democracy is a form of legitimate rule to recruit honest and capable persons, reflecting the Western concept of democracy.[21] Often, a government that favors the middle class has been called "a government for the rich, not for the poor." This political dilemma, which mirrors Thailand's economic dilemma, results in political instability that hinders reform. Although the middle class has consistently voiced its preference for greater political freedom and for a more democratic system of government, it has never learned to solve the political paradox that democracy cannot survive as long as the huge socioeconomic gap persists between urban and rural areas or between the rich and the poor.

An attempt to address the political dilemma through constitutional means has been made in recent years. Between 1932 and 1997 Thailand had no fewer than 15 constitutions. The 1997 constitution has been named the "Thai people's constitution" because the process of drafting it involved a great deal of public participation. This made the sixteenth constitution completely different from previous charters, most of which were drafted in close collaboration with military juntas. The 1997 constitution addresses the so-called social contract between the state and the people. In 1996, a 99-member constitutional Drafting Assembly was formed. One member was elected in each province, totaling 76 members; 23 additional members were appointed from political and academic circles. The draft of the present constitution was passed by the Parliament in October 1997. There are several key challenges to the new constitution. Public participation and access are encouraged: As a matter of fact, petitions with fifty thousand signatures are permitted to propose either legislative initiatives or dismissals of cabinet members or senior government officers.

In sum, the reform of the Thai constitution has been expected to increase not only the degree of democratization, but also the degree of decentralization and the degree of citizen participation. This should provide for a more equitable distribution of political as well as economic power among the people. And in these ways, it demonstrates that the ultimate solution to Thailand's crisis must be political as well as economic.

Notes

1. Ammar Siamwala, *Can a Developing Democracy Manage Its Macroeconomy? The Case of Thailand* (Bangkok: Thailand Development Research Institute, 1999).
2. Siamwala, *Can a Developing Democracy?*
3. Richard F. Doner and Ansil Ramsey, "Thailand: From Economic Miracle to Economic Crisis," in *Asian Contagion: The Causes and Consequences of a Financial Crisis,* ed. K. D. Jackson (Boulder, Colo.: Westview Press, 1999), 171–207.
4. Peter G. Warr, "Capital Mobility and the Thai Crisis" (paper presented to conference on International Capital Mobility and Domestic Economic Stability, Australian National University, July 1999), 5.
5. Warr, "Capital Mobility."
6. Peter G. Warr, "The Thai Economy," in *The Thai Economy in Transition,* ed. Peter G. Warr (Cambridge: Cambridge University Press, 1993), 1–80.

7. Karl D. Jackson, "Introduction: The Roots of the Crisis," in *Asian Contagion*, 1–27.
8. Ammar, *Developing Democracy*, 309.
9. Donor and Ramsay, "Thailand": and Ammar, *Developing Democracy*.
10. Ammar, *Developing Democracy*, 310.
11. Kitti Limskul, "The Financial and Economic Crisis in Thailand: Policy Response, Impact on the Social Sector, and Counter Measures" (Mimeo: Faculty of Economics, Chulalongkorn University, 1999).
12. Ammar, *Developing Democracy*.
13. Ammar, *Developing Democracy*.
14. National Economic and Social Development Board (NESDB), *Newsletter: Indicators of Well-being and Policy Analysis*, vol. 2, no. 4 (1998).
15. National Economic and Social Development Board (NESDB), *Newsletter: Indicators of Well-being and Policy Analysis*, vol. 3, no. 1 (1999).
16. Warr, "Capital Mobility and the Thai Crisis."
17. Donor and Ramsay, "Thailand."
18. English translation taken from Apichai Puntasen, "Reviewing ASEAN Economic Crisis: Lessons for Future Sustainable Development" (paper presented to conference on Globalization and the Economic Crisis in East Asia: Our Common Challenges, Center for Social Development Studies and the Japanese Studies Network, Thailand, March 1999).
19. Puntasen, "Reviewing ASEAN Economic Crisis."
20. Aneg Laothamatas, "A Tale of Two Democracies: Conflicting Perceptions of Elections and Democracy in Thailand," in *The Politics of Election in Southeast Asia*, ed. R. H. Taylor (New York: Cambridge University Press, 1996), 201–223.
21. Laothamatas, "A Tale of Two Democracies."

11

Korea's Recovery Program

Jaebong Ro

PRIOR TO 1996 THERE WERE NO CLEAR WARNING SIGNS of economic crisis in Korea. The only hint came from the current account, which recorded a negative balance throughout the early 1990s. Then Korea's trade account deficit dramatically rose from prevailing levels of 2–3 percent of GDP to 4.4 percent in 1996, as the price of semiconductors plummeted and the cost of imported petroleum started to climb. Foreign loans also loomed on the horizon. Long- and short-term liabilities rose steadily during the early 1990s and then soared suddenly upward, as repayable loans jumped from 24.2 percent of GDP in 1994 to 31.4 percent in 1996.

The financial sector was more fragile than it appeared. After adoption and implementation of the BIS standard for the ratio of assets to liabilities, it was reported that the ratio never fell below 8 percent.[1] However, it turned out that the BIS figures released by most banking institutions were misleading and did not fully reflect their financial condition. Through a variety of loopholes, the impairments of weak assets were hidden and inaccurate write-downs of impaired assets bulked up the BIS figure. After adjustment and correction, the BIS ratio dropped from 11 percent to 8 percent.

Another indication of the financial sector's ill health was the deteriorating earnings and finance structure of conglomerates, known as *chaebols*. Because most of the outstanding short-term and long-term loans were made to conglomerates, their ability to repay was pivotal to the creditors. During the early 1990s the Korean economy generally improved—but the earnings of the *chaebols* declined. Most conglomerates were criticized for overexpansion—via overborrowing—and for not focusing on their core businesses. This trend led to investments in low NPVs (net present values), which damaged the financial structure of the conglomerates and eventually led to their inability to repay their loans.

In late October 1996 Standard & Poor's suddenly lowered Korea's credit rating. Because of the chain of bankruptcies among *chaebols* and financial institutions, along with the government's ineffective efforts to improve the situation, S&P came to regard Korea as an unstable economic environment. This decision led to an increase in interest rates on foreign loans. Investment in Korea was swiftly withdrawn as the country's business stability came into question. Because of the small size of the Korean market, this rapid change in the flow of foreign direct investment (FDI) caused a foreign exchange crisis and created a panic situation.

And so Korea—widely deemed a "tiger" or a "miracle" because of its phenomenal economic growth—fell victim to Asia's financial crisis in late 1997. This triggered the most severe economic downturn in modern Korean history. It spared no sector, nor any individual, from hardship. As the number of nonperforming loans skyrocketed, financial institutions were unable to perform their basic functions, leading to the collapse of the *chaebols* that had been seen as the driving force behind Korea's economic expansion over the previous three decades. Foreign currency reserves were depleted so rapidly that the Korean economy was on the brink of issuing a debt moratorium. The once-proud Korean *won* depreciated, losing more than 50 percent of its value.

There was no shortage of finger-pointing. Some blamed overconsumption, while others criticized the overcapacity of Korean conglomerates. Some pointed to mismanagement by the Korean government, while others focused on the volatility of international capital flows. Academic research has noted that conglomerates lost their competitiveness and efficiency by focusing on expansion. Their massive borrowing and bad decision-making prevented them from repaying their loans. Banks and financial institutions were forced to declare bankruptcy, and economic turmoil became inevitable. The lowering of Korea's credit rating by S&P caused a panic that led to the rapid withdrawal of FDI. This, in turn, devaluated the Korean *won* and eventually provoked Korea's crisis.[2]

In retrospect, it appears that Korea's leadership has focused all its efforts on responding to the symptoms of the crisis—rather than to underlying causes. Foreign exchange reserves, as low as $3.9 billion in 1997, now exceed $96 billion. An economic downturn of 6.7 percent in 1998 turned to a positive rate of 10.9 percent for 1999. By restructuring the financial and corporate sectors and the labor market, Korea has eliminated inefficiency and factors leading to insolvency in order to gear up the economic system to truly accommodate a market economy. Nevertheless, there remains a series of latent factors of instability—such as concerns over delayed restructuring, reform fatigue within society, and collective egoism. In other words, Korea's economic reform is partial and incomplete. Major second-stage reforms must be pushed through. And if these changes are made, completion of the restructuring agenda and the consequent boost in growth potential will ensure stable economic growth in the years to come.

This chapter seeks to evaluate the government's effort in dealing with the financial crisis over the past three years from an unbiased perspective. It is my hope that this essay will contribute to the ongoing search in Korea for the most appropriate economic policy. Toward this end, I focus on the details of the restructuring needed in the major areas of the economy—including the financial, capital market, corporate, and labor sectors. I conclude with an examination of the government's actions to date.

Economic Turnaround—Spectacular but Incomplete

In the wake of the economic crisis, the principal indicators of Korea's economic conditions showed nothing but turmoil. Signs of a turnaround were surfacing by the end of 1998, however, the economy has since been on the road to recovery. The financial and foreign exchange markets have stabilized with the *won*/dollar exchange rate at the 1,200 level (down 40 percent from its peak of 1,964), and interest rates down significantly from over 20 percent to single digits. In addition, usable foreign reserves reached a record high of $96 billion in December 2000. Foreign investment has also improved a great deal. In December 2000, total FDI was about $15.7 billion, a 125.1 percent increase compared to the figures of the latter stages of 1997 (see table 11.1).

Meanwhile, total external liabilities decreased from $159 billion to $136 billion from 1997 to 2000 and the structure of external debt improved dramatically. The ratio of short-term liabilities dropped from 716.6 percent in

TABLE 11.1
Foreign Direct Investment in Korea, 1995–2000

	*(Units: US$ millions, %)**					
	1995	*1996*	*1997*	*1998*	*1999*	*2000*
$ Amount	1,947 (47.8%)	3,203 (64.5%)	6,971 (117.6%)	8,853 (27.0%)	15,541 (75.6%)	15,690 (1.0%)
N Cases	873 (35.1%)	967 (10.8%)	1,055 (9.0%)	1,400 (32.7%)	2,086 (50.1%)	4,140 (97.0%)

*Parentheses indicate percentage increase over previous year.
Source: Korean Ministry of Commerce, Industry and Energy.

November 1997 to around 46 percent by the end of 2000. Driven by continuous stock purchases by foreign investors and record low domestic interest rates, the Korea Stock Price Index (KOSPI) surpassed 1,509 points in January 2000, up from a low of 298 points in June 1998.

At the onset of the crisis, industrial production posted negative growth in 1998. In 1999 this figure rebounded to record high positive growth. In turn, the capacity utilization ratio in the manufacturing sector has increased steadily. This is in line with overall economic growth, which has resumed after contracting more than 6 percent in 1998. Another positive sign is a sizeable trade surplus, although it is shrinking in size (see table 11.2).

Not all indicators show improvement. The unemployment rate is currently lingering at over 4 percent and the number of unemployed has exceeded 890,000. These statistics are much higher than in 1995–96, just before the financial crisis. These developments have fueled a sharp increase in the demand for welfare benefits, which has further burdened the Korean economy. In addition, the structure of the trade surplus is very unhealthy. The huge trade surplus in 1998 was entirely attributable to decreased imports, as exports remained unchanged from the previous year. This dramatic drop in imports bodes especially ill for Korea, as its key industrial and export sectors are heavily reliant on imported raw material and capital goods. Thus, the drop in imports underscores the corporate sector's perception of dire straits and an ominous future.

Overview of Reforms

What was initially thought in 1997 to be a mere spillover or "contagion effect" from Southeast Asia revealed that the Korean economy possessed deep structural

TABLE 11.2
Major Economic Indicators for Korea, 1996–2000

	1996	*1997*	*1998*	*1999*	*2000*
GDP growth rate (%)	6.8	5.0	−6.7	10.9	8.8
Interest rate (%)	12.57	24.31	8.30	9.85	8.12
Industrial production (% change)	8.5	4.7	−6.5	24.2	16.8
Exports (US$ billions)	129.7	136.2	132.3	143.7	172.3
Imports (US$ billions)	150.3	144.6	93.3	119.8	160.5
Consumer price index (%)	4.9	4.5	7.5	0.8	2.3
Unemployment rate (%)	2.0	2.6	6.8	6.3	4.1
Average exchange rate (*won*/dollar)	844.20	1,415.20	1,207.80	1,145.40	1,259.70

Sources: Ministry of Finance and Economy, *Monthly Economic Trends,* various issues; Bureau of Statistics, *Korea's Major Economic Indicators,* various issues; and Bank of Korea, *Monthly Bulletin,* various issues.

problems. As foreign capital flowed out of the country, the need for fundamental reforms throughout the entire economy became inevitable. In response, the Korean government embarked on a rigorous, comprehensive reform program to revive the ailing economy and restore confidence. The main objective of the ongoing reforms in Korea has been the restoration of economic growth. While Korea may no longer be able to sustain the high growth rates of the past, realizing its potential economic growth rate is crucial.[3]

Another problem stems from the need to regain competitiveness. In the years preceding the crisis, Korea's productive efficiency continuously fell as wages climbed; technology development stagnated; and other factors, such as prices, interest rates, and real estate, remained above international levels. Restructuring and reform measures are needed to address these disturbing trends.

Meanwhile, Korea cannot overlook the ongoing liberalization of world markets. Globalization trends have become so pervasive that governments have been forced to reexamine their economic role. Policy makers have had to take into account many new limitations on their capacity. For instance, the WTO has severely restricted the government's ability to adjust or even maintain tariff rates. Further, all countries in the global economy are vulnerable to highly volatile international capital markets. Thus, financial and monetary policies cannot be effective without considering international conditions. Regional movements also affect government economic policy. Korea must alter some of its trade and investment policies to bring them into line with the Trade and Investment Liberalization and Facilitation (TILF) initiative of the Asia-Pacific Economic Cooperation forum (APEC).[4] Furthermore, the upcoming free trade agreement (FTA) between Korea and Chile will require changes in related policies. At the same time, the trade diversion effects of exclusive FTAs and regional trade compacts are topics of growing concern.

Korea's reforms to date have essentially sought to mitigate distortions stemming from inappropriate regulations and practices accumulated during the decades of high growth. First of all, financial markets have largely been closed off from the market mechanism and thus are not internationally competitive. Relatively heavy governmental control over the economy has inevitably been accompanied by unproductive political and bureaucratic influence. For instance, some large business groups ran their inefficient businesses with a "too-big-to-fail" mentality, based on implicit government guarantees of solvency. This mentality permeated decision-making on borrowing and lending. Since the financial crisis has decimated the capital structure, due diligence and other credit-based processes used in the past may require even more improvement. For such reasons the financial sector lies at the heart of Korea's restructuring and reform process.

Korea's domestic capital market has also remained somewhat closed to foreign investment. In recent years the government has deregulated much of the market, with a particular focus on improving the FDI environment. However, further deregulation is necessary in order to attract FDI, which can provide the capital and technology needed for sustained growth. At the same time, the regulatory framework should be reviewed and rebuilt. This does not imply the imposition of new regulations, but instead focuses on strengthening the supervisory function of various capital market agencies in order to monitor and prevent unhealthy practices and trends. In the early 1990s, the Korean government had a tendency to implement deregulation without instituting the necessary supervisory mechanisms. As a result, big business groups were able to finance their operations with an unhealthy amount of short-term loans from foreign financial institutions, contributing significantly to the financial crisis.

Another area requiring reform is the corporate sector. Excessive borrowing has notably weakened the financial status of Korean firms. In addition, inefficient corporate governance lets business owners avoid legal responsibility for operations over which they exert complete control. The government must strive to improve corporate management, not by direct intervention, but by a regulatory framework that enforces high standards.

The labor market needs to be addressed. Korean labor unions have gained notoriety in international investment circles, as they continue to pursue an interest in managing firms (in which they have no ownership), rather than concentrating on wages, welfare, and working conditions. The government should try to achieve social and political consensus to change such attitudes. At the same time, the social safety net should be enlarged to help workers forced out of work by ongoing corporate restructuring. Even after full recovery, unemployment is expected to remain at 4 percent, a level that will require an appropriate social welfare mechanism long after the crisis ends.

In addition to these sectoral reforms, Korea should consider further trade liberalization. Immediately prior to the crisis, Korea was vigorously pursuing trade liberalization; however, the financial crisis has forced the government to devote its efforts to more pressing demands. Now that there are signs of recovery, the government should return to its past trade liberalization policy. Further, such initiatives will open up more markets to Korea and improve its competitiveness in international markets. To demonstrate that it is a responsible member of the international community, Korea must ensure that it fully complies with international trade agreements, especially those of the WTO. Korea should also become more aggressive in pursuing both regional and bilateral cooperation. Regional initiatives should include cooperation in APEC, dialogue in partnership with ASEAN members, and cooperation in Northeast

Asia. Bilateral cooperation initiatives should look to Japan, Australia, and the United States as potential partners.

Restructuring the Financial Sector

As the principal trigger of the economic crisis in Korea, the financial sector has been the target of fundamental restructuring and major reforms. The objectives are to restore market confidence in the financial system and develop the sector into an international industry by enhancing its overall competitiveness. The Korean government has introduced measures to comply with international "best practices." Transparency is increasing new financial supervisory efforts and improving more strictly enforced accounting standards.

In 1998 Korea completed a major overhaul of the financial sector that affected both commercial banks and nonbank financial institutions. An unprecedented number of financial institutions have had their licenses revoked or operations suspended. In total, 96 banks and nonbank financial institutions were directly affected by the restructuring. During the initial stages of the economic crisis at the end of 1997, 13 of the 25 commercial banks satisfied the BIS ratio requirement of 8 percent. Upon review by the Financial Supervisory Commission (FSC) of the 12 banks failing to meet the BIS standard, five were deemed unviable and subsequently liquidated through purchases and acquisitions (P&A) in July 1998. The other seven banks were allowed to operate on the condition that they implement necessary corrective actions. In response to the government's efforts to reform banking institutions, the 20 remaining banks have embarked upon rigorous corrective measures imposed by the FSC, including disposal of nonperforming loans, new equity capital infusion, management reform, and mergers. By October 1998, four mergers had been announced, while two banks were to be sold in an open auction to foreign investors. Through the end of the following year, the government forced distressed banks out of the market through mergers, assets and liability transfers, and disposition of assets. The number of banks dropped from 33 in the latter stages of 1997 to 23 at the end of 1999.

Financial institutions that were deemed unhealthy but showed intent to survive were provided with public funding in hopes of promoting rehabilitation. At the end of 1999, public funds in the amount of 64 trillion *won* were created for the purpose of handling nonperforming loans and raising funds from the stock market. Of this amount, 45.2 trillion *won* and 18.8 trillion *won* were distributed to the banking sector and nonbank financial institutions, respectively.

Meanwhile, the first stage of restructuring came to a close in 1999, and moves for the second stage of restructuring were initiated in 2000. During this second stage, evaluations on the rehabilitation plan and self-sustained viability of banks were conducted and institutions with low viability were provided public funding to support incorporation into the finance holding company.

At the end of 2000, public funds worth 40 trillion *won* were set aside for the nonbanking sector and six banks to handle accumulated nonperforming loans. The more highly rated banks—those that did not receive public funding—plan to pursue expansion and efficiency through free market business activities such as mergers and acquisitions, establishment of subsidiaries, and aggressive use of CRV (corporate restructuring vehicles) to reduce ill-credit bonds.

In the case of nonbank financial institutions (NBFIs), the government has applied essentially the same restructuring principles from 1997 through 1999. The FSC initially conducted a thorough review of NBFIs and has closely monitored self-rehabilitation measures under the initiative of major shareholders. Institutions with inadequate plans for rehabilitation became subject to corrective measures or closure. By the end of October 1998, 36 NBFIs had their licenses revoked and 55 had licenses suspended. Six securities firms and six insurance companies, along with 325 merchant banks and mutual financing companies, were also cleared out from the market.

In 2000, the second stage of restructuring was well under way in the nonbanking sector. Merchant banks in financial distress were merged into Hananro Merchant Bank; market standards that would support these banks to transform into a single investment bank were designed and adopted. Also, prompt collective action (recommendations, standards, and enforcement in management) was applied to insurance companies and merchant banks that showed little potential for survival on their own.

Additional efforts focused on the modernization of the financial supervisory framework. In December 1997, financial reform laws were passed to unify all financial regulatory and supervisory functions under the FSC, functions previously dispersed between the Bank of Korea and the Ministry of Finance and Economy (MOFE).[5] In addition, the four financial regulatory agencies were formally consolidated into the Financial Supervisory Service (FSS) under the direction of the FSC. The ultimate goal of the FSC is to raise Korean financial supervision levels to international standards. In this endeavor, the FSC has set up new paradigms through the use of indirect regulatory methods, the negative-pledge system, and the application of transparent and objective principles in its practices.

To enhance the transparency of financial institutions, the FSC has adopted the mark-to-market accounting method, which values assets at their current market values. In addition, accounting standards for public disclosure and those for supervision, formerly integrated, are now administered separately. Moreover, the FSC has increased regular public disclosure items to the levels required by the International Accounting Standards. With regard to loans, the government has strengthened loan classification standards and provisioning requirements; in accordance with international standards, loans in arrears for three months or longer are classified as substandard or below, while loans in arrears between one and three months are classified as precautionary. The more conservative standard is essential for the better supervision of financial institutions (see table 11.3). In 1999, prompt collective action was applied to financially distressed banks to prevent financial insolvency, improve standards on security evaluation, and adopt forward-looking criteria that comply with international standards and reflect the debtor's true ability to repay.

The reforms in Korea's financial sector are truly monumental, and without the financial crisis they would not have been implemented so soon. Almost every conceivable reform measure has been implemented and, at least on paper, Korea's financial regulations and degree of liberalization are on a par with those of the most advanced nations. Difficult challenges nonetheless remain. First, Korea must confront the excessive number of remaining bad loans. Public funds worth 110 trillion *won* were consumed supporting banks in financial distress. In 1998, public funds worth 64 trillion *won* were created, but 40 trillion additionally created in 2000 due to the accumulation of nonperforming loans during the restructuring period. The accumulation was a result of passiveness in disposing of distressed financial firms, which naturally increases the tax burden on citizens. If financial and business reforms do not meet expectations, the business sector will further deteriorate and public revulsion will accumulate.

Widening loan exposure is also needed. According to one estimate, the ten largest conglomerates received more than half of all domestic loans in early 1999. Since banks were often heavily exposed through loans to only a few of the large *chaebols,* the bankruptcy of the Kia and Hanbo Groups triggered immediate and severe difficulties for several financial institutions. In addition, such loan concentration deprives even highly promising small and medium-sized enterprises of opportunities to finance their operations. Although improvement will take time, the number of loans to smaller-sized companies needs to be increased.

TABLE 11.3
Changes in Loan Classification Standards

Time overdue	*Old*	*New*
1–3 months	Normal	Precautionary
3–6 months	Precautionary	Substandard or Doubtful
6+ months	Substandard or Doubtful	Substandard or Doubtful

The informal but very close relationship between regulators and regulated financial institutions must be eliminated. The practice of hiring retired regulators to fill executive positions at financial institutions is widespread.[6] Such collusion has weakened supervision and lowered the efficiency of financial institutions. Changing the practice is difficult because it is pursued in a context of unstated but tacit favor-seeking. Even so, a determined government should be able to change the situation.

Capital Market Liberalization

The Korean government, recognizing the need to fully integrate its domestic capital market with global markets, has focused its strategy for developing capital markets on two interrelated policy initiatives: market liberalization and market augmentation. In the hope that market liberalization would directly increase Korea's access to foreign capital and technology (while market augmentation would improve the operational efficiency of the capital market), Korea in 1998 began implementing a rigorous plan to rapidly liberalize its capital markets. The government adopted many bold measures that year, including the elimination of the limit on foreign equity ownership and the removal of restrictions on foreign investments in bonds and short-term money market instruments.

The Korean government has actively sought to attract FDI. Accordingly, the investment climate in Korea has improved remarkably: hostile M&As were fully liberalized, restrictions on foreign exchange transactions were relaxed, and the real estate market was opened to foreign buyers. Furthermore, out of a total of 1,121 classified sectors, only 2 are still closed to FDI—which means that 99.8 percent of the Korean economy is open to the world. The 27 sectors that currently remain only partially opened will be further liberalized in the near future.

In its efforts to attract investment, the Korean government in November 1998 enacted the new Foreign Investment Promotion Act (FIPA), providing foreign investors with improved support services and increased incentives. The new FIPA streamlined and reorganized all previous FDI laws to increase investor convenience and provided greater autonomy to local governments in attracting FDI. With regard to investment promotion, one-stop service through the Korea Investment Service Center (KISC) at the Korea Trade-Investment Promotion Agency (KOTRA) has been established to facilitate FDI in Korea. Other measures, including tax exemptions and reductions, have also been instituted.

Although capital market liberalization contributed to removing cross-border barriers, more needs to be done to foster a more attractive FDI environment.

First, many complicated and vague regulations should be eliminated or clarified, since FDI-related areas like taxation, advertising, and banking continue to lack transparency. Also, regulations must be more strongly enforced. For instance, real estate owners often demand illegal side contracts to reduce their tax burden. Second, cost evaluation standards should be more clearly defined. Koreans often evaluate costs and prices on the basis of mixed standards derived from book value, personal contribution to the business, and a number of intangible factors. This differs from the Western method of using such standardized factors as cash flow, discount rate, and calculated forecasts. Without clear standards, foreign purchases of assets and M&A activity are less likely to take place. While the government cannot and should not intervene in the evaluation process of private firms, it can promote the adoption of such international standards.

Corporate Sector Reform

The economic crisis made corporate reform a top priority for the Korean government. This led to a wide range of new initiatives starting in late 1997. Corporate reforms have mainly focused on such areas as eliminating cross-debt guarantees, promoting transparency, strengthening the rights of shareholders, improving capital structure, and strengthening cooperation between small and large businesses.

Conglomerates were required to eliminate their existing cross-debt guarantees by March 2000, and since April 1998 have been prohibited from issuing new guarantees. To improve transparency, corporations were requested to produce consolidated financial statements (CFS) beginning in fiscal year 1999. As a result of these measures, internationally accepted standards of corporate transparency and accountability have been adopted. In addition, voting rights of minorities have been strengthened, as the representation requirement was reduced from 1 percent to 0.01 percent for class action suits. Moreover, the boards of listed companies since 1998 have been required to include at least one outside director.

Along with these measures, bankruptcy-related laws were streamlined in February 1998 to expedite the closure of nonviable companies. In May 1998, creditor banks established a formal review committee to assess the viability of 313 client firms showing signs of financial weakness. Upon completion of their evaluation, creditor banks listed 55 corporations as nonviable. To facilitate the closure of these nonviable corporations, their banks have been prohibited from extending them new credit. Financial assistance across affiliate companies for bailout has also been prohibited. In addition, in November 2000, the government downgraded the credit rating of 39 firms out of 38 in workout cases, 48 under court receivership, and 17 in cooperative lending. The creditor banks classified 52 out of 287 financially troubled firms as subject to potential closure (11 went into court receivership, 18 were liquidated, 20 were sold, and 3 were closed via merger).

Regarding workout programs for corporate debt, legal procedures related to corporate rehabilitation and bankruptcy filing were simplified to facilitate rulings on the closure of nonviable firms and to ensure better representation of creditor banks in the resolution process. In effect, these improvements reduced the complicated steps that previously required for closure proceedings.

Meanwhile, the government acknowledged the agreement on corporate restructuring among financial banking institutions (December 2000) to promote recovery and efficiency in handling noncollectable bonds and to adopt CRV standards (October 2000). Moreover, the prepackaged bankruptcy standard was implemented in early 2001 to swiftly handle financially afflicted firms.

A major goal of the government in reforming the corporate sector has been the restructuring of the conglomerates. The five largest conglomerates and creditor banks reached an agreement on debt reduction and other restructuring measures based on the agenda for conglomerate reform announced in early 1998. In early September of that year, the top five conglomerate leaders announced plans calling for the restructuring of key industrial sectors through mergers and business swaps referred to as "Big Deals" in Korea (table 11.4).

The Big Deals represent an expedient way for large conglomerates to focus on their core competencies, reduce overcapacity in key industries and overlapping investments, and create efficient management structures. All these deals were finalized in 1999 with the exception of the petrochemical industry. Currently, the petrochemical industry is still in the progress of self-initiated reform. The government is working to strengthen competition by making continuous efforts into advancing business skills and attracting foreign direct investment.

Although some progress has been made, more action is necessary in the corporate sector. Besides excessive debt and overcapacity, the most significant problem is corporate governance. The decision-making process at most conglomerates is highly concentrated, with the chairman frequently making decisions of great importance with little input or discussion. A good example is the case of the Samsung Group. Samsung was profitable with relatively little debt. Despite the fact that it had no expertise in the field, Samsung's owner decided to enter the automobile industry. The automobile market was already crowded and the production utilization ratio was about 50 percent. Samsung's large initial investment was financed by profitable firms within the group as

TABLE 11.4
Large-Scale Business Restructuring: Big Deals

	(As of end 1999)	
Industry	*Companies*	*Details*
Semiconductors	Hyundai Electronics and LG Semiconductor	Hyundai Electronics acquire LG microchip
Petrochemicals	Samsung Chemical and Hyundai Petrochemicals	Consortium with equal ownership
	SK and LG Chemical	Consortium in progress
Aerospace	Hyundai, Daewoo, and Samsung	The establishment of a public entity for the three *chaebols*
Rolling Stock Manufacturing	Hyundai Precision and Industries, Daewoo Heavy Industries, and Hanjin Industries	The establishment of a public entity for the three corporations
Power Plant Equipment	Hyundai, Samsung, and Korea Heavy Industries & Construction	Three corporations exchange assets
Vessel Engines	Samsung and Korea Heavy Industries & Construction	Korea Heavy to take over Samsung, establish an integrated public entity vessel engine production division
Oil Refining	Hyundai Oil Refining and Hanhwa Energy	Hyundai to take over Hanhwa

Source: Korean FSC website (www.fsc.or.kr/).

well as by cross-guaranteed debt. All the group's affiliates suffered major losses when the Samsung Motors experiment came to an ignominious end.

The government has been trying to improve corporate governance by reducing the limitless power of corporate owners. To this end, it recommends that conglomerates promote professional managers rather than owners to top executive ranks. In September 1999, a set of criteria on transparency that meet with global standards (i.e., OECD Principles of Corporate Governance) was established by the government. In addition, the Korea Stock Exchange formed standards for recognizing firms that demonstrate outstanding corporate governance.

Another problem is the tendency of almost all conglomerates toward business expansion and diversification rather than concentrating on their core businesses. For instance, heavily indebted Hyundai started a new tourism business in North Korea, planning to invest $900 million. This phenomenon produces the burden of both overfinancing and inefficient management.

Reforming the Labor Sector

The economic crisis has served as a reminder of the need for labor market reform in Korea. Recognizing that the inefficiency of the labor market undermines the economy's overall competitiveness, the government has focused on greater labor market flexibility, along with the creation of a social safety net.

Greater labor market flexibility was legally instituted with the revised Labor Standard Act (LSA) passed in February 1998, allowing layoffs attributable to managerial difficulties. This was a big step because implicit lifetime employment guarantees had been pervasive in Korea. Further, a provision of the revised LSA, the two-year grace period for employment adjustment for managerial reasons, was subsequently abolished, allowing for worker layoffs with sixty days' notice to the workers' representative or union. This amendment has facilitated necessary corporate sector restructuring and allowed firms to function more competitively. In addition, flexible work hours and the dispatched worker system were introduced.[7]

Aside from these reforms, the Korean government addressed the social impact of high unemployment. Priority has been given to projects with job-creating potential, such as public-works projects, and the promotion of major state-owned corporations and regional economic projects, with resources being drawn from the supplementary budget. Furthermore, a social safety net has been established for the unemployed. Various policies for job creation include the promotion of SMEs (small and medium enterprises) and venture firms, and financial support and tax benefits for business start-ups. Also, the provision of short-term jobs and reinforcement of vocational training are being implemented to enhance employment. Moreover the government increased the budget for basic living expenses, increased the work project budget for people on public assistance, began subsidizing school tuition, and has expanded social safety-net spending to 720 billion *won*—with 500 billion allotted to the poor (see table 11.5).

In the short term, job creation and the social safety net are important measures for dealing with the high unemployment rate. However, what ultimately must occur is a change in labor union practices that will promote labor flexibility. There is serious mistrust between organized labor and management. In order to remedy this, the government launched a Tripartite Commission in September 1999 for labor sector reforms consisting of labor, management, and government representatives. The efforts for reaching an agreement between labor and management materialized in the reduction of working hours (October 2000) and the follow-through of collective bargaining was assured by the government (December 2000).

TABLE 11.5
Extraordinary Unemployment Measures: Resources and Beneficiaries

Program	*Budgetary Allocation (100 million won)*	*No. of new jobs or beneficiaries (1,000 persons)*
1. Job creation	64,457[a]	233
2. Provision of short-term jobs	10,500	248
Jobs for the highly educated	2,552	51
Internships for high school graduates, etc.	948	34
Public works projects of local governments	7,000	163
3. Reinforcement of vocational training	1,028	(27)
4. Promotion of social safety net	7,208[b]	(323)
Total	83,193	481(350)

[a]Includes a supplementary budget of 11,509.
[b]Includes a supplementary budget of 2,561.
Note: Figures in parentheses refer to the numbers of beneficiaries from the program.
Source: Korean MOFE, "Trends of Government Revenue and Expenditure," February 1999.

Conclusion

It has been several years since the restructuring of the Korean economy began. The results have been mixed. Whereas reform in the capital market has proceeded at a rapid pace, with most of the remaining technical problems expected to be rectified soon, realizing full reforms in the financial sector will require more time and greater effort. In the case of the corporate and labor sectors, greater diligence on the government's part will be required. The efforts targeting corporations face resistance from the large business conglomerates, while the efforts targeting labor are often blocked by unions. Further hampering the reform effort is the fact that the government can not directly implement the needed changes. Therefore, it must instead try to persuade business and labor interests to participate.

In order to enhance these restructuring efforts, legal and regulatory reforms have been pursued with the goal of increasing transparency. Lack of transparency hinders supervision of the financial sector and discourages FDI. Greater transparency in both corporate- and labor-sector operations and regulations is needed. Strict implementation of laws and regulations governing businesses is also important. Some conglomerates have received preferential treatment from the government in the form of emergency and/or low-cost loans as they teetered on the edge of bankruptcy. This has reinforced belief in Korea's traditional "too-big-to-fail" maxim. Korea must eliminate any basis for the continuation of such a belief; otherwise it will be difficult to regain competitiveness.

The bureaucratic system also needs improvement. The Korean government should introduce new and creative ideas and expertise into its bureaucracy. To this end, the system of recruiting officials should be changed. Almost all high-level officials are presently recruited through an official examination. While this system is successful in the sense that it is based purely on merit, it fails to test creativity and specialized knowledge. Thus, the government should hire more contract-based, high-level officials from the private sector.

Meanwhile, political realities have often slowed reform efforts. For instance, politicians courting the labor vote may choose to block needed restructuring in the labor sector. Corporate sector restructuring may be delayed because of the special relationship between the business community and the political elite. This kind of political influence reduces economic efficiency while acting as an obstacle to restructuring efforts.

For Korea to overcome problems still lingering in the aftermath of the crisis, the government must exercise stronger governance while simultaneously fostering cooperation. In the case of the financial and capital sectors, where the markets have become increasingly interwoven on a global scale, it is beyond the power of a single national government to pursue effective reforms. Therefore, it is of great importance that Korea cooperate with other countries at the regional and international level. In this sense, initiating cooperation among countries requires a strong government role. Similarly, in order to strengthen the regulatory framework of the financial sector and establish a secure social safety net, the government needs to act aggressively. By contrast, deregulation of financial and capital markets essentially means relinquishing government control. The same applies to trade liberalization in the context of globalization. In order to simultaneously restructure corporate governance and deal with labor unions, the government must carve out a strong role for itself in directing, as opposed to directly controlling, the actual process.

Finally, since the various sectoral reforms are interrelated, the Korean government should prepare a comprehensive reform package. The nonperforming loans of financial institutions reflected the corporate sector's low profitability and vulnerable financial status. Thus, simultaneous action in both the corporate and financial sectors will be necessary if the reforms are to succeed. Similarly, improving the profitability of the corporate sector is related to labor market flexibility, and financial market restructuring is interconnected with capital market liberalization.

Lessons from the Korean Crisis

Soon after the financial crisis struck, the growth rate of the Korean economy plummeted from 5.0 percent in 1997 to negative 6.7 percent in 1998. The unemployment rate rose sharply from 2.6 percent in 1997 to 8.4 percent into the first quarter of 1999, causing extreme social instability. However, the solidarity of Koreans resulted in a surprisingly successful economic recovery from the crisis, recording a 10.9 percent growth rate within just one year after the eruption of the crisis. This experience yields some valuable lessons.

First, external balance and stability is as important as achievement of domestic macroeconomic goals. Given that financial crises occur when deepening external imbalance leads to the collapse of credibility, as in the form of a sudden capital outflow, there is need for a policy mix that aims at macroeconomic stability and balance both at home and abroad.

Second, although insolvent companies exited and the financial sector recovered its soundness due to public funding, it still remains necessary for companies and financial institutions to become profitable and competent on a sustainable basis. It is very likely that corporate and financial restructuring will be truly completed when insolvent economic actors turn into profitable and efficient actors.

Finally, it should be remembered that social cohesion is a key to successful restructuring. The unity and willingness of the Korean people in the early phase of the crisis made a substantial contribution to improving overseas credibility. Many Koreans responded to the drop in foreign reserves by donating personal valuables, especially gold, to the government; and despite the rise in unemployment, labor resisted the temptation to go out on strike. However, social unity is possible to crumble as a sense of weariness spreads over the whole of society, the income gap between the rich and the poor widens, and the lower-income class expands in absolute and relative magnitude.

Notes

1. The BIS ratio is used to assure that asset-liability ratio does not pose a threat of default.
2. Inseok Shin et al., "Korea's IMF Program—Three Years" (Seoul: Korea Institute for International Economic Policy, 2000).
3. The potential economic growth rate is estimated to be 3–5 percent, though predictions vary according to different models.
4. In November 1994, APEC members proposed to establish a free trade and investment regime in the Asia-Pacific region by no later than 2010 for industrialized economies and 2020 for developing economies; to expand and accelerate trade and investment facilitation programs; and to intensify development cooperation. See APEC Economic Committee, "The Impact of Trade Liberalization in APEC" (November 1997).
5. The dichotomy of regulatory structure resulted in inconsistent supervisory practices and inadequate coordination among regulatory bodies.
6. In Japan, this is called *amakudari*, or "descent from heaven."
7. A dispatched worker is a temporary employee on the payroll of an employment agency, but assigned to another employer. The labor unions voiced strong objections to adopting this system, citing its instability.

12

Currency Crises in Asia and Latin America

Shoji Nishijima

MARKET LIBERALIZATION SPREAD WIDELY THROUGHOUT developing countries during the 1990s. Fundamental policy reforms—privatization, deregulation, liberalization of trade and capital—progressed much faster than had been generally expected. In response to these reforms, an enormous amount of foreign capital flowed into these "emerging markets" and supported high economic growth with favorable macroeconomic performance. As an inevitable consequence of hasty liberalization, however, excessive dependence on foreign capital led to currency instability.

Beginning with Mexico in late 1994, a plague of currency crises moved around the world—striking Asia in 1997, Russia in 1998, and Brazil in 1999. But the causes and trajectories of these crises are not identical. In particular, there is a conspicuous difference between Asia and Latin America with respect to the contagion process. While the Brazilian crisis of 1999 had serious impacts on neighboring countries, it did not lead to widespread infection—as occurred in Asia—and the recovery process in Brazil was much faster and more vigorous than in Asian countries.

The purpose of this chapter is to analyze the currency crises in Asia and Latin America and the challenges for currency stabilization. I begin by describing the background of the currency crises and focus on inconsistent macroeconomic policies in the context of rapid liberalization. I introduce a theoretical model that incorporates both macro fundamentals and agents' expectations in the development of economic crises. The model implies that a deterioration of macro fundamentals would increase the likelihood of currency crisis through changes in the behavior of governments and private agents. I then offer a comparison of the macro fundamentals of five afflicted countries in Asia and Latin America, and emphasize the role of the banking sector in accounting differences between the two regions. A conclusion examines future tasks for the stabilization of national currencies.

Economic Reform and Currency Crisis

One of the crucial elements in the hasty process of policy reform in many developing countries is the simple fact that, by itself, innovation does not necessarily guarantee consistency in policy. For example, a combination of trade liberalization and fixed exchange rates (or dollar-peg systems) is likely to produce serious policy contradictions. By reducing risk, a fixed exchange-rate system was indispensable to Asian countries seeking to attract dollar-denominated investments, and it was also indispensable for Latin American countries as an anchor against inflation. Yet fixed exchange rates inevitably lead to currency appreciation, and that weakens international competitiveness. At the same time, trade liberalization generally increases imports much faster than exports, since it takes a good deal of time to improve export competitiveness through increased productivity and product differentiation. As a consequence of these two policies, the trade balance tends to deteriorate and sooner or later become unsustainable, a process that leads to market expectations about the collapse of the exchange rate regime.

Another inconsistency comes from the juxtaposition of capital liberalization and fixed exchange rates. A well-known theorem of open macroeconomics maintains that it is not possible to have free capital movements, fixed exchange rates, and an independent monetary policy at the same time.[1] Nevertheless, many of the countries stricken by crisis tried doggedly to do just that. In fact, capital liberalization opened the door for developing countries to attract foreign capital. Net resource flows (the sum of long-term debt, portfolio and equity investment, direct investment, and grants) increased dramatically from $35.3 billion in 1991 to $127.7 billion in 1997 in Asia, and from $30.7 billion in 1991 to $136.9 billion by 1998 in Latin America. But if capital inflows exceed current account deficits, as we shall see below, they tend to produce currency overvaluation, which makes it more difficult to sustain the fixed exchange rate. One way to avoid this dilemma—as in China, Malaysia, and Chile—is to impose some form of capital control; another is to abandon the fixed exchange rate. In this sense, the currency crises have helped to bring about necessary adjustments from fixed to flexible exchange-rate systems.

A third instance of policy inconsistency derives from the sequence of financial market liberalization. Many developing countries liberalized domestic financial markets by abolishing regulations and controls on financial institutions; such reforms were intended to eliminate deleterious policy distortions and to strengthen competition. But if financial markets are liberalized without building appropriate institutional frameworks—such as prudential regulations and an independent central bank—the resulting competition encourages over-lending and risky money-raising methods and tends to undermine the system as a result. In both Asia and Latin America, financial market liberalization preceded the imposition of vital institutional reforms. And if foreign capital is liberalized at the same time, the danger can only be magnified. Borrowing foreign capital in international markets inevitably includes the risk of devaluation. Once an exchange rate is devalued, indebtedness in terms of national currency will increase in direct proportion to the devaluation, which could lead to insolvency for financial institutions. Such instability has proven to be a crucial condition for speculative attacks on currency.

In sum, a currency crisis is virtually an inevitable result of hasty liberalization under two conditions: (1) if the reforms ignore potential contradictions between trade and financial policies, and (2) if the reforms do not include sufficient institutional safeguards to ensure prudent and disciplined behavior on the part of key players in the public and private sectors. In the following section, I examine alternative explanations for currency crises and introduce a conceptual synthesis.

Theoretical Analyses of Currency Crises

In the economics literature there are two types of arguments for explaining balance of payments crises or currency attacks. What might be called a first-generation model, developed by Paul Krugman, focused on macroeconomic fundamentals as a main cause of crisis.[2] The model describes a process in which poor macroeconomic fundamentals, resulting from inappropriate fiscal and monetary policy, produce macro imbalances that make the fixed exchange rate unsustainable. The model is very distinctive in the sense that it can explain a currency attack before the depletion of foreign reserves. It assumes that investors have precise knowledge not only of macro fundamentals but also of the "shadow exchange rate" (that is, the hypothetical exchange rate under a flexible system). Thus prescient investors could correctly predict whether they would gain from currency attack or not. Moreover, under the assumption of perfect foresight, it is possible to know the exact timing of currency attack by linearizing the model. One of the crucial implications of the Krugman analysis concerns the importance of establishing good macroeconomic fundamentals through sound fiscal and monetary policies.

The second-generation model, generally called a "self-fulfilling" model, emphasizes changes in the expectations of investors. One such study argues that a currency attack could lead to collapse of a fixed exchange-rate system even in an economy with sound macro fundamentals.[3] For one reason or another, investors may exert a concerted attack on a currency—either through explicit cooperation or through "herding," the term often used to describe a run on banks. Under these conditions the government is forced to devalue, and the crisis becomes self-fulfilling. The point of this model is that currency attacks can occur regardless of policy inconsistency or macroeconomic fundamentals, while the first-generation model explains crisis as a result of unsustainable macroeconomic policies. The second model generally has two equilibriums because of the assumption of imperfect foresight, but it cannot determine which equilibrium is realized (whether an attack occurs or not) depending on the extent of changes in investors' expectations and on exogenous contingent events.

It must be stressed that these two models are not contradictory; rather, they are complementary. If we acknowledge that investors' expectations are affected by "the state of the economy" (for instance, by the fundamentals), the two models can be reconciled. In fact, one of the contributions of the second-generation model is to open a way to understand currency crises by introducing the changes in investors' expectations that are influenced by the state of the economy.[4] Private agents generally form their expectations about a prospective change in the exchange-rate regime by observing the state of the economy. On the other hand, the government usually makes its decision about the exchange rates by looking at the state of the economy and at the private agents' expectations. Therefore bad fundaments tend to trigger a speculative attack, while good fundamentals tend to prevent it. In this sense, an incorporation of the state variables that reflect macroeconomic fundamentals into the second-generation models constitutes an appropriate and viable step.

A Synthesis of Currency Crisis Models

The basic idea for a model that combines macroeconomic foundations and investors' expectations comes from Sachs, Tornell, and Velasco.[5] Their work focuses on insufficient foreign reserves, exchange rate appreciation, and soundness of the banking system as crucial factors that affect expectations of private agents. They allow for the possibility of a multiple equilibria model by introducing behavioral assumptions for both governments and investors.

Consider a government that is managing a fixed exchange rate. The rate can be maintained as long as foreign reserves are sufficient to finance a capital outflow. But once the outflow exceeds the reserves, devaluation occurs;

the magnitude of the devaluation depends on the state of the economy in general and on the banking system in particular. As for private agents, it is assumed that capital movements depend on the anticipated exchange rate. In the event that the devaluation is expected to exceed a critical value, the investors initiate capital flight—and retain funds in the country as far as devaluation is expected to be less than the critical value. Under such assumptions, "there is a peculiar circularity here: the devaluation depends on a capital outflow, but the capital outflow depends on the expectation of a devaluation."[6]

As an appendix to this chapter I construct a simple formal model that takes account of this idea about the circular relationship between capital outflow and anticipated devaluation (see Technical Note). First I specify the dynamics of capital outflows and expected rate of devaluation, which raise the possibility of multiple equilibria. Then I introduce the critical values regarding capital outflow and expected rate of devaluation that are assumed to be influenced by macroeconomic fundamentals. The implication of the model is very straightforward: When macroeconomic fundamentals deteriorate, the possibility of crisis increases through changes in the critical value. The model can thus be regarded as a synthesis of the first- and second-generation models that captures the effects of macroeconomic fundamentals on the behavior of both governments and investors. Building upon these insights, the following section examines and compares the macro fundamentals of the Asian and Latin American countries that underwent currency crises during the 1990s.

Macro Fundamentals in Asia and Latin America

In the 1990s, a series of currency crises spread like a contagion through Asia and Latin America. But the causes and processes of the crises were not necessarily the same, reflecting the particular characteristics of each country. Table 12.1 compares various aspects of crises of five countries: Mexico, Thailand, Indonesia, Korea, and Brazil. Table 12.2 displays their macroeconomic indicators. It is apparent from these tables that the various crises had both common and divergent dimensions. I first examine the macroeconomic fundamentals that were common to the crisis countries.

Common Features

The first shared characteristic is that many of these countries adopted fixed exchange-rate systems, either outright or in the form of a system pegged to the dollar—a de facto fixed-exchange rate. Both Mexico and Brazil had adopted

TABLE 12.1
Currency Crises in Five Countries

	Mexico	*Thailand*	*Indonesia*	*Korea*	*Brazil*
Timing of crisis	December '94–March '95	July–December '97	October '97–June '98	November '97–January '98	January–May '99
Macro problems	Current account deficit, unsound banking system	Current account deficit, unsound banking system (bubble)	Unsound banking system	Excessive investment and unsound banking	Overvaluation and budget deficit system
Short-term foreign debts	*Tesobonos*	Borrowing of banks	Borrowing of private sectors	Borrowing of banks	Borrowing of private sectors
Foreign reserves	Depleted before devaluation	Lost in the futures market	Not depleted	Lost by debt payments of banking sector	Not depleted
Trigger to crisis	Capital flight	Speculation of hedge funds	Capital flight and contagion	Denial of rollover and contagion	Capital flight and contagion
Destabilizing factors	Lack of information about *Tesobonos* and expectation for default of bonds	Loss of forward position of Central Bank, and bad loans of private banks	Short-term debts of private sector, and presidential scandal	Short-term debts	Slow fiscal reforms and replacement of Central Bank president
Political risk	Presidential election (December '94)	Unstable condition	Presidential election (March '98)	Presidential election	Presidential election (October '98)
Warning signal	Rapid accumulation of *Tesobonos*	Burst of the bubble and bad loans	No particular signal	No particular signal	Capital flight after Russian crisis
Financial liberalization	During 1980s	In 1990s; opened BIBF in 1993	In 1970s	Maintained regulations	In 1990s
IMF rescue package	2/95 $51.6 billion	8/97 $17.2 billion	11/97, 1/98 $40.0 billion in total	12/97 $570 billion in total	11/98 $41.5 billion

Sources: Mexico, Thailand, Indonesia, and Korea: T. Itou, "Asian Currency Crisis and IMF," *Keizai Kenkyu,* Vol. 50, No.1, January 1999 (in Japanese), p. 89; and Brazil: S. Nishijima, and E. Tonooka, "Crise cambial brasileira: fundamentos vs. ataque auto realizável," *Kobe Economic & Business Review,* 44, March 2000.

TABLE 12.2
Major Macro Fundamentals in Five Countries

		Current Account/ GDP %	*Foreign Reserves (US$ billions)*	*Real Exchange Rates*	*Short-Term Debts/ Total %*	*Short-Term Debts/ Reserves %*	*Domestic Credit/ GDP %*
Mexico	1992	−6.90	19.2	0.680	21.8	128.0	31.3
	1993	−5.97	25.3	0.623	27.5	143.3	31.4
	1994	−7.21	6.4	1.000	28.1	610.5	34.5
	1995	−0.49	17.0	1.031	22.4	218.8	28.1
	1996	−0.69	19.5	0.777	19.1	154.0	17.0
	1997	−2.14	28.9	0.675	19.1	98.8	28.7
	1998	−4.19	31.9	0.724	17.2	86.3	26.6
Thailand	1994	−5.71	30.3	1.000	44.8	96.4	92.0
	1995	−8.23	36.9	0.928	49.5	111.3	99.5
	1996	−8.32	38.6	0.927	41.4	97.3	100.7
	1997	−2.03	26.9	1.627	37.2	129.5	132.7
	1998	12.63	29.5	1.127	27.3	79.6	133.0
Indonesia	1994	−1.64	13.3	1.000	18.1	146.1	50.6
	1995	−3.34	14.9	0.951	20.9	174.2	51.8
	1996	−3.46	19.4	0.917	25.0	166.2	54.2
	1997	−2.33	17.5	1.817	24.1	187.9	57.8
	1998	4.65	23.6	1.862	13.3	85.2	59.2
Korea	1994	−0.96	25.8	1.000	32.5	122.7	57.7
	1995	−1.74	32.8	0.938	54.3	142.1	56.6
	1996	−4.44	34.2	0.991	57.5	194.9	61.0
	1997	−1.72	20.4	1.915	39.3	262.8	69.4
	1998	12.8	52.1	1.213	20.2	54.0	79.0
Brazil	1994	−0.21	38.5	1.000	20.8	81.6	57.7
	1995	−2.62	51.5	0.730	19.2	59.2	36.6
	1996	−3.05	59.7	0.734	19.6	59.4	38.0
	1997	−3.79	51.7	0.729	17.4	66.6	40.0
	1998	−4.46	43.9	0.762	10.8	57.2	49.1

Source: IMF: International Financial Statistics, World Bank, *Global Development Finance, 2000.*

exchange rate bands (predetermined zones within which rates might fluctuate) prior to the attacks on their currencies. Thailand and Korea were working with currency "baskets" that were weighted 90 percent by the dollar. Indonesia adjusted its exchange rate to the dollar by use of a "crawling peg system," which allowed for gradual devaluations vis-à-vis the dollar. A dollar-peg system can play an effective role in the control of inflation, but it can also lead to massive capital inflow, since foreign investors usually are not cognizant of the exchange rate risks that exist under fixed exchange-rate systems.

Second, a fixed exchange-rate system tends to appreciate the value of domestic currency unless inflation is completely controlled. Moreover, if foreign capital inflow exceeds current account deficits, the excess dollars in the exchange markets lead to overvaluation of the domestic currency, which in turn exacerbates current account deficits. When the government tries to finance the current account deficits by stimulating capital inflow, the result will be a cycle of transactions that accelerate overvaluation and worsen current account deficits. When these deficits reach serious dimensions, or if capital inflows diminish for some reasons, foreign investors will then regard the dollar-peg system as unsustainable, and they will have incentives to launch a currency attack.

This seems to be what happened in the 1990s. Compared with the base year of 1994, in which the real exchange rate (given by the wholesale price index) is normalized to one, table 12.2 demonstrates that most of the afflicted countries had a large appreciation in the year preceding their crises: Mexico in 1993, Brazil in 1998, and Thailand and Indonesia in 1996. Korea, in contrast, did not show any sign of appreciation in 1996.

A third common feature is the fact that many of these countries experienced financial instability even before the currency crisis began. Even before the peso crisis, for example, the Mexican banking sector was vulnerable due to the liberalization and privatization of Mexico's financial sector. Financial liberalization in 1988 generated a rapid increase in bank lending stimulated by the boom in domestic consumption. That lending bubble eventually resulted in financial instability for Mexican banks because of the accumulation of nonperforming loans.

In Thailand, the asset bubble had already burst in 1996, bringing about a sharp decline in real estate and stock prices. Balance sheets of the banks that took part in the bubble economy had deteriorated considerably. Table 12.2 shows clear signs of the investment boom in Thailand, in which the domestic credit/GDP ratio increased sharply, from 92.0 percent in 1992 to 132.7 percent in 1997. Then the Thai economy turned. The Bangkok Bank of Commerce declared bankruptcy in 1996, and sixteen nonbank institutions collapsed in the following year. The Thai government injected huge amounts of liquidity into these financial institutions, but much of the money was simply lost in fruitless efforts to prolong the lives of collapsed institutions.

In Indonesia, the financial liberalization that began in 1988 stimulated the establishment of many new banks. But these new banks lacked adequate financial discipline, and they soon accumulated bad debts because of numerous fraudulent loans. Indonesia was just one among many countries that had already veered toward financial instability before the beginning of any currency crisis.

Fourth, the crisis countries depended too heavily on short-term capital. Excessive dependence on short-term portfolio investment is likely to lead to a currency crisis. A good example of this risky practice can be observed in the case of Mexico in the mid-1990s. Mexico received inflows of substantial amounts of capital that were invested in short-term government bonds such as *Cetes* (which were peso-denominated) and *Tesobonos* (which were dollar-denominated). By the end of 1994, the accumulated stock of *Tesobonos* reached $29 billion (with $17 billion held by foreign investors). And the share of short-term foreign debt compared to total foreign debt came to 28.1 percent. With this undue preponderance of short-term foreign debt, and also because of Mexico's political instability and an increase in the U.S. interest rates, investors soon came to anticipate the collapse of the Mexican exchange-rate regime. They reshuffled their portfolios from *Cetes* to *Tesobonos* and began to withdraw their capital in order to avoid exchange-rate risks. Subsequently, foreign reserves plummeted from $29.3 billion in February 1994 to around $17 billion by mid-1994. To make matters worse, when investors realized that nearly $10 billion in bonds were scheduled to mature in the first three months of 1995, they rushed to sell their Mexican bonds. Finally, with its foreign reserves nearly depleted, the Mexican government decided to adopt a flexible exchange-rate system.

Asian countries, on the other hand, had borrowed heavily from international banks, and the preponderance of that borrowing was in short-term debt. In 1996, for instance, the ratio of short-term debt to total debt reached 41.4 percent in Thailand and 57.5 percent in Korea (see table 12.2). This practice always raises a risk that is similar to the risk inherent in excessive short-term portfolio investment, as in the case of Mexico: Large-scale short-term debt makes a recipient country highly vulnerable to capital flight. Once international banks become reluctant to extend further credit or refuse to roll over short-term loans into longer-term loans, private agents who borrowed foreign money would face a liquidity shortage. This would, in turn, increase the expectation of a default, thereby leading to a sudden flight of capital.

Capital flight is also likely to occur when short-term debt exceeds the stock of foreign reserves. In Korea, most of the short-term debt was held by the banking sector, and its ratio to foreign reserves reached 260 percent when the currency crisis hit in 1997. Indonesia also had a very high ratio of short-term debt to foreign reserves, nearly 197.9 percent in 1997. Thailand opened an offshore market in 1993 and attracted huge amounts of foreign loans. Eventually, Thailand's ratio of short-term debt to foreign reserves reached 129.5 percent in 1997. In contrast, Latin American countries generally had a lower ratio of short-term debt to foreign reserves, particularly in the case of Brazil, which had a proportion of only 57.2 percent in the year preceding the currency crisis.

Crucial Differences

Although a substantial current account deficit is one of the best indicators of an impending crisis, there are still differences among countries in their sensitivities to this kind of imbalance. Mexico and Thailand had high current account deficits in the periods preceding their respective crises: 7.12 percent for Mexico in 1994 and 8.32 percent for Thailand in 1996. But other countries had smaller deficits: 3.46 percent for Indonesia in 1996, 4.44 percent for Korea in 1996, and 4.46 percent for Brazil in 1998. Most striking about Korea is the rapid growth of its deficit, from less than 1 percent in 1994 to 4.44 percent in 1996.

Second, there were differences in the level of foreign reserves held at the onset of crises. In Mexico, for example, foreign reserves were depleted by nearly $25 billion in 1994 alone, because the Mexican government tried to defend its fixed exchange rate by selling dollars. Thailand's reserves dwindled to $5 billion because of mismanagement in the forward exchange in the face of an attack on the Thai currency. On the other hand, Indonesia and Brazil maintained reasonable levels of reserves when they were forced to devalue.

Third, the types of investors who were responsible for capital flight differed among countries. In Mexico, these investors were mainly residents of Mexico, and they were generally more pessimistic than foreign investors. The Thai crisis was undoubtedly caused by speculation by foreign investors, especially managers of hedge funds. But there was no clear evidence of speculation by foreign investors in Korea and Indonesia. Indonesia suffered from the capital flight of overseas Chinese. In Korea, a crisis was triggered by the refusal of international banks to roll over its short-term debts.

Fourth, the character of the economic boom preceding the crises differed from country to country. As mentioned above, financial instability often preceded a currency crisis. In many cases, those financial instabilities resulted from a sudden collapse of an overheated economy. With the collapse of the asset bubble, Thai real estate and stock prices plunged sharply in 1996. The downdraft brought about numerous bank failures, as well as bankruptcies among nonbank financial institutions. In contrast, Mexico had a consumption boom, rather than an investment boom, led by the expanding importation of consumption goods from 1991 through 1994. This expansion was covered by concurrently expanding foreign capital inflows. Indonesia did not have a clear bubble, although there were some signs of an asset bubble, particularly in Jakarta. Korea had excessive investments by *chaebols* (large Korean business conglomerates) that caused the balance sheets of the banking sector to deteriorate. Brazil had a boom in the stock market, but not in real estate. These differences in the characteristics of boom economies played an essential role in the nature and course of subsequent crises.

Fifth, the timing of IMF rescue offerings varied from country to country. The IMF programs were implemented after the depletion of foreign reserves in Mexico and Thailand. But Indonesia received the IMF rescue money when it had rather large reserves and the macroeconomic situation was not particularly critical. Even so, after the implementation of the IMF program, speculation spread that the Indonesian government would not respect or could not honor its agreement with the IMF, and immediately the Indonesian currency, the *rupiah,* started to devalue. And there was another problem that was peculiar to Indonesia. When the IMF's recommended increase in energy prices was implemented, the political situation deteriorated rapidly and made the economy even more unstable. In Korea, the agreement with the IMF was concluded in December 1997, when foreign reserves had begun to decline sharply because international banks declined to roll over debts. Huge losses from Korean investments in Indonesia had a direct impact on the abrupt devaluation of the *won* in November 1997. And although Brazil suffered from huge capital flights after the Russian crisis of August 1998, it still had enough foreign reserves when the agreement with the IMF was concluded in November 1998. But the IMF program could not forestall the Brazilian currency crisis of January 1999.

Sixth, one of the important differences between Asian countries and Brazil lies in their respective fiscal positions. While Asian countries generally had fiscal surpluses, Brazil had continued to maintain large fiscal deficits: –7.2 percent of GDP in 1995, –5.9 percent in 1996, –6.1 percent in 1997, and –8.0 percent in 1998. These deficits diminished the credibility of Brazil's fiscal policies. Further exacerbated by the Russian crisis, capital flight became serious in the second half of 1998. But the Brazilian government was constrained from proactively allaying investors' anxieties over its fiscal situation because of political pressures that militated against remedial measures in the run-up to the Brazilian presidential election. With such a fiscal imbalance, the market predicted a resurgence of inflation that would make the dollar peg unsustainable. Even the agreement with the IMF about a rescue package could not calm the market's concerns. In January 1999, triggered by the dismissal of the president of the Brazilian central bank, investor anxiety reached its peak, and capital flight began in earnest. The crisis finally forced the Brazilian government to abandon its exchange-rate regime.

Through this comparison of Asia and Latin America, we have seen that there are both common and different elements to the causes and processes of their respective currency crises. But the soundness of their banking sectors is surely one of the most salient factors. Generally speaking, banking sectors in Asian countries have not been as healthy as are those in Latin America. This is especially so because many Latin American countries had already restructured their banking sectors in order to remedy financial instabilities that had emerged before 1997. This difference alone offers one of the most powerful explanations for differences in the course of (and recovery from) the currency crises of the 1990s. Although Brazil could not prevent the onset of the crisis, it managed to avert a deepening of the crisis because of healthy condition of its banks. Brazil did not go from currency crisis to banking crisis, as occurred in Asia, and as a result Brazil enjoyed a relatively smooth and speedy economic recovery. This relatively favorable experience is one of the most important reasons why the Latin American countries did not "catch" the crisis in the same way that it spread in Asia. (Argentina, Mexico, and Chile experienced only modest fallout from the Brazilian crisis.)

The Soundness of the Banking Sector

As shown by theoretical models and empirical evidence, when economic fundamentals deteriorate, the collapse of the exchange-rate regime becomes more likely. When we speak of the deterioration of fundamentals, we are referring to factors such as insufficient foreign reserves, overvalued exchange rates, an unsound banking system, current account deficits, massive capital inflow or outflow, budget deficits, and an excessive ratio of short-term debt to long-term debt. In this section, I now focus on the soundness of financial sectors.

There appears to be a two-way causal relationship between financial instability and currency crises.[7] As discussed in the preceding section, financial instability was one of the most significant causes of the currency crisis in Asia. But the equation runs in the opposite direction as well: In the Asian countries, the currency crisis provoked a serious banking crisis. Let us examine more closely the mutual causality between currency crisis and banking crisis.

From Banking Crisis to Currency Crisis

When a banking crisis hits, resident depositors and nonresident investors alike usually pull their resources out of home-country financial institutions and place them in less risky financial institutions in foreign countries. Such capital flight leads to the gradual (or sometimes abrupt) depletion of foreign reserves, rendering fixed exchange rates unsustainable. Particularly when investors are motivated by "herd behavior" or they behave in a concerted way in a speculative attack, capital flight tends to be serious.[8] Moreover, if the monetary authority acts as a "lender of last resort" to bail out banks, then the subsequent banking crisis will aggravate capital flight by providing enough resources (money) to buy foreign currency, thereby depleting foreign reserves.[9]

Second, financial liberalization without adequate and prudent regulation is likely to lead to excessive borrowing from foreign sources by both financial sectors and nonfinancial sectors alike. This practice is even more likely under a fixed exchange-rate system in particular, because the exchange-rate risk is not readily apparent. Therefore, banks are likely to borrow excessive money from abroad and lend it to domestic private sectors. Where possible, private enterprises themselves also seek to raise money directly from abroad. But foreign borrowing can quickly become disproportionate when asset prices are soaring. In Thailand the establishment of an offshore market (Bangkok International Banking Facilities, or BIBF) in 1993 significantly promoted capital inflow.

Investors are even more inclined to indulge in high-risk investments when credit is abundantly available. These high-risk investments naturally increase the number of nonperforming loans. The banks' balance sheets inevitably begin to deteriorate and the banks' credibility begins to decline. When credibility is lost, new borrowing or debt rollover becomes less readily available and the market begins to anticipate the imminent default of borrowers. If such expectations become pronounced, capital flight ensues. As more banks (and their private borrowers) become insolvent, the likelihood of a currency crisis will increase, especially as a result of deepening investor anxiety about the default of banks and their corporate clients.

Third, an unhealthy banking sector makes it difficult for monetary authorities to adopt necessary policy measures to defend the domestic currency. And the vitiation of that ability is particularly unfortunate because interest rate policy is one of the most useful measures against capital flight because it can attract foreign capital just by increasing the differential between domestic and foreign interest rates. When the banking sector is vulnerable, however, raising interest rates can have the effect of degrading banks' balance sheets by increasing insolvencies in the nonfinancial (corporate) sectors. These failures tend to produce nonperforming loans, which would, in sufficient numbers, ultimately bring about bank failure.

If the political and ideological setting does not permit such banking crises to follow their natural courses, the government must then perforce abandon its system of fixed exchange rates, rather than defending it by introducing tightening policies, such as raising interest rates. If investors correctly parse such government behavior, they will foresee an immense collapse of the fixed exchange-rate system, leading to a precipitous outflow of capital.

What forces can lead a nation's entire banking sector to become unstable and vulnerable? As discussed previously, there have been many instances in which hasty financial liberalization brought about the instability of banking sectors. Generally, financial liberalization has the salutary effects of eliminating policy distortions, increasing financial market competition, and improving resource allocations by applying greater efficiencies. From the standpoint of financial institutions, liberalization can allow them to benefit from higher profits while enjoying the advantages of "risk sharing" of their investments by diversifying both their operations and assets, and enhancing their "economy of scope." In reality, however, financial markets are usually incomplete due to factors such as asymmetric information, externalities, and so on. If the introduction of liberalization does not bring with it an institutional and regulatory framework that proscribes moral hazards for financial institutions, then an impetuous brand of liberalization surely will eventuate—and that outcome generally destabilizes the financial system.

Under the strong market competition brought about by liberalization, several risks are expected to increase:

1. *Credit risk:* Liberalization intensifies competition among financial institutions, thereby favoring a predilection for lending to high-risk, high-return projects that have a high probability of insolvency.
2. *Market risk:* Liberalization increases the volatility of asset prices, and could cause unexpected losses as a result of fluctuations in interest rates, exchange rates, and financial asset prices.
3. *Management risk:* Liberalization exposes and exaggerates the risks arising from any limitations of management capabilities (inadequate risk-screening abilities, excessive expansion of credit and operations, lack of in-house discipline, and so on).

As a result of the greater exposure to these various risks under haphazard liberalization, bad loans accumulate and banks' asset profiles deteriorate. When external capital markets are liberalized at the same time, domestic financial institutions actively acquire foreign currency funds in order to fortify their positions. These holdings naturally expose them to risks connected to fluctuations in exchange rates and foreign interest rates.

In many developing countries, financial liberalization in the 1980s and 1990s destabilized certain national financial markets because liberalization was not accompanied by the institutional structures necessary to establish a prudent financial system. Table 12.2 lists the ratio of domestic credit to GDP as an indicator of the soundness of several national banking sectors. Every country shows a clear sign of a lending boom in the years preceding the onset of crisis, implying a deterioration in the soundness of the banking sector.

From Currency Crisis to Banking Crisis

To reverse the equation once again, a currency crisis tends to aggravate instability in the banking sector, because exchange rate devaluations tend to increase foreign debt in terms of (devaluated) local currency held by local banks or corporations. In Mexico, Thailand, and Indonesia, currency crises propelled generally unsound banking practices into outright financial crises. This degeneration was given a further kick downward by substantial local devaluations, which magnified these countries' economic depressions and prolonged their recoveries. Table 12.3 shows the ratio of nonperforming loans to total loans for five countries. It clearly indicates that the ratio of nonperforming loans increased after a currency crisis, particularly in Thailand and Indonesia, where the ratios ballooned from less than 10 percent nonperforming to more than 50 percent. In Thailand, the banking sector held huge amounts of foreign debt, while the nonfinancial sector was the major debtor in Indonesia. In either case, devaluation reduced the solvency of the borrowers and led to the banking crisis.

The Brazilian case seems to be an exception. Brazil reduced its percentage of nonperforming debts from 10.5 percent before the crisis to 5.8 percent after the crisis. This fine performance shows a telling contrast with the dubious record of the Asian countries in this regard. Brazilian banks borrowed huge amounts of money from international banks in the 1990s. By the end of 1998, the total foreign debt owed by the Brazilian banking sector reached $52.7 billion. This amount was enough to cause the market to fear default by Brazilian banks if devaluation occurred. But in reality, Brazilian banks did not suffer losses from the devaluation in January 1999, because Brazil avoided exchange-rate risks by hedging in the futures markets and investing in dollar-indexed bonds. By the end of 1998, Brazil's total stock of dollar-indexed bonds was about $68 billion, of which banks held $65 billion. The point is that banks could gain huge windfall profits by

TABLE 12.3
Ratio of Nonperforming Loans to Total Loans

	Before Crisis	*Peak*	*Current*
Brazil	10.5% (12/98)	10.5% (12/98)	5.8% (12/00)
Mexico	7.3% (12/94)	12.2% (01/97)	17.6% (06/99)
Thailand	8.3% (06/97)	52.3% (05/99)	34.7% (11/00)
Indonesia	9.3% (03/97)	58.7% (12/98)	23.9% (11/00)
Korea	6.3% (09/97)	8.5% (03/99)	7.1% (09/00)

Source: Central Banks of each country and BIS, 70th Annual Report.

holding dollar-indexed bonds when devaluation occurred. Table 12.4 shows the profit rates of banks, which increased after devaluation. The data indicate that Brazil's banking sector managed to improve its financial position even in the face of a currency crisis.

Finally, we must consider the differences between the corporate sectors of Asia and Latin America. Their experiences through their respective currency crises figured heavily in accounting for the different courses assumed by Asia and Latin America in their banking crises. Latin America had a long history of high inflation that precluded the development of efficient financial intermediation. So the Latin American corporate sectors have not borrowed heavily from banks. This means that even though the corporate sectors drifted into insolvency due to devaluation, its effect on the banks' loan profiles would be relatively modest. This factor, perhaps more than any other, prevented the currency crisis from turning into a banking crisis in Latin America. In Asia, by contrast, corporations borrowed very heavily from banks. As a result, the insolvency of the corporate sector created difficulty for the banking sector through the accumulation of nonperforming loans.

Future Tasks

Theoretically, an economy cannot pursue a dollar-peg system, a liberalized capital market, and an independent monetary policy at the same time. With this rule in mind, a currency crisis that brings the demise of the dollar-peg system can be seen as an inevitable adjustment, ineluctably compelled by the incompatibility of these three policies. If this adjustment is large and sudden, then it is called a currency crisis. As mentioned previously, the five countries under consideration here made a determined effort to maintain these three

TABLE 12.4
Profitability of Banks Before and After Devaluation in Brazil

	Group 1		*Group 2*		*Group 3*		*Total*	
	1989	*1999*	*1989*	*1999*	*1989*	*1999*	*1989*	*1999*
Net Profit/Net Wealth (ratio of total value)	5.8	9.9	−15.6	17.1	−4.1	17.8	−0.3	13.3
Net Profit/Net Wealth (average)	6.3	9.8	6.3	14.4	6	10.2	6.1	10.8

Note: Figure for 1999 is the ratio of the first quarter of 1999 over that of 1998. Group 1 is the banks that have the gross wealth greater than 1.5% of the total gross wealth of the largest 176 banks, and 0.15% to 1.5% for Group 2, and less than 0.15% for Group 3.
Source: FGV, *Conjuntura Econômica*, Dezembro, 1999, 53, No. 12.

policies. Without exception, they all fell victim to the crises that plagued Asia and Latin America.

From this failure, there emerges a possible prescription to prevent the recurrence of such crises. The solution is to abandon at least one of these three policies. But the task is not quite that simple. In practical experience, three remedies have been attempted:

1. Adopting a flexible exchange-rate system in place of a dollar-peg system. This approach was followed by Mexico, Thailand, Indonesia, Korea, and Brazil after their currency crises.
2. Adopting a capital-control system while maintaining the dollar peg. China and Malaysia took this course after their currency crises; Chile did so until 1998.
3. Abandoning monetary policy independence, but maintaining the dollar peg. Hong Kong and Argentina applied this method, with the addition of a currency board system.

Capital liberalization generally improves resource allocation in both reforming countries and in the world as a whole. But there is a scenario in which capital control is justified from a macroeconomic point of view.[10] When an economy receives capital inflows that are substantially greater than the current account deficits, there is an excess supply of dollars in the exchange market. If a flexible exchange-rate system is adopted, the local currency would then appreciate. This would, in turn, lead to a further worsening of current account deficits.

One way to avoid such a dilemma is by adopting capital controls to restrict the further influx of capital. China introduced a system of capital controls before 1997, and when Malaysia returned to the fixed exchange-rate system, it adopted capital control in August of 1998. Chile implemented its *encaje* (deposit) plan arrangement to control short-term capital inflows in June of 1991. Under this arrangement, investors were obliged to deposit a specified proportion of their Chilean investment capital in the Central Bank for one year without interest (this proportion declined from 30 percent to 10 percent). This was considered to be a form of insurance against unproductive investments, such as lending and portfolio investment. In 1998 the *encaje* policy was abolished, but there still remains a great controversy as to its merits. According to the Economic Commission for Latin America and the Caribbean (ECLAC), *encaje* helped to contain short-term capital inflows and to preserve the terms of capital.[11] But the ECLAC study emphasized that Chile's sound banking system and strong macroeconomic fundamentals had played an important role in the success of the system.

Under a currency board system, the monetary base changes according to the changes in foreign reserves. Because of this mechanism, monetary policies are usually not considered to be entirely independent. (Nevertheless, currency boards have a strong antipathy to doing anything that might precipitate a currency crisis.) When capital outflow reduces the money supply, the system then recovers capital by increasing interest rates.

Argentina adopted a quasi–currency-board system in April of 1991. But the Argentine experience showed that currency boards do not necessarily possess the power to prevent currency crises. Argentina was subjected to serious speculative attacks during the Mexican and Brazilian crises. After the Brazilian crisis, the Argentine government was confronted with strong pressure from the market to abandon its currency board because of the shortage of foreign reserves and Argentina's lack of viability due to unfavorable macroeconomic conditions. The Argentine experience also yielded another lesson: Currency boards can only be effective in environments with strong macroeconomic fundamentals. Unfortunately, Argentina had difficulty in paying its foreign debts, and finally decided to adopt a flexible exchance-note system in February 2002.

Five of the countries that I have examined (and Argentina as well) are now under flexible exchange-rate systems. But that does not necessarily guarantee that the risk of currency crises has been eliminated. A currency crisis can be broadly viewed as excessive volatility of exchange rates, to such an extent that it might cause serious harm to an economy. And occasional, wide swings in exchange rates are not phenomena that can simply be legislated or administrated out of existence. Recall the turbulence of exchange rates in Indonesia, Korea, and Brazil, even after those countries changed to flexible exchange-rate regimes. Those countries still have much to do in order to secure the stability of their exchange rates.

Banking Reform and Regulation

In the preceding section, I underscored the importance of the soundness of the banking sector as a means to prevent or moderate currency crises. However, market imperfections (such as incomplete information) are particularly acute in Asia and Latin America. Due to the prevalence of insider information, unscrupulous dealings can be ubiquitous in the financial markets. Managers, shareholders, depositors, and even government and regulatory authorities are not always free from moral hazards. Therefore, regulation is necessary to control abuses. If such regulation is malfeasant, corrupt, or simply inadequate to the task, the well-being of the banks is endangered and the financial system may be destabilized.

The special vulnerability of banking systems is only magnified by poor corporate governance. And corrupt or incompetent administration of private banks is more readily permitted to persist in the presence of an underdeveloped legal and regulatory environment. When laws governing areas such as corporate activity, bankruptcy, contracts, and property rights are inadequate, then corporate misconduct may undermine lending discipline, leading to the increased incidence of bad debts and difficulties in recovering collateral. Regulatory reform in the areas of accounting systems and the disclosure of information are particularly important, as these provide information that is vital to the effective governance of a bank's financial condition and the extent of its risk-taking. Lastly, as a backstop to effective corporate administration of the banking system, legal regulatory authorities must be prepared to impose restraints or corrective measures on excesses, corruption, or malfeasance.

The stable and efficient functioning of a banking system that is capable of wielding effective financial intermediation and settlement requires several layers of regulation: (1) regulations to police unscrupulous or deleterious forms of competition, (2) regulations requiring sound management practices, (3) regulations requiring oversight and inspection by outside authorities, and (4) provisions for various safety nets. These may take the form of rescue loans extended to failing banks by central authorities acting as the lender of last resort; and deposit insurance, which can stabilize depositors' expectations; and so on. Prudent external regulation can reduce the risks in a bank's asset profiles and can assist in bringing sound management practices to bear by asserting control over a bank's balance sheet. These measures may entail the regulation of capital ratios, of large-scale lending practices, of liquidity reserves, and of prime-asset ratios.

Certainly, most of the national economies that I have discussed have suffered from periods of regulatory mayhem. For instance, Mexico went through its peso crisis at the end of 1994 and Brazil experienced financial instability after the Real Plan in 1994. Both of these crises occurred in relatively underdeveloped regulatory environments. Considerable progress has been made since then with the restructuring of financial systems. This reconstruction has taken several routes: by strengthening the supervisory functions of central authorities, by the introduction of prudential rules, and by the introduction of competitive spurs in the form of foreign banks that have been permitted to enter native financial arenas as a consequence of liberalization.

Although progress has been made in reinforcing the soundness of the banking systems in Asia and Latin America, there remains considerable room for improvement. Mexico in particular still has a serious fiscal burden from its restructuring program (known as FOBAPROA, *the Fondo Bancario de Protección de Ahorro*). On the other hand, the banking systems in the Asian countries have only recently initiated reforms after their recent currency crises, and they are still struggling with such ponderous problems as huge nonperforming loans. To create a sound banking system in Asia, special attention must be given to establishing prudential regulation, restructuring corporate sectors, developing well-run local banks, and determining appropriate levels of foreign debt.

Macroeconomic Stability

Under the flexible exchange-rate system, monetary policy is independent and it should play an important role in currency stabilization. Regulatory manipulation of interest rates and the money supply can be effective policy measures. Governments can and should implement monetary policies with the purpose of stabilizing prices and exchange rates. In Brazil, the government has pursued an "inflation-targeting policy," using its flexible exchange-rate system, rather than dollar pegging, as a price anchor. In this strategy, interest rate policy plays a key role. But the difficulty of calibrating optimal interest rates is compounded when investor anxiety rises to a high pitch over the government's excessive debt burden.[12] This problem must be resolved in a definitive way in order to restore investor faith in the Brazilian economy.

On the other hand, the Asian countries have enjoyed relatively stable macroeconomics due to their relatively propitious fiscal positions (especially when compared to Latin America). As long as the Asian countries develop sound banking systems and secure appropriate levels of capital inflow, they should be able to maintain macroeconomic stability without special difficulties.

When macroeconomic imbalance occurs, it becomes essential to identify correctly the underlying reasons for the imbalance in order to determine the best course of remediation. To understand this point, it may be useful to review the history of macroeconomic management in the Asian currency crisis of 1997. In response to the crisis, Asian countries implemented corrective policies prescribed by rescue programs agreed upon with the IMF. Traditional IMF rescue programs in the developing countries (mainly in Latin America) have assumed that macroeconomic instability is caused by large fiscal imbalances. The basic prescription recommended by the IMF for the treatment of the problem has been a combination of two reforms: tightening fiscal policy and devaluation. These measures were usually thought to be effective palliatives for economic ailments. But in the Asian crisis, the real reason for the problem was not excessive government spending, but private sector overinvestment supported by foreign borrowing. So the policy reforms required by the IMF agreements failed to restore economic health to the Asian countries. Instead, they deepened the depression caused by the crisis and accelerated the already plunging depreciation of the local currencies. After all, the traditional prescription offered by the IMF, which might have been an effective remedy for Latin American problems, was not the correct approach to relieve Asian economic ailments. And therefore, I must conclude that remedial policies in pursuit of macroeconomic stability can only be effective if they are applied in accordance with a correct analysis of the problem in the first place.

While a policy of very high interest rates (reaching 50 percent per year) was helpful to Brazil in preventing a resurgence of inflation and attracting foreign capital, it only contributed to economic depression in the Asian countries. Real world experience with various economic curatives has turned a spotlight on one overriding truth: Macroeconomic stability is the sine qua non to avert exchange rate turbulence and associated economic imbalances.

Domestic Savings

A fundamental cause of currency crises lies in the lack of sufficient domestic savings. Such accumulations of social capital are needed in order to build investment for development. Historically, the saving rates in Latin American countries have been very low relative to those in the Asian countries. The savings rates in countries such as South Korea and Malaysia exceed 35 percent; the corresponding rates in countries such as Mexico, Argentina, and Brazil are only around 20 percent. A low domestic savings rate means that investment necessary for development cannot be financed domestically, and therefore it must depend on foreign investment (which presumably has been made possible by the accumulation of savings in the country from which it came).

One key reason for the low savings rate in Latin America is the chronically high rate of inflation. In effect, inflation brings about the transfer of real income from the public to the government—this is the so-called inflation tax. And inflation has other effects: It causes a predilection for nonproductive investment in land and other real estate, U.S. dollars, and gold, while at the same time suppressing the propensity to hold financial assets such as savings deposits.

Another cause of low savings is a marked inequality of income. Those in low-income groups have insufficient funds for saving, while those in the high-income bracket have a strong tendency to hedge against inflation by investing in real estate or by investing their funds overseas. In order to encourage savings, it is necessary to construct an institutional framework for that purpose. For instance, Chile succeeded in increasing savings through privatization of its pension system. It is also essential for the efficient mobilization of capital resources to increase savings through the development of financial intermediation by banks and other institutions. Borrowing money from abroad is not itself an inherently harmful practice. But too much dependence on it can entail drawbacks, including the ultimate risk of destabilization.

Conclusion

The growing specter of recurrent currency crises is only one aspect of the problems visited upon Asia and Latin America under globalization. Certainly, economic liberalization has led to remarkable economic recoveries and dramatic increases in trade and investment in these regions. However, in most cases, reforms leading to liberalization have been implemented precipitately. And undue haste has brought with it economic and social problems—for example, rising unemployment, deepening inequality of income, financial instability, and currency crises. Of course, there is no guarantee that globalization will vouchsafe a wholly congenial outcome for Asia and Latin America. After all, the countries of these regions bring their own historical, social, and political backgrounds—and their own problems—to the table.

Unplanned and overly hasty economic liberalization has been shown to bring crisis and destabilization. These problems have made clear the need for the development of appropriate institutional frameworks and have underscored the importance of implementing policy in a consistent manner. Experience has shown that the liberalization process must be planned. And such plans must carefully take into account the background and unique characteristics of each country in order to tailor specific policies on the speed, scope, and sequencing of reform measures. This need-specific approach is clearly more useful than a one-size-fits-all uniform program that, in fact, fits no one individual country very well at all.

In the process of planning economic reforms for both Asia and Latin America, the most important factor that the liberalization process should take into account is social stability. This is particularly important because liberalization tends to create winners and losers whose newly exaggerated opposition might aggravate social instability. This unrest could undercut the liberalization process itself. In order to avert this sort of harmful rebound, policy makers in both the Asian and the Latin American countries must be prepared to devise programs that are congruent with the goals of social justice. They must be cognizant of the need to establish appropriate institutional frameworks to moderate the side effects of liberalization, and they must be apprised of the importance of implementing economic policies in a fully consistent manner.

Leaders in the private sector must improve their ability to adjust and respond to new and changing economic circumstances. To put it succinctly, leadership in both the public and private spheres must improve their governance in order for their nations and businesses to meet the exigencies of changing circumstances and derive the greatest common benefit from economic liberalization.

One can already begin to discern the outlines of changes in the attitudes and capabilities of governments and other institutions in both Asia and Latin America. These countries are now engaged in a process of consolidating the various institutional mechanisms of democracy, and their markets have been opened to global competition as a consequence of liberalization. The spread of democracy has encouraged wider popular participation in the political process. This broader democratization is effectively altering the political landscape: In such reformed political climates, no longer do the institutions of government and the private sector serve only the special interest groups and the privileged classes.

Progress is also being made in bringing institutional reforms to the public sector. These reforms consist of the establishment of institutional checks and balances among the forces of government. That is, these countries are restructuring their governments so as to divide authority between their legislative and executive branches and so as to promote the separation of powers at local as well as national levels.

The increasing integration of national economies into the global economy brings with it the spread of global standards and it compels newly globalized economies to face the necessity to change. In this new environment, private sectors now seek rules requiring fair competition, rather than government protection, as they did formerly. Government and other forms of bureaucratic institutions are driven to greater public openness in the conduct of their business. Under the day-to-day condition of greater institutional transparency, private agents can reduce transaction costs. In addition, citizens of these reforming countries are increasingly asserting their demands through group actions and the formation of voluntary organizations and NGOs. These organizations serve the social goal of monitoring the conduct of institutional leaders.

As public pressure to disclose information mounts, it becomes more difficult for old bureaucratic and political systems to monopolize power. Authoritarian figures who derived their power from former institutional bases are losing their legitimacy, and the scope for arbitrary behavior by bureaucrats is also being lost. Under the impact of these changes, societies are becoming more disciplined, and politicians and bureaucrats are being left with no choice but to abandon their opportunistic behavior.

In Asia and Latin America, the reform of governments and institutions through the strengthening of the rule of law has just begun. Through these changes, governments and institutions will be able to improve the quality of their governance and their capacity for devising and implementing correct macroeconomic policies.

Notes

1. See the Mundell-Fleming model in Rudiger Dornbusch, *Open Economy Macroeconomics* (New York: Basic Books, 1980).
2. P. Krugman, "A Model of Balance-of-Payments Crises," *Journal of Money, Credit, and Banking* 11, no. 3 (1979): 311–325.
3. M. Obstfeld, "Rational and Self-fulfilling Balance-of-Payments Crises," *American Economic Review* 76, no. 1 (1986): 72–81.
4. R. Flood and N. Marion, "Perspectives on the Recent Currency Crises Literature," *NBER Working Paper,* No.6380 (1998).
5. J. Sachs, A. Tornell, and A. Velasco, "Financial Crises in Emerging Markets: The Lessons from 1995," *Brookings Papers on Economic Activity,* 1 (1996): 147–215.
6. Sachs, Tornell, and Velasco, "Financial Crises," 157.
7. G. Kaminsky and C. Reinhart, "The Twin Crises: The Causes of Banking and Balance-of-Payments Problems," *Board of Governors of the Federal Reserve System* (1996). This article explores reciprocal causality between banking crises and currency crises with data from twenty countries from 1970 to 1995.
8. A. Devenow and I. Welch, "Rational Herding in Financial Economics," *European Economic Review* 40, nos. 3–5 (1996): 603–615.
9. R. Chan and A. Velasco, "Financial Crisis in Emerging Markets: A Canonical Model," *NBER Working Paper,* No.6606 (1998).
10. M. Dooley, "Capital Controls and Emerging Markets," *International Journal of Finance and Economics* 1, no. 3 (1996): 197–206.
11. Economic Commission for Latin America and the Caribbean (ECLAC), "Chilean Policy on Foreign Capital: A Focus on Encaje" (January 1999).
12. S. Nishijima and E. Tonooka, "Crise cambial brasileira: Fundamentos vs. ataque auto-realizável," *Kobe Economic & Business Review,* no. 44 (March 2000): 15–51.

Technical Note: A Synthetic Model for Currency Crises

Let us first specify the dynamics of capital outflows and expected rate of devaluation. Capital outflow K is assumed to increase when the actual expected rate of devaluation is greater than its long-run level $D(K)$, which would be established after adjustments at given K. Then, the adjustment process of capital outflow is specified as:

$$\dot{K} = \delta\ [D - D(K)],\ D'(K) > 0,\ D''(K) > 0 \tag{1}$$

where $\dot{K}$ is the change of capital outflows, δ is the adjustment coefficient, and $D(K)$ denotes the expected rate of devaluation in the long run after the completion of adjustments at given K. It is assumed that private agents know the correct level of $D(K)$. In other words, private agents decide on capital outflows considering the difference between the actual expected rate of devaluation and $D(K)$ as far as δ is positive, because $D > D(K)$ denotes a situation in which private agents are currently perceiving a higher possibility of the collapse of a fixed exchange rate regime in the near future.

On the other hand, the adjustment process of expectation about devaluation is given as:

$$\dot{D} = \lambda\ [K - K(D)],\ K'(D) > 0,\ K''(D) > 0 \tag{2}$$

where $\dot{D}$ is the change in expected rate of devaluation and λ is the adjustment coefficient. $K(D)$ represents capital outflows after the completion of adjustments at a given value of D. Private agents revise their expectations, taking account of the difference between the actual capital flows and $K(D)$ at some future point in time. When actual capital flows are greater than those in the long run, private agents foresee a more likely collapse of the exchange-rate regime, and thus they revise their expectations to anticipate a higher rate of devaluation.

Under such specifications, the system generally has two equilibrium conditions, and one cannot determine a priori which equilibrium state will take precedence: the lower equilibrium where the fixed exchange rate system is maintained, or the higher equilibrium where a speculative attack ensues. Moreover, the model is limited to predicting mutually exclusive outcomes: If one of the two equilibria is stable, the other must be unstable. This means that the system can describe only two outcomes: Either a fixed exchange rate is always maintained, or a speculative attack occurs. However, if we introduce two additional variables to the model—the critical levels of capital outflows and of the expected rate of devaluation—the system then has the capability of predicting two stable equilibria. In this state, the model predicts a situation in which both a sustained exchange rate and a speculative attack could occur, depending upon the nature and severity of contingent shocks (political instability, rumor, balance-of-payments crises in other countries, and so on).

Here we assume behavioral rules for private agents: There is, for them, a critical level of the expected rate of devaluation at which they decide whether or not to launch a speculative attack. If the agents' expectations exceed the critical level, they would decide in favor of an attack (with ensuing capital outflow). Of course this critical level depends on macro fundamentals, and it will be lower when fundamentals are unfavorable. The lower the level of foreign reserves, for instance, the lower is the critical level of the expected rate of devaluation by which the agents decide upon a speculative attack.

For its part, the government has a rule for determining whether to maintain or abandon the fixed exchange rate. If the actual level of capital outflows exceeds the critical level, the government has to abandon the fixed exchange rate. This critical level is also dependent on macro fundamentals: the worse the fundamentals, the lower the critical level.

Figure 12.1 shows the case in which the critical level about the expected rate of devaluation (D^*) is introduced to the process of adjustment of capital outflows. Formally, the meaning of the critical level is expressed by a change in the sign of the coefficient δ, depending on whether the actual expected rate of devaluation is greater than the critical level or not.

$$\text{If } D < D^*, \delta < 0.$$

$$\text{If } D^* < D, \delta > 0.$$

The negative sign of δ in the case of $D < D^*$ means that, even though the actual level of the expected rate of devaluation is greater than it would be in the long run, private agents do not increase their capital outflows (contrary to the adjustment process of equation 1), because they believe that the exchange rate will remain stable, since the actual level of expectation is lower than the critical level. By contrast, a positive sign for δ means that private agents become bearish and increase their capital outflows (thus initiating a speculative attack) in anticipation of a collapse of the exchange-rate system.

By linearizing equations 1 and 2, let us examine the stability condition

$$\begin{bmatrix} \dot{D} \\ \dot{K} \end{bmatrix} = \begin{bmatrix} -\lambda K'(D) & \lambda \\ \delta & -\delta D'(K) \end{bmatrix} \begin{bmatrix} D - D_0 \\ K - K_0 \end{bmatrix}$$

$$\text{Trace} = -\lambda K'(D) - \delta D'(K) < 0$$
$$\text{Determinant} = \lambda\delta[K'(D)\, D'(K) - 1]$$

where D_0 and K_0 denote the steady state of D and K. In figure 12.1, the equilibrium point B located in the area of $D^* < D$ is stable, because of $\lambda, \delta > 0$, $K'(D) > 1$, and $D'(K) > 1$, the stability condition, Trace < 0 and Determinant > 0, is satisfied. The equilibrium point A located in the area of $D < D^*$ is also stable as far as $|\lambda|$ is sufficiently large, because, from $\delta < 0$, $1 > K'(D)$,

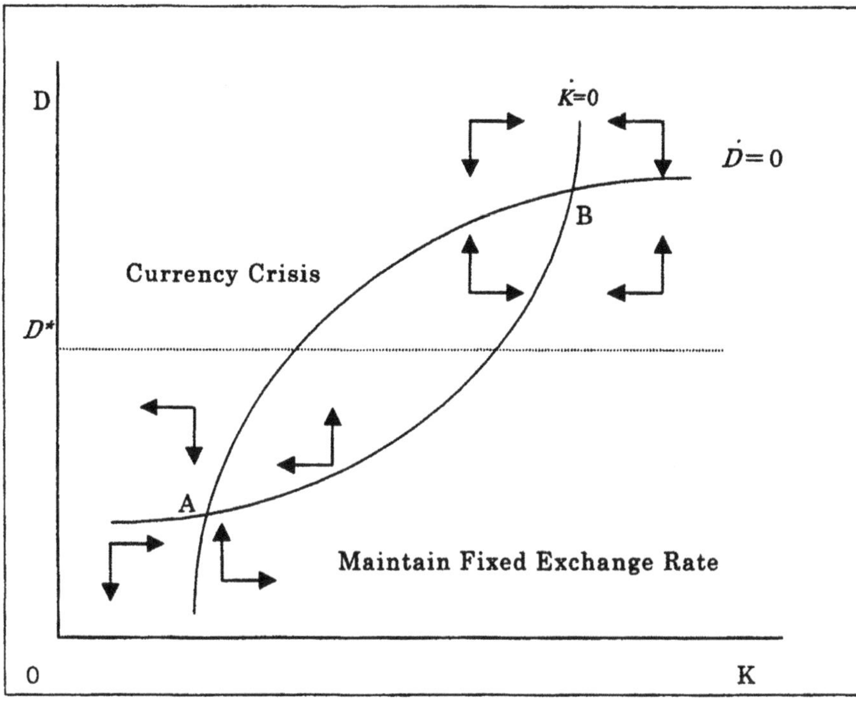

FIGURE 12.1
Two Stable Equilibria Model in the Case of D*
Source: Author.

and $1 > D'(K)$, the stability condition Trace < 0 and Determinant > 0 is guaranteed. Therefore by introducing a critical level of expected rate of devaluation, the model has the possibility that both equilibria would be stable.

From the model with two stable equilibrium conditions, we can derive several implications. Depending on the location of the starting point (initial condition) that is determined by a contingent event (see examples above), either a currency attack or maintenance of fixed exchange rate could result. If the starting point is in the area of "Currency Crisis" in the figure, it reaches to the equilibrium point B (where a currency attack would occur). On the other hand, if the starting point is in the area of "Maintenance of Fixed Exchange Rate," the equilibrium point A would be established (and a currency attack would not occur). Depending on the location of D^*, however, the probability of currency crisis or that of sustained fixed exchange rate would change. If D^* is located nearer to the origin (more downward in the graph), the initial condition is more likely to be located in the area denoting a currency attack.

The point here is that the critical level is dependent on speculators' collective assessment of performance of macro fundamentals such as foreign reserves, exchange rate overvaluation, the banking system, and the like. If the fundamentals are unfavorable, the critical level at which investors decide on a speculative attack would be lower (D^* line shifts downward), and the area denoting speculative attack would enlarge. Then the model implies that the probability of speculative attack would increase as fundamentals deteriorate, even at the same level of initial condition. On the contrary, when fundamentals improve, the area for currency attack contracts and the probability of a currency crisis will diminish.

Figure 12.2 shows the case in which the critical level of capital outflow K^* is introduced, and the sign of the adjustment coefficient λ in equation 2 is dependent on it. Following the same reasoning as in the previous case, the model can have two stable equilibrium conditions and predict a currency attack depending on the critical level of capital outflows. Here the critical level at which a government decides to abandon (or sustain) the fixed exchange-rate regime

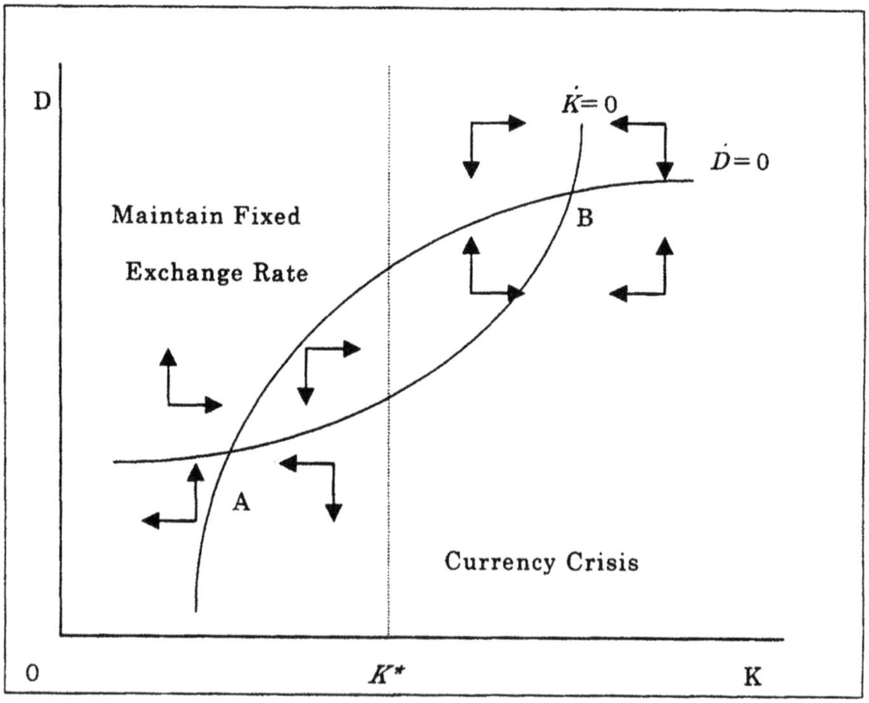

FIGURE 12.2
Two Stable Equilibria Model in the Case of K*
Source: Author.

is also affected by macroeconomic performance. When the fundamentals are weak, the government would decide to devalue at a lower level of capital outflows (K^* shifts to the left) and the likelihood of a currency crisis would increase. But here we must observe a caveat: Stability of the two equilibria is not guaranteed when both critical levels are introduced at the same time.

In sum, by introducing two concepts—critical levels regarding the expected rate of devaluation and of capital outflows—we have derived a simple model in a multiple equilibria framework that combines main features of first- and second-generation models. The new model thus represents a synthesis. Depending on the nature and the extent of contingent incidents, it predicts that both a currency attack and maintenance of fixed exchange rate system could occur. It also demonstrates that, by influencing the decisions of private agents and of governments, macrofundamentals play an important role in establishing or affecting the probability of the collapse of the exchange-rate system.

13

Searching for the Exits: Perspectives on Crisis Management

Gilson Schwartz

THE ASIAN AND LATIN AMERICAN CRISES have often been described either as part of a financial "contagion" process or as moments of a crisis affecting the foundations of the international financial system. Conversely, there is also a widespread, commonsense belief in the convergence of the global system toward perpetual and irreversible market-driven progress that will naturally encompass both developed and developing economies. From this perspective, crises in emerging markets reflect information asymmetries, imperfect or populist policies, and other, mostly local, institutional inefficiencies.

My purpose here is to explore these conflicting views through a comparative account of Asian and Latin American postcrisis strategies and agendas. An analysis of these crises and their recovery processes in terms of development models and economic policy regimes should lead to a new perspective. After all, ideological controversies aside, there is a fundamental structural dimension to the comparison between Asia and Latin America. This should be brought into the analysis as a nonfinancial element in the development of expectations concerning emerging markets (expectations relating to the introduction of new technologies, for instance, and to opportunities for private capital accumulation through large-scale privatization).

Deregulation on a global scale became the main policy regime of the 1980s, and the acceleration of cross-border transactions clearly derives from the growth and liberalization of trade and investment flows. Blown by the winds of competition and the need to operate on larger scales, banks and corporations were able to build truly global, real-time, online communication systems dedicated to the clearance of financial transfers.

Within this context, however, capital flight became more frequent by the late 1990s, while the volatility of capital flows increased as well. Open economies are obviously more exposed to the effects of these waves, so it is not by chance that such countries as China and India resisted contagion. And in the case of Malaysia, for instance, the centralization of exchange operations and a rapid and absolute suspension of foreign financial commitments proved to be efficient remedies; despite dire warnings from the critics, these measures did not lead to a permanent closing of the country to foreign investments.

Virtually all other developing countries engulfed in the neoliberal utopianism of the 1980s suffered from episodes of capital flight. The universality of the virus-like spread of the crisis did not prevent numerous authors, academics, policy makers, regulators, and businesspeople from blaming domestic factors as the source of trouble. A variety of different arguments emerged:

- Reform was not enough (fiscal reform in Brazil, reform of chaebols in South Korea, for instance).
- Deregulation and transparence/governance were not enough (asymmetries in information led to incorrect inputs in an otherwise correct decision-making paradigm).
- Multilateral financial institutions (such as the International Monetary Fund [IMF]) were inefficient or led to the aggravation of crises in Indonesia, South Korea, or Brazil (this view presents a variation of the "moral hazard" argument).
- A process of "overinvestment" exhausted the real marginal efficiency of capital (especially in Asia), along with a classical boom-and-bust cycle (involving speculation on land and real estate).
- Gains in competitiveness and the shift to an export-led model were not rapid enough (especially in Latin America).

The focus on local imbalances and/or inefficiencies is clearly reflected in the postcrisis agendas. However, it should be fruitful to examine the sequence of events in both regions in order to identify—as reflected in differences of approach and strategy—the likelihood of sustainable development models despite and beyond the financial crises. A comparative evaluation of postcrisis environments in Latin America and Asia can help lead to a more nuanced appreciation of the local versus global etiology of the financial crisis, and also toward a redefinition of development models that extend beyond the financial realm.

This chapter begins with a review of Latin America's recovery process, followed by a similar exercise for the Southeast Asian region. I then present a comparative framework, and final remarks address the nature of the crisis and possible ways out of the crisis in terms of development models and economic policy regimes.

Latin America

Latin America experienced the first financial disruption of the 1990s during the Mexican crisis of 1994. It also experienced the last emerging market crisis of the decade, during the Brazilian exchange rate crisis of January 1999.

During the 1990s Latin America was an eager follower of the "Washington consensus," adopting structural reforms in such areas as trade policy, financial liberalization, tax regimes, liberalization of external capital transactions, and privatization. (For some countries, these reforms began in the mid-1980s, and the Chilean experience dates back to the 1970s.) Leaders throughout the region embraced these changes once it became "accepted that the old model of state-directed, import-substituting industrialization was not sustainable and had to be replaced."[1]

Trade reform and domestic financial liberalization were the first measures to be widely adopted in the region, followed by capital account liberalization by the mid-1990s. Privatization and tax reforms have displayed less regional convergence. However, the ideological consensus became so strong that in 1997 the World Bank finally published a standard, recipe-like opus that mirrored and updated the older Washington consensus approach—*The Long March: A Reform Agenda for Latin America and the Caribbean in the Next Decade*.[2]

The depth of this ideological consensus is such that it encompasses both structural reform processes and macroeconomic policy regimes, even when analysts make a clear distinction between these two levels. For instance, Samuel Morley and his coauthors stress that "changes in macroeconomic management have succeeded in lowering inflation to the lowest level in 50 years and have restored the credibility of Latin America in the eyes of international lenders," so that "there is little controversy about these measures or about the fact that they have been successful." But then, shifting their focus, they contend that "that is not nearly as true of the structural reforms," since it is impossible to determine "whether the success of Argentina after 1990 is due to the Menem government's structural reforms or the fact that its macroeconomic reforms stopped hyperinflation."[3] This issue, conditioned by subjective evaluations, is a key aspect of the local versus global debate on the etiology of and remedies for the recurrent crises in the region or, for that matter, in emerging markets at large. I return to this question in final remarks of this chapter.

In point of fact, it was the abandonment of one fundamental rule of economic policy making that led to recoveries in one country after another: the departure from exchange rate target zones (also known as exchange rate "anchors"). The floating of the Mexican peso after the 1994 crisis provided an example of an alternative with relatively good results that came to be adopted by Brazil, Chile, Colombia, and Ecuador in 1999 (Ecuador being the exception in terms of aftershocks and the subsequent dollarization of its economy). Later, in 2001, Argentina felt the full force of a crisis of confidence in its fixed exchange rate regime. As the nation's economy was spiraling downward, there were two stark alternatives: outright dollarization or floating of the peso.

And yet this view does not pay due attention to the fact that at crucial moments, such as in Brazil in 1999, the currency float was not a matter of choice but rather a necessity in response to a speculative run against the *real* (even after an International Monetary Fund [IMF] package had come to the rescue of the frail exchange rate regime, a situation that occurred also in Asia).

Therefore, the "success" of the postcrisis regimes cannot be explained by the emergence of sustainable new models. Rather, it must be seen as a recovery led by new capital inflows aimed at devalued assets (such as insolvent companies and banks) or by the return of domestic capital after the abandonment of the wrong policy regime (in this case, looking for the financial gains guaranteed by high, defensive interest rates and the availability of a safety net that the IMF and other institutions could not suspend thereafter).

Moreover, economic performance has proved to be uneven in Latin America—Mexico was able to benefit from the still-burgeoning U.S. demand, whereas South American economies were subject to severe economic contractions. Moreover, the crisis in Argentina and the maintenance of high interest rates in Brazil indicate that the region is still far from entering a new, sustained phase of economic development.

From this perspective, it is clear that the financial crisis in the Southern Cone meant a severe deadlock for the Common Market of the South (MERCOSUR). This was essentially due to the extreme contradiction between the Argentine and the Brazilian exchange rate regimes (not only after the 1999 crisis of the *real* but mostly after the 2000–2001 confidence crisis affecting the peso). Under renewed external stress, Argentina resisted devaluation of the peso and contracted dramatically, jeopardizing fiscal adjustment and thus solvency and convertibility, while the Brazilian economy was able to adjust through movements of the exchange rate. (Flexibility has its limit, however, so Brazil's Central Bank maintains a very high real interest rate—this erodes the fiscal balance and can lead to renewed crises of confidence). This difference between the two countries not only undermined prospects for Argentine exports to Brazil, but also reduced investment in

Argentina—diverting companies to Brazilian locations, a tendency that could, in turn, lead to a reduction of intraregional trade. As political and economic crises mounted in late 2001/early 2002, Argentine authorities finally abandoned the dollar peg and permitted the peso to float. The peso promptly plummeted in international markets. At the same time, the devaluation reduced bilateral tensions with Brazil and may have strengthened the internal cohesion of MERCOSUR.

It is important to note, however, that the banking systems in Latin America were strengthened before the financial crisis of 1998–1999, probably as a result of improved supervisory and regulatory measures after the Mexican crisis of 1994–1995. These initiatives led to important restructuring policies and to the authorization of acquisitions by foreign financial institutions. In other words, banks and other financial institutions in Latin America, supported by state-led restructuring programs, adjusted more readily to external shocks and were able, as in Brazil, to become the actual beneficiaries of volatile capital flows, high interest rates on public debt, and changing market shares. This contrasts with the Asian crisis, which was more directly triggered by corporate governance problems and had a strong negative impact on regional banks.

At the same time, numerous analyses have stressed the role of foreign direct investment (FDI), especially those attracted by privatization processes and acquisition opportunities, in the performance of Latin American foreign accounts after the capital flight episodes. For optimists, this should be taken as the most promising sign of the irreversible integration of the region into the global economy. Such investments are seen as long-term commitments that give rise to increasingly sophisticated information systems that boost the region's economic potential.

For the skeptics, these FDI flows may be welcome from the perspective of productive globalization, but their consequences are riskier from a long-term financial standpoint. First, the available privatizable assets are finite and, given the frustration with and criticism of recent privatization processes, political opposition to privatization may grow. Moreover, even pro-market governments in Mexico and Chile have never privatized what they see as strategic assets for public finance and development strategies (like copper or financial institutions). Second, there is a rising concern about the sustainability of current development models, since past FDI will lead to future outflows (profit remittances, royalties and dividends, etc.) without a corresponding contribution to trade balance performance. This is particularly true with FDI, and privatizations have focused largely on infrastructure and the service sector.

In terms of foreign trade, the outlook is grim once oil exports (an item that favors Mexico and Venezuela, in particular) are factored out. As a result of the

Asian crisis, prices of Latin American commodities have been depressed, while the gradual recovery from the Mexican and Brazilian crises has led to the growth of imports.

Southeast Asia

Southeast Asia, much like Latin America, witnessed economic liberalization and rising FDI flows during the 1990s. While investment was drawn to Latin America as a result of structural reforms and macroeconomic stabilization, the attraction to Asia was based on the success of export-led models, the consistency of intraregional trade and investment flows, and the linkage to a global technological restructuring sustained by growing demand for electronic components (semiconductors). As a matter of fact, one of the reasons for the crisis in the region was the collapse of the microchips market in 1996. Moreover, during the 1990s, other exports faced growing competition from China, which devalued its exchange rate in 1994.

This linkage to a new generation of export-led industrial projects obviously contrasts with the Latin American dependence on privatization and FDI flows that targeted domestic markets. Although these structural features of development models in the two regions are therefore distinct, Asian governments also embarked on liberalization strategies that increased their exposure to global, volatile capital flows.

If there were exchange rate problems in Asia, they resulted from the widespread policy of pegging currencies to the U.S. dollar. Appreciation of the dollar (vis-à-vis the yen, for instance, which favored Japanese exports to the United States over Korean exports) began in 1995. By 1997, the dollar had appreciated by 50 percent with respect to the yen and by 23.9 percent with respect to the mark. South Korea, for instance, managed its exchange rate policy mostly with respect to the U.S. dollar. Exchange rate "anchors" in Asia therefore served not only as a subsidy for FDI, but also as an inducement for portfolio investments and credit. From this perspective, if both the Asian and Latin American crises reflected liquidity conditions in global financial markets, it was mostly the effect of capital inflows on the exchange rate that caused critical conditions to develop.

It must be stressed that, in this context, issues of corporate governance and structural reform in Asia became a priority (especially in the eyes of Western financial public and private institutions) only *after* the crisis, while concerns about institution-building and market-oriented reforms were expressed in Latin America *before* the crises (where these issues were mostly linked to the frailty of fiscal reform and to the persistence of inflation).

This circumstance could in itself leave room for doubt about the relevance of corporate governance—not only as an explanation for the crisis itself, but also as the most important factor in recovery (as compared with the determination of exchange rate regimes by global, short-term capital flows). In South Korea, for example, financial liberalization accelerated after 1995—yet without the necessary improvement in prudential regulation—as a result of the country's entry into the OECD.

This is not to say that governance issues as such are negligible or irrelevant. But it is necessary to emphasize the financial nature of the crisis in order to understand the recovery process. One important example is Korea, where the standard IMF recipe was abandoned very soon in favor of a three-part strategy that involved (a) rapidly declining interest rates in 1999, (b) socialization of losses through public debt issues in order to bail out the banking system, and (c) an export-led recovery that favored an early reduction of Korean liabilities with the IMF. Improved regulation of financial activities also contributed to the Korean recovery; in this respect, the function of the state as a lender of last resort has proved to be a key aspect of both Asian and Latin American recovery strategies.

The nature of regional integration projects and their resilience in the face of crisis also differ markedly in Asia and Latin America. While MERCOSUR was hard hit by the crisis and there is continuing skepticism about Argentina's economic policy, the crisis in Asia led to important initiatives that may extend and deepen the "open regionalism" approach to economic integration. One key development has been the reaction to inadequate policies proposed by the IMF and growing support for some type of Asian Monetary Fund. China, which initially opposed the idea, now supports it. The Philippines and Hong Kong are proposing the creation of a regional currency. Hence, there seems to exist clear progress toward the creation of new regional institutions in East Asia.[4]

Intraregional trade is also a key aspect of the Southeast Asian recovery. Intraregional exports, which accounted for 22.7 percent of total exports in 1990, were 31.8 percent of the total in 1999. Intraregional imports have risen from 21.6 percent to 32.3 percent of the total during the same period (in both cases, excluding trade with Japan, which accounted for 13.2 percent of exports and 22.4 percent of imports in 1999). In other words, almost half of Asian trade flows are intraregional. According to the Asian Development Bank, "intraregional trade has lent the recovery a welcome self-sustaining quality."[5]

Even so, FDI inflows are still below pre-crisis levels and, in this respect, questions about governance and confidence-building may exert considerable influence in the long term. This is especially true in face of the slowdown in the U.S. economy, which leads to a fall in the demand for Asian exports of manufactured goods and electronic components. Moreover, private capital flows are still very unequally distributed among the affected economies (FDI to Indonesia, the Philippines, and Thailand either slowed down or became more negative in 2000).

There is also considerable doubt as to the feasibility of a new "flying geese" phenomenon in regional development, due, for instance, to ASEAN countries' difficulties in "catching up" (especially in technology-intensive sectors) or to the entry of China into the World Trade Organization. (It must be stressed that Chinese competition was one of the external factors that explain the 1997–1998 crisis in Southeast Asian economies, so it is also likely that in the future, as China benefits from its World Trade Organization [WTO] entrance, investment will be directed to its territory).

One optimistic hypothesis is that capital flows will be lower for a long time to come, but that they will be of better quality—not only in terms of the types of flows and sectoral allocation, but also in terms of the quality of information underlying the decision-making process among investors. So far, however, it is clear that the recovery is far from complete. Bank loans, for instance, have not recovered since the 1997–1998 crisis and there are loan repayments yet to take place in the ongoing financial restructuring process.

Structural Issues

Conventional wisdom frequently espouses widely held beliefs related to Latin American and Asian "structural" imbalances and problems. One of the most common views is that Latin American countries lack savings. This has led, at different times, to reform proposals that favor liberalization of domestic financial markets, and especially to policies against so-called financial repression, a financial development model that initially developed with Asian economies in mind.

The practical consequence of these proposals has been the further opening of domestic banking systems, deregulation of capital markets, and chronically high interest rates. At the end of the day, these have not solved the "savings gap" anywhere. In Asia, financial liberalization, especially the accelerated liberalization and opening of capital markets, has been aptly described by many analysts as one of the major causes of speculative bubbles and mismanagement of financial institutions, not to mention exchange rate crises.

Within the Keynesian framework, at least, savings are a function of income, not of interest rates. Modest rates of economic growth and highly skewed patterns of income concentration, rather than institutional fragilities of the financial system, thus explain the low level of savings in Latin America. In other words, the insufficiency of savings can be traced back to equity and policy issues that are underestimated by the standard "low savings" argument.

Another common oversimplification differentiates the nature of governance problems: Asia is said to have a problem with governance of the private sector (corporate deficits, cross-shareholding among companies, cronyism, and the like), while Latin America has a problem with the public sector (such as fiscal deficits, corruption, and waste). This is clearly not a general rule: Brazil, for instance, stands out as one of the principal "cases" made by the IMF in terms of successful reforms of the public sector, especially with respect to accountability. The banking crisis in Brazil, on the other hand, made it clear that very serious governance problems could be identified in the private sector. Or take China, whose "domestic" financial system cannot be analyzed separately from the sizeable network of overseas Chinese capital. Other "anomalies" prevail both in Asia and Latin America: Chile imposed capital controls in order to fend off inflows that could lead to exchange rate appreciation, while Malaysia took emergency measures in order to reduce the dangers of capital flight. In both countries these unorthodox approaches have had quite positive effects, despite harsh criticism from orthodox economists and ultraliberal technocrats.

Perhaps the root of the "evil" in these simplifications lies in the U.S.–based perspective on what should be taken as a benchmark (or an ideal) for governance both in the private and in the public sector.

Looking for the "Way Out"

Recovery, which is probably occurring as fast as the events that precipitated the crisis, is due mostly to external conditions and should not be taken for granted either in Southeast Asia or in Latin America. Moreover, external risks are still relevant. In both regions, renewed depreciation or pressures on currencies, along with equity losses, have been recently mounting. The financial restructuring in Southeast Asia, moreover, involves not only financial institutions but, especially in the case of South Korea, a far-reaching restructuring of the corporate sector.

The "landing" of the U.S. economy remains the key common risk factor for developing economies. Although the "soft landing" scenario is still the most probable, an increased volatility in asset prices is also evident. The crises in Asia, Russia, and Latin America have provoked a "flight to quality" that could not be totally reversed in a global economy affected by rising interest rates in the U.S. and a depreciation of the euro. Paradoxically, the U.S. economy itself may be trapped in a speculative bubble further inflated by the crises in developing economies.

It is also possible that any "landing" in the U.S., hard or soft, would bring the recovery in developing economies to a halt, given the weight of the U.S. market in interregional trade. The depreciation of the euro and the slow recovery of Japan would be unlikely to offset the negative effects of a cooling U.S. economy.

In Latin America, the absence of industrial policies to foster trade balance performance, along with restrictive fiscal policies in the context of anti-inflationary policies, impose limits on economic recovery. In Asia, it might be argued that intraregional trade, along with corporate and banking restructuring, could support higher levels of economic growth even in the face of slowing global growth.

Perhaps for Asia the way out is "in": strengthening of domestic institutions containing the effects of the crisis through intraregional trade and investment flows, supported by an Asian Development Fund and by a new wave of Japanese and Chinese economic expansion. For Latin America the way out is not so clear: The Mexican economy is too dependent on U.S. markets, Argentina is locked in a self-destructive monetary regime, and the Brazilian domestic market cannot lead regional recovery, as became clear with the MERCOSUR stalemate. There is no self-evident solution.

Notes

1. Samuel A. Morley, R. Machado, and S. Pettinato, *Indexes of Structural Reform in Latin America*, Serie Reformas Económicas (Santiago, Chile: ECLAC, January 1999).
2. S. Javed Burki and Guillermo Perry, *The Long March: A Reform Agenda for Latin America and the Caribbean in the Next Decade* (Washington D.C.: World Bank, 1997).
3. Morley et al., *Indexes.*
4. Proposed by Japan in the wake of the 1997 crisis. See Fred Bergsten, *The New Asian Challenge* (Institute for International Economics, Working Paper 00-4, March 2000).
5. *Asia Recovery Report 2000* (Asian Development Bank, October 2000).

PART IV

THE ROLES OF MAJOR POWERS

PART IV TURNS TO GEOPOLITICAL ISSUES and the ways that leading powers—Japan, China, and the United States—might (or might not) affect prospects for closer collaboration between countries of Asia and Latin America. Unlike most analyses, this book examines and compares the foreign policies of these three countries both within and beyond their respective spheres of regional influence.

Keiichi Tsunekawa traces the recent history of Japanese policy toward Southeast Asia and Latin America, calls attention to the novelty of the Asia–Latin America connection, and emphasizes the ambiguity of Japan's position—as an Asian country and also as a close ally of the United States. He explains that Japanese decision-makers began to see the connections between policies toward Asia and Latin America as a result of concerns that the North American Free Trade Agreement (NAFTA) and the prospective Free Trade Area of the Americas (FTAA) might have a diverting effect on trade and investment. In response, Japan began moving to launch FTA talks with Mexico and Chile in 1999–2000. Japan's interest in the bi-regional relationship received a further boost from the creation of the Forum for East Asia–Latin American Cooperation (FEALAC) in 2001. Despite its vague initial goals, FEALAC can be seen as helping Japan coordinate its Asian and Latin American policies, and, notably, raise its foreign policy profile as distinct from that of the United States. While Japanese–U.S. ties remain vital and close, Japan's willingness to work within the ASEAN-plus-three framework and its reaching out to Latin America for economic ties signals perhaps a more assertive foreign policy line—and one especially tailored to meet new economic exigencies.

Jiang Shixue offers an overview of Chinese policy toward Latin America and the developing world, especially in anticipation of its own emergence as an international power. From the Chinese perspective, closer ties with Latin America have three foundations: shared hopes for a more equitable distribution of international power, the growing potential for trade and investment, and Beijing's concern over Latin America's diplomatic connections with Taiwan. For its part, Latin America can hardly afford to neglect China's massive market potential and increasing political weight in international affairs. The bilateral ties are, to be sure, constrained by geographical distance, the scarcity of transportation linkages, and widely distinct cultures and customs. Yet greater communication and trade links will eventually overcome these challenges. Sino–Latin America relations have a curious albeit unsurprising gateway—namely Cuba—but also a new lubricant, the Asia–Pacific Economic Cooperation (APEC) forum. Indeed, Shixue posits that APEC—rather than FEALAC—may well become the foremost conduit for building the economic and diplomatic ties between China and Latin America.

Peter Smith provides an analysis of U.S. foreign policy and its evolution in regard to Asia and Latin America in the aftermath of the Cold War. During the 1990s, he points out, geopolitical issues remained important in U.S. relations with Asia, while geoeconomic issues tended to dominate the inter-American agenda. Although U.S. policy lacked consistency and clarity, the United States wielded extraordinary power throughout the world—and the American public was largely unconcerned. That changed abruptly after the terrorist attacks of September 2001. The U.S. response to those attacks has been effective in ways, but it also raises deep questions about the future direction and extent of U.S. action. It is too early to say whether these developments will lead to formation of a new world order.

All in all, these chapters yield several hints about the likely shape of things to come: China is eager to enhance its relations with Latin America and other areas of the developing world; Japan wants both to strengthen new relations with Latin America and also retain close ties to the United States, and will try to avoid the need to choose between these two; and the United States is determined to maintain its global primacy, and has also come to recognize the merits of multilateral cooperation. The result is a complex panorama for nations of Asia, Latin America, and the developing world in search of a new and stable world order. It reminds us of the Chinese characters for "crisis"—one depicting danger, the other opportunity.

14

Japan and the Asia–Latin America Connection

Keiichi Tsunekawa

UNTIL RECENTLY, THE JAPANESE GOVERNMENT and private Japanese enterprises treated Asia and Latin America as separate policy targets rather than as a unified field of diplomatic and economic activities. The connections between the two regions had scarcely been considered due to the lack of well-developed economic and political relations. To be sure, modest economic connections between the two regions reach back to the sixteenth century, when galleons transported goods across the Pacific. In the nineteenth and early twentieth centuries many Chinese and Japanese migrated to Latin America. After World War II, Japanese corporations invested in natural resources and manufacturing in Latin America. Trade between Asia and Latin America has intensified since the early 1980s, but interregional trade is still very modest in comparison with intraregional trade (and in comparison with trade between individual Asian or Latin American countries and the United States). As a result, Japanese leaders have not found it necessary to devise a policy regarding closer relations between Asia and Latin America—until now.

The advent of NAFTA, the North American Free Trade Agreement, finally compelled Japanese leaders to consider the need for connecting their Asian and Latin American policies. The conclusion of NAFTA and the prospect of the even broader Free Trade Agreement of the Americas (FTAA), which would bring about the economic integration of practically the entire Western Hemisphere, made Japanese leaders worry that trade and investment would be diverted from Asia to Latin America. In fact, some Japanese corporations, especially the makers of electric and electronic products, relocated some of their plants from Southeast Asia to Mexico. South Korean and Taiwanese companies also increased their investments in Mexico.

In practice, the loss of trade and investments as a result of NAFTA was less egregious than expected by some authorities. That was due to the fact that, among other reasons, Asian economies were growing rapidly at the time of the initiation of NAFTA. Moreover, the prospect of the formation of the FTAA waned due to the Clinton administration's failure to obtain authorization for fast-track negotiations from Congress. In the meanwhile, the financial crisis that hit Asia in 1997 and 1998 forced Japanese leaders in both the public and private sectors to concentrate on the recovery of the Asian economies. Consequently, they set aside their concerns about Latin America for a while. Nevertheless, the concern about an exclusive trading zone in the Americas continued to linger among Japanese and Asian leaders.

In December 1998, at the second meeting of the heads of the governments of "ASEAN-plus-three" (the ASEAN countries plus Japan, China, and South Korea), Singapore Prime Minister Goh Chok Tong proposed a new forum for dialogue between Asia and Latin America. The Japanese government agreed to the idea in principle, although without much enthusiasm. However, the formation of the interregional forum that came to be named Forum for East Asia–Latin America Cooperation (FEALAC) persuaded the Japanese government to consider further the relationship between the two regions, along with Japan's role in the formulation of that relationship. The process of policy formulation has only recently gotten under way. Therefore, this paper will limit its analysis to the consideration of possible Japanese policy regarding interactions between Asia and Latin America.

In the following section, I trace the process of the formation of FEALAC. It will be shown that the member countries discovered that their initial concern was not so much to facilitate cooperation based on well-defined common interests, as is typical in such negotiations. Rather, they determined that their role was to discover and define what their common interests were in the first place. This chapter then turns to a review of Japan's foreign policy and its evolution over the past fifty years. Next, I consider how Japan has applied its policies toward Asia on the one hand and Latin America on the other. Finally, I discuss how Japan's policy toward FEALAC compares to the general pattern of Japanese foreign policy. In that discussion, I give special emphasis to identifying what particular interest Japan has in the further development of Asian–Latin American relations.

The Meaning of FEALAC

During a visit to Chile in September 1998, Prime Minister Goh Chok Tong of Singapore became the first national leader to propose an interregional forum between Asia and Latin America. (Goh Chok Tong had, on a prior occasion, advocated the formation of an earlier interregional forum. When he visited France in 1994, he proposed ASEM—the Asia-Europe Meeting). Expressing his support for the Asia–Latin American conference, Singapore's Foreign Minister Jayakumar characterized the purpose of the proposed forum as being to connect the "missing link" and to exploit the "enormous economic potential" of the two regions.[1]

Two months later, and with Chilean President Eduardo Frei's full endorsement, Mr. Goh offered his proposal to found the new forum to the heads of the governments of the ASEAN-plus-three. They decided to accept Mr. Goh's proposal and subsequently assigned their respective foreign ministries the job of exploring the agenda and the methods of the proposed forum. The first Senior Officials' Meeting (SOM) was held at Singapore in September of 1999 to discuss those subjects. Twelve Latin American countries (the Rio Group) and fifteen Asian countries were invited to the meeting, which was, at that time, called East Asia–Latin America Forum (EALAF). The Asian delegation was larger than the original ASEAN-plus-three because Australia and New Zealand had also been invited.[2]

In contrast to the ASEM meetings, there was a conspicuous lack of enthusiasm among the participants of EALAF, as testified by the way that the latter was formed. First, unlike EALAF, ASEM was planned from the outset to be a meeting of the heads of the member governments, rather than officials at the ministerial level. The meetings of foreign ministers, finance ministers, and trade affairs ministers were arranged only after the first summit, which was held in March of 1996. In contrast, EALAF was intended to be no more than a meeting of foreign ministers.

Second, only seventeen months elapsed between Goh's proposal at Paris and the first ASEM summit, while the preparation for the first foreign ministers' meeting of EALAF (in March 2001) took two and a half years. At this meeting, in which three more countries from Latin America (Costa Rica, El Salvador, and Cuba) were admitted as members and the participants agreed to change the name of the entity to FEALAC, thirteen out of thirty member countries including Japan failed to send their foreign ministers.

Third, the membership of ASEM was discussed intensively from the beginning and was determined before the first summit meeting. Initially, Japan wanted to invite Australia and New Zealand but was strongly opposed by Malaysia, presumably because membership in ASEM was regarded to have more than just a symbolic meaning. [3] The ASEAN-plus-three resemble the putative members of Mahathir's controversial East Asia Economic Group (EAEG). The exclusion of Australia and New Zealand, therefore, could be seen to imply that the membership could reserve the right to apply exclusionary tactics in any of its decisions. Ultimately Japan backed down and Australia and New Zealand were excluded after all.

In contrast, no serious discussion seems to have taken place before Australia and New Zealand were admitted to FEALAC. However, as late as August of 2000 (almost two years after Goh first made his proposal), at the second SOM in Santiago, Malaysia once again raised the issue of exclusiveness. This time, Malaysia broached the issue by questioning the proposed name of the organization. Malaysia argued that the use of the expression "East Asia" was not appropriate since two "non-Asian" countries (Australia and New Zealand) were included. Other countries did not support Malaysia this time, but the episode demonstrated that FEALAC was launched without a serious discussion of the nature of its constituency.

Even after holding two SOMs, the group still could not agree upon a formal document that defined its agenda and its purposes. The original framework paper prepared by Singapore stated that the "purpose of the Forum is to promote better understanding, dialogue, and cooperation so as to achieve more effective and fruitful relations between the two regions." The paper listed three "key objectives," defined as follows: to (1) increase mutual understanding, trust, dialogue, and friendly cooperation; (2) tap the potential of cooperation in economics, trade, investment, finance, science and technology, environmental protection, culture, sports, and people-to-people exchanges; and (3) expand common ground on important international political and economic issues.[4] This document points to broad issues but offers no concrete proposals. Rather than addressing specific matters, forum participants merely agreed at the first SOM, and confirmed at the second SOM and at the first foreign ministers' meeting, that individual countries would realize "national projects" voluntarily. These projects ranged from the building of databases to a journalist exchange program. Under such circumstances, the commitment of the member countries was very limited.

Japan made only two modest proposals for FEALAC, neither of which revealed any great sense of urgency on the part of the Japanese. One was the expansion of the Japan-Singapore Partnership Program for the 21st Century, in which trainees would be invited not only from Asian but also from Latin American countries to attend training courses on finance, information technology (IT), and small- and medium-sized enterprises. The other proposal was to convene symposiums of intellectuals from both regions that would explore measures to cope with common problems and to expand inter-regional relations.[5] On the occasion of the first foreign ministers' meeting, Japan added two more modest proposals: sponsorship of symposiums of young leaders from both regions and the invitation of young diplomats for joint language training programs.

In short, FEALAC was instituted because the participants shared a vaguely felt sense of the potential benefits of cooperation, and not because they believed that they had any urgent necessity to concur on the basis of common interests and concerns. Under the circumstances, the Japanese government did not treat FEALAC as a particularly high priority. Their lack of concern was demonstrated when they shifted responsibility for FEALAC from the Foreign Ministry's Bureau of Asian Affairs to its Bureau of Latin American Affairs. (The change occurred sometime between the first and the second SOM.)[6] Considering the paramount importance given to Asia in the overall foreign policy of Japan, this shift suggests the low status of FEALAC in the minds of Japanese policy makers.

Nonetheless, FEALAC clearly could be useful for Japan. It could serve as a means not only to coordinate its policies on Asia and Latin America, but also to redefine aspects of its policy toward the United States. To understand how Japan can pursue its foreign policy interests by participating in Asian–Latin American interactions in general, and FEALAC in particular, I now examine Japan's postwar foreign policy with particular attention to Japanese policy regarding Asia and Latin America.

Japan's Postwar Foreign Policy

Many authors cite the first *Blue Book on Foreign Policy* published by the Japanese Foreign Ministry in 1957 as the document that defined the basic policy framework for the postwar period.[7] It listed three central principles of Japan's foreign policy.[8] The first was that Japan would use the United Nations as the main arena of its diplomatic activities. The second was that Japan would cooperate with the "liberal countries." The third was the firm maintenance of its position as a member of the community of Asian nations. These three principles have been maintained over the past fifty years, although the relative importance of each has varied from time to time.

The emphasis on the United Nations can be understood if one remembers the constraints imposed upon the Japanese government by domestic public opinion and by the "Peace Constitution" that followed the Second World War. Under the postwar constitution, Japan disavowed the use of military force to solve its disputes with other countries. Naturally, the Japanese people heartily supported this restriction because they had only recently gone through the trauma of devastating war and defeat. They showed a clear preference for the use of peaceful policy instruments, and a firm rejection of military options.[9] For the majority of the Japanese people, the UN has been the "embodiment of the pacifist ideals," although the UN Charter actually permits collective security (meaning military) activities.[10] Therefore, pursuing Japan's foreign policy through the auspices of the United Nations seemed to be the best alternative, and the means most acceptable to the Japanese public.

Unfortunately, the Cold War and its escalation, which had started before Japan's accession to the United Nations, made the international body less effective as an instrument of peaceful diplomacy. As a consequence, and also as a result of pressure from the United States, Japan was persuaded to rebuild its military capability. But faced with domestic opposition to heavy rearmament (and also acting from his own convictions), Prime Minister Yoshida opted for a small-scale and gradual rearmament. Japan would depend mostly on a bilateral treaty with the United States for its national security.[11]

In addition to its role as the guarantor of Japanese security, the United States was important to Japan as a market for its recovering industries. In 1950, the United States purchased 22 percent of Japanese exports. The figure increased to 27 percent in 1960, while the European Community bought just 4.7 percent in the same year.[12] Cooperation with the "liberal countries" primarily meant cooperation with the United States.

The deepening military and economic dependence on the United States led to a nationalist reaction from both the right and the left. The right wing wanted heavier rearmament and the revision of the "Peace Constitution." The left wanted to preserve the constitution but to abolish the Japan–U.S. Security Treaty and to oust U.S. military forces from Japan.[13] Both the constitution and the security treaty survived, but the search for an "autonomous foreign policy" attained a new importance in the development of Japanese foreign policy. Autonomy, in this context, meant action independent of the United States.

Autonomous foreign policy was first attempted in economic matters in Asia. During the immediate postwar period, the Japanese government put priority on economic recovery and regarded China as the key to it. In 1940, 51 percent of Japanese exports went to China, followed by all other Asian countries combined with 17 percent.[14] Moreover, the Nationalist Party government of Chiang Kai-shek seemed conciliatory to Japan in the years immediately after the war. So, the Japanese government hoped to reestablish diplomatic and commercial ties with China as soon as possible in order to promote Japan's export business. Disappointing Japan's hopes, the Nationalist Party lost the civil war and was forced out of the mainland in 1949. The Japanese government then tried to negotiate with Communist China in spite of U.S. opposition. This attempt failed and Japan had to be satisfied with a limited "private" trade agreement with China that was concluded in 1958.

After the Chinese market was lost, the Japanese government directed its attention to Southeast Asia and South Asia. During the 1950s, the government repeatedly proposed to combine the financial resources of the United States with Japanese technology and the natural resources of Asia to foster the economic development of Japan and Asia.[15] Japan no doubt regarded Asia as the region most crucial to Japan's economic interests. Consequently, one of the earliest expressions of Japan's autonomous foreign policy was glimpsed when the Japanese government sent a delegation to the first Asia-Africa conference of "nonaligned" nations held in Indonesia in 1955. Japan sought to make a favorable impression on its Asian neighbors even though it knew that Washington deplored the anti-Western tendencies of the conference.[16]

An emphasis on economic affairs could be added as the fourth principle of Japan's postwar foreign policy. The Yoshida administration laid down the basic policy line on this matter. Yoshida fostered the idea that Japan should strengthen itself as a "commercial state" by using Japanese resources for economic recovery and development while depending on U.S. military power for its security.[17] During that era, serious domestic conflict between conservative and socialist forces made it difficult for the government to take a clear-cut position on political or ideological affairs. Throughout the 1950s, a national consensus emerged on one issue: The government would avoid being involved in political or military conflicts and instead it would concentrate its efforts on economic interactions with other countries regardless of their political or ideological tendencies. This policy was called "economic diplomacy."

In short, Japan's postwar foreign policy was marked by a certain contradiction: Military and economic dependence on the United States was contrasted by the pursuit of an autonomous foreign policy in its economic relations with other countries, especially in Asia. This contradiction can be understood only by looking at Japan's lack of meaningful military power, the pacifist social norm, and its emphasis on economic development.

The contradictions between two of the cornerstones of Japan's foreign policy did not come to light until around 1970, as we shall soon see. But prior to reaching a deeper understanding of the matter, Japan seemed to have been unaware of its own contradictions. This was largely due to a benevolent U.S. hegemony under which Japan was able to concentrate its energy on its own economic development without having to share the burden of maintaining national and international security (except for a few cases such as Japan's relationship with China and Taiwan).

The relative decline of the U.S. economy and the failure of its Vietnamese policy led to the gradual lessening of American hegemony and its attention to Asian affairs. President Nixon issued what came to be called the Nixon Doctrine in February 1970, announcing his intention to reduce the U.S. military presence in Asia. The following year Nixon shocked Japan by announcing his intention to visit China. This announcement was made without prior consultation with Japan, whose desire for rapprochement with China had been strongly opposed by the U.S. government. Subsequently, President Nixon delivered two more shocks: the termination of dollar-gold convertibility and the imposition of a 10 percent import surcharge. In 1973, Japan (and, of course, the world) faced still another jolt in the form of the oil embargo. Japan was especially hard hit because of its almost total dependence on imported petroleum. The U.S. government declined Japan's request for help in obtaining supplies of oil.[18]

These events led Japanese leaders to realize that Japan could no longer rely quite so heavily on the United States, either for its national defense or for securing its supply of natural resources. The latter problem came to be perceived as a security issue because the Japanese realized that their economy could not survive without a secure supply of energy and natural resources. This realization led to the formulation of a new national security policy known as the Comprehensive National Security Policy. It featured the strengthening of Japanese military capability along with new directions in foreign policy that had the express purpose of securing the supply of natural resources.[19] In pursuit of these goals, Japan would need to use its new economic strength to expand its military power and to establish friendlier relationships with countries rich in needed resources.

Japan's effort to move in these new directions was somewhat restrained by opposition among its own people, and from its Asian neighbors, to any substantial Japanese military buildup. Hence, in order to secure peaceful stability in the region, Japan used economic aid to foster economic development among its neighbors in Asia. Japan's plan was to mitigate struggles among contending forces by stimulating their economic development. At the same time, the Japanese government began to use the official development assistance (ODA) program to cultivate friendships with countries that were rich in resources.

These policies were not always inimical to the aims of American foreign policy. But, to the extent that they were, Japan was now powerful enough economically to pursue an autonomous foreign policy even when the policy did not comply with U.S. preferences (as in the case of its policy toward the Arab world during the 1970s).[20]

The pursuit of its economic interest, including the securing of sufficient natural resources, never ceased to be an important objective of Japan's foreign policy. But, at the same time, the country's rising economic power tended to undercut the moral basis of the "economic diplomacy" that had solely sought Japan's own economic interest. Japan's economy grew rapidly during the fifties and sixties, and by the late sixties its economy became the second largest in the world. Accordingly, when Japan was admitted into the G-7 concert in the latter half of the seventies, the G-7 members urged it to offer more assistance to countries beyond the Asian regions adjacent to Japan. As a result, the ODA budget was expanded and aid was offered to non-Asian regions such as Latin America, the Middle East, and Africa. Much Japanese aid was given to resource-rich countries such as Brazil, Mexico, and several nations in the Middle East. Still a portion of its aid was offered to less-developed areas, such as sub-Saharan Africa and Bolivia and Paraguay, even though such aid did not directly serve Japan's economic interests. At the same time, the Japanese government increased the share of the "untied" part of the assistance.[21] It also began to implement the "capital recycling policy" during the latter half of the eighties, by which it committed up to 63 billion dollars for five years to alleviate the debt burdens of the developing countries.[22]

Finally, the pacifist attitude of Japanese society eased somewhat. By the early nineties, the majority of the Japanese people were ready to accept some form of military participation in international affairs. After a nationwide controversy over the Gulf War, the National Diet enacted the United Nations Peacekeeping Operations (PKO) Law in 1992. The new law allowed Japan's Self Defense Forces, for the first time, to be dispatched abroad on the condition that they not engage in combat operations.[23] The first PKO mission was sent to Cambodia in 1992. That mission was followed by dispatches to Mozambique (1993), the Golan Heights (1996), and East Timor (2002). All of these missions employed small, lightly armed forces under United Nations command. Clearly, the main principles of Japanese foreign policy, as described in the 1957 Japanese Foreign Ministry *Blue Book*, can be seen at work in these initiatives. One can see, for example, that the principle of working through the United Nations has been staunchly maintained. Furthermore, the Japanese are still cautious about the use of military forces in international conflicts. They continue to prefer economic instruments of policy regardless of whether the purpose is Japan's own "comprehensive security" or a less-selfish contribution to peace and prosperity in the world.

Although Japan's military and economic dependence on the United States persisted, the decline of U.S. hegemony in the world and the solidification of the Japanese economy increased Japan's need and capability to pursue a more independent foreign policy for its national security after the 1970s. At the same time, Japan relaxed its economic diplomacy, except for measures to ensure the supply of natural resources. Instead, the Japanese government turned to using economic resources for less-selfish diplomatic purposes—for example, lending assistance to poor or indebted countries, and alleviating international conflicts. In the process, the geographical scope of Japan's foreign policy expanded beyond Asia, although Asia has never lost its primacy in Japan's foreign relations.

Japan's Relationship with Asia

As discussed above, Asia was the main arena of Japan's economic diplomacy during the 1950s and '60s. During those years, Japan suffered disappointments in two of its diplomatic goals in Asia: It failed to secure the Chinese market or to persuade the United States to finance economic development in Southeast Asia. In an attempt to recover from these setbacks, and in an effort to promote the Japanese economy, the Japanese government arranged to use reparation payments to the Asian countries for damages incurred during the Second World War.[24] That is, the reparation payments were used to purchase Japanese merchandise. Furthermore, in 1957, the Kishi Administration proposed to establish a Southeast Asia Development Fund. This initiative did not materialize, but the 5.4 billion yen earmarked for the fund were used in 1961 to establish the Overseas Economic Cooperation Fund (OECF).[25]

During the 1960s, the Japanese government extended its ODA to Asian countries. The purpose of its effort was twofold: to lend some support to the United States, which was becoming involved in an exhausting war in Indochina, and also to benefit Japanese businesses through "tied" aids.

In 1966, a minister-level forum on Southeast Asian development was organized by a Japanese initiative. This was the first international conference hosted by Japan after World War II.[26] However, the Southeast Asian countries were anxious about the increase of Japanese influence in the region and the forum soon lost its momentum. The Asian countries presented Japan with yet another disappointment when they selected Manila, not Tokyo, as the location of the headquarters of the newly established Asian Development Bank. This turn of events was particularly upsetting to Japan, which was one of the largest contributors to the bank.[27] Such incidents underscored an increasingly clear reality: Asian leaders feared the resurgence of Japan as a regional power.

Ironically, Japan itself was very cautious about undertaking initiatives with political and military implications during that period. The best example of Japanese reserve was the case of the Asia Pacific Council (ASPAC). When the South Korean government proposed this forum for the purpose of engendering political and military cooperation in the region, the Japanese government hesitated to participate. It decided to join ASPAC only when Korea agreed to make the forum no more than a consultative body and to restrict its area of concern to nonmilitary matters.[28] Once again, economic diplomacy was the main feature of Japan's foreign policy toward Asia.

In the 1970s, Japan faced growing Asian antagonism toward the expansion of its economic presence. In 1972, a boycott of Japanese merchandise spread throughout Thailand. Two years later, Prime Minister Tanaka was met by anti-Japanese demonstrators in Bangkok and Jakarta. Japan came to realize that it needed to pursue a less selfish foreign policy in Asia. Japan believed that it needed to contribute to peace and prosperity in the Asian countries, but without raising concerns about the resurgence of Japanese hegemony.

As the American presence diminished in Asia, Japan approached new avenues of independent diplomacy in the region. The Japanese government established diplomatic relations with China in September 1972 and with North Vietnam the following year. The negotiations with North Vietnam had begun even before the Paris Peace Accord was signed. After the Saigon government was defeated in 1975, ASEAN countries tried to normalize their relationships with Vietnam. The ASEAN initiative coincided with the Japanese search for peace and stability in Southeast Asia. Recognizing the moment of opportunity, Prime Minister Fukuda issued the Fukuda Doctrine in 1977. In that document, the Japanese government announced its intention to serve as an intermediary between ASEAN and Vietnam and to promote peaceful coexistence between the two. Because Japan's main policy instrument was economic assistance for development, the foreign ministry intended that the aid money to Vietnam would be used to purchase merchandise from the ASEAN countries, thus benefiting both.[29] Economic prosperity resulting from development was expected to alleviate ideological differences, just as had happened in postwar Japan. This form of diplomacy represented a benchmark in postwar diplomacy in Japan. For the first time, Japan turned from diplomatic initiatives that were crafted solely to serve its own economic development. Instead, economic power was used for diplomatic purposes with political and military implications.

This new kind of diplomatic initiative was begun during the period in which the United States lost a firm sense of direction in its Southeast Asian policy after its retreat from Vietnam. The Foreign Ministry of Japan asserted that this policy was a "positive diplomatic initiative taken by Japan for the first time after World War II."[30]

The new diplomacy encountered difficulties, however, when conflict arose between Vietnam and China. The situation became even more serious when Vietnam invaded Cambodia in order to topple the pro-China government in 1978. Under U.S. pressure, Japan suspended economic assistance to Vietnam in 1980. Nevertheless, despite pressure from the Americans, Japan persisted in its conciliatory posture toward Vietnam and supported the ASEAN policy for peaceful dialogue. In its efforts to rebuild peace in Cambodia in the years between 1988 and 1993, Japan again offered abundant economic assistance with the intention of fostering compromise between the contending forces.[31]

The 1970s and 1980s were a period of rapid economic growth for many Asian countries. South Korea and Taiwan led the trend, followed by the Southeast Asian countries. The development of the latter countries became especially rapid in the second half of the eighties, largely due to the expansion of Japanese investment. However, Asian leaders became increasingly concerned about the future of the trade system. Their doubts were heightened by the slow progress of the Uruguay Round, the prospect of further integration of the European Community, the frequent application of protectionist measures such as the "Super 301" by Washington, and the conclusion of the U.S.–Canada Free Trade Agreement. This concern led to the formation of APEC—the forum for Asia Pacific Economic Cooperation.

Japan and Australia took the initiative in the formation of APEC, but there was a difference of opinion between them with regard to the proposed membership. Australia envisaged a solely Asian constituency, while Japan wanted to invite the United States and Canada, too. Japan's Ministry of International Trade and Industry (MITI), the principal promoter of APEC in Japan, hoped to keep U.S. protectionism in check by including America in the Asia-Pacific network of cooperation.[32] The Japanese view prevailed at last and APEC began in 1989 with the participation of Japan, Australia, New Zealand, South Korea, six ASEAN countries, the United States, and Canada. Later, Japan successfully opposed Mahathir's proposal to form an East Asian Economic Group with the exclusive participation of the ethnically Asian countries, excluding not only the United States but also Australia and New Zealand.

During the first half of the 1990s, Japan maintained its opposition to excluding the United States from the framework of economic cooperation in Asia. At the same time, the Japanese government opposed the U.S. attempt to use APEC as the venue in which to negotiate a NAFTA-like regional free trade agreement. Japan supported ASEAN's approach of a voluntary, non-exclusionary liberalization that came to be called "open regionalism." Actually, open regionalism meant two things for Japan. Japan opposed excluding the United States, and it opposed an exclusive regional free trade regime.

Japan's opposition to the establishment of any exclusive regional free trade zone arose from its identification of itself as a commercial state. It feared that Japanese firms and products could face discrimination from an exclusive regional economic bloc (in which Japan might not be included). Therefore, Japan preferred the multilateral and nondiscriminatory General Agreement on Tariffs and Trade/World Trade Organization (GATT/WTO) framework. This position of espousing nonexclusivity, however, made for an uncomfortable contradiction with its own domestic protectionism in the agricultural and fishery sectors. The insistence upon open regionalism gradually degenerated into a pretext for domestic protectionism.

After 1999, the idea of open regionalism began to meet with growing skepticism in certain quarters of the Japanese government and the private sector. A series of international events help to explain this development. First, both NAFTA and the European Union (EU) were perceived as a success, while the Millennium Round of the WTO came to a standstill. Liberalization within the APEC framework did not show any progress after 1995 either.

In light of these events, a research group in Keidanren, the largest business association in Japan, published a report in April 1999 calling for a free trade agreement (FTA) between Japan and Mexico. The following month, a White Paper by MITI admitted for the first time that regional integration could be compatible with the multilateral approach.[33] MITI's White Paper of 2000 made a full-scale study of the effects of regional integration and came to the same conclusion: that it could complement the multilateral trade regime of the WTO.[34] A research group was organized within the MITI-affiliated Institute of Developing Economies to study the possibility of concluding an FTA with South Korea in December 1998. Another research group to explore a possible FTA with Mexico was formed three months later in the Japan External Trade Organization (JETRO), another affiliate of MITI. Then a binational research team was formed in March 2000 to consider forming an FTA with Singapore. Later in the same year, a new research group was formed in JETRO envisaging a FTA with Chile. Officials within the foreign ministry who were formerly more cautious about the regional and bilateral approach to trade agreements were now increasingly going over to this view. Finally, in January 2002, the Japanese government signed its first bilateral FTA—the Japan-Singapore Economic Agreement for a New Age Partnership.

In the meantime, Japan had at last come to accede, in 1996, to an exclusively Asian grouping for regional cooperation. But prior to that, in April 1995, when the ASEAN economic ministers invited their counterparts from Japan, China, and South Korea for an unofficial meeting, Japan proposed to invite Australia and New Zealand. It did not wish to give the impression that it had condoned Mahathir's idea of an exclusive East Asian grouping. ASEAN did not concur with Japan's position and, as a consequence, the meeting did not materialize. However, when the Asia-Europe Meeting (ASEM) was launched in 1996, Japan finally accepted the ASEAN-plus-three formulation. Although Japan initially proposed to invite Australia and New Zealand, Malaysia was strongly opposed to this position and Japan relented. As a result, the first meeting of the heads of the ASEAN-plus-three governments was held in an informal session in February 1996 to prepare for ASEM.[35]

Japan moved toward a more regionally based approach in the aftermath of the Asian financial crisis of 1997–1998. This time, the main actor in Japan was the Ministry of Finance, which was regarded as one of the most pro-Western entities in the Japanese bureaucracy. The seriousness of the crisis and the perceived slowness and ineffectiveness of the response by the International Monetary Fund (IMF) and the United States encouraged the ministry to advocate a more regional approach to cope with the crisis. An early attempt in this direction, the initiative to form an Asian Monetary Fund, failed due to opposition from the United States and China. The Japanese government then agreed to a cofinancing arrangement with the IMF, committing $19 billion dollars to help Thailand, South Korea, and Indonesia. The Japanese government also offered unilateral financial assistance. For this purpose, it announced in September of 1998 the New Miyazawa Initiative, with funding amounting to $30 billion. The second stage of New Miyazawa Initiative was announced in May 1999, with the offer of an additional 2 trillion yen (equivalent to $18 billion). On the occasion of the finance ministers' meeting of the ASEAN-plus-three held in May 2000, the participants agreed to adopt the Chiang Mai Initiative. In it, they determined to bolster the preexisting network of bilateral agreements for currency swaps in order to avert another financial crisis.[36]

The first formal summit of the ASEAN-plus-three was convened in December 1997, in the midst of the financial crisis. The group convened regularly thereafter. In the fourth summit, held in November 2000, the leaders agreed to establish a working group to study the possibility of an East Asian Free Trade Area.[37]

Japan's policy regarding the membership of the group of countries for regional cooperation in Asia changed during the 1990s; it went from insisting on the inclusion of the United States to accepting a more exclusionary framework. However, this change does not mean that Japan abandoned its long-held policy objective of maintaining close economic and political ties with the United States. The bilateral relationship with the United States continues to occupy a very important position within Japan's overall foreign policy. After all, Japan still depends on the United States both militarily and economically. Nonetheless, Japan is now more ready to work within the given framework of ASEAN-plus-three, at least in the field of economic cooperation.

Japan's Relationship with Latin America

Compared with Asia, Latin America has not been a high priority region in Japan's foreign policy except for a brief period in the seventies when Latin America attained prominence as a region rich in natural resources.

Japan's postwar relationship with Latin American was largely left in the hands of private initiatives, except for the government policy of sending some ninety thousand immigrants to various Latin American countries. During the fifties and sixties, Japanese companies expanded their exports to the region in spite of the fact that their Latin American customers, unlike those in Asia, purchased Japanese goods without the incentive of Japanese reparation money or "tied" ODA funds.

What was more impressive during this period was the amount of Japanese investment in Latin American manufacturing industries. In 1971, Japan had an accumulated external investment of $1.3 billion dollars in manufacturing around the world—26.6 percent of this total was in Latin America, while Asia and the United States received 36.8 percent and 21.5 percent respectively.[38] Latin America was thus important for Japanese companies more as an investment site than as a trade partner. This is largely because major Latin American countries imposed heavy import restrictions on metal products and machinery. As a consequence, Japanese companies made their largest investments in Latin America in metal production and transportation equipment. In the case of Asia, by way of contrast, the textile industry was the most important industry for Japanese investors.

The oil embargo of the mid-seventies heightened Japan's sense of vulnerability by revealing Japan as a nation deeply dependent on imports for its supplies of energy, mineral resources, and food. As a result, government and business leaders came to regard Latin America as a highly important source of natural resources, and they began to visit the region more frequently than before. Japanese companies participated in many important projects for development as joint-venture partners of Latin American governments and companies, and Japanese firms frequently provided technical assistance to those ventures. In many cases, Japan's public financial institutions, such as the Japan Export-Import Bank and the OECF, offered low-cost credits to finance such projects. For example, a variety of development projects were arranged between Brazil and Japan to produce iron ore, steel, aluminum, paper pulp, and soybeans.[39] In Mexico, the government and the private sector of Japan made a strong effort to secure Mexico's commitment to the increase of the supply of oil for Japan. As an inducement, the Japanese provided financial and technical support to the Mexican government to build a new steel production complex at Lázaro Cárdenas City on the Pacific coast.

In the late seventies, the Japanese government and the private sector began to take a strong interest in the Panama Canal. The construction of a new canal or the expansion of the existing one was seen by the Japanese planners as urgently needed to secure an alternative sea lane for its trade and, more specifically, to transport natural resources to Japan from such South American countries as Brazil and Venezuela.[40]

In response to Japan's increased economic interaction with Latin America, the foreign ministry decided in late 1979 to establish a Bureau of Latin American Affairs. (It had been formerly joined with the section for North American affairs.) MITI moved more slowly, finally establishing an office for Oceanian and Latin American affairs in 1984. But we need to recall that JETRO, which was affiliated with MITI, had already established a network of offices in major Latin American cities.

The debt crisis that afflicted Latin America after 1982, and declining prices of natural resources, lowered the status of the region in the eyes of Japanese companies. The attractiveness of the region as a trade partner and as an investment site decreased due to the severe recession—a sharp contrast with Asia, which received massive amounts of Japanese investment during the same period.

However, the debt crisis led the Japanese government to revise its policies in the Americas, including its relations with the United States. Previously, Japan fully relied on the United States for the maintenance of security and stability and pursued its own economic interest in the region. The crisis, however, was too serious for the United States to handle alone. But Japan had another reason to intercede in the crisis. The trade imbalance between Japan and the United States had become a point of antagonism between the two countries in the 1980s. The Japanese government felt the necessity to appease Washington by giving its support in issues that were believed to be of vital interest to the United States.[41] The debt problem of Latin America was certainly one of those issues. The Japanese government participated in Secretary Brady's debt reduction plan for Latin American countries under its "capital recycling program." For example, Japan offered Mexico $2 billion dollars to realize the Brady Plan there.[42]

Japan's policy for Central America was another example of its efforts to complement U.S. policy. In support of the Reagan administration's struggle against a left-wing regime in Nicaragua during the 1980s, Japan reduced its ODA to that country while increasing aid to nearby capitalist countries such as Costa Rica, Honduras, and Jamaica. This seemingly pro–U.S. policy resembled Japanese policy for Southeast Asia during the sixties, in which Japan reduced economic assistance to North Vietnam while expanding ODA to the capitalist countries in the region.

In the year 2000, the Japanese government also decided to cooperate with Plan Colombia, which aims at coping with the widespread violence related to drug production and trafficking and guerrilla warfare. Japanese contributions are limited in both their amount and scope. Japan plans to participate only in "alternative crop" production projects and to contribute humanitarian aid. Still, the active participation of Japan in these matters helped induce the skeptical European countries, which disliked the military part of Plan Colombia to decide finally to cooperate with the United States.[43]

However, as Hiroshi Matsushita points out, Japan did not always follow the U.S. lead in Latin America. Matsushita lists and analyzes three such instances: the armed conflict over the Falkland/Malvinas islands, the peace process in Central America, and the conflict over Noriega's rule in Panama.[44] We can add that neither did Japan endorse American policy toward the Fujimori government in Peru. Japan's persistent support for Fujimori can most plausibly be explained by his overwhelming popularity among the Japanese people and their political leaders as the first person of Japanese descent to become president of a foreign country. Under these circumstances, the Japanese government believed that it did not have a viable alternative other than supporting him. However, there are some signs that the Japanese government tried to adjust its Fujimori policy to fit U.S. preferences. For example, on the occasion of the 1992 *autogolpe* (a coup organized by the incumbent government to extend its powers), a high-level foreign ministry official was sent to Peru to urge Fujimori to call for elections to the constitutional assembly as soon as possible. On the occasion of the 2000 presidential election, Japan participated in the Organization of American States (OAS) election observation mission.

These are instances in which Japan's policy was not necessarily congruent with U.S. preferences. Matsushita gives several reasons for these divergences. In the Malvinas case, Japan was reluctant to harm its traditional friendly relations with Latin American countries that strongly supported Argentina. Japan also feared persecution of Japanese immigrants living in Argentina. In the Noriega case, Japanese leaders had established close relations with Noriega and his cronies through working on the new Panama Canal project. As for Central America in the 1980s, Matsushita only writes without explanation that Japan preferred a peaceful solution.

Here, however, we need to recall one of the basic principles of Japan's postwar foreign policy: its preference for nonmilitary means to solve any international conflict. For example, just as Japan kept searching for a peaceful solution for Indochina even after having cut off aid to Vietnam, the Japanese government supported the peace initiative of the Contadora Group—even though the U.S. government regarded the group's efforts as useless. Unlike Washington, the Japanese government heartily supported the Esquipulas II accord. Japan offered abundant aid to reconstruct Central American economies once peace was reestablished.[45] Once again, Japanese involvement had political and military implications. But the policy instrument was economic, just as it was in Japan's involvement in the peace process in Southeast Asia.

Regional economic integration was a new issue area for Japan's policy makers working in the area of Latin American affairs. On the occasion of the NAFTA debate, private-sector leaders and the Japanese public were critical of the proposed treaty. They feared that Japanese companies would face disadvantages, especially in sectors such as automobile and textile production, banking, and government procurement. Japanese leaders issued contradictory statements saying that they welcomed the treaty but hoped it would not discriminate against nonmembers. More generally, they feared that NAFTA, together with the European Union (EU), could strengthen the movement toward regional economic blocs in the world. As of 1993, Japanese leaders overwhelmingly supported the multilateral approach.

In practice, Japanese companies found that they could adjust to the NAFTA regime without much difficulty. Nevertheless, their complaints persisted, especially about the disadvantages stemming from the abolition of Mexico's maquiladora system. Partly to overcome the disadvantages, the Japanese government began in 1999 to study the possibility of an FTA with Mexico.

In contrast to its attitude toward NAFTA, Japan was mostly favorable toward the Common Market of the South (MERCOSUR) and other regional trade regimes in Latin America. The Japanese did not regard these organizations as likely to discriminate against Japanese firms vis-à-vis their American or European rivals. Rather, they were seen as facilitating the enlargement of the potential market for Japanese products, and providing economies of scale in production and marketing.

In conclusion, although Latin America seldom occupied the center stage of Japan's foreign relations, its Latin American policy shares several characteristics with its Asian policy. First, the government needed to balance two policy principles: cooperation with the United States on the one hand, and the search for autonomous foreign policy on the other. The latter motive was, naturally, followed more cautiously in Latin America. Second, although the change came to Latin America slower than in Asia, the economic diplomacy dominant during earlier decades gave way to less selfish policies such as debt reduction programs and the contribution to the peace-building process in Central America. Third, Japan always preferred peaceful means to solve international conflicts. Japan's policy instrument for that purpose has almost exclusively been economic aid for development in both Asia and Latin America.

Japan's Interest in Asia–Latin America Interactions

The most important dimension in the relations between Asian and Latin American countries is, no doubt, economic. Although the amount of trade is still limited, the outlook for future expansion is encouraging. Even more encouragement can be taken from the rapid recovery of the Asian economies after the crisis of 1997–1998, and the renewed growth of the Latin American economies after their lost decade. For most Asian countries, Japan is the largest trade and investment partner. And for most Latin American countries, Japan is a more important economic partner than any other Asian country. The same Japanese manufacturers, commercial concerns and financial firms have business interests on both sides of the Pacific. Therefore, closer economic cooperation between Asia and Latin America will certainly benefit Japanese businesses. However, a deepening of Japan's involvement in Asia–Latin American interactions will require a redefinition of its relationship with the United States. To enhance our understanding of this point, we must recall some recent trends in Japan's foreign policy.

First of all, the occasions for autonomous policies have become more common, especially in Asia. Japan strengthened its commitment to the ASEAN-plus-three framework of cooperation in the latter half of the 1990s while allowing APEC to lose its momentum. This framework gave birth to the Chiang Mai agreement for foreign-currency swaps.

In contrast, Japan has played a more subordinate role in Latin America because Japan does not regard it as a high priority region and because Japan is well aware that the United States traditionally regards Latin America as within its sphere of influence. On the other hand, Japan has hesitated to support the United States in its unilateral military actions. Japan has preferred nonmilitary options pursued through international diplomatic forums such as the UN and the OAS. In the economic field, the Japanese government and the business sector were dismayed when the Japanese presence in Mexico was decried in the United States in order to criticize the maquiladora system and rally support for NAFTA. Japanese leaders also fear that the prospective FTAA could be disadvantageous for Japanese and Asian interests. Once again, Japan needs to engage in a balancing act: It needs to accommodate the United States in certain matters, but at the same time it needs to defend the preferences and interests of its own enterprises and those of its Asian partners in Latin America.

These sensitive issues explain in part Japan's cautious approach toward FEALAC. First, there is the issue of Japan's willingness to fight for open regionalism. Japan welcomed the participation of Australia and New Zealand. But ultimately, as mentioned above, Japan's point of view was rejected by its partners, and those countries were excluded from ASEM. This fact together with the increasing consolidation of the ASEAN-plus-three framework could give the impression that the Asian countries were rapidly weakening in their commitment to open regionalism. If Australia and New Zealand are also excluded from FEALAC—a forum that encompasses the region regarded by the Americans as their own backyard—Washington could certainly be expected to react with dismay. By including those Anglo-Saxon countries in FEALAC, Japan can send the message to the United States that it has no inclination to tolerate exclusivist policies in either Asia or Latin America.

Second, Japan proposes to avoid redundancies between FEALAC and APEC. The implication is that the subjects related to economic integration are to be entrusted to APEC since the working groups dealing with various aspects of integration already exist in APEC. The Japanese government prefers to deal with multiple subjects in FEALAC. The word "multiple" here means political, social, and cultural issues in addition to economic issues.[46] Apparently, the Japanese government wants to avoid giving the impression that FEALAC is solely devoted to economic matters between Asia and Latin America. This attitude of the Japanese government can only be understood as an attempt to avoid a negative U.S. reaction toward FEALAC.

Still, Japan has no intention to totally exclude economic subjects from FEALAC dialogue, regardless of the potential for alarming the United States. In particular, there are two issues that could be addressed by FEALAC that could engender uneasy feelings among U.S. policy makers. First, Japan may agree to discuss policy regarding harmonization in standards and conformity assessment systems, e-commerce regulations, competition rules, investment rules, paperless trade, and the like. Some of these issues are already being dealt with by APEC working groups. However, APEC includes only three Latin American countries while FEALAC membership now covers fifteen, including all of the large Latin American economies. Obviously, then, involvement of FEALAC in similar discussions would pose a greater cause for concern to the United States. Moreover, those issues are now common currency among Japanese policy makers in both the public and private sectors as subjects to be included in the bilateral agreements for economic integration. These are often called the "new age" agreements because they contain stipulations about new issues such as IT-related businesses. The readiness of Japanese policy makers to discuss these kinds of policy measures can be partially explained by the domestic constraint against ordinary FTAs in Japan. The strenuous resistance by the agricultural and fishery interests and their political and bureaucratic representatives make it difficult for Japan to negotiate trade liberalization. Therefore, in order to avoid political complications, the policy makers prefer to stress nontrade issues both in regional and bilateral negotiations. Even if trade liberalization were not included, however, any agreement on the above policy areas could not but affect U.S. business interests.

A second potentially contentious issue is the FTAA. Japan and other Asian countries have every reason to worry about the possible terms of the FTAA agreement. If it stipulates rigid rules of origin for the products that the Asian countries will export to the Americas, or if Asian companies receive disadvantageous treatment in comparison with companies from the FTAA countries, many actual or potential business opportunities will be lost to the Asians. FEALAC will provide Asian countries with the opportunity to get information about the progress of FTAA negotiations and the opportunity to introduce their own views. In this dialogue, the country most likely to be helpful to

Japan will be Brazil. Besides being the most important Latin American partner in trade and investment for many Japanese companies, Brazil is the leader of MERCOSUR and will also lead the final stage of negotiations with the United States over the FTAA.

Japan's recent effort to launch negotiations for bilateral agreements with Mexico and Chile can also be interpreted as having double meanings with regard to Japan's relationship with the United States. On the one hand, by including the Latin American countries, in addition to Singapore and South Korea, as its potential partners, Japan can avert giving the impression that it is lending its support to an exclusively Asian form of regionalism. On the other hand, the initiative is a clear sign from Japan that it will not sit idly by and just watch the expansion of regionalism in the Americas. The conclusion of bilateral agreements across the Pacific will serve Japan as a preemptive measure against some of its concerns about an FTAA regime that may pose a threat to Japan's commercial interests. Furthermore, if Japan succeeds in concluding a "new age" agreement with Mexico, Chile, or both, it will serve other Asian countries as a model for their own potential agreements with Latin American countries. This intrusion into the traditional U.S. sphere of influence could antagonize certain factions in American business and government.

Economic relations between Asia and Latin America are still limited in size and scope. The formal dialogue between the regions is in its early and protean stages. It is too soon to predict exactly in which direction the interregional dialogue will move. Whichever direction it takes, however, Japan will need to continue its delicate balancing policy. It still depends on the United States to provide its security and to serve as a large market for its exports. Japan does not necessarily need to tailor its actions to please the United States, but it certainly must avoid causing needless antagonism. At the same time, Japan needs to defend its economic interests and those of its Asian neighbors in the pursuit of new trade relations in the Americas. Japan must also deepen cooperation within the ASEAN-plus-three framework, and it must search for an autonomous foreign policy based on the use of economic and not military power.

Notes

1. "Asia, Latin America Tie the Knot," *Asia Times Online*, September 7, 1999.

2. For details about the beginning of FEALAC, refer to Shuichi Takano, "Higashi Azia Raten Amerika Foramu—Genjo to Shourai no Hatten no Kanousei" [East Asia–Latin America forum: Current conditions and future prospects], *Raten Amerika Jiho* 42, no. 11 (November 1999): 2–6. *Raten Amerika Jiho* is a monthly journal

published by the Latin American Society and subsidized by Japan's Ministry of Foreign Affairs. Many articles written by Foreign Ministry officials appear in the journal. Takano's is one of them.

3. Susumu Yamakage, "Nihon no Tai-ASEAN Seisaku no Henyo—Fukuda Dokutorin wo Koete Aratana Renkei he" [Transformation of Japan's policy toward ASEAN: new links beyond the Fukuda doctrine], *Kokusai Mondai*, no. 490 (January 2001): 66.

4. "Framework for a Proposed Forum for Dialogue and Cooperation between East Asia and Latin America" (mimeograph prepared and presented to the second SOM by the government of Singapore, August 2000.)

5. See Takano, "Higashi."

6. The head of the Japanese delegation for the first SOM was Deputy Director General of the Bureau of Asian Affairs. He was replaced by Deputy Director General of the Bureau of Latin American Affairs at the second SOM.

7. Akio Watanabe, *Azia Taiheiyo no Kokusai Kankei to Nihon* [International relations in the Asia Pacific and Japan] (Tokyo: University of Tokyo Press, 1992), 84; Sueo Sudo, "Nihon Gaiko ni Okeru ASEAN no Ichi" [The position of ASEAN in Japan's diplomacy], *Kokusai Seiji*, no. 116 (October 1997): 148.

8. Ministry of Foreign Affairs, *Waga Gaiko no Kinkyo, Showa 32 Nenban* [Blue book on foreign policy, 1957] (Tokyo: Ministry of Foreign Affairs, 1957), 7–8.

9. Peter Katzenstein, *Cultural Norms and National Security: Police and Military in Postwar Japan* (Ithaca: Cornell University Press, 1996), 116.

10. Robert M. Immerman, "Japan in the United Nations," in *Japan: A New Kind of Superpower?* eds. Craig C. Garby and M. B. Bullock (Washington, D.C.: Woodrow Wilson Center Press, 1994), 185.

11. Masataka Kosaka, "Nihon Gaiko no Bensho" [Dialectics of Japan's diplomacy], in *Kouza Kokusai Seiji 4: Nihon no Gaiko* [Series international politics 4: Japan's diplomacy], eds. Sadashi Aruga et al. (Tokyo: University of Tokyo Press, 1989), 298–99.

12. Yano Kota Kinenkai, ed., *Suji de Miru Nihon no Hyakunen* [One hundred years of Japan in statistics], 3d ed. (Tokyo: Kokuseisha, 1991), 323–25.

13. For a detailed description of the controversy over the Constitution and the Japan–U.S. Security Treaty, see chs. 4–6 of Akihiko Tanaka, *Anzen Hosho—Sengo 50 Nen no Mosaku* [National security: a search during the fifty postwar years] (Tokyo: Yomiuri Shimbunsha, 1997).

14. Yano Kota Kinenkai, *Suji.*

15. Watanabe, *Azia Taiheiyo,* 83–84.

16. Sumio Hatano, "Sengo Nihon no 'Azia Gaiko'" ['Asian diplomacy' in postwar Japan], in *Higashi Azia Kokusai Kankei no Dainamizumu* [Dynamism of international relations in East Asia], ed. Motohide Saito (Tokyo: Toyo Keizai Shinpousha, 1998), 92.

17. Kosaka, "Nihon Gaiko," 299.

18. Makoto Iokibe, "Kokusai Kankyo to Nihon no Sentaku" [International environment and choices of Japan], in *Kouza Kokusai Seiji 4,* 39.

19. Takeshi Igarashi, *Nichibei Kankei to Higashi Azia* [Japan–U.S. relationship and East Asia] (Tokyo: University of Tokyo Press, 1999), 172–73.

20. Iokibe, "Kokusai Kankyo."

21. According to Robert M. Orr, 71 percent of all ODA loan procurement contracts went to Japanese companies in 1981; within six years, this figure dropped to 56 percent, less than for many other countries. Orr, "Collaboration or Conflict? Foreign Aid and U.S. Japan Relations," in *Japan's Role in International Politics since World War II*, ed. Edward R. Beauchamp (Garland Publishing, Inc., 1998), 142.

22. Akio Hosono, "Raten Amerika wo Meguru Kokusai Kankei to Nihon no Tai-Raten Amerika Seisaku" [International relations of Latin America and Latin American policy of Japan], in *Raten Amerika no Kokusai Kankei* [International relations of Latin America], eds. Akio Hosono and Keiko Hata (Tokyo: Shinhyouron, 1993), 15.

23. Mike M. Mochizuki, "Japan as an Asia-Pacific Power," in *East Asia in Transition: Toward New Regional Order*, ed. Robert Ross (New York: M.E. Sharpe, 1995), 154.

24. Hatano, "Sengo Nihon," 91.

25. Mie Ohba, "Chiikishugi to Nihon no Sentaku" [Regionalism and choices of Japan], in *Azia Seiji Keizai Ron—'Azia no Naka no Nihon' wo Mezashite* [Political economy of Asia: Japan's search for a "firm position in Asia"], eds. Akira Suehiro and Susumu Yamakage (Tokyo: NTT Publishers, 2001), 261.

26. Watanabe, *Azia Taiheiyo*, 92.

27. Ohba, "Chiikishugi."

28. Hatano, "Sengo Nihon," 93.

29. Sudo, "Nihon Gaiko," 154.

30. Hatano, "Sengo Nihon," 101.

31. Hatano, "Sengo Nihon," 102–104; Sudo, "Nihon Gaiko," 155–57.

32. Susumu Yamakage, *ASEAN Pawaa—Azia Taiheiyo no Chukaku he* [Power of ASEAN: toward the core of the Asia Pacific] (Tokyo: University of Tokyo Press, 1997), 228–30.

33. MITI, *Tsusho Hakusho Heisei, 11 Nenban* [White paper on trade 1999] (Tokyo: MITI, 1999), 287–90.

34. MITI, *Tsusho Hakusho Heisei, 12 Nenban* [White paper on trade 2000] (Tokyo: MITI, 2000), 104–25.

35. Ohba, "Chiikishugi," 273.

36. Yamakage, "Nihon no Tai-ASEAN," 68.

37. Ohba, "Chiikishugi," 282.

38. MITI, *Wagakuni Kigyo no Kaigai Jigyo Katsudo 1972* [Japanese enterprises' business activities abroad 1972] (Tokyo: MITI, 1973).

39. Ernani T. Torres, "Brazil-Japan Relations: From Fever to Chill," in *Japan, the United States, and Latin America: Toward a Trilateral Relationship in the Western Hemisphere*, eds. Barbara Stallings and Gabriel Székely (Baltimore: Johns Hopkins University Press, 1993), 129, 135–36.

40. Charlotte Elton, "Panama and Japan: The Role of the Panama Canal," in *Japan, the United States, and Latin America*, 212–14.

41. Yasutomo makes a more general argument that Japan started to use its ODA as a means to alleviate the trade friction with the United States in the 1980s. Dennis T. Yasutomo, "Nihon Gaiko to ODA Seisaku" [Japan's diplomacy and ODA policy], in *Nihon no ODA to Kokusai Chitsujo* [Japan's ODA and international order], ed. Takeshi

Igarashi (Tokyo: Japan Institute of International Affairs, 1990), 92. In reviewing the Latin American policy of Japan, Purcell and Immerman came to the same conclusion. See Susan Kaufman Purcell and Robert M. Immerman, "Japan, Latin America, and the United States: Prospects for Cooperation and Conflict," in *Japan and Latin America in the New Global Order,* eds. S. K. Purcell and R. M. Immerman (Boulder, Colo.: Lynne Rienner Publishers, 1992), 128.

42. Hosono, "Raten Amerika," 16.

43. Mitsuo Sakaba, "Barankameha karano Messeiji—Koronbia no Wahei to Kaihatsu heno Shien" [A message from Barrancameja: assistance for peace and development in Colombia], *Raten Amerika Jiho* 43, no. 8 (August 2000): 14–15. Sakaba was Deputy Director General of the Bureau of Latin American Affairs and led the Japanese delegation to the Madrid Conference for Support for Colombia held in July 2000.

44. Hiroshi Matsushita, "Japanese Diplomacy toward Latin America after World War II," in *Japan, the United States, and Latin America,* 90–94.

45. Watanabe, *Azia Taiheiyo,* 206.

46. Shogo Toyota, "Higashi Azia Raten Amerika Foramu—Shourai heno Kanousei" [East Asia–Latin America forum: promise for the future]," *Raten Amerika Jiho* 43, no. 10 (October 2000): 7–8.

15

China, Latin America, and the Developing World

Jiang Shixue

CHINA'S FOREIGN POLICIES HAVE TENDED TO FOCUS MAINLY on the developed countries, particularly the United States, and on its neighbors, including Russia (or the USSR in the past). But China has also paid considerable attention to developing areas like Latin America and Africa, and relationships with (and within) the "Third World" have formed a central pillar of Chinese diplomacy.

As a matter of fact, Latin America has been important to China for at least three reasons. First of all, as a developing country, China finds it politically necessary to stand alongside Latin America in the struggle for the establishment of a just international order. Second, in order to reduce trade dependence upon the United States and other developed countries, China has been attempting to develop economic relations with Latin America. No less important is the possibility that China wishes to gain access to the rich natural resources in Latin America for its own urgent needs. Last, but not least, the Taiwan issue has yet to be resolved. Indeed, with the passage of time, this issue has become an increasingly conspicuous part of China's diplomatic efforts, and the Chinese government refuses to relinquish sovereignty over Taiwan. As of 2001 there were still twenty-nine countries that have "diplomatic relations" with Taiwan, and fourteen of them are found in Latin America.

I begin this chapter with a general overview of China's foreign policies in order to show how its policies toward Latin America fit within a general framework. Subsequent sections evaluate the development of Sino–Latin American relations, followed by a discussion of China's relations with Cuba—the only socialist country in the Western Hemisphere. Finally, I conclude with an exploration of ways that China's role in the Asia Pacific Economic Cooperation (APEC) forum can help promote Asian–Latin American ties.

China's Foreign Policies: Past and Present

China's foreign policies over the past half-century have witnessed important changes and adjustments, which might be categorized into two subphases: the Cold War era and the post–Cold War era.

The Cold War (1949–1989)

When the People's Republic of China was founded on October 1, 1949, the West, led by the United States, fiercely attempted to isolate the new socialist nation. Therefore, China's most pressing task was to break through this isolation by seeking assistance from the developing countries, including those in Latin America, as well as from the Soviet Union. In the words of Chairman Mao Zedong, China needed to "build a new stove to make meals"—meaning that the new China would not recognize the diplomatic relations the old China built with foreign powers, and would also rid itself of the humiliating diplomacy imposed by the imperialists before 1949. Chairman Mao also stated the need to "clean the house before inviting guests," meaning that the new China would eliminate the privileges and influence of imperialism in China. In reality, the foreign policy of the new China was "leaning towards one side," meaning the new China would establish diplomatic relations mainly with socialist and other countries friendly to China so as to build an international front against imperialism.

Needless to say, it was a great encouragement for China that the victory of its socialist revolution served as an inspiration to emerging national liberation movements in many parts of the Third World. China adopted a policy of sincere support for these movements in many ways.

In the 1950s, China recorded at least two remarkable diplomatic achievements: the announcement of the Five Principles of Peaceful Coexistence and participation in the Asia-Africa Conference in Bandung, Indonesia. On December 31, 1953, when he met with the visiting Indian delegation about a border dispute, Chinese Premier Zhou Enlai said, "I believe that relations between China and India will improve. . . . China has established the principles governing Sino-Indian relations. They are mutual respect for sovereignty and territorial integrity; mutual non-aggression; non-interference in one another's internal affairs; equality and mutual benefit; and peaceful coexistence." It was later recognized that the fifth principle could be achieved only if the first four were implemented. These principles, later known as the Five Principles of

Peaceful Coexistence, were written into the Sino-Indian treaty signed on April 29, 1954, regarding their border dispute. That same year, the Five Principles were written into China's first constitution. During his visit to India and Burma in June 1954, Zhou reaffirmed China's Five Principles and received positive reactions from the two hosts. On subsequent occasions Chairman Mao Zedong also expressed his hope that the Five Principles would be incorporated into the foreign policies of other countries. This aspiration was realized at the Bandung conference of 1955, where Premier Zhou Enlai and the Chinese delegation played a significant role; ultimately, participants adopted Ten Principles that were based on China's Five Principles.

From the late 1950s to the late 1960s, the world order was increasingly influenced by the hegemonic rivalry between the United States and the Soviet Union. As a large country close to one of the two superpowers, and eager to play a role in the world arena, China was deeply influenced by this world situation. As a result, China made determined efforts to forge relations with the developing countries of Asia, Africa, and Latin America. Many agreements of economic cooperation were signed between China and countries in these regions. At the same time, through dialogue and negotiation, China successfully settled historic border disputes with such countries as Burma, Nepal, Mongolia, Afghanistan, and Pakistan. Moreover, relations with European countries and Japan were starting to move forward in a positive way.

Although China's relations with the developing world and some Western countries seemed to be moving forward by the late 1950s, its ties with the Soviet Union were beginning to fray. The leaders of the Soviet Union had been trying hard to make China accept policies that served the Soviets' global strategic vision, and even attempted to persuade China into giving up its positions on such important issues as Taiwan and the Sino-Indian border dispute. China's firm stand, as well as a number of other factors, resulted in the USSR's decision to "punish" China by withdrawing economic and technological assistance in the early 1960s.[1]

In the 1950s and 1960s China's relations with the United States continued to be sour, particularly during and after the Korean War. Even so, by the end of the 1960s China had established diplomatic relations with more than fifty countries, while continuing to play a significant role in maintaining world peace. U.S. efforts to isolate socialist China had failed.

In the early 1970s, China made remarkable progress in its foreign diplomacy on at least two fronts. First, China regained its legitimate seat in the United Nations in October 1971, which made it possible for China to play an increasingly essential role in international affairs. Second, U.S. President Richard Nixon paid an official visit to China on February 21, 1972, which led to a breakthrough in Sino–U.S. relations.

China's position in the world arena again received notice when Mao Zedong put forward his view of the "three worlds" in February 1974. As he explained to a visiting leader, the United States and the Soviet Union were the First World; in the middle was the Second World, which included Japan, Europe, Australia, and Canada; and the developing countries were the Third World. This classification was reminiscent of then-common notions about the "third world" and the Cold War, of course, but was significant in two ways: First, it came from the standpoint of a developing nation; second, it implied that countries of the Third World should work together in the pursuit of their interests.

After the third plenary session of the Chinese Communist Party's Eleventh National Congress in 1978, China implemented significant adjustments in many areas, including foreign policy. Deng Xiaoping changed the tone that directed people's understanding of the major themes of the era.[2] When he met with the visiting Brazilian president J. P. Figueiredo in Beijing in May 1984, Deng said that there were many problems in the world, and the two most conspicuous were peace and development. Later on, he expressed again his idea that the most important problem in the world could be summarized in just "four words": East, West, North, and South. East–West was related to peace, and North–South was relevant to development.[3] This definition has facilitated the formulation of China's foreign policies in the new international environment, and has helped pave the way for further development of its relations with other countries, including those of Latin America.

The Post–Cold War Era (1990–present)

When the Cold War ended, China started to reevaluate the world order and the need to adjust its foreign policies. The vision of both the government and academics was that China could enhance its position in the changed world scenario.[4] For example, in the early 1990s, Deng Xiaoping said that in the emerging world order China could be one of the poles of a multifaceted world power structure, and that the end of the Cold War could be a good opportunity for both China and the world.

Generally speaking, the majority of the Chinese people, particularly academics, believe that China's foreign diplomacy in the new century should be based upon three pillars.[5] First, development is and will continue to be a dominant issue. As Deng Xiaoping said repeatedly, China should continue to better itself. Indeed, only by maintaining rapid economic growth can China play an important role in the world.

Second, the defense of sovereignty is still at the top of China's foreign policy agenda. China shares borders with fifteen countries, and its border disputes with some of these countries have yet to be resolved. Around China there are several "hot" spots, and Japan appears to be intensifying its military ties with the United States.[6] Within China, separatist forces, supported by some foreign countries, are found in Taiwan, Tibet, and even Xinjiang province (actually not a province, but an autonomous region).

Finally, as a socialist country with (1) a long history of rich culture and civilization, (2) more than 1.2 billion people, (3) nuclear weapons and long-range missiles, and (4) a permanent seat on the UN Security Council, China deserves an important role in the world arena.[7] In the words of one scholar, "China should make great contributions to the world. . . . [T]he complexity of [current] world politics and the imperatives of progress all require China to gradually strengthen its self-awareness and to act like a big country."[8]

But how to act like a "big country"? Some Chinese scholars are suggesting that China cannot escape from the historical pattern whereby any country wishing to become a world power has grown beyond its own region. According to this logic, China should strive to play an important role in the affairs of the Asia-Pacific region.[9]

Sino–Latin American Relations: A Historical Overview

Initial contacts between China and Latin America date back to the 1570s, when Sino–Latin American trade started to flourish across the Pacific. Via Manila, China exported silk, porcelain, and cotton yarn to Mexico and Peru in exchange for silver coins and other items. In the middle of the nineteenth century, peasants from southern China went to South America and the Caribbean as "contract laborers" working in mines and plantations.

After the founding of the People's Republic of China, Mexico, Argentina, Chile, and a few other Latin American countries contacted China regarding possible diplomatic relations. For a number of reasons their overtures were not successful. In the 1950s, some Latin American countries simply followed the United States in the attempt to isolate China. For instance, in January 1950, before the UN Security Council was about to vote on the Soviet proposal that Taiwan's seat in the UN should be replaced by the People's Republic of China, the United States learned that Ecuador was planning to sever its relations with Taiwan. Washington informed the foreign ministry of Ecuador that, although Ecuador had its own independent right to make any international political decisions, severing relations with Taiwan would have a significant influence upon the outcome of the vote in the Security Council. Because of these pressures from the United States, the Ecuadorian representative to the UN, Homero Viteri-Lafronte, acknowledged that although Ecuador's vote had limited impact on its own, it would have great significance for the United States. Therefore, said Viteri-Lafronte, Ecuador would follow Washington's wishes and not do anything that could risk damaging U.S. interests. Shortly thereafter the Truman administration issued a letter to Latin American embassies in Washington, saying that countries of the Americas should do their best to bring their foreign policies into complete alignment—under the aegis of the United States.[10]

Fidel Castro's victory in 1959 attracted immediate moral and political support from China. As a matter of fact, Cuba became the first Latin American country to recognize the new China.[11] In September 1960 Chinese Premier Zhou Enlai told Castro, "if necessary, China will furnish all necessary assistance to the Cuban people in their fight for freedom."[12] In April 1961, U.S. President Kennedy, then seen by many as "inexperienced in foreign affairs," approved an exile invasion of Cuba at the Bay of Pigs. The Chinese government made an official statement, with strong wording, denouncing the American action. Throughout the whole country, public rallies were held to voice support for the Cuban people's stand against U.S. imperialism. Subsequently, before disputes gradually erupted between the two socialist countries in the mid-1960s, China and Cuba signed several agreements of economic cooperation.[13]

In the 1960s China also voiced support for other Latin American countries struggling against the United States. When a demonstration calling for the return of the Panama Canal was suppressed by the U.S. army in January 1964, leading to twenty-two deaths, Chairman Mao Zedong immediately expressed his anger: "The Chinese people will always stand on the side of the Panamanian people, fully supporting their fight against the American aggressors and their just struggle to take back the Panama Canal."[14] When the United States forcibly intervened during the Dominican Republic's internal political instability in April 1965, Chairman Mao made a similarly worded statement denouncing the U.S. action.

Despite the "Cultural Revolution"—which had disastrous consequences for China's political, economic, and social development, as well as for its relations with other countries—Chinese diplomacy continued to progress in certain areas. On December 15, 1970, for instance, Chile and China established diplomatic relations. After U.S. President Nixon made his historic visit to Beijing in 1972, many Latin American countries started to change their attitudes toward China and even expressed their interest in developing relations with it. As table 15.1 shows, the 1970s witnessed the establishment of diplomatic relations between China and more than ten Latin American countries.

Many Latin American countries supported China's reentry into the United Nations in 1971, and China used many occasions to voice its support for Latin

TABLE 15.1
Calendar of Diplomatic Recognition between China and Latin American Countries

Country	*Date*
Cuba	1960
Chile	1970
Peru	1971
Mexico	1972
Argentina	1972
Guyana	1972
Jamaica	1972
Trinidad and Tobago	1974
Venezuela	1974
Brazil	1974
Suriname	1976
Barbados	1977
Ecuador	1980
Colombia	1980
Antigua and Barbuda	1983
Bolivia	1985
Grenada	1985–1989*
Nicaragua	1985–1990*
Belize	1987–1989*
Uruguay	1988
The Bahamas	1997
St. Lucia	1997

*When Belize, Grenada, and Nicaragua established "diplomatic relations" with Taiwan, the People's Republic of China severed its ties with the three countries.

America's call for the establishment of a new world order. At a banquet for the visiting Mexican President Luis Echeverría on April 20, 1972, for example, Chinese Premier Zhou Enlai declared that

> Latin America is emerging on the world stage with a new face. . . . The struggle led by Latin American countries to defend the maritime sovereignty limit of 200 nautical miles has inspired and motivated people around the world to wage a struggle against maritime imperialism. . . . The Chinese government and the Chinese people firmly support the just struggle of the Latin American people, and believe that a united Latin America, through its struggle, will win a great victory over the expansionary influence of imperialism, and new and old colonialism.[15]

In the early 1970s, China also supported Latin America's call for the establishment of a nuclear-free continent. In November 1972, foreign minister Ji Pengfei announced that China would neither use nor threaten to use nuclear weapons toward the nuclear-free countries or zones in Latin America; that

China would not test, manufacture, locate, or store nuclear weapons in Latin America; and that it would not transport nuclear weapons through Latin America's sovereign land, sea, or air space. Soon thereafter, the Chinese government presented a note to Mexico affirming that China respected and supported the just call of Latin American countries to establish a nuclear-free zone in the region. China's position on this issue won immediate praise from Latin America.

Sino–Latin American Relations in the New Century

As mentioned earlier, China's reforms and opening-up to the outside world since 1978 has provided the country with new opportunities to revise and strengthen foreign policy. Since then, Sino–Latin American relations have been moving forward steadily. As of the writing of this chapter, China has established diplomatic relations with nineteen Latin American countries.

The Communist Party of China (CPC) always plays a decisive role in the nation's foreign policy making. During the "Cultural Revolution," it must be admitted, the CPC made some mistakes in this arena. At that time, the CPC believed that the major themes of the era were war and revolution, and that if revolution could not stop a war, then war would stop revolution. Now the CPC's general stance toward international relations is based on four principles: autonomy, full equality, mutual respect, and mutual noninterference. And in particular, the CPC has formed explicit and productive relationships with political parties in Latin America.[16]

First, the CPC seeks ties with not only the ruling parties, but also with opposition parties. In Argentina, for instance, before the election in 1983, many people believed that the Radical Party would not win. But the CPC still invited the party's leader Raúl Alfonsín to visit China. After winning the presidency with 52 percent of the vote, the grateful president sent a large delegation to China, apparently in appreciation of China's earlier invitation. On China's side, the CPC continued to maintain relations with the Peronist Party, whose leader Carlos Saúl Menem won the presidential elections of May 1989. In November 1989, only five months after the Tiananmen Square incident of June 4, President Menem sent his brother, Senate President Eduardo Menem, to visit Beijing at a time when the West was sanctioning China. The Argentine guest even invited Chinese President Jiang Zemin to visit Buenos Aires in May 1990. In November 1990, President Menem became the first Latin American head of state to visit China after the June 4 incident.

Second, by taking advantage of "party diplomacy," the CPC has developed relations with parties in the countries that have not yet established diplomatic relations with China. This is particularly significant in the case of Bolivia and Uruguay, since before China established formal diplomatic relations with these two countries, the CPC had good contacts with the political parties there. To date, the CPC has established relations with various political parties in the majority of the Latin American countries that have no diplomatic ties with China. For instance, it has good contacts with the major parties in Paraguay, the only South American country that recognizes Taiwan. It is reported that these parties have reached a consensus that the Paraguayan government should improve the relationship between China and Paraguay.

Third, the CPC seeks to develop party relations so as to draw lessons and experiences from the Latin American process of economic development and political governance. The CPC also helps both sides to create opportunities for economic cooperation. For instance, returning from a visit to Brazil and Uruguay in June 1996, a high-level CPC delegation succeeded in helping a Chinese company in Shenzhen to sell telecommunications equipment to these two South American countries. After a party delegation from Honduras visited China in 1991 and asked China to make investments there, the CPC's Department of International Liaison even facilitated the building of a clothing factory in Honduras by a Chinese investor.

China has also made efforts to develop relations with the multilateral and regional organizations of Latin America. For instance, since the establishment of political dialogue between China and the Rio Group in 1990, nine talks have been conducted at the foreign-ministry level. China has always praised the important role of the Rio Group and considered it to be an important political force among developing countries, as well as a reliable partner in international affairs. In June 1994, China became the first Asian country to be an observer to the Latin American Integration Association. In May 1997, China was admitted into the Caribbean Development Bank, and in September 1993, China officially applied to join the Inter-American Development Bank. Meanwhile, the Common Market of the South (MERCOSUR) is becoming an important integration organization in the Western Hemisphere, and China has held two official talks with this group following the establishment of a dialogue mechanism.

On the whole, bilateral relations between China and Latin American countries are now on good terms. However, there is still room for improvement. As a matter of fact, the Central American and Caribbean subregions represent weak spots from the standpoint of China's foreign policy, since Taiwan has a strong foothold there.[17]

It is well known that the effectiveness of mainland China's efforts to counter Taiwan's "dollar diplomacy" is often thwarted by the United States. President Clinton's permission for Taiwan's then-president Lee Teng-hui to visit the

United States in 1995 was a notable example. As for the countries of Central America and the Caribbean, it is evident that the governments in these subregions would not dare to recognize the People's Republic of China before getting the nod from the U.S. government. Apparently, it is Washington's desire to prevent a unified China from rising in East Asia, and it is in America's national interest to maintain the status quo between China and Taiwan.

Taiwan's apparent success in carrying out its "dollar diplomacy" is easily understood. As a Chinese proverb goes, "Whoever has the milk can be my mother." Lured by generous economic assistance from Taiwan, some Central American and Caribbean countries have repeatedly proposed in vain that the Chinese province of Taiwan be "readmitted" into the UN. But as many observers acknowledge, if the 1.2 billion people of mainland China do not agree, Taiwan's independence will be nothing more than a daydream.

It is increasingly recognized that, in the age of globalization, politics tend to be economic in nature, and economic issues are often linked to politics. Indeed, to develop bilateral relations, it is important to expand economic ties. In demonstration of this point, China and Chile signed a bilateral trade agreement in October 1952, the first such agreement between China and a Latin American country. Since then, Sino–Latin American trade has grown steadily. By 1960, two-way trade between China and Latin America had risen to more than US$30 million as compared with only US$7 million in 1955. In 1970 and 1978 it surpassed US$100 million and US$1 billion, respectively. With the rapid development of diplomatic relations across the Pacific since the late 1970s, Sino–Latin American trade increased impressively. By 2000, as shown in table 15.2, two-way trade between China and Latin America had risen to more than US$12 billion.

During the 1990s, China's once-frequent trade deficit with Latin American countries shifted to become a small surplus. In 1997, for example, China enjoyed a surplus of US$837 million, and in 1998 and 1999 its surplus stood at US$2.3 billion. China's exports to Latin America are mainly machinery (tractors, machine tools, engines, ships, hydroelectric generators, and the like), electronics (TV sets, refrigerators, and other household devices), textiles, clothing, medical products, cosmetics, and light industrial products. From Latin America, China imports such goods as iron and copper ore, fish meals, petroleum, wool, machinery, steel, edible oil, sugar, paper pulp, and leather, among others.

China's major trade partners in Latin America are quite concentrated in number. As table 15.3 indicates, China's five largest trade partners—Brazil, Chile, Argentina, Panama, and Mexico—accounted for three-fourths of its trade with the entire region in 1999.

TABLE 15.2
Sino–Latin American Trade, 1950–2001 (US$ millions)

Year	*Volume of Trade*
1950	2
1955	7
1960	31
1965	343
1970	146
1975	476
1980	1,331
1985	2,572
1990	2,294
1995	6,114
2000	12,600
2001	14,938

Source: *Zhonguo haiguan tongji (China Customs Statistics),* various issues.

It should be pointed out that Sino–Latin American trade accounts for a small share in each side's overall foreign trade (less than 2 percent for each). However, the outlook for increased trade appears promising. This is simply because: (1) Latin America has a wealth of natural resources, and China's rapid economic development will need more such input to sustain growth. (2) There is some economic complementarity between the two sides. (3) As both China and Latin America undergo economic reforms, markets are opening

TABLE 15.3
China's Major Trade Partners in Latin America, 1999 (US$ millions)

Country	*Volume of Trade*
Brazil	1,845
Chile	1,269
Argentina	1,086
Panama	1,038
Mexico	951
Peru	441
Cuba	289
Uruguay	213
Venezuela	188
Colombia	125

Source: *Zhonguo haiguan tongji (China Customs Statistics).*

and investment regulations are becoming more liberal. (4) Latin America cannot afford to neglect China's huge market potential, especially since China has now joined the World Trade Organization (WTO). Moreover, as it diversifies its external economic strategy, Latin America will also need China and other East Asian countries. (5) In the age of globalization, China and Latin America have common interests involving such issues as South-South cooperation.

In recent years it has been increasingly recognized, by both the Chinese government and academics, that Sino–Latin American economic cooperation is all the more important insofar as China can meet some of its resource needs from the other side of the Pacific. It is true that China is a nation with a great amount of natural resources. Because of its huge population, however, China is also lacking resources in terms of per capita distribution. Take forest and timber for example. According to recent statistics, China's forest area is 1.2 million square kilometers, and timber resources are about 10 billion cubic meters. These two absolute numbers are huge compared to many other countries in the world. But in per capita terms, China's forest area is merely 0.10 hectare, and timber resources are less than 10 cubic meters, as compared with the world average of 1.07 hectare and 83 cubic meters, respectively.[18] Up to 1998, it has been reported, 230 million cubic meters of timber were cut down each year in China, causing wide-ranging soil erosion and floods. Needless to say, importing timber from Latin America or other parts of the world is strategically important to China.

Despite these mutual interests, the further development of Sino–Latin American economic relations confronts two major obstacles. First, the geographical distance between the two regions is certainly an unfavorable factor. So far there is no direct air link between China and any Latin American country, and the limited maritime routes are affected by distance, weather, and other impediments (customs procedures, problems in loading and unloading, and so on). As a result, delays are very common. Second, exchanges of market information are difficult, and mutual understanding is lacking. This is due not only to the geographical distance but also to languages, cultures, and customs, to name a few.

These two obstacles have existed for a long time. In recent years, the use of antidumping measures seems to have added another obstacle to the development of Sino–Latin American economic relations. On April 15, 1993, Mexico decided to levy antidumping tariffs on ten categories of imports from China. This was the first action ever taken in Latin America to limit Chinese exports. Since then Argentina, Brazil, Chile, Colombia, Ecuador, and Venezuela have all employed this trade practice against China.

Several features characterize Latin America's antidumping policies. First, this practice tends to cover a wide range of Chinese products. Second, the antidumping tariffs levied are very high. For example, Mexico once levied a tariff of 1105 percent on Chinese shoes—a rate that was equivalent to a total ban on this product. Third, Latin American countries still believe China's economy is commanded by central planning. Lastly, certain Latin American countries seldom follow international norms—they tend to levy tariffs before carrying out an actual investigation.

Expanding its market share in Latin America has been part of China's objective to reduce its dependence upon the United States, Japan, and Europe. China has therefore been trying very hard to find ways and means to increase economic relations with Latin America. One recent measure has been called "processing with our own materials," which means that China ships the production lines and intermediate goods to Latin America instead of selling the final products. This idea seems feasible, particularly in the case of TV-set production, since China's own capacity is showing signs of exceeding its domestic market needs.

Government officials, businesspeople, and scholars from both China and Latin America have frequently suggested that both China and Latin America should think of more effective ways to sustain the momentum of economic cooperation that has been underway over the past several decades. One such way would be for them to make more foreign direct investments in each other's economies.

By the end of 1998, China had made 246 investments in Latin America, totaling around US$290 million. Major investments include an iron ore mine in Peru, oil fields in Mexico and Peru, agriculture and textiles in Mexico, timber in Brazil, fish meals and timber products in Chile, fisheries and TV sets in Argentina, motorcycles in Colombia, shrimp raising in Ecuador, and gas production in Venezuela and Peru. By the end of 1998, there were also seventy-seven Latin American investment projects in China, totaling US$8.3 billion.[19]

The movement toward regional economic integration in Latin America, exemplified by MERCOSUR, offers both opportunities and challenges for China. On the positive side, it is likely that highly competitive Chinese enterprises will take advantage of the free movement of goods and capital among the Latin American countries. On the negative side, however, is the possibility of trade diversion, which is not favorable to China and other Asian countries.

Another way to promote Sino–Latin American cooperation is in the field of science and technology. In this regard, China and Brazil may serve as good examples. A satellite has been sent into orbit jointly by the two nations, and it is reported that a second launching is planned for the near future. Finally, given their tremendous labor resources and growing infrastructures needs, construction contracts may be another area of cooperation.

Recently many people have noted that, while Latin America is labor-intensive compared to more developed regions, this advantage has been fading away since

China and India, among others, have entered the world market with cheaper labor. Indeed, China and Latin America might face friction in competing for world market shares in the sense that China's labor cost is lower than that of Latin American countries. However, this kind of friction is unavoidable insofar as competition is becoming ever fiercer in the age of globalization.

Even so, it remains important to recall what Deng Xiaoping said in 1988: "People are saying that the 21st century is the Pacific era. . . . I firmly believe that at that time there will also be a Latin American era, and I hope the Pacific era, Atlantic era and the Latin American era appear at the same time." He also said, "China's policy is to develop and maintain good relations with Latin American countries, and make Sino–Latin American relations a model of South-South cooperation."[20]

China's Relations with Cuba

As mentioned earlier, it was through Cuba that China "entered" Latin America in the diplomatic arena, and the two countries enjoyed a short honeymoon thereafter. In fact, it was the Cuban Revolution that encouraged China to take a new look at revolutionary movements on the other side of the Pacific.

China-Cuba relations were greatly affected by the split between China and the former Soviet Union. In the early 1960s, faced with a tight American embargo and sanctions, Cuba acquired strategic assistance from both the former USSR and China, and Cuba seemed to take a neutral stand toward the Sino-Soviet divide. At the end of 1964 a delegation of communist parties from nine Latin American countries, led by a high-level Cuban official, visited both Moscow and Beijing. They urged the leaders of both large socialist countries to halt their public disagreements. Authorities in Beijing did not accept what they regarded as pro-Soviet suggestions, however, and this caused discontent among their Cuban counterparts.

On March 13, 1965, at a public rally, Castro implicitly criticized China's leaders and their external and internal policies. In September of that year, Cuba denounced the Chinese embassy in Havana for having violated Cuba's sovereignty by distributing printed matter. The sour relations between the two socialist countries were worsened by the fact that Moscow was providing Cuba with more economic aid than Beijing. Cuba was also not happy to see that China and the United States had started to move closer in the early 1970s. Therefore, despite efforts made by Chinese leaders to improve relations with the Caribbean island nation, bilateral contacts remained very low-level.[21]

The exchange of visits between Chinese Foreign Minister Qian Qichen and his Cuban counterpart Malmierca in 1989 marked the full resumption and development of Sino-Cuban relations. In 1993 Chinese leader Jiang Zemin paid a visit to Cuba, and in 1995 Cuban leader Fidel Castro went to China. Since the early 1990s, in fact, the two socialist countries have been cooperating closely on many international issues. China supports Cuba's struggle to defend its sovereignty and counter U.S. imperialism, while Cuba actively backs China's application to join the World Trade Organization (WTO) and China's positions on human rights, Taiwan, and Tibet.

With the improvement of political relations, bilateral economic cooperation has also been proceeding smoothly. In 1999, two-way trade amounted to US$288 million. China imports raw sugar and some medicine from Cuba, and exports food, machinery, medicines, and light industrial products. In July 1997, the first Sino-Cuban joint venture, making plastic slippers, was established in Cuba. In the current era China-Cuba relations have come to be based mainly on realistic cooperation with mutual understanding and benefits—in contrast to the early 1960s, when ties were mainly based on ideology.

China and APEC

At present, the Asia-Pacific Economic Cooperation (APEC) forum is the only institutionalized regional economic organization that includes members from both sides of the Pacific. Although the idea of forming a free-trade area around the Pacific Rim was expressed as early as the mid-1960s, real actions were not taken until the late 1980s. Following the suggestions put forward by the then–Australian Prime Minister Hawk, foreign ministers and trade/economic ministers from twelve Asia-Pacific countries met together in Canberra, Australia, in November 1989. Hence, this meeting was considered to be the official establishment of APEC. Begun as an informal dialogue group, APEC has since become the primary regional vehicle for promoting open trade and practical economic cooperation. Its goal is to advance Asia-Pacific economic dynamism and promote a sense of community.

Even before APEC came into being, China took an active attitude toward Hawk's idea of forming an organization of regional cooperation in the Asia-Pacific area. Because of the Tiananmen Square incident, China was excluded as a founding member of APEC. It was not until November 1991 that the People's Republic of China, Hong Kong, and Chinese Taipei (Taiwan) were admitted into APEC.

APEC is the only regional organization that China has joined. There are several reasons why China attaches great importance to its role and position in APEC. First of all, around 80 percent of China's foreign trade is with APEC members. The United States, Japan, and Hong Kong are China's main trade partners, and the ASEAN countries and South Korea are also becoming important trade partners for China. In addition, about 90 percent of the flow of foreign capital into China comes from APEC member countries.

Second, by joining APEC, China was seeking to curtail the pace and impact of globalization. Ever since the open-door policy was adopted at the end of the 1970s, China has increasingly recognized that, with the rapid development of the globalization process, it absolutely must integrate itself into the world—but in a gradual way. In 1994 APEC members agreed to complete the process of trade/investment liberalization by 2010 for developed economies and by 2020 for developing economies, including China. This schedule is consistent with China's own timetable for opening its domestic market. Within APEC, in other words, China can learn by doing—and accumulate experience and knowledge about ways of integrating its economy with the outside world.

Third, APEC membership made it possible for China to accelerate and promote its campaign to enter the WTO, a step that was finally taken in late 2001. Even then, APEC provides China with an alternative forum for discussing and resolving economic disputes with other major powers, especially the United States. Through APEC, China wishes to ease trade conflicts with others through diverse and creative forms of dispute resolution.

Finally, it is beneficial for China, the largest developing country in the world, to play an important role in establishing a new international economic order. Years of reform have made China's economy develop at a very fast rate. Some of its neighbors are concerned about the future possibility that China will threaten their security, based on groundless reasoning about some kind of alleged "China threat." Within the APEC community, China can build a better image of confidence and responsibility through dialogues and negotiations with other APEC members. At the same time, China can make known its own proposals and express its wishes to other developing members in order to bargain more effectively with the developed members on both economic and political matters.

While on the one hand China looks positively upon APEC, on the other hand China maintains that it has to take into account its own national realities in dealing with the trade/investment liberalization issues within the APEC framework. There are several key concerns. First, despite its rapid economic growth rates, China is still a developing country that cannot be compared with the industrialized nations in many areas. Moreover, the objective of establishing a socialist market economy has yet to be realized. Therefore, it is too early to expect China to integrate its economy fully and speedily into the world economy. Second, around 80 percent of China's population resides in rural areas. With low productivity and high production costs, they cannot compete in the world market. Third, in addition to the agricultural sector, other sectors such as automotive, electronics, telecommunications, and financial services, among other services, are still in need of protection. Until they grow stronger, it is not wise to open these sectors to competition from mighty transnational corporations.[22]

Despite China's insistence on recognition of its national realities, it has taken an active and positive attitude toward various APEC activities. In the past seven years, for instance, Chinese President Jiang Zemin has participated in each APEC Economic Leaders' Informal Meeting, during which he has made important speeches elaborating China's policies, initiatives, principles, and positions on economic cooperation among APEC members and on some other issues.[23]

First, at the Bogor meeting in November 1994, Jiang Zemin put forward the five principles of economic cooperation in the Asia-Pacific region: (1) mutual respect and consensus; (2) gradual progress and steady development; (3) mutual opening up without exclusion; (4) extensive cooperation, mutual benefit, and reciprocity; and (5) common prosperity. Second, at the Osaka meeting in 1995, Jiang Zemin announced that, starting in 1996, China would reduce its import tariffs by at least 30 percent. Third, at the Subic meeting in 1996, Jiang Zemin announced that China would reduce its average import tariff rate to around 15 percent by the year 2000. President Jiang also praised what was called the "APEC approach." "Since its establishment," he said, "APEC has accumulated some experience in the course of practice and gradually come up with [a] unique way of cooperation. This has come to be known as the 'APEC approach.' It has such features as recognition of diversity; emphasis on flexibility, gradual progress and openness; adherence to mutual respect, equality, mutual benefit, consensus and voluntarism; and [the] combination of individual and collective actions."[24] And at the Kuala Lumpur meeting in 1998, Jiang Zemin said that the Chinese government would allocate $10 million to set up the China APEC Fund on Scientific and Industrial Cooperation, which will help finance cooperation between China and other APEC members in the field of science and technology.

In addition to the informal meetings of APEC economic leaders, China has also been an active participant in all kinds of ministerial meetings and consultations. The Ninth APEC Informal Leadership Meeting will be held in Shanghai in November 2001, with China as the official host.

To date, three Latin American countries have become APEC members: Mexico, Chile, and Peru.[25] It is said that Ecuador and other Latin American countries are hoping to follow suit. At the various meetings mentioned above, Chinese leaders and other high-level officials exchanged views and arguments with their counterparts from other member countries, including those from Latin America. Therefore, APEC seems to have served as a valuable bridge connecting China and other Asia-Pacific and Latin American countries.

There is another new "bridge" that has been built across the Pacific between Asia and Latin America—the East Asia–Latin America Forum (EALAF), first mooted by Singapore Prime Minister Goh Chok Tong during a visit to Chile in October 1998. "I conceived the EALAF as a multi-dimensional dialogue. It was to help break down barriers and encourage the evolution of more concrete links," said Prime Minister Goh.[26] The first EALAF, attended by senior officials from twenty-seven East Asian and Latin American countries, was held in Singapore in early September 1999. The second meeting was held among foreign ministers in Chile in the first quarter of 2001; it was there that the group changed its name to FEALAC (Forum for East Asian–Latin American Cooperation).

According to the foreign ministry of Singapore, the Forum will contribute to a stable international order by interconnecting two important growth areas of the world. However, the full potential of linking the two regions is likely to take a decade or more to be realized, due to the lack of historical contact, awareness, and understanding between both regions. The launch of the forum thus represents the start of a long-term process to bring that synergy to fruition.[27]

China has sent high-level delegations to the EALAF/FEALAC meetings. It is China's belief that close cooperation between East Asia and Latin America will help elevate the position of developing countries and also facilitate the establishment of a new political and economic order. China has also proposed that the forum allow only sovereign nations to participate, and that it take advantage of the complementarity of both regions to promote economic cooperation in the new century.[28]

Conclusion

Since 1949, China's foreign policies have changed from time to time. No matter what kinds of shifts there are in the future, however, it appears clear that China will continue to devote a great deal of attention to the Third World.

Latin America is important for China in at least three areas. Politically, China needs Latin America and other developing regions to maintain the momentum of its struggle against imperialism and hegemonic powers. Economically, China considers Latin America to be a source of trade and investment opportunities, and a potential supplier of natural resources. Diplomatically, mainland China considers Latin America to be a place where it needs to contain Taiwan's "dollar diplomacy."

Unlike Chile or some other Latin American countries, China has not designed a "trans-Pacific" strategy to reach out to Latin America. However, it is expected that in the new century the above three aspects will still dominate China's policies towards Latin America, and Sino–Latin American relations will continue to develop on the basis of the Five Principles of Peaceful Coexistence.

APEC appears to offer an appropriate venue for China to develop its multilateral ties with Asia-Pacific and Latin American countries. Indeed, because of China's participation in APEC, Asia-Latin American interactions have been proceeding smoothly and positively in the past decade, and will continue to move forward rapidly in the new millennium. As Chinese president Jiang Zemin said repeatedly during his trip to Latin America in April 2001, "The 21st century will be a century of China and Latin America cooperating in all areas hand in hand, and it will also be a century of the peoples in China and Latin America building a better tomorrow."

Notes

1. Within one month of July 1960, the Soviet leaders called back 1,390 experts and terminated 12 bilateral treaties and more than 300 agreements of technological cooperation.

2. In an article published in 1924, Soviet leader Joseph Stalin considered war and revolution to be the defining characteristics of the age. This ideology had great influence upon China's diplomacy until the end of the 1970s.

3. Deng Xiaoping, *Deng Xiaoping wenxuan* [Selected works of Deng Xiaoping], Vol. 3 (Beijing: Renmin Chubanshe [People's publishing house], 1993), 56–57.

4. Chinese analysts have naturally had different opinions regarding the prospects for peace and development in the world. For instance, one scholar argued that the NATO bombing of Yugoslavia meant the end of the opportunities offered by peace and development. (See Zhang Wenmu: *Kesuowo zhanzheng yu zhongguo de jiyu* [The Kosovo War and China's security strategy in the new century], *Zhanglue yu guanli* [Strategy and management], no. 6, 1999.

5. Wang Yizhou, "Mianxiang 21 shiji de zhongguo waijiao: 3 zhong xuqiu de xunqiu jiqi pingheng" [Seeking and balancing the three requirements: China's diplomacy in the 21st century], *Zhanglue yu guanli* [Strategy and management], no. 6, 1999.

6. China has fresh memories of Japan's past actions. In the post–Word War II era, Japan became one of the major economic powers and, as the leaders of both governments have maintained, the two "close neighbors separated only by a strip of water" should work towards a peaceful future.

7. In 1996, China vetoed a UN resolution to send a peace-keeping mission to Guatemala. This was only the third veto it had used since it reentered the UN in the early 1970s, and it taught a lesson to those countries that tried to intervene in China's internal affairs. China withdrew its veto on this UN resolution in early 1997, after talks were held between China and Guatemala.

8. Wang Yizhou, "Seeking and Balancing," 26. (Apparently, the term "big country" used here simply means a world power.)

9. See, for example, Ye Zicheng, "Zhongguo shixin daguo zhanlue shizaobixin" [The inevitability of China's foreign diplomacy as a world power], *Shijie jingji yu zhengzhi* [World economics and politics], no. 1, 2000.

10. *Foreign Relations of the United States*, Vol. 2, 1950. Quoted from Tao Wenzhao, "Meiguo, laiyi yu shongguo zai lianheguo de daibiaoquan," [The United States, Trygve Lie, and China's representation in the UN], Meiguo yanjiu [American studies], no. 4, 1996. See www.state.gov/www/about_state/history/frusX/.

11. It is reported that, during a rally held in Havana on September 2, 1959, Castro proclaimed: "The Revolutionary Government of Cuba would like to ask the Cuban people if you would like Cuba to establish diplomatic relations with the People's Republic of China." The rally roared with enthusiasm, raising their hands and chanting, "Yes, yes!" Then, walking toward the nearby head of the New China News Agency stationed in Havana, Castro said, "Here is the Chinese representative. From now on, I declare that Cuba has cut its relations with the puppet regime of Chiang Kai-shek (in Taiwan)." For a more vivid account of the scene, see Wang Taiping, ed., *Xin zhongguo waijiao 50 nian* [Fifty years of the new China's foreign diplomacy], (Beijing: Beijing Chubanshe [Beijing publishing house], 1999), 1636–1637.

12. Quoted from Zhang Guang, *Zhongguo de waijiao zhengce* [China's foreign policies], (Beijing: Shijie Zhishi Chubanshe [World Affairs Press], 1995), 91.

13. Sino-Cuban relations turned for the worse in the mid-1960s for both political and economic reasons. Politically, this was related to the Sino-Soviet rupture, during which Cuba sided with the Soviet Union. Economically, Cuba had been complaining that China was not providing enough economic aid.

14. Quoted from Zhang Guang, *Zhongguo de waijiao zhengce,* 91.

15. Taiping, *Xin zhongguo waijiao 50 nian,* 1660.

16. Huang Wendeng, "Dengxiaoping lilun yu zhongla dangji guanxi" [Deng Xiaoping theory and relations between the communist party of China and Latin American political parties], *Ladingmeizhou yanjiu* [Latin American studies], no. 6 (1998): 1–7.

17. Paraguay is the only South American country that has not recognized the People's Republic of China.

18. Guo Yuanzheng, "Lizuo kechixu fanzhan, jiakuai kaituo lamei ziyuan shichang" [Opening the natural resources market at a quicker pace, on the basis of sustainable development], *Ladingmeizhou yanjiu* [Latin Americans], no. 1 (1999): 18.

19. Wang Jian, "Zhong la jingmao guanxi xianzhuang ji qianjing" [Status quo and prospects for Sino–Latin American trade], *Ladingmeizhou yanjiu* [Latin American studies], no. 2 (2000): 12–13.

20. Quoted from the *Renmin ribao* [People's Daily], October 8, 1995.

21. Taiping, *Xin zhongguo waijiao 50 nian,* 1640–1645.

22. It is interesting to note that disputes have emerged in recent years among Chinese intellectuals regarding the prospects for these "weak" sectors. While some believe that it is highly necessary to continue protecting "infant" industries, others argue that foreign competition should be brought in to make them stronger.

23. Quoted from the Chinese Foreign Ministry's website, at www.fmprc.gov.cn/english/dhtml/.
24. In 1993, Mexico became the first Latin American country to join APEC. It was followed by Chile in 1994 and Peru in 1998.
25. Quoted from www.mfa.gov.sg/abtspore/index.htm.
26. Quoted from www.mfa.gov.sg/abtspore/index.htm.
27. As a token of support for the forum, China announced that the Chinese Foreign Ministry would organize a course for the Latin American diplomats in Beijing so as to promote mutual understanding between the diplomats of both sides.

16

The United States: Building a New World Order?

Peter H. Smith

> Out of these troubled times . . . a new world order can emerge: a new era—freer from the threat of terror, stronger in the pursuit of justice, and more secure in the quest for peace. An era in which the nations of the world, East and West, North and South, can live in harmony.
>
> —George H. W. Bush (1991)

THE UNITED STATES HAS FOLLOWED AN UNCERTAIN PATH since the ending of the Cold War. It has been especially unclear whether or how the United States would attempt to preserve its global power, revamp the international system, or construct a new world order. These concerns have presented special challenges to East Asia and Latin America and to the development of closer relations between these two regions. What have been the basic patterns of U.S. foreign policy during the 1990s, and what implications might they have for East Asia and Latin America?

This chapter begins by surveying the global position of the United States at the conclusion of the Cold War and tracing underlying elements in U.S. foreign policy during the 1990s. Subsequent sections explore U.S. relations with Asia and Latin America under Presidents Bush (the elder) and Clinton. The essay then presents an analysis of the still-evolving administration of George Bush (the younger) and its response to the terrorist attacks of September 11, 2001. A brief conclusion offers speculation about prospects for a new world order.

I write this chapter within one year of the devastating assaults on New York City and Washington, D.C., which led to the death of nearly three thousand human beings. The attacks have deeply affected national priorities for the

United States and its relations with other countries throughout the world in ways that are still difficult to grasp and impossible to foresee. This essay is therefore highly tentative.

Supremacy and Constraints

When the Cold War suddenly ended in 1989–1991, pundits and politicians in the United States hastened to proclaim the final victory of capitalism over communism. Francis Fukuyama gave highbrow formulation to this impulse in his celebrated 1989 essay "The End of History," which claimed that the world was bearing witness "not to an 'end of ideology' or a convergence between capitalism and socialism, but to an unabashed victory of economic and political liberalism." Communism was as dead as fascism; authoritarian doctrines were relics of the past. The implication was that the world had reached "the end point of mankind's ideological evolution and the universalization of Western liberal democracy as the final form of human government." As a process of ideological and intellectual struggle, history had arrived at a terminal point.[1] While Fukuyama did *not* mean to imply that all forms of conflict and change would disappear, as some of his critics inaccurately claimed, he seriously underestimated the power of ideas and identities most likely to shape the newly emergent world: ethnicity, religion, and nationalism.

Although it had historic consequences for the world as a whole, the fall of communism was an essentially European affair. What happened in Eastern Europe did not occur throughout Asia. China and North Korea remained resolute communist states, while Russia and the United States both maintained their military presence in the region. Instability and tension continued to prevail along the Asia/Pacific front.

The most immediate result of the end of the Cold War was the emergence of the United States as the world's sole superpower. The implosion of the Soviet Union meant that the United States would have no serious military rival anywhere: it could enjoy a "unipolar moment" of unchallenged strategic and tactical superiority, as epitomized by its overpowering performance during Operation Desert Storm against Iraq's Saddam Hussein in 1991. Moreover, the United States had the world's largest economy, one that expanded sharply during the course of the 1990s. As shown by table 16.1, the United States had less than 5 percent of the world's population in 1999 but produced nearly 29 percent of the total economic output. Its nearest rival, Japan, produced just half that much, and the number three country, Germany, produced just half as much as Japan. The United States economy was overwhelmingly larger than those of Latin America, including Mexico and Brazil.

TABLE 16.1
Gross National Product and Population Size: Selected Countries, 1999

	GNP		*Population*	
	US$ Billions	*% World*	*Millions*	*% World*
United States	8,351.0	28.6	273	4.6
Japan	4,078.9	14.0	127	2.1
Germany	2,079.2	7.1	82	1.4
China	980.2	3.0	1,250	20.9
Korea	397.9	1.4	47	0.8
Indonesia	119.5	0.4	207	3.5
Brazil	742.8	2.5	168	2.8
Canada	591.4	2.0	31	0.5
Mexico	428.8	1.5	97	1.6
Russia	332.5	1.1	147	2.5
Argentina	277.9	0.9	37	0.6
Chile	71.1	0.2	15	0.3

Source: World Bank, *World Development Report 2000/2001: Attacking Poverty* (New York: Oxford University Press, 2000), table 1 (pp. 274–275).

Yet supremacy was not without its complications. One problem was the control of nuclear weapons. During the Cold War only two major command posts—one in the United States, the other in the Soviet Union—were positioned to launch a nuclear exchange. Fragmentation of the USSR meant that its former dependencies, most conspicuously Ukraine, would acquire command and control of these weapons systems; moreover, erstwhile allies and client states, no longer beholden to the major powers, could pursue nuclear strategies of their own. There thus emerged a growing number of claimants on power and prestige—midlevel nations with nuclear capability, such as India and Pakistan, and pariah "weapons states" like Iraq and North Korea—that threatened drastic alteration of the military calculus.

Adding to this irony, U.S. firepower appeared to be of limited utility. The challenges and conflicts of the 1990s did not lend themselves to military solutions. The Gulf War of 1991 was seen as a glaring exception. The protracted, contradictory, and painful struggles of Somalia, Bosnia, and Kosovo seemed to represent the norm. Military prowess was becoming a hollow shell.

Another key development was the increasing importance of nongovernmental actors and forces—multinational business firms, international traders, migrant workers, private organizations, and other participants in emerging networks of "transnational interdependence." Technological innovation, demographic expansion, spreading communications, atmospheric pollution, and other nonpolitical factors were coming to have more impact on the daily lives of citizens than the policies of governments. Currency traders could make decisions around the clock, billions of dollars could move at the push of a button. The power of the market, in particular, was challenging (or, better said, disregarding) the power of the state. Governments were in retreat.

Transnational activities often took illicit form. Arms trafficking, drug smuggling, and clandestine migration took place in explicit violation of state policies and/or multilateral regimes. Criminal organizations and terrorist groups flourished as well. Gangster operations and terrorist cells represented formidable obstacles to the construction of a new international order and, especially, to effective governance by nation-states.

These trends became painfully apparent on September 11, 2001, when the United States was unable to prevent attacks on American soil and citizens by small groups of individuals who hijacked commercial airliners and plowed them at full speed into the World Trade Center and the Pentagon. Even more tellingly, it was entirely unclear whether the U.S. military response—bombings and commando raids in Afghanistan, where suspected terrorist leader Osama bin Laden maintained headquarters—would prove to be effective. High-powered armaments seemed strangely irrelevant to this emerging drama. Much of Afghanistan had already been destroyed in a decade-long war against invading Soviet troops during the 1980s; it was a "failed state" par excellence. Ousting Afghanistan's Taliban government was one thing; rebuilding (or building) the nation was another; destroying bin Laden's international network was something else again. And as the United States imposed its military strength throughout the region, it risked a bitter long-term backlash throughout the Muslim world.

Policy and Policy Making

Under such circumstances it was uncertain whether the post–Cold War world would manage to achieve a workable code for international behavior. The situation was confusing. As political scientist Joseph A. Nye Jr. wrote in 1992, "No single hierarchy describes adequately a world politics with multiple structures. The distribution of power in world politics has become like a layer cake. The top military layer is largely unipolar, for there is no other military power comparable to the United States. The economic middle layer is tripolar and has been for two decades. The bottom layer of transnational interdependence shows a diffusion of power."[2] This configuration was unlikely to produce stability. There was no clear-cut mechanism for resolving disputes or preventing violence: not a balance of power, as in the nineteenth century; not mutual bipolar deterrence, as during the Cold War; and not single-power hegemony, despite the military preeminence of the United States.

U.S. policy was thrown off course. Without an identifiable enemy and without a sense of mission, there were no longer any organizing principles: "In the post–Cold War era," as one insider noted in 1994, "no one knows what foreign policy ought to be." In short order, though, the United States adopted an overriding goal—maintaining the nation's position as the only remaining superpower. No longer engaged in a sweeping ideological crusade, Washington would pursue practical advantage and power enhancement in a world of traditional realpolitik. In skeletal form, post–Cold War foreign policy came to have three basic priorities:

1. Preservation of supremacy as the world's sole superpower
2. Promotion of U.S. economic strength and prosperity
3. Support for democratic change and human rights

It was assumed that all of these goals were mutually reinforcing: geoeconomic and geopolitical strength went hand-in-hand; democratization, for its part, would gain allies and open markets. But when hard choices arose, Washington steadfastly pursued the top two priorities—political and economic power—at the expense of democracy and human rights.

Formulation of these objectives did not lead to a coherent strategy. At times Washington resorted to use of military force, in such distant locations as the Sudan and Kosovo, often in the guise of "humanitarian interventions" that were followed by (usually abortive) efforts at "nation-building."[3] On other occasions it blithely ignored blatant violations of fundamental human rights. The record was somewhat more consistent in the field of economics, where the United States ardently promoted market liberalization and commercial opening, often through an expanding web of free-trade agreements. Official spokespersons vigorously asserted that open economies would lead to open polities and that, as a result, America's efforts would expand and consolidate "market democracies" around the globe. That was a dubious claim.

The 1990s turned out to be a decade of remarkable prosperity and power for the United States. Success came easily—almost too easily. As Henry Kissinger noted with evident perplexity, Americans appeared to take their position for granted:

> At the dawn of the new millennium, the United States is enjoying a preeminence unrivaled by even the greatest empires of the past. From weaponry to entrepreneurship, from science to technology, from higher education to popular culture, America exercises an unparalleled ascendancy around the globe. . . .
>
> Ironically, America's preeminence is often treated with indifference by its own people. . . . Especially in the 1990s, American preeminence evolved less from a strategic design than a series of ad hoc decisions designed to satisfy domestic

> constituencies while, in the economic field, it was driven by technology and the resulting unprecedented gains in American productivity. All this has given rise to the temptation of acting as if the United States needed no long-range policy at all and could confine itself to a case-by-case response to challenges as they arise.[4]

The market would take care of economics, and economics would take care of geopolitics. There was no need for foreign policy.

Such attitudes were widespread in the United States. A 1994 poll by the Chicago Council on Foreign Relations found that foreign policy issues accounted for less than 12 percent of major concerns cited by the general public and a sample of national leaders. By 1998 the figure was down to 7.3 percent for the public (and up to 19.5 percent for the leaders, largely because of the Asian economic crisis). The interpretation was self-evident: "Most Americans do not see the United States as facing major international problems. . . . When fewer dramatic international crises are bedeviling the United States, public focus on foreign policy wanes. The findings suggest that there is satisfaction with the U.S. position in the world, and even a measure of disconnection from international events, which seem to pose less of an immediate threat to people's lives."[5] The only exception to this rule was concern about international terrorism, especially in the wake of bombing attacks on U.S. embassies in Nairobi and Dar es Salaam in 1998.[6] But even that seemed like a distant threat.

Complacency led to ambivalence about America's role in the world. The 1998 survey found that 28 percent of the general public espoused an isolationist stance, 61 percent supported "an active role" for the United States, and 11 percent had no opinion. As might be expected, the elite was much more internationalist—with 96 percent in favor of activism and just 3 percent in favor of isolationism. Paradoxically, though, the general public was more willing to back unilateral action—with 72 percent agreeing that the United States "should act alone if it does not have the support of its allies," compared with just 48 percent of the leaders.[7] Elaborating on this point, studies by the Pew Research Center found that "influentials" (analogous to leaders in the Chicago survey) tended to advocate a proactive American role in shared multilateral leadership, for the United States to be a kind of *primus inter pares*, while the general public supported multilateral cooperation—but without special U.S. responsibilities as leader. There was broad support for multilateralism, but a significant difference of opinion about the *kind* of multilateralism that would be most appropriate.

Surveying the world, both the general public and national leaders attributed special significance to Europe, Russia, and China. Asia as a whole was viewed as important but less so than Europe; Latin America was farther down the ladder. Thus countries of East Asia were regarded as more "vital" to U.S.

national interests than were nations of Latin America. As shown by table 16.2, 87 percent of the public in 1998 perceived a vital U.S. interest in Japan and 74 percent saw a vital interest in China, as did 94–95 percent of the leaders. Mexico and Brazil attracted much less concern from the general public (66 percent for Mexico and only 33 percent for Brazil). And while 93 percent of America's leaders saw vital interests in Mexico, only 75 percent held the same view of Brazil (even this figure represented a substantial increase over 1994, presumably because of that country's impending financial crisis). Both the public and leaders regarded South Korea as more important than Brazil. Cuba was fast losing its relevance, even for the general public.

Within Asia, American concerns were undergoing marked change. In the 1990 survey, 63 percent of American leaders regarded economic competition from Japan as a serious threat; by 1998 this was true for only 14 percent. By contrast, worries about China were on the rise. The emergence of the People's Republic of China (PRC) as a world power was seen as a potential threat by 40 percent of the U.S. public in 1990 and just 16 percent of the leaders; by 1998 these figures had risen to 57 percent for the public and 56 percent for the leaders. Such context helps explain U.S. policy toward Asia in the 1990s.

U.S. Policy toward Asia, 1989–2001

Asia was a problem area for the United States. In the economic realm, it was strong and getting stronger. Recovering from the devastation of World War II, Japan entered the ranks of advanced industrial nations during the 1960s and

TABLE 16.2
Perceptions of Vital U.S. National Interests, 1994–98

	1994		*1998*	
	Public (%)	*Leaders (%)*	*Public (%)*	*Leaders (%)*
Mexico	76	98	66	93
Brazil	34	49	33	75
Cuba	67	—	50	—
Japan	85	96	87	94
China	68	95	74	95
Korea	65	90	54	82

In response to the following question: "Certain countries of the world are important to the U.S. for political, economic, or security reasons. . . . For each [country to be named], tell me whether you feel the U.S. does or does not have a vital interest in that country."
Source: John E. Reilly (ed.), *American Public Opinion and Foreign Policy 1999* (Chicago: Chicago Council on Foreign Relations, 1999).

1970s; such nearby countries as South Korea, Taiwan, Singapore, and Hong Kong—nicknamed the "four little tigers"—made equally impressive strides in the 1970s and '80s. By the mid-1990s East Asia was widely regarded as having the "most dynamic" regional economy in the world. And in the political realm, communist regimes continued to hold sway over mainland China, North Korea, and Vietnam. Of course the practical meaning of communist doctrine would undergo significant modification, but leaders in these countries harbored profound reservations about unfettered capitalism and unlimited U.S. power. As a sign that the Cold War was over, though, President Clinton announced the normalization of diplomatic relations with Vietnam in 1995 and made a state visit to that country in 1999.

During the course of the 1990s, U.S. policy toward Asia would focus on three basic concerns: (1) regional security, (2) trade and economic development, and (3) democracy and human rights.

Regional Security

A key to regional security was the "forward deployment" of American troops in East Asia, especially Japan. During the first Bush administration, some thought that it would no longer be necessary (or desirable) for the United States to continue this practice. In 1990 the Pentagon proposed a three-stage reduction of U.S. forces in East Asia over a ten-year period; and in 1992, two massive U.S. military bases were closed down in the Philippines. These developments immediately prompted concern among the region's governments—particularly Japan, South Korea, and the Association of Southeast Asian Nations (ASEAN)—which regarded the U.S. military presence in East Asia as insurance against instability and a guarantee against external aggression. In their eyes, an American withdrawal would result in a dangerous power vacuum.

After brief hesitation, the Clinton administration decided to maintain the forward deployment. In October 1993, a so-called bottom-up review called for approximately a hundred thousand American troops in Northeast Asia. In 1995 the Department of Defense (DOD) reaffirmed its intent to exercise leadership in the region and proposed a halt to troop reductions planned under George Bush I. Moreover, it asserted that the deployment of American military forces should serve as the bedrock for a "deep security engagement" throughout East Asia. Three years later, the DOD's East Asian strategy report confirmed this view once again.

The policy led to strenuous negotiations with Japan. In September 1994, officials from the two countries declared that the U.S.–Japan security alliance remained a critical factor in regional peace and stability, while Tokyo agreed to pay almost $5 billion, or about 70 percent, of the cost of maintaining U.S. forces in Japan. Years later the Clinton-Hashimoto Joint Declaration upgraded the alliance to cover a wider portion of East Asia and recommended significant changes in Japan's internal security procedures, including the removal of political constraints preventing the Japanese government from using its Self-Defense Forces in an East Asian emergency. Forward deployment was firmly in place.

This did not sit very well with the People's Republic of China, which was, of course, one of the principal targets of the U.S. strategy. Tensions flared repeatedly between the two countries. In 1994 the Pentagon revealed that China's modernization program had made the PRC a credible military threat to U.S. national security. The next year PRC leaders objected vigorously when the Clinton administration permitted Taiwan's President Lee Teng-hui to make a private visit to Cornell University in June 1995, thus jeopardizing the "one-China" policy that was a pillar of the Washington-Beijing relationship. In March 1996, during presidential elections in Taiwan, the PRC conducted three major military exercises and threatened to use force if necessary to reunite Taiwan with the mainland; Washington responded by dispatching two aircraft carrier battle groups to the Taiwan Straits and warning the PRC against the use of force. In May 1999 relations were strained again by the bombing of the Chinese Embassy in Belgrade during the U.S.–led North Atlantic Treaty Organization (NATO) campaign against Yugoslavia, apparently as a result of a CIA targeting error, but the two sides managed to settle the issue within a matter of months. The United States and China—the one an undisputed superpower, the other aspiring to become one—were jostling for advantage but unwilling to engage in direct confrontations.

Still another challenge came from North Korea and its nuclear-weapons program. The fear was that the North Korean regime, enigmatic and unpredictable, might threaten a nuclear strike in order to compensate for its isolation and weakness. After Jimmy Carter made a visit to Pyongyang in 1994, the Clinton administration decided to provide North Korea with positive incentives for responsible behavior. In subsequent negotiations Pyongyang agreed to freeze its program in return for aid in building conventional reactors (that would not produce bomb-grade material) and in finding alternative sources of energy. Four years later North Korea test-fired a ballistic missile over Japanese airspace, and the Clinton team began seeking a freeze on Pyongyang's missile program along the lines of the nuclear freeze. Relations improved with the formation of a high-level Trilateral Coordination and Oversight Group (TCOG) to coordinate North Korea policy. Pyongyang delayed its response on the missile question until fall 2000, when the Clinton administration had only a few months left in office, so the agreement could not be completed in time. In view of North Korea's assurances that it would continue its moratorium on the testing of long-range ballistic missiles, the United States began to ease longstanding economic sanctions in June 2000. (This entire question resurfaced again in late 2002.)

Trade and Economics

As suggested by the dénouement with North Korea, economic relations were linked to regional security in two basic ways—through the existence or threat of U.S. trade sanctions against recalcitrant regimes, and through the idea that expanding investment and commerce would contribute to stability. Washington had practical interests as well: expanding markets for U.S. exports, and reducing the nation's chronic trade deficit.

In March 1993 Assistant Secretary of State for East Asian and Pacific Affairs Winston Lord intimated that, in the aftermath of the Cold War, economics would supplant military considerations on America's foreign policy agenda. The Clinton administration pledged to seek greater access to Asian markets in order to reduce the bilateral trade imbalances with key Asian economies. Lord's general theme—the creation of a "New Pacific Community"—was developed around the notion that no region would be as important to the United States in the next century than Asia. Several months later Clinton initiated the summit process for the Asia-Pacific Economic Cooperation (APEC) forum. While upgrading of APEC was widely welcomed in Asia, the U.S. endorsement of a formal timetable for creating a free-trade arrangement in the region was not well received. Asians advocated a heavier emphasis on such shorter-term programs as cooperative infrastructure development, exchange of trade and investment data, harmonization of customs standards, and other forms of trade promotion. The ASEAN nations in particular saw U.S. proposals for a free-trade arrangement as premature.

A longstanding source of the U.S. trade imbalance was Japan. To be sure, the 1985 Plaza Agreement had helped boost U.S. exports through appreciation of the yen, and a 1990 agreement was intended to reduce "structural impediments" to U.S. trade and investment. But by 1992 the U.S. trade deficit with Japan ballooned again, while massive Japanese investments (at home and in the United States) made Americans uneasy about the rising strength of this once-defeated enemy. Early in the Clinton term, U.S. trade officials threatened Japan with economic sanctions unless Tokyo opened its markets to U.S. exports and took steps to lower the trade imbalance. Arduous negotiations ensued: In June 1995, the two countries agreed to expand U.S. automotive exports to the Japanese market just hours before $5.9 billion in tariffs to block imports of Japanese luxury cars were to take effect.

As for China, the Clinton administration pursued a two-pronged strategy. First, Washington sought to fully integrate China into the global trading system as a way of nurturing economic reforms in that country and of increasing China's stake in the stability and prosperity of East Asia. Second, it aimed to expand U.S. access to the Chinese market. In late 1999 the United States and China finally agreed on ways to reduce tariffs and other trade barriers, thus paving the way for China's accession to the World Trade Organization (WTO). The following year the U.S. Congress approved Permanent Normal Trade Relations for China.

During Clinton's second term, economic relations with Asia were dominated by the region's financial crisis. In mid-1997 Thailand freed the *baht* from the dollar, crippling investor confidence and triggering a financial crisis throughout Southeast Asia and South Korea (see chapters 10 and 11 in this volume). Cautious because of lingering congressional resentment over the Mexican bailout of early 1995, the Treasury Department worked through the International Monetary Fund (IMF) to pull Asia out of the crisis. In October 1997, the U.S. contributed $3 billion to an IMF-led bailout of Indonesia; in December, South Korea agreed to the terms of a $55 billion IMF bailout, to which the U.S. contributed $5 billion. U.S. demand for Asian goods also boosted the prospects for recovery. Russia was the next to be infected, and the United States rushed to provide emergency cash for fear that its old nuclear rival would disintegrate and lose control over its weapons.

Democracy and Human Rights

Tiananmen set the tone for U.S. human rights diplomacy. After the Chinese crackdown against demonstrators in Beijing in 1989, the United States promptly suspended high-level official exchanges, weapons exports, and other trade and investment programs. At the G-7 Houston summit in mid-1990, Western nations called for political and economic reforms in China.

Trade thus became tightly connected to human rights. In May 1993, the Clinton administration decided to formally link the renewal of China's most favored nation trading status (MFN) to its progress on human rights. In addition, Washington pledged to promote human rights through a wide variety of mechanisms—by making foreign aid contingent on the recipient's human rights record, expanding international radio broadcasting to Asia, and supporting progressive nongovernmental organizations (NGOs). Focus on worker rights in Malaysia and Indonesia, the problem of East Timor, and the caning of an American youth in Singapore strained relations with much of Southeast Asia. Singapore, a country that had been a stalwart supporter of U.S. bases in the Philippines and the most enthusiastic advocate of free trade, joined Malaysia as a vocal critic of America.

Sino-American relations suffered additional strain over such issues as Beijing's (unsuccessful) bid for the 2000 Olympic Games, the imposition of sanctions against China's sale of missile technology to Pakistan, and the search of a Chinese cargo ship allegedly carrying precursors for chemical weapons to the Middle East. Beijing made only the most begrudging concessions on human rights, thus presenting Clinton with a dilemma: Either carry out an ill-conceived threat, or lose credibility. Faced by this choice, Clinton eventually backed down and severed the linkage between China's trade status and its human rights record. With the United States no longer in opposition, China gained membership in the World Trade Organization in November 2001.

U.S. Policy toward Latin America, 1989–2001

Latin America presented the United States with a very different kind of situation. Washington had held sway throughout the Americas for most of the twentieth century. And with the ending of the Cold War, U.S. hegemony within the region was suddenly uncontested. The European Community focused its energy and resources on the rehabilitation and reincorporation of Eastern Europe; the Soviet Union withdrew from the hemispheric arena and then collapsed, leaving Russia to cope with enormous domestic challenges; Japan, ever mindful of its relationship with the United States (and beset by its own economic problems), proved reluctant to meddle in the Americas; and China, despite its headlong rush toward economic growth, was not yet in any position to pursue an aggressive strategy toward Latin America. There were no strong external competitors for the United States.

Nor were there serious internal threats. In fact, Latin America was enjoying an unusual degree of political democracy, at least in the sense of holding free and (more or less) fair elections. Democratization had spread throughout most of the region during the course of the 1980s, reaching Mexico in the late 1990s and leaving only Cuba as a holdout. Of course there were limitations to the *quality* of democratic life in Latin America, and there would be authoritarian setbacks in such countries as Peru and Venezuela. Generally speaking, though, electoral democracy had firmer foundations in Latin America than in East Asia. In consequence, human rights did not comprise a central theme on the inter-American agenda of the 1990s.

Instead the inter-American agenda focused on social and economic issues—drugs, migration, trade, and investment—matters not of high politics but of mid-level priority. Moreover, such questions touched directly on domestic concerns within the United States; within the academic literature, they came to be known as "intermestic" issues.

Largely as a result, policy making became decentralized. Interagency infighting had long been a feature of the Washington scene, but it reached new heights (or depths) during the 1990s. Different agencies had different policies: The Department of the Treasury had one policy for Latin America, Commerce had another, the State Department had another, INS another, and so on. There was little discernible effort to reconcile these policies. The State Department and/or the White House might have been expected to perform this role. Under Bill Clinton they did not. It remained an open question whether this would change under a different president.

At the same time, Congress came to play a central part in policy formation. Rather than evaluating foreign-policy issues on their merits, however, legislators tended to respond to constituent demands in order to enhance prospects for their own reelection. Frequently, too, they engaged in "log-rolling" deals on issues that bore no substantive connection to each other. And to the extent that the interests of individual congresspersons diverged from those of the White House, there was bound to be discord and confusion. This was especially true after November 1994, when the Republican Party captured majorities in both the U.S. Senate and the House of Representatives. This dynamic led to inconsistent outputs.

It also produced anomalies. Perhaps the most striking was the continuation of hostility toward Cuba. Although the Cold War had come to an end, although the Cuban military presented no discernible threat to the United States (or any other country of the hemisphere), and although the U.S. business community was losing out on attractive investment opportunities in Cuba, Washington refused to abandon its forty-year-old economic embargo of the island or its virulent opposition to Fidel Castro. This provided a striking contrast to evolution of the U.S. stance toward Vietnam. Such obstinacy could be explained only by the political strength of the right-wing Cuban exile community in the state of Florida; as such, it illustrated the influence of domestic interests on U.S. policy toward the hemisphere.

The War on Drugs

Illicit drugs posed a major problem for U.S. society. Approximately 14 million Americans were consuming illegal substances on a current basis (that is, within the past 30 days). This represented a substantial decline from the 1979 high of 25 million but an increase over the 1992 low, and it still represented nearly 6 percent of the household population aged twelve or older. There were nearly 10 million current users of marijuana, by far the nation's favorite illicit drug, and about 1.5 million current users of cocaine. Especially intractable was "frequent" usage of cocaine: The number of those who consumed on a weekly basis (and were thus addicted) had remained close to 600,000 since the mid-1980s. There was a rise in the number of heroin addicts (also around 600,000) and a notable increase in experimentation with illicit drugs by American teenagers. The implication was inescapable: Nearly 20 years after Ronald Reagan declared a "war on drugs," consumer demand remained steady and strong. And as the Office of National Drug Control Strategy reported in 1997: "Illegal drugs continue to be readily available almost anywhere in the United States. If measured solely in terms of price and purity, cocaine, heroin, and marijuana prove to be more available than they were a decade ago when the number of cocaine and marijuana users was much higher."[8]

In response, the United States made determined efforts to suppress the production and transit of illicit drugs throughout the hemisphere. The presumption was that a reduction in supply from Latin America would push up the retail price of drugs in the United States—and this in turn would lead to a reduction in demand. Without supply there could be no demand; it was as simple as that. Washington therefore adopted two basic approaches: elimination of the sources of supply by destroying crops and laboratory facilities, and interdiction of shipments bound for the U.S. market. As the federal allocation for antidrug efforts continued to expand, from $2.7 billion in fiscal year (FY) 1985 to $19 billion in FY 2000, the commitment to supply reduction remained remarkably firm, claiming just about two-thirds of the total budget.

Another policy tool was the annual process of "certification," mandated by Congress as an amendment to the Foreign Assistance Act of 1986. According to the statute, governments that failed to cooperate with the United States on drugs would lose foreign assistance and face U.S. opposition in multilateral lending organizations. In 1996 and 1997 Colombia was denied certification; in 1998 it received a national interest waiver. And almost every year, the evaluation of Mexico led to high drama: In 1998 the Clinton administration decided to certify Mexico against opposition from a significant number of lawmakers and law enforcement authorities. Although the rituals of certification provoked recurrent controversy, Washington persevered with the process.

Near the end of his second term, Clinton gave his approval to a $1.3 billion aid package for Colombia, which was facing major threats from guerrilla organizations and drug trafficking groups. Anxious to prevent a "failed state" in the Americas, Washington granted massive amounts of military assistance—presumably to pursue the war on drugs, although many critics claimed that the military aid would also be used in the decades-old civil war between the guerrillas and the government (especially because the guerrillas were often in league with the traffickers). It was not clear, at this writing, what would be the result.[9] What was clear was the continuation of the U.S. consumption of drugs.

Undocumented Migration

Just as illicit drugs made their way into the United States, so did undocumented migrants. Despite expansions in U.S. quotas for legal immigration from the 1960s through the 1980s, people continued to enter the country without official authorization, in violation of U.S. law. Responsible demographers estimated the total stock of "illegal aliens" in the early 1990s to be between 2.5 and 4 million, with Mexico accounting for 55–60 percent of the total. A subsequent study put the stock of illegal Mexicans around 2.3–3.4 million as of 1996.

Periodically, the United States took measures to stanch this flow. The Immigration Reform and Control Act of 1986 (IRCA) contained three principal provisions: (a) economic sanctions for American employers who "knowingly employ, recruit, or refer for a fee" undocumented workers; (b) permanent amnesty to undocumented workers who could prove continuous residence in the United States since January 1982; and (c) partial amnesty for undocumented workers in the agricultural sector. Ultimately, IRCA represented a compromise between those political forces opposing unauthorized migration (from organized labor to racist reactionaries), and Latino leaders expressing concern about the potential aggravation of ethnic prejudice. In the end, IRCA achieved mixed results. The employer sanctions portions proved to be toothless, but as a result of the provisions for amnesty, nearly 3 million people acquired legal status in the United States.

During the 1990s the United States redoubled efforts to deter illegal immigration. A tough stand on this issue became a hallmark of the Clinton administration, which took office in the midst of a crisis over an influx of rafters from Haiti. Washington increased the INS budget from $1.4 million in FY 1992 to $2.6 million for FY 1996. It sharply expanded the size of the border patrol. And it launched concentrated efforts at key crossing points: In 1993 the administration proclaimed Operation Hold-the-Line in El Paso, Texas (formerly known as Operation Blockade); in 1994 it launched Operation Gatekeeper in San Diego; and in 1997 it initiated Operation Rio Grande in McAllen, Texas. An INS strategic plan called for a long-term effort to extend such concentrated enforcement operations across the entire Southwestern border.

It was unclear whether such efforts would ever be effective. One visible result was to redirect large numbers of migrants toward perilous inland terrain, where deserts and mountains posed major hazards to pedestrians, leading to the deaths of hundreds of Mexicans every year—at the rate of one per day. The result was a strain on relations, especially with Mexico. After all, annual remittances to Mexico were $5 billion or more, and the northward exodus provided the country with a social safety valve. Latin American governments also sought to protect their country from abuse, mistreatment, and harassment within the United States. Undocumented migration tended to create bad feelings on all sides, and stepped-up-measures to deter the flows only tended to exacerbate these tensions.

The Movement for Free Trade

During the 1990s the dominant axis of inter-American relations would come to deal with economic issues. Early in the decade a spirit of optimism suffused Washington and many capitals of Latin America. As economic matters moved to the forefront of the inter-American agenda, officials came to agree that the Cold War had distorted U.S.–Latin American relations by introducing an ideological factor that was extraneous, artificial, and deleterious. In the newly emerging world, they further concurred, the economic interests of the United States and Latin America converged with one another. Steadfast pursuit of economic goals would therefore lead to a happy and harmonious relationship. It was economics, rather than politics, that defined true and legitimate national interests.

Reflecting such convictions, a movement in favor of "free trade" swept through the Americas. By far the most ambitious and far-reaching example of regional integration concerned the North American Free Trade Agreement (NAFTA) between Mexico, Canada, and the United States. Unveiled in August 1992, the pact was signed that October in the midst of the U.S. presidential campaign, and took effect in January 1994. Building on a preexisting free-trade accord between Canada and the United States, NAFTA created one of the two largest trading blocs in the world. With a population of 370 million and combined economic production of approximately $6 trillion as of 1992, North America could be a worthy rival to the European Union.

NAFTA promoted the free flow of goods between member countries by eliminating duties, tariffs, and trade barriers over a period of fifteen years. Sixty-five percent of U.S. goods gained duty-free status immediately or within five years; half of U.S. farm goods exported to Mexico immediately became duty-free. There were special exceptions for certain "highly sensitive" products in agriculture, typically one of the sectors most resistant to economic integration; phase-outs on tariffs for corn and dry beans in Mexico and orange juice and sugar in the United States would extend to the year 2009. Tariffs on all automobiles within North America would be phased out over ten years, but rules of origin stipulated that local content would have to be at least 62.5 percent for vehicles to qualify. Not surprisingly, Asian governments regarded this clause as highly protectionist, a thinly disguised effort to exclude Japanese industries and products from the North American market.

NAFTA opened Mexico to U.S. investments in various ways. Under the treaty U.S. banks and securities firms could establish branch offices in Mexico, and U.S. citizens could invest in Mexico's banking and insurance industries. While Mexico continued to prohibit foreign ownership of oil fields, in accordance with its constitution, U.S. firms became eligible to compete for contracts with Petróleos Mexicanos (PEMEX) and to operate, in general, under the same provisions as Mexican companies.

One item was most conspicuous by its absence: Beyond a narrowly written provision for movement of corporate executives and selected professionals, the treaty made no reference at all to large-scale migration of labor. The continuing flow of "undocumented workers" from Mexico into the United States remained a major source of conflict and contention in the bilateral relationship. Apparently sensing that there was no ground for reasonable compromise, NAFTA negotiators decided to avoid the question altogether.

Commerce promptly increased. Two-way trade between Mexico and the United States climbed from $83 billion in 1993 to $100 billion in 1994, $108 billion in 1995, and $157 billion in 1997. By this time the United States was exporting more to Mexico than to China, Korea, and Singapore combined, and Mexico displaced Japan as the second largest trading partner of the United States (Canada remained in first place). There were numerous explanations for this expansion in trade, among them conclusion of the Uruguay Round of General Agreement on Tariffs and Trade (GATT) negotiations, but NAFTA no doubt had an impact. According to an understated and somewhat technical report from the White House in mid-1997, NAFTA resulted in "a modest increase in U.S. net exports, controlling for other factors," and boosted jobs in the export sector by 90,000–160,000.[10]

NAFTA also weathered a currency crisis in Mexico. As described in chapter 9 of this volume, the newly inaugurated administration of Ernesto Zedillo confronted a massive run on the peso in December 1994. The resulting crisis threatened to decimate foreign investments in Mexican securities, derail Mexico's pattern of growth, discredit free-market reforms, and destroy the credibility of NAFTA itself. Faced by such prospects, the Clinton administration managed to put together a multilateral package of nearly $50 billion, including $20 billion from the U.S. government, but the peso continued to slide. To combat inflationary pressures (and meet the demands of international creditors) the Mexican government adopted rigorous adjustment programs. Overall, the Mexican GDP declined by more than 6 percent in 1995, then began a gradual recovery. NAFTA thus survived its most stringent test.

Beyond NAFTA, the next step was presumed to be a free trade zone embracing all of the Americas. As George Bush *père* proclaimed when launching the Enterprise for the Americas Initiative in June 1990, the ultimate goal was to create a free trade zone "stretching from the port of Anchorage to the Tierra del Fuego." And in December 1993 Vice President Al Gore pronounced his vision of "a Western Hemisphere Community of Democracies" that would consolidate political and economic harmony throughout the region, with NAFTA as "a starting point."

Yet a hemispheric free trade zone faced formidable obstacles, both economic and political. The commercial rationale was much less compelling than in the case of NAFTA. In point of fact, trade relations between the United States and Latin America *outside of Mexico* were declining in importance to the United States over time. Moreover, a hemispheric scheme could result in substantial trade diversion, especially for countries of South America (most notably Brazil). Second, prospects for joining NAFTA were highly uncertain, since the treaty did not define criteria for admission—which meant, in effect, that member countries could establish arbitrary or impossible accession criteria if they so chose. Third, and perhaps most fundamentally, the hemispheric project lacked clear political motivation. And without such motivation, there could be no lasting integration.

Then the heads of state took center stage. In December 1994, the Clinton administration hosted a grandiose "Summit of the Americas" in the Latinized city of Miami. The meeting's ostensible goal was to develop a blueprint for hemispheric collaboration into the twenty-first century. Eager to capitalize upon this opportunity, leaders agreed to initiate a Free Trade Area of the Americas (FTAA). And as a sign of good faith, NAFTA members invited Chile to commence negotiations on accession. Confidently predicting that FTAA "will stretch from Alaska to Argentina," Clinton boasted that the Miami accord marked "a watershed in the history of the hemisphere."

Obstacles promptly arose. In September 1997, President Clinton submitted to Congress a proposal for renewal of "fast-track" consideration of international trade agreements. (Despite its name, "fast track" referred not to the speed of deliberation but to the stipulation that Congress would have to vote on trade agreements as complete packages, yes or no, rather than amending them.) Fast track had become a staple of trade policy since the early 1970s, as it enabled representatives from the United States—and other countries—to reach agreements with the assurance that they would not be subjected to crippling revisions by special interests in Congress. Yet as controversy mounted, one expert made the astute observation that "Fast track has become a referendum on NAFTA." This meant trouble for the Clinton bill. A *Wall Street Journal/NBC News* poll in early 1997 showed that 43 percent of Americans believed that NAFTA had a negative impact on the United States. And in September, a *Business Week*/Harris Poll revealed that only 42 percent of the public had a positive opinion of NAFTA; 36 percent had a negative view and 22 percent were undecided or unsure. More to the point, a strong majority—54 percent—did not favor extension of NAFTA to other countries of Latin America, and an identical percentage opposed renewal of fast-track authority. "NAFTA has become a dirty word politically," as one advocate of free trade ruefully acknowledged. Fairly or not, NAFTA seemed to be suffering from a political malady common to integration schemes: Benefits would be long-term and diffuse, while costs were short-term and concentrated. And as a result, Congress did not approve fast-track authority.

This failure overshadowed U.S.–Latin American relations for the remainder of the decade. A second Summit of the Americas in Santiago, Chile, in 1998 was unable to make much headway on the FTAA project. As Clinton's second term drew to a close, it was possible to imagine three general scenarios for hemispheric trade. One envisioned prolongation of the status quo, with a three-member NAFTA as the only formal trade accord connecting Latin America to the United States. A second possibility might be called "NAFTA-plus"—that is, a scenario under which NAFTA would undergo limited expansion to include three or four other countries of Latin America. The process would begin with Chile, which had been invited to begin negotiations at Miami in December 1994, and then move on to other countries. In fact, however, the list of viable candidates seemed to be very short. A third possibility still envisioned the achievement of an FTAA on a hemispheric basis—not through NAFTA, but through broad negotiations among thirty-four partner countries. In that case, it seemed likely that the eventual degree of integration would be relatively shallow.

Parenthesis: Asian–Latin American Relations

During the post–Cold War period, the United States paid little (if any) attention to emerging relationships between Asia and Latin America. Such cooperation seemed to pose neither challenge nor threat. To the extent that Washington policy makers considered the question at all, it appears that they regarded APEC as the solution—since it included three Latin American countries as well as nations of the Asia-Pacific region. There is no evidence that they took much notice of the launching of the Forum for East Asia–Latin America Cooperation (FEALAC) in 1998–99. So long as U.S. officials regarded FEALAC as innocuous or insignificant, they would not insist on taking part (or taking over, as authorities from other countries might have said). If and when it became truly important, however, it seemed likely that Washington would not want to be excluded.

George W. Bush—The Changing of the World?

During the presidential campaign of 2000, Republican candidate George W. Bush expressed frequent disdain for post–Cold War foreign policy—especially under Bill Clinton. Mindless of his own inexperience in international affairs, the Texas governor denounced what he considered to be excessive reliance on multilateral consultation, over-commitment of military forces, naive campaigns on behalf of human rights, and hapless engagement in nation-building efforts. By contrast, Bush vowed, his administration would take a no-nonsense approach: The United States would pursue its national interests with as little entanglement as possible with other countries.

Once in office, the new administration began living up to its promises. To the shock of U.S. allies, the foreign-policy team came out in opposition to the Anti-Ballistic Missile Treaty, the Comprehensive Test Ban Treaty, the Small-Arms Control Pact, the Biological Weapons Protocol—and the Kyoto Protocol on environmental protection. At the same time Bush expressed support for the Nonproliferation Treaty, the Missile Technology Control Regime, the Biological Weapons Convention, and the Chemical Weapons Convention. As explained by Richard Haass, Bush's director of policy planning at the State Department, "What you're going to get from this administration is 'à la carte multilateralism.' We'll look at each agreement and make a decision, rather than come out with a broad-based approach."[11] Allies in Europe and elsewhere were deeply skeptical. As German analyst Theo Sommer said of the U.S. president: "He does not concede, he does not give up, he does not surrender. He offers everyone consultations, partners and rivals alike; he promises to keep in touch; that is why, he assures everyone, you cannot talk about an American go-it-alone attitude. Yet the conversations are aimed at conversion, not compromise."[12]

The president appeared to take a different tack on dealing with Mexico, the country of which he had greatest personal knowledge prior to becoming president. During his first year in office he met with Mexico's President Vicente Fox on several occasions: The two struck up a genuine friendship and vowed to resolve pressing bilateral issues, including the problem of undocumented migration. More broadly, Bush strongly advocated creation of a Free Trade Area of the Americas and pledged to give high priority to hemispheric relations. In April 2001 he reiterated these views at the third Summit of the Americas, held in Quebec City, and returned to Washington with an avowed determination to seek congressional approval for fast-track, now renamed trade promotion authority. (He would receive that endorsement in mid-2002.) For the first time in decades, Latin America appeared to be near the top of the U.S. presidential agenda.

In the meantime, Washington's high-handedness spawned serious tension with Russia and China. Bush's relentless insistence on expanding NATO eastward, scrapping the Anti-Ballistic Missile (ABM) treaty of 1972, and pursuing a missile defense program raised major concerns for Russian leader Vladimir V. Putin. And whereas Clinton had frequently referred to China as a "strategic partner," Bush began alluding to the PRC as a "strategic competitor." He took an unusually hard line in his interpretation of U.S. military obligations to Taiwan. And in April 2001, a U.S. EP-3 spy plane collided in mid-air with a Chinese fighter jet, and the damaged American aircraft made an emergency landing on the PRC island of Hainan. The U.S. crew was detained for eleven days amid rising tension; eventually the crew was released and the EP-3 was dismantled and returned to the United States, but mutual suspicions lingered.

It soon appeared that countries around the world were chafing under U.S. primacy. The United Nations voted the United States out of the UN Commission on Human Rights for the first time since its inception in 1947.[13] In July 2001 Russia and China signed a "friendship treaty," their first accord since 1949, and declared joint opposition to America's plans for missile defense. Shortly thereafter 178 countries voted for a global-warming treaty with the United States alone in dissent. Next, 148 countries pushed to move forward with enforcement measures to ban germ warfare despite American objections. These were not turning points but warning signs, indications of an underlying shift from the 1990s. As Henry Kissinger reluctantly observed, "The matter-of-fact acceptance of our hegemony is wearing off."[14]

September 11, 2001

Then came the horrendous attacks of September 11, when terrorists hijacked commercial airliners and crashed them into the World Trade Center in New York and the Pentagon in Washington, D.C. As fear and mourning gripped the nation, Americans rediscovered a sense of purpose and collective mission. Firefighters and policemen became national heroes, New York mayor Rudy Giuliani earned accolades for leadership, tales of courage and caring offered inspiration to an apprehensive citizenry. Many called out for revenge.

Almost immediately, suspicions focused on Al Qaeda, a terrorist network organized by the mysterious Osama bin Laden. Son of a Saudi billionaire, bin Laden was a fundamentalist Muslim who had fought alongside of Afghan *mujahedeen* in their successful guerrilla war against the Soviet Union. A religious fanatic, bin Laden went on to declare an Islamic jihad—against Israel, against modernity, and against the United States. As economic, social, and political conditions deteriorated in the Arab world, bin Laden was able to recruit desperate young people who were prepared to sacrifice their lives for the sake of the cause.[15] Bin Laden's network was thought to be responsible for at least two attacks in the late 1990s—the bombings of U.S. embassies in Nairobi and dar es Salaam in 1998, and the explosion of the Navy destroyer *Cole* in 2000. His ultimate intention appears to have been the formation of a pan-Islamic theocratic state, one that would uphold religious tradition and assert itself as a major world power. Forced to leave his native Saudi Arabia and later Sudan, he had found safe haven in Afghanistan, then under the control of a relentlessly fundamentalist movement known as the Taliban.

It was only a matter of days before the U.S. government articulated its response to 9/11. In a memorable speech on September 20, George W. Bush launched an all-out war on terrorism. He described his nonnegotiable demand that the Taliban turn Osama bin Laden over to U.S. authorities, thus issuing a public ultimatum. He vowed to use military force as necessary. He called for sacrifice and patience from the American people. And he set ambitious and far-reaching goals. "Our war on terror begins with Al Qaeda," the president said, "but it does not stop there. It will not end until every terrorist group of global reach has been found, stopped, and defeated." Promising to challenge and dismantle "the global terror network," the president went on to declare that "Our response involves far more than instant retaliation and isolated strikes. Americans should not expect one battle, but a lengthy campaign, unlike any other we have seen. It may include dramatic strikes, visible on television, and covert operations, secret even in success. We will starve terrorists of funding, turn them against one another, drive them from place to place, until there is no refuge or rest."

Bush delivered a stern warning to governments around the world. The United States, he said, "will pursue nations that provide aid or safe haven to terrorism"—not only Afghanistan under the Taliban, but other countries as well. As a result, the president continued, "Every nation in every region now has a decision to make. Either you are with us, or you are with the terrorists. From this day forward, any nation that continues to harbor or support terrorism will be regarded by the United States as a hostile regime." There was only one choice—black or white. Bush made no mention of international law, world tribunals, or the United Nations.

The American public stood firmly behind its newly focused leader, whose approval ratings approached unheard-of levels around 90 percent. Surveys found that between 85 percent and 92 percent of Americans advocated the use of military force "against groups that are identified as responsible." CBS/*New York Times* polls revealed that two-thirds of Americans would support military action "even if it means that innocent people are killed." Similarly, an *NBC News* poll found 78 percent in agreement with the statement that "combating terrorism is worth risking civilian casualties in Afghanistan." At the same time, Americans thought the anti-terrorist campaign should employ a full arsenal of strategies—not only military force but also diplomatic efforts, financial and economic instruments, enforcement of the law, and secret intelligence. And in general, they expressed strong support for multilateral cooperation. A Harris poll found 95 percent support for the need to "build a strong international coalition of many countries to support us"—remarkably, "even if this means exercising more restraint than we'd like." Similarly, an Associated Press poll revealed that 90 percent said that the UN, much maligned in U.S. conservative circles, should "play a major role in pulling countries together to fight terrorism."

The Bush administration designed a two-part strategy. One element involved formation of a multilateral alliance against terrorism and/or Al Qaeda and/or Afghanistan's Taliban regime. The strongest support came from the United Kingdom; under pressure, NATO declared itself under potential attack. Vladimir Putin of Russia also joined the U.S. side, partly in hopes that this would bolster his own campaign against "terrorist" forces in Chechnya. Arab and Islamic states were circumspect, condemning the September 11 attacks but refraining from endorsement of U.S. policies. Many other nations shared this view.

As these events took place, East Asia and Latin America took sides with the United States—but cautiously. The Organization of American States unanimously approved a resolution denouncing the September 11 assaults, pledging to combat terrorism, and offering to take action "as appropriate." Similarly, leaders from East Asia (plus three countries of Latin America) agreed at the APEC meeting to condemn the September 11 attacks "in the strongest terms" and to proclaim that it was "imperative to strengthen international cooperation at all levels in combating terrorism." Notably absent from the APEC declaration, however, was any expression of support for U.S. military action in Afghanistan; notably present was a pointed affirmation that the United Nations should play "a major role" in the anti-terrorist campaign, "especially taking into account the importance of all relevant UN resolutions." China was especially concerned about a U.S. military build-up so near its own borders. It was also apparent, in many countries, that popular opinion was equivocal (one poll in Thailand showed that 47 percent of respondents wanted their government to adopt a "neutral" attitude). Indeed, it seemed that many observers shared the opinion expressed so succinctly by Cuba's Fidel Castro—against terrorism, and also against war.

The second element in Bush's anti-terrorist strategy involved military strikes against Afghanistan. Bombing sorties began on October 7, less than a month after the initial attack. On-the-ground raids by commando units followed about two weeks later. Afghan civilian casualties quickly mounted in number. American firepower took a staggering toll, especially on the ruling Taliban. By December 2001 the U.S.–led coalition was able to patch together an interim government under the moderate leadership of Hamid Karzai, a genial figure and a practicing Muslim. That turned out to be the easy part. Al Qaeda was another matter. Fully one year after 9/11, the elusive Osama bin Laden was still at large (amid rumors of his death), less prominent leaders were holding his organization together, and hundreds if not thousands of shock troops were poised to launch further terrorist attacks. What the Pentagon called the "long shadow war" was still in its early stages.[16]

In his January 2002 state-of-the-union address, President Bush expressed determination to continue and extend the anti-terrorist campaign. "What we have found in Afghanistan confirms that, far from ending there, our war against terrorism is only beginning. . . . Thousands of dangerous killers, schooled in the methods of murder, often supported by outlaw regimes, are now spread throughout the world like ticking time bombs, set to go off without warning." Sharply critical of regimes that permitted or supported terrorist action, he denounced three governments—Iraq, Iran, and North Korea—as constituting an "axis of evil." While the United States would like to have international support for its policies, it would be willing to act on its own: In the president's words, "Some governments will be timid in the face of terror. And make no mistake about it: If they do not act, America will." The world, and the United States, must be committed to a long-term effort: "Our war on terror is well begun," in the president's words, "but it is only begun. The campaign may not be finished on our watch—yet it must end and it will be waged on our watch."

By March 2002, six months after the September attacks, President Bush announced the second phase of the war against terrorism—the post-Afghanistan phase. This would be, in his words, "a sustained campaign to deny sanctuary to terrorists who would threaten our citizens from anywhere in the world." Once again, he challenged governments around the globe: Any state failing to cooperate with the United States would be viewed as a foe. Against terrorists, he proclaimed, "there can be no immunity, and there can be no neutrality." For its part, the United States would commit substantial resources to the campaign—troops, training, and financial and logistical support.

It soon became clear that the United States was building a rationale for attacking Iraq. A prime component of the so-called axis of evil, Iraq was said to be developing biological and other weapons of mass destruction. It posed a threat to diplomatic negotiations in the Middle East. And its still-surviving leader, Saddam Hussein, was a nemesis—not only to the United States and to the West, but also to the Bush dynasty. Speaking both on and off the record, U.S. officials made clear their belief that, one way or another, Saddam would have to go. The question was when and how this might be accomplished.

Ultimately, the war on terrorism led to fundamental revisions in U.S. military doctrine. Strategy during the Cold War was based on the idea of "mutual assured destruction." The United States would employ its nuclear arsenal only in response to nuclear attack; so long as a retaliatory "second strike" could be sufficiently devastating, the threat would serve as an effective deterrent. In March 2002, a Nuclear Posture Review within the Department of Defense identified non-nuclear states as potential targets—including Iraq, Iran, Syria, and Libya—all officially identified as "state sponsors" of terrorism.[17] For the anti-terror campaign, the United States would require a new generation of nuclear missiles, weapons designed to destroy underground command posts and biological weapons facilities. The report expressed concern about nuclear states as well, especially North Korea and China (one of the scenarios justifying nuclear deployment was depicted as "a military confrontation over the status of Taiwan"). Russia was mentioned but described as a friendly power. The most serious threats were seen to come not from major powers, in fact, but from rogue states in the less developed world; accordingly, the United States would train its mighty arsenal upon the poor. The report thus argued in favor of a fundamental shift in strategy, a stance that one analyst described as "unilateral assured destruction."[18]

In a June 2002 commencement address at West Point, President Bush made clear the conviction that Cold War doctrines were now obsolete. Against terrorists, he insisted, notions of "containment" and deterrence were irrelevant. The United States must now be prepared to strike first. "If we wait for threats to fully materialize," he said to the uniformed cadets, "we will have waited too long. We must take the battle to the enemy, disrupt his plans and confront the worst threats before they emerge." A corollary of this doctrine was, of course, the need for nearly flawless gathering and analysis of intelligence. As reports of shocking failures in the U.S. intelligence community prior to 9/11 swirled about the capital and country, there was little assurance that this condition could be fulfilled.

For hawks within the Bush administration, the war on terror was becoming the foundation for a wholly new formulation of U.S. foreign policy. "For the first time since the dawn of the Cold War," G. John Ikenberry wrote in September 2002, "a new grand strategy is taking shape in Washington." Insisting on the need to maintain U.S. primacy, this incipient doctrine identified principal threats to security as coming not from rival powers but from terrorist groups with potential access to weapons of mass destruction. Dismissing the concept of deterrence as outdated, it claimed a right for the United States to use preemptive or preventive military force—if necessary, in unilateral fashion. By implication, this outlook redefined (and restricted) traditional terms of state sovereignty, discounted international rules and treaties, and attached little value to the goal of international stability. Framed almost completely in response to 9/11, the so-called Bush doctrine was intellectually bold and internally consistent. That did not mean that it would be effective or appropriate.[19]

Even as it jettisoned military doctrines, the war on terror came to resemble the Cold War in other, fundamental ways. As during the Cold War, the United States now had an enemy—a different kind of enemy, to be sure, but an enemy nonetheless. It had an all-consuming mission. And it subsumed almost all other interests to the pursuit of this goal. As William M. Arkin observed, "What makes the new crusade so natural to the Bush team is that it looks so much like the old one: It is not conventional terrorism, but the possibility of terrorism with weapons of mass destruction, or WMD, that has galvanized the administration. With that possibility comes a renewed appetite for covert action and human agents, a need to root out internal security risks, a rise in Cold War-style government secrecy."[20] Geopolitics returned to the fore. Ends came to justify means. Concerns about human rights, which had made so much progress during the 1990s, faded into the background. Once again, Americans came face-to-face with a painful dilemma: They supported the campaign against terrorism, but they became concerned about protection of their civil liberties.

Questions and Concerns

As the United States pressed on with its offensive, serious questions emerged—about the campaign and its implications. One had to do with the depth of American involvement in Afghanistan and South and Central Asia. Even in its early stages, the U.S. effort began to show distinct signs of "mission creep." The initial goal was to capture Osama bin Laden and destroy the Al Qaeda network. To do that, however, the United States realized it would have to overthrow the Taliban regime. And once that was done, the United States would have to find a way to install a government that would be (a) acceptable to Washington, (b) legitimate within Afghanistan, and (c) unthreatening to the neighboring countries—such as Pakistan, India, and China. As Serge Schmemann of the *New York Times* put it, "Getting rid of the Taliban means putting something else in power to prevent Afghanistan from reverting to a blood-soaked breeding ground for new jihads."[21] In other words, the United States would have to become deeply involved in the arduous and expensive task of "nation-building"—precisely the sort of effort that George W. Bush had so vigorously criticized during his presidential campaign. Would the United States follow through? How and with what effect?[22]

A second issue related to the breadth of the U.S. anti-terrorist effort. How far would the United States go? "Terrorism" is a highly elastic concept. By the

U.S. government's own definition, the term refers to "premeditated, politically motivated violence perpetrated against noncombatant targets by subnational groups or clandestine agents, usually intended to influence an audience." International terrorism means "terrorism involving citizens or the territory of more than one country." And an international terrorist network, by extension, is "any group practicing, or that has significant subgroups that practice, international terrorism." Hundreds of terrorist incidents occur around the world each year. In its report on terrorism during the year 2000, the U.S. government designated twenty-eight groups as "foreign terrorist organizations" and listed seven countries as "state sponsors" of international terrorism: Cuba, Iran, Iraq, Libya, North Korea, Sudan, and Syria (but not, remarkably, Afghanistan).[23] In his September 20 speech, Bush had vowed that the U.S. campaign would not end "until every terrorist group of global reach" had been destroyed. And as he said on a subsequent occasion, "Ours is a war against terrorism in general.... [S]uccess or failure depends not on bin Laden, success or failure depends upon routing out terrorism where it may exist all around the world. He's just one person, a part of a network."[24] Was the president saying that the United States would pursue each and every one of the organizations identified as "terrorist" by the U.S. State Department? Would some groups but not others qualify as having "global reach"? Might the campaign extend to Singapore, Indonesia, or even Colombia? Or would the Bush administration be content with wrapping up Al Qaeda alone? Where and when might the campaign come to an end?

This problem became all the more vexing in light of the fact that "terrorism" was not an ideology, cause, belief, country, or nation-state—but a tactic. Anyone could use it. Stamping out one practitioner, such as Al Qaeda, or even all known practitioners as of any given moment, such as the organizations listed by the U.S. government, does not guarantee that some other group will not decide to employ the tactic in the future. Of course it is possible to outlaw these heinous methods, but such agreements would have no more power than international law. And though it is possible to impose (or threaten to impose) enormous costs on those who resort to terrorism, this may or may not be sufficient to deter desperate or even fanatical people from taking the chance. As almost every observer has said, the campaign against terrorism would be unlike any war—not only because of the enigmatic nature of Al Qaeda and similar networks, but also because the "enemy" was an instrument and not a mission.

Another concern related to Washington's stance toward multilateralism. Was the creation of the anti-terrorist coalition merely a matter of convenience? Or did it signify a more meaningful embrace of multilateral cooperation as a key component of U.S. foreign policy? Evidence remained ambiguous. On the one hand, the Bush administration in May 2002 reached an arms-reduction agreement with Russia, took the lead in establishing a consultative NATO-Russia Council, and invited NATO to redefine its mission in a world-wide war on terrorism. On the other hand—and at just about the same time—the administration withdrew support from the International Criminal Court at The Hague, thus "unsigning" a treaty that had been endorsed by the outgoing Clinton administration (but not yet ratified by Congress). Critics of the Court insisted that it would relinquish U.S. national sovereignty to an international prosecutor who could in principle launch investigations against American officials and military officers. Many close U.S. allies, including almost all of NATO, firmly opposed the U.S. decision. One result, as noted by Senator Russell D. Feingold (D-Wisconsin), was a loss of U.S. credibility. "As we continue to fight terrorism worldwide," he said, "we are asking countries around the globe to honor important commitments, to crack down on the financial and communications networks of terrorists and international criminals, and to share sensitive intelligence with the United States. This is not the right time to signal a lack of respect for multilateralism."

In sum, it appeared that the president and his team would continue to espouse multilateralism "à la carte." After all, the anti-terrorist campaign was fundamentally a unilateral effort: While the United States sought support from other countries, it did not ask for their assistance or advice in planning the campaign itself.[25]

Concern was mounting over the extent to which the United States, with its focus on the anti-terrorist campaign, would pay insufficient attention to other pressing issues. One illustration of this problem emerged from the Asia Pacific Economic Cooperation (APEC) summit meeting in Shanghai in October 2001, where Bush would meet President Jiang Zemin of China for the first time and have an opportunity to address regional leaders about the querulous state of the global economy. For Bush, however, the APEC meeting essentially became an opportunity to strengthen the coalition against Osama bin Laden and the Taliban regime. As the president declared upon arrival, "I've come to Shanghai because China and other Asia Pacific nations are important partners in the global campaign against terror."[26] For people in other parts of the world, there were serious concerns that had nothing to do with the vicious attacks of September 11. Would they be able to make their voices heard?

The anti-terrorist campaign led to sweeping changes in regional priorities for U.S. foreign policy. Central and South Asia and the Middle East—broadly speaking, the Muslim world—vaulted to the top of the ladder. East Asia retained its importance—but not for economic reasons, as proclaimed in the mid-1990s, but because of North Korea's membership in the "axis of evil," because of Al Qaeda sympathizers and cells in parts of the region, and because of China and Japan's roles as major powers. By contrast, Latin America lost huge amounts of ground. Briefly privileged by Bush's expressions of personal interest, the region fell off the proverbial radar screen—and suffered from inattention as Argentina and the rest of South America plunged into economic and institutional crises. Initially embraced as a special partner, Mexico saw its hopes completely dashed for significant reform of U.S. immigration policy. "In these difficult times," said a disappointed Vicente Fox in May 2002, "Latin America seems to have been abandoned to its fate."[27]

Trade policy became a source of friction and frustration. The United States had, of course, long presented itself to the world as a champion of free trade. But in March 2002 the Bush administration raised tariffs on imported steel; two months later it increased subsidies to American farmers by 80 percent over the decade to come. International reaction was swift and to the point. Javier Solana, the EU's foreign policy chief, proclaimed that the farm bill had created the "most profound" disagreement between Europe and the United States—worse even than the disputes over steel tariffs, the Kyoto environmental treaty, or the International Criminal Court. The Cairns group, an association of agricultural exporting nations, asserted that "the sheer size of the subsidy package will inevitably hurt farmers around the world, particularly in developing countries." APEC representatives denounced the U.S. measures as protectionist. And in Brazil, especially, government authorities maintained that the U.S. actions seriously jeopardized prospects for creation of a Free Trade Area of the Americas.[28]

Concluding Speculations

It became commonplace, in the wake of the September 11 attacks, to declare that the world had undergone a total change, that nothing would be as it was before. In many ways that was true for American citizens, whose sense of security and innocence was suddenly destroyed. Their anxiety would soon be heightened by a mysterious epidemic of anthrax, as envelopes containing life-threatening spores were sent to the offices of prominent American authorities through the U.S. Postal Service. (It was unknown, as of this writing, who was behind this dastardly plot.)

The most visible change was the realignment of governments, siding with the United States in the name of anti-terrorism. The near-unanimity on this position was altogether remarkable—but it did not necessarily portend the arrival of a new world order. It should be remembered that this was a coalition of *established governments*—and established governments, almost by definition, are opposed to terrorist groups (which usually seek their overthrow).

This was not a global alliance of citizens. Moreover, the U.S.–led campaign created new opportunities for besieged leaders to label their opponents as "terrorists" and therefore as a threat to civilization, not just to their own rule.

The focus on security gave new authority and salience to governments and states, as distinct from economics and markets. Anti-terrorism was a state issue par excellence. The events of September 11 silenced voices that had long proclaimed the withering away of the state and the irrelevance of governments. Nor was there any question that international issues, and foreign policy, would once again become paramount concerns for American citizens. Questions about "stateness" recaptured attention in academic and policy circles, both in reference to "failed states" that might harbor terrorists (such as Afghanistan) or "strong states" that could bring terrorists to heel.

Also significant was the fact that the U.S. coalition was formed around a single issue—the attacks and aftermath of September 11. That was the sole criterion for alignment with (and gratitude from) the Bush administration. Gone were concerns about human rights, democratic practice, or related issues. The only relevant question was whether governments would enlist in the American-led campaign. To peoples still living under autocratic rule, this might seem like a betrayal. In time, this could come back to haunt the United States.

There emerged, in this context, a paradox of power. U.S. supremacy became a source of vulnerability. Terrorists focused their anger and their plots against the United States precisely because it was the strongest nation in the world: Being a target was the cost of being Number One. But beyond that, too much power became a liability. As Timothy Garton Ash wrote, "The fundamental problem is that America today has too much power for anyone's good, including its own. . . . [T]he problem with American power is not that it is American. The problem is simply the power. It would be dangerous even for an archangel to wield so much power."[29] Lopsided worlds tend to be inherently unstable. It could be argued, in fact, that the United States would serve its own best interests by helping to create a more balanced, multipolar world order.[30]

In the long run, the war against terror held uncertain prospects for global stability. Especially as tensions continued to rise in the Middle East, there loomed the possibility that Arabs and Muslims would regard a prolonged U.S.–led military campaign against (or within) Islamic states an assault upon their culture and religion. And even in the wake of military triumph in Afghanistan, there remained the twin challenges of (a) reconstructing that long-suffering nation, and (b) building support among moderate Muslims around the world—while effectively crushing Al Qaeda's international network. Failure to meet these challenges could degenerate into a confrontation between Islam and the West, a much-feared "clash of civilizations."

There was also an optimistic scenario, a prospect that the coalition could hold together beyond the Afghan campaign and become the basis for constructing a new world order. This hope was elegantly expressed by none other than Mikhail Gorbachev, who had his own firsthand knowledge of the perils of waging military campaigns in Afghanistan. Writing in the *New York Times*, the erstwhile Soviet leader appealed for wisdom: "It would be wrong," he said, "to use the battle against terrorism to establish control over countries or regions. This would discredit the coalition and close off the prospect of transforming it into a powerful mechanism for building a peaceful world. Turning the coalition against terror into an alliance that works to achieve a just international order would be a lasting memorial to the thousands of victims of the September 11 tragedy."[31]

Notes

1. Francis Fukuyama, "The End of History," *The Public Interest* (1989).

2. Joseph S. Nye, Jr., "What New World Order?" *Foreign Affairs* 71, no. 2 (Spring 1992): 83–96, with quote on 88.

3. See David Halberstam, *War in a Time of Peace: Bush, Clinton, and the Generals* (New York: Scribner, 2001).

4. Henry Kissinger, *Does America Need a Foreign Policy? Toward a Diplomacy for the 21st Century* (New York: Simon & Schuster, 2001), 17–19.

5. John E. Reilly, ed., *American Public Opinion and U.S. Foreign Policy 1999* (Chicago: Chicago Council on Foreign Relations, 2000), 10. In 1986, by comparison, foreign policy problems accounted for 26 percent of concerns among the general public and 42 percent among the leaders.

6. Reilly, *American Public Opinion,* 11, 15.

7. Reilly, *American Public Opinion,* 4–5, 12.

8. Office of National Drug Control Strategy, White House, *The National Drug Control Strategy, 1997* (Washington: The White House, 1997), 21.

9. See Julia E. Sweig, "What Kind of War for Colombia?" *Foreign Affairs* 81, no. 5 (September/October 2002): 122–141.

10. *Study on the Operation and Effects of the North American Free Trade Agreement* (Washington: The White House, 1997), iii.

11. Thom Shanker, "Spinning à la Mode," *New York Times Week in Review,* August 5, 2001, 5.

12. Thom Shanker, "White House Says the U.S. Is Not a Loner, Just Choosy," *New York Times,* July 31, 2001, A1, A10.

13. This prompted Maureen Dowd to write, with characteristic hyperbole, "Doesn't W. realize that EVERYBODY in the world HATES us? Not Mexico. Maybe not Monaco. But EVERYBODY ELSE! Even the Swedes can't stand us, for Pete's sake." *New York Times,* May 6, 2001.

14. *Newsweek*, August 6, 2001.

15. See cover story by Fareed Zakaria, "Why They Hate Us: The Politics of Rage," *Newsweek*, October 15, 2001.

16. Mark Hosenball, "A War Yet to be Won," *Newsweek*, September 11, 2002, 30–32.

17. See U.S. Department of State, *Patterns of Terrorism 2000* (Washington D.C., 2001), and *Patterns of Terrorism 2001* (Washington D.C., 2002).

18. John H. Cushman, Jr., "Rattling New Sabers," *New York Times*, March 10, 2002, A1, A7.

19. G. John Ikenberry, "America's Imperial Ambition," *Foreign Affairs* (September/October 2002): 44–60, esp. 49–55, with quote on 49; and Doyle McManus, "U.S. Foreign Policy Assertive, Divisive: Strategy," *Los Angeles Times*, September 1, 2002, A1, A24.

20. William M. Arkin, "A Policy in from the Cold," *Los Angeles Times*, Opinion, May 26, 2002, M1, M6.

21. Serge Schmemann, "After the War, Rebuild a Nation. If It's a Nation," *New York Times*, Week in Review, October 21, 2001, 1, 16.

22. Michael Massing, "Losing the Peace? As Afghanistan Struggles to Recover, the U.S. Prepares to Move On," *The Nation*, May 13, 2002, 11–18.

23. U.S. Department of State, *Patterns of Global Terrorism 2000*, vi and passim. The report on 2001 designated thirty-three groups as terrorist and listed the same countries as state sponsors of terrorism. See also Sebastian Junger, "Terrorism's New Geography," *Vanity Fair* (December 2002): 194–206.

24. *New York Times*, October 12, 2001, B4.

25. See Michael Hirsh, "Bush and the World," *Foreign Affairs* 81, no. 5 (September/October 2002): 18–43.

26. David E. Sanger, "Bush Meets Jiang," *New York Times*, October 20, 2001, A1, B4. See also Sanger, "Bush's New Focus Requires a Shift in His China Policy," *New York Times*, October 18, 2001, B3.

27. Quoted in Sebastian Rotella, "U.S. Foreign Policy Assertive, Divisive: Reactions," *Los Angeles Times*, September 1, 2002, A13.

28. See Peter H. Smith, "From NAFTA to FTAA? Paths toward Hemispheric Integration," in *NAFTA in the New Millennium*, eds. Edward J. Chambers and Peter H. Smith (La Jolla and Edmonton: Center for U.S.–Mexican Studies, University of California, San Diego, and University of Alberta Press, 2002), ch. 20.

29. Timothy Garton Ash, "The Peril of Too Much Power," *New York Times*, April 9, 2002, A31.

30. Benjamin Schwarz and Christopher Layne, "A New Grand Strategy," *The Atlantic Monthly*, January 2002, 36–42.

31. Mikhail S. Gorbachev, "A Leading Role for the Security Council," *New York Times*, Week in Review, October 21, 2001, 15.

POSTSCRIPT

Forging the New Relationship: Proposals for Policy

WHAT IS TO BE DONE? We close this volume by returning to the themes posed in our introduction—the promise of closer relations between Asia and Latin America. The connection is stronger than most people realize, it has significant potential for future development, and, in our view, it could have beneficial effects for the world community at large.

We believe that intensification of these trans-Pacific ties will be good for leaders and citizens in both of the regions; that, by example and by momentum, it will serve to strengthen links among developing areas (South-South ties); and that it can provide a model for links between developing areas and advanced industrial countries (North-South ties).[1]

In all these ways, we think that strengthened Asian–Latin American ties can help promote globalization with equity—what we might call "globalization with a heart." Globalization, as shown in chapter 1 of this book, can be defined as the contemporary flow of goods, capital, information—and migrant labor—between countries and regions. It accelerates change and creates instability. It offers benefits for some and imposes costs on others. By globalization with equity, we are referring to a process that entails:

- Economic growth in all parts of the world
- A significant reduction of poverty (with eventual eradication as the common goal)
- A visible reduction of inequalities within and between regions and nations

- The development of multilateral entities with authority and capacity to monitor and regulate transnational flows, and to establish and implement rules that are effective and fair

As should be readily apparent, we are imagining a process of globalization that is qualitatively different from currently prevailing patterns and norms.[2]

How can improved Asian–Latin American ties help achieve this lofty goal? And what can be done to strengthen the linkages between these two regions? In this brief conclusion, we approach these questions through three analytical perspectives: (1) ways to foster direct relationships between Asia and Latin America, (2) potential roles of major powers, and (3) implications of alternative scenarios for global world orders.

Cross-Regional Connections

We see every reason to believe that trade and investment between East Asia and Latin America will increase within the near future. Chapters 2–4 make this point with emphasis. We urge regional leaders to anticipate potential opportunities and to take advantage of them. As suggested by chapter 5, we expect that the business community will play a major role in this process.

Contributions in this volume—especially chapters 9–13 on financial crises—clearly demonstrate the need for "second-generation" economic reforms in both Asia and Latin America. Most of these reforms relate to questions of "governance" (of transactions, bureaucracies, and corporations). They present the public sector with a major responsibility. We think these steps are essential—not only for the benefit of the individual countries involved, but also because of the need to reignite economic growth within and across the two regions.

And in this connection, we advocate an intensive process of "mutual learning" between officials and leaders of the two regions. As maintained in chapters 6–8, Latin America still has much to learn from Asian strategies for economic development (note: we are careful here to avoid the notion of a single Asian "model" of development). And as the chapters on currency crises indicate, key countries in both regions fell victim to similar forces and fates. In order to prevent recurrences of such crises, or at least to find ways out of them, analysts and policy makers from the two regions should make serious efforts to learn from each other's experience. This process should occur not only within governmental agencies or official think tanks but also within universities, nongovernmental organizations, the media, and other institutions of civil society.

Institutional Linkages

Given the promise and potential of these cross-regional ties, we believe it is time to strengthen institutions. We do not call for the creation of a new entity. Rather, we recommend that leaders take decisive steps to develop existing (or prospective) institutions.

Bilateral free trade agreements (FTAs) are one such institution. Key examples are the recently concluded FTA between Chile and Korea, and possible FTAs between Japan and Chile, and Japan and Mexico. We suggest that governments in both regions explore the desirability and feasibility of additional FTAs, either with individual countries or with groups of countries (such as the Common Market of the South [MERCOSUR] or the Association of Southeast Asian Nations [ASEAN] group). At the same time, we regard bilateral and minilateral agreements as only modest steps forward, since they tend to involve very small numbers of partners and to have discriminatory impacts on nonmembers.

More inclusive, of course, is the forum for Asia-Pacific Economic Cooperation (APEC)—which embraces the United States, most of Asia (including Japan), and three Latin American countries (Mexico, Chile, and Peru). It is an advantage for APEC that it includes the United States; one disadvantage, from our standpoint, is that it includes only three Latin American countries. We are further concerned that APEC lost a good deal of momentum in the wake of the Asian crisis of 1997–1998, and that governments have begun to seek new venues (such as the "ASEAN-plus-three" forum established by Japan).[3]

Even so, we believe that APEC still has an important role to play in integrating Latin America with Asia. For this to happen, though, we suggest that

- APEC's Latin American members—Mexico, Peru, and Chile—make periodic reports to Latin American countries on APEC deliberations (through meetings of the Sistema Económico Latinoamericano, SELA, and/or through other forums)
- Brazil be invited to attend APEC meetings as an "observer," at least until such time as APEC decides to open a new round of formal admissions

For the foreseeable future, the limitation on Latin American membership is a serious obstacle for APEC.

We have high hopes for the recently established FEALAC, the Forum for East Asia–Latin American Cooperation (as described in chapters 4 and 15 and elsewhere in this volume). One of FEALAC's special features is its membership—which encompasses virtually all of Latin America, including Cuba, but not the United States. At the same time, it is a very thin institution.

What might be done to strengthen FEALAC? First, we think that the organization's agenda should be broadened to deal with issues of mutual concern. These might include:

- patterns and processes of democratic reform (and, especially, the evolution of civil-military relations), a concern in many countries of both regions;
- progress (or lack of progress) on negotiations for a Free Trade Area of the Americas (FTAA), which represents a potential threat to Asia;
- drug trafficking and drug control policy challenges that reach within and across the two regions;
- treatment of ethnic minorities;
- gender relations;
- environmental protection; and
- terrorism and anti-terrorist measures, including modes of intelligence-sharing and broader international cooperation.

Clearly, we are hoping that FEALAC will deal with difficult and controversial topics. That is the only way that it can gain weight as an institution.

In order to manage an agenda of this magnitude, FEALAC needs to strengthen its insitutional capacity. We therefore present some procedural suggestions:

- FEALAC meetings should be regularized, and a summit meeting for heads of state should be held within the next two or three years.
- Task forces should be established to examine and report upon selected issues at determined intervals.
- FEALAC should establish academic study centers, much along the lines of existing APEC Study Centers; these centers could conduct research on issues of common concern and forge productive links to academic communities throughout the member countries.
- FEALAC should take proactive steps to inform the general public and policy community about the nature and promise of Asia–Latin America connections, heighten awareness about the issues, and create a political base for further cooperation.

We think it would be premature to establish a permanent secretariat for FEALAC. The history of international organization is replete with examples of overbureaucratized agencies. We would not rule out a FEALAC secretariat in the future; but to justify such a step, we think it needs to develop its agenda and define its roles in the meantime.

Nor do we think that FEALAC should broaden its membership to include the United States at this time. The East Asia–Latin America relationship needs time, space, and opportunities to develop on its own. We suspect that the institutional presence of the United States, the world's most powerful country, would inhibit and constrain this process. Nor would we support FEALAC membership for any country (or group of countries) from outside of East Asia or Latin America—not the European Union, not Russia, not Canada. The Asia–Latin American connection needs to evolve by itself.

Academic and Cultural Exchange

As mentioned above, we think that FEALAC Study Centers could make important contributions to high-level research on issues of common concern. We are also pleased to observe that, in one of its first communiqués, FEALAC stressed the importance of academic and cultural exchange.

We urge schools and universities to take up this challenge as well. Students in Asia need to learn more about Latin America; students in Latin America need to learn more about Asia. We salute the efforts of pioneering institutions and professional associations, but we think that the educational mission requires more attention and resources in both regions.

School and university curricula will need to offer courses in the languages, histories, and cultures of the other regions; faculty and student exchanges should be fostered to the maximum possible extent; and modern information technology—such as teleconferencing and computerized translation—can promote communication between leaders and citizens of the two regions.

Professionals in the media—television and radio, as well as print media—should become involved in this process. The goal here is not only to improve the expertise of journalists; it is also to improve understanding and heighten awareness within the general publics.

Universities can make significant contributions through the organization of conferences and seminars on cross-regional issues. Academic institutions in developed countries—including the United States as well as Japan—should dedicate resources for this kind of activity.

One of the keys to more intensive interaction between Asians and Latin Americans is to identify encouraging venues that are neutral (and nonthreatening). Prominent universities are uniquely positioned to offer these opportunities.

Cooperation in Multilateral Arenas

We think it is essential that regional and cross-regional associations become building blocks for a truly integrated global community. Toward this end, Asia and Latin America should not only strengthen cross-regional links; they should also use these linkages to help strengthen multilateral organizations.

In an ideal world, this agenda leads in two directions: strengthening the World Trade Organization in the economic realm, and strengthening the United Nations in the political realm. Meaningful achievement of these ends will require serious and sustained attention to dissident voices. After all, the major complaint of demonstrators in Seattle, Quebec, and Genoa has pointed to a serious concern—that globalization has not promoted equity (or, in more moderate terms, that it has not promoted sufficient equity with sufficient speed).

To be specific, we recommend that countries of Asia and Latin America consult with one another as meetings take place and issues emerge. We do not mean to suggest that the two regions should attempt to form a geoeconomic bloc or geopolitical alliance. But we think they should consult with one another and vote in common when it serves their interests. This could greatly strengthen their positions. And if they vote against each other, either individually or collectively, the reasons should be clearly understood by both sides.

To promote the processes of coordination and information-sharing, we have two specific suggestions for Latin America:

- Countries of the region might consider supporting the Japanese quest for a permanent seat on the UN Security Council, and
- Nations that currently do not have diplomatic relations with the People's Republic of China might reconsider their position.

In return, leaders and peoples of Asia can demonstrate increased sensitivity to Latin American desires to become players on the world stage, rather than minor figures in the "backyard" of the United States. This aspiration is especially strong for Mexico and Brazil, two of the countries with closest linkages to East Asia.

Roles of Major Powers

Directly or indirectly, the actions of major powers will have significant impacts on prospects for trans-Pacific linkages. We believe that it is in their interest to promote these links, as they will provide the basis for a more stable and prosperous world community. We urge leaders of major world powers to take a long-term view of these developments and to act in their enlightened self-interest.

Perhaps the most challenging task is to stimulate economic growth. This is obviously something that they want to do. But we think it worthwhile to stress the importance of stimulating growth in such a way as to benefit developing economies as well as the advanced industrial world. This means openness instead of protectionism, transfer rather than monopolization of technology, regulation and/or legalization of labor migration, and—to be more specific—reduction of barriers to agricultural goods from developing countries. To quote one of our contributors:

> Both the United States and Japan are in strong positions to influence the main currents of trade and investment in the communities of the Pacific Rim. Their ability to do so is certainly bolstered by the fact that they are major suppliers of capital to the region. Both nations, however, have critics who maintain that the United States and Japan have not been sufficiently responsive to the needs of developing countries, including those in Asia and Latin America. These critics would urge the United States and Japan to become catalysts for creating harmony in the face of the inevitable conflicts that will arise as the developing nations are subjected to the tumultuous process of economic globalization. They believe that the United States and Japan should assume leading roles in sustaining world economic growth—but with greater prudence.

As another colleague added, "The future connection between the regions will basically depend on how the regions can realize long-term economic growth and social justice. It is obvious that if both regions cannot attain these objectives, economic relations will stagnate. And that will pose a serious obstacle for establishing a new world order."

For Asia and Latin America to implement second-generation reforms, as mentioned above, they will need to cultivate transparency. In the political realm, this means democratization. We therefore urge the major powers—especially Japan and the United States, the two current powers with standing interests in both regions—to support the processes of democratization in whatever ways are possible. Or, to put it another way, they should avoid steps that contradict or ignore the imperatives of political change. For Japan, this would mean reconsideration of a good deal of its official development assistance (ODA) program; for the United States, it offers a word of caution about the single-minded nature of the anti-terrorist coalition forged in the wake of the September 11 attacks.

Aside from such traditional mechanisms as trade, foreign direct investment (FDI), market opening, and technological assistance, major powers should focus efforts and energies on such problems as environmental degradation, poverty alleviation, and improvement of public health (with special emphasis on such epidemics as HIV/AIDS, which is widespread in parts of Asia and Latin America).[4] One particularly effective means might be to work through nongovernmental organizations and other elements in civil society.

We have broad recommendations for each of the major powers analyzed in chapters 14–16 of this book—Japan, China, and the United States.

Japan should increase its involvement in both Asia and Latin America. This will help avert the possibility of Japanese "isolation," especially in the wake of its decade-long recession, and bolster its long-term economic and political prospects. For these reasons Japan should be more open about technology transfer, investment strategies, and its domestic distribution channels—which have created de facto trade barriers. More ODA should be extended on a multilateral rather than bilateral basis. We recognize that greater Japanese involvement in Latin America may involve, as another colleague has suggested, "a redefinition of Japan's relationship with the United States"—in other words, less acceptance of the idea that Latin America falls within an exclusively U.S. sphere of influence. Latin American countries would certainly prefer to be treated as a full-fledged partners; moreover, Japan has legitimate interests of its own within Latin America. We also urge Japan to give increased attention and support to FEALAC.

As a still-emerging power, China is in the process of establishing and consolidating links throughout Asia and Latin America. We hope this process will continue. And as it does, we hope that Chinese leaders will recognize the paramount importance of fair, effective, and transparent rules for international conduct. Big countries must respect the same rules as small countries.

As the world's preeminent power, the United States might need to change the most. Our own view is that global domination can be dangerous—the tragic events of September 11 testify to that. The ultimate goal of U.S. leadership should be to transform the current situation into a stable world order. This will mean accepting a decline in relative power, refraining from unilateral decisions, and recognizing that U.S. actions—however trivial they might seem—can have major consequences for less-developed countries of the world. As part of this package, Washington should encourage the formation of transregional relationships. They are unlikely to produce anti-American alliances. On the contrary, they will contribute to global stability in the long run.

Global Scenarios

The twenty-first century has begun in an atmosphere of uncertainty and instability. The global distribution of power is shifting and uneven; informal (and formal) rules for conduct are neither binding nor fully enforced; and prospects of terrorism and other threats are revising the global agenda and patterns of international alignment.

As though to emphasize this sense of indeterminacy, we can see several potential patterns of interaction for the future. They take the form of six distinct scenarios.

Scenario 1: Global Hegemony for the United States

According to this view the United States will reign supreme in economic, military, and political affairs. This vision has gained plausibility as Europe and Japan faced unwelcome problems. As the U.S. economy recovered strongly in the mid-1990s, the European Union foundered—with growth rates often less than 2 percent, and unemployment climbing well into double digits (reaching 22 percent in Spain). Japan also found that its "bubble" was bursting, as growth rates slipped to 1 percent or less for several years and scandals gripped the once-prestigious banking sector. The economic crisis that gripped Southeast Asia in 1997 and the Russian meltdown in 1998 likewise weakened potential power centers. It has thus become imaginable that American supremacy would be accompanied or assisted by stagnation in Europe, depression in Asia and Russia, retrenchment in Japan, and instability in China. As a sole hegemon, the United States would be in a position to lay down and enforce international rules of the game.

Scenario 2: Intensification of Multipolarity

The international system of the twenty-first century could come to contain a half-dozen major powers—as Henry Kissinger has predicted, "the United States, Europe, China, Japan, Russia, and probably India—as well as a multiplicity of medium-sized and smaller countries."[5] The United States would be important but not dominant in such a world, and codes of behavior would result from agreement and cooperation among the diverse power centers. This view tends to focus on the long-term distribution of demographic and economic resources, rather than on short-term commercial or political developments.

Scenario 3: Clash of Civilizations

A variation on this theme, propounded by Samuel P. Huntington, foresees the consolidation of eight or nine "civilizations" (Western, Latin American, African, Islamic, Sinic, Hindu, Orthodox, Buddhist, Japanese). These broad cultural groupings would transcend nation-states and shape the outlooks, associations, and interests of key actors in the world. Conflicts between them would be frequent (sometimes violent), compromise scarce, and tension permanent. There would probably be mounting antagonism between "the West and the rest," as rising cultures of the world seek to acquire and assert commensurate shares of power.[6]

Scenario 4: Formation of Rival Economic Blocs

This idea envisions a small number of powerful economic and political blocs, each headed by a major power. A common version portrays three regional units: a "European" bloc, dominated by Germany and the European Union (EU), with a sphere of influence stretching through Eastern Europe to parts of the Middle East and much of Africa; an "Asian" bloc, led by China or Japan (or both), extending throughout the Asia-Pacific to the borders of South Asia; and an "American" bloc under the United States, embracing the entire Western Hemisphere. This might not be an easy arrangement to manage. Alarmists predicted that "the twenty-first century will be a century of economic warfare," while the respected economist C. Fred Bergsten once made a similar point with more caution: "the end of the Cold War could sharply heighten the prospect of trade war." Without the common cause of anti-communism, leading powers would be tempted to seek economic advantage from one another. Moreover, three-player games tend to be notoriously unstable, since everyone fears that the other two will line up against it on a permanent basis: "given the inevitable self-perception of vulnerability on the part of each of the three parties, two will tend to ally against the third under conditions of rough tripolar equality—perhaps in an effort to create their own so-called 'bipolar' dominance." This would strengthen the hand of parochial forces—protectionists in America, traditionalists in Japan, regionalists in Europe—and precipitate a self-destructive cycle. "The target would probably seek to form (or expand) its bloc of nearby supporters, and the other areas would respond in kind. All economies would suffer, and risks of trade warfare would become real."

Scenario 5: North-South Separation

In this perspective there might develop a "North-North" axis of economic and political cooperation encircling the upper half of the globe—from the United States to the European Union through East (or Central) Europe to Russia and Japan. Capital and commerce would flow freely around this circuit and promote accelerated growth. With a few exceptions, however, the South would be left out. Economic benefits would become increasingly concentrated in the North, resulting in a stark separation between haves and have-nots. As Charles William Maynes once observed, "The key division in world politics is likely to become the North-South divide. The reasons are the relationship between poverty and people and the clash between economics and demographics."[7] Consolidation of a North-North axis could provoke serious problems. An abandoned South would be liable to become ever more dispirited, desperate, and reckless. Moderate leaders would lose credibility. Radicals of one stripe or another—nationalists, populists, *ayatollahs* (if not leftists)—would come into power. With little to lose, they would be tempted to pursue high-risk strategies of confrontation. The world would become increasingly dangerous, and temptations for military action would escalate. Clearly, it would not be in the long-term interests of the North to have an angered and impoverished South on the other side of the equator.

Scenario 6: Globalization with Equity

A final scenario, by far the most optimistic, envisions progressive and multilateral movement toward a global regime that could establish and uphold widely accepted rules of the game. This benevolent scene would be most likely to occur in the economic realm—perhaps under the aegis of the World Trade Organization (WTO). At the same time great powers, including the United States, would devote fewer resources to military armaments and more to economic development. By creating a positive-sum game, the promotion of economic development would, in turn, reduce the likelihood of international conflict; the curtailment of military spending would diminish the need for armed defense. The world would become a kinder, gentler, more livable place.

We recognize that partial and nascent elements of all six scenarios are apparent at the present time.[8] We realize that two or more (or perhaps all) scenarios might coexist in complex combinations. They might also appear in sequence—Scenario 1 might lead to Scenario 2, and then to 4, and so on. We expect that the ultimate shape of these panoramas will be determined largely, but not exclusively, by the major powers (whichever they might be).

Our central concern at this juncture is to present hypothetical connections between these scenarios and Asian–Latin American relationships. In our view, three of the six scenarios are overtly hostile to the development of East Asia–Latin America ties:

- Rival economic blocs—because Latin America would belong to the "American" bloc, one of whose chief competitors would be the Asian bloc
- The "clash of civilizations"—on the ground that, at least as interpreted by Samuel Huntington, East Asia and Latin America would be on opposite sides of the civilizational divide (this would depend, of course, on the operational alignment of the civilizations that he identifies)
- North-South separation—since this would divide East Asia (with Japan and possibly South Korea classified as belonging to the "North")

Two scenarios would have ambiguous, uncertain, or neutral implications for an Asian–Latin American connection:

- Increasing multipolarity—depending upon the number, location, and relative strength of the poles, multipolarization could either create new options for the developing world or lock them into "spheres of influence."
- Prolongation of U.S. hegemony—if America's supremacy were seen to be impregnable, Washington might regard the Asian–Latin American relationship as innocuous or mildly beneficial; but if the United States were

> to feel unsure of its position, it would either oppose or want to gain control of such an alliance.

The one scenario that is clearly supportive of an Asian–Latin American connection (and other cross-regional connections) would be globalization with equity. Under this circumstance the choices would be free, alignments fluid and open, the playing field level for all—and the game would be positive-sum. Moreover, the major powers—especially the United States—would be more likely to accept or support a meaningful Asian–Latin American relationship in this context. (Washington would almost certainly oppose such a relationship under any of the three hostile scenarios sketched out above; it might tolerate or support an Asian–Latin American link under conditions of multipolarity or U.S. hegemony, depending on specific circumstances.)[9]

In sum, this analysis indicates that prospects for Asian–Latin American relations are, realistically speaking, contingent upon the shape of global alignments. It also suggests the importance of avoiding hostile scenarios and cultivating positive ones.

This leads to a further point: By changing the direction of causality, we can grasp how important it is for East Asia and Latin America to become proactive participants in the process of constructing a new world order. They should not merely await the decisions and determinations of major powers. By forming the kinds of connections that we have espoused, they can reduce the chances that negative scenarios—the "clash of civilizations" or North-South separation or rival economic blocs or prolongation of U.S. hegemony—will come into being. By strengthening linkages between their leaders and societies, East Asia and Latin America can help lay the foundations for a future of globalization with equity. They can demonstrate the benefits of cross-regional collaboration, encourage others to follow their path, and—not to be too Machiavellian about it—narrow the range of plausible options. The shaping of a new world order is a challenge and task for all nations.

Notes

1. The presence of Japan, as an advanced industrial nation, adds a note of ambiguity. For this reason we believe that Japan has a special role to play in fostering the inter-regional relationship.

2. See Joseph E. Stiglitz, *Globalization and Its Discontents* (New York: W. W. Norton, 2002).

3. For recommendations regarding APEC see Richard E. Feinberg and Ye Zhao, eds., "Assessing APEC's Progress: Trade, Ecotech, and Institutions," a Project of the

APEC International Assessment Network (Singapore: Institute of Southeast Asian Studies, 2000).

4. In fact Brazil has become a pioneer in the treatment of HIV/AIDS, and has much to offer to countries of Latin America and Asia.

5. Henry A. Kissinger, *Diplomacy* (New York: Simon & Schuster, 1994), 23–24.

6. Samuel P. Huntington, "The Clash of Civilizations?" *Foreign Affairs* 72, no. 3 (Summer 1993): 22–49, and *The Clash of Civilizations and the Remaking of World Order* (New York: Simon & Schuster, 1996). For provocative commentary on this thesis see *Foreign Affairs* 72, no. 4 (September/October 1993): 2–26.

7. Charles William Maynes, "America without the Cold War," *Foreign Policy* 78 (Spring 1990): 3–25, with quote on 22–23.

8. There is sharp disagreement about the extent to which the September 11 attacks and aftermath correspond to a "clash of civilizations." See articles by John Keegan and John O'Sullivan in *San Diego Union-Tribune*, Insight: Opinion & Commentary, October 14, 2001; and Edward W. Said, "The Clash of Ignorance," *The Nation*, October 22, 2001, 11–13.

9. This point has been developed more fully by Peter H. Smith, "The United States and the Asia–Latin America Connection" (presentation to conference on Asia and Latin America: Connections and Comparisons, Kobe University, October 2000).

Suggested Readings

Books

Aggarwal, Vinod K., and Charles E. Morrison. *Asia-Pacific Crossroads: Regime Creation and the Future of APEC.* New York: St. Martin's Press, 1998.

Birdsall, Nancy, and Jaspersen, Frederick, eds. *Pathways to Growth: Comparing East Asia and Latin America.* Baltimore, Md.: Johns Hopkins University Press, 1997.

Bryceson, Deborah, Cristobal Kay, and Jos Mooij, eds. *Disappearing Peasantries? Rural Labour in Africa, Asia, and Latin America.* London: Intermediate Technology Publications, 2000.

Collier, Paul, Jan Willem Gunning, et al. *Trade Shocks in Developing Countries: Volume 2, Asia and Latin America.* Oxford: Clarendon Press, 1999.

Curtis, Gerald L., ed. *The United States, Japan, and Asia.* New York: Norton, 1994.

Fukuchi, Takao, and Mitsuhiro Kagami, eds. *Perspectives on the Pacific Basin Economy: A Comparison of Asia and Latin America.* Tokyo: Institute of Developing Economies, 1990.

Gereffi, Gary, and Donald L. Wyman., eds. *Manufacturing Miracles: Paths of Industrialization in Latin America and East Asia.* Princeton: Princeton University Press, 1990.

Haggard, Stephan. *Pathways from the Periphery: The Politics of Growth in the Newly Industrializing Countries.* Ithaca: Cornell University Press, 1990.

Haggard, Stephan, and Robert R. Kaufman. *The Political Economy of Democratic Transitions.* Princeton: Princeton University Press, 1995.

Hosono, Akio, and Neantro Saavedra-Rivano, eds. *Development Strategies in East Asia and Latin America.* New York: St. Martin's Press; London: Macmillan Press, 1998.

Kagami, Mitsuhiro. *The Voice of East Asia: Development Implications for Latin America.* Tokyo: Institute of Developing Economies, 1995.

Kagami, Mitsuhiro, and Masatsugu Tsuji. *Privatization, Deregulation, and Economic Efficiency: A Comparative Analysis of Asia, Europe, and the Americas.* Cheltenham, UK; Northampton, Mass.: Edward Elgar, 2000.

Lowenthal, Abraham, and Gregory Treverton, eds. *Latin America in a New World.* Boulder, Colo.: Westview, 1994.

McGuire, James W. *Rethinking Development in East Asia and Latin America.* Los Angeles: Pacific Council on International Policy, 1997.

Naya, Seiji, et al., eds. *Lessons in Development: A Comparative Study of Asia and Latin America.* Panama and San Francisco: Institute for Contemporary Studies, International Center for Economic Growth, 1989.

Nishijima, Shoji, and Peter H. Smith, eds. *Cooperation or Rivalry? Regional Integration in the Americas and the Pacific Rim.* Boulder, Colo.: Westview Press, 1996.

Purcell, Susan Kaufman, and Robert M. Immerman, eds. *Japan and Latin America in the New Global Order.* Boulder, Colo.: Lynne Rienner, 1992.

Ravenhill, John. *APEC and the Construction of Pacific Rim Regionalism.* Cambridge: Cambridge University Press, 2001.

Smith, Peter H., ed. *Latin America in Comparative Perspective: New Approaches to Methods and Analysis.* Boulder, Colo.: Westview Press, 1995.

Stallings, Barbara, and Gabriel Szekely, eds. *Japan, the United States, and Latin America: Toward a Trilateral Relationship in the Western Hemisphere.* Baltimore, Md.: Johns Hopkins University Press, 1993.

Stiglitz, Joseph E. *Globalization and Its Discontents.* New York: W. W. Norton, 2002.

Tulchin, Joseph S., and Ralph H. Espach, eds. *Latin America in the New International System.* Boulder, Colo.: Lynne Rienner, 2001.

Articles, Chapters, and Working Papers

Campos, Nauro F., and Jeffrey B. Nugent. "Development Performance and the Institutions of Governance: Evidence from East Asia and Latin America." *World Development* 27, no. 3 (March 1999): 439–452.

Chan, Steve. "Japan and the United States as Development Models: Classifying Asia Pacific and Latin American Political Economies." *Comparative Political Studies* 34, no. 10 (December 2001): 1134–1158.

Chan, Steve, and Cal Clark. "Do MNCs Matter for National Development? Contrasting East Asia and Latin America." Pp. 166–187 in *Foreign Direct Investment in a Changing Global Political Economy,* edited by Steve Chan. New York: St. Martin's Press, 1995.

Felix, David. "Industrial Development in East Asia: What Are the Lessons for Latin America?" *UNCTAD Review* (1994): 123–142.

Frankel, Jeffrey A., and Sergio L. Schmuckler. "Crisis, Contagion, and Country Funds: Effects on East Asia and Latin America." Pp. 232–266 in *Managing Capital Flows and Exchange Rates: Perspectives from the Pacific Basin,* edited by Reuven Glick. Cambridge: Cambridge University Press, 1998.

Fukuyama, Francis, and Sanjay Marwah. "Dimensions of Development." *Journal of Democracy* 11, 4 (October 2000): 80–94.

Gereffi, Gary. "Rethinking Development Theory: Insights from East Asia and Latin America." Pp. 26–56 in *Comparative National Development: Society and Economy in the New Global Order,* edited by Douglas Kincaid and Alejandro Portes. Chapel Hill: University of North Carolina Press, 1994.

Goldberg, Linda S., and Michael W. Klein. "Foreign Direct Investment, Trade, and Real Exchange Rate Linkages in Southeast Asia and Latin America." *National Bureau of Economic Research* Working Paper 6344 (December 1997).

Haggard, Stephan. "Regionalism in Asia and the Americas." Pp. 20–49 in *The Political Economy of Regionalism,* edited by Edward Mansfield and Helen Milner. New York: Columbia University Press. 1997.

Higgott, Richard, and Nicola Phillips. "Challenging Triumphalism and Convergence: The Limits of Global Liberalization in Asia and Latin America." *Review of International Studies* 26, no. 3 (July 2000): 359–379.

Hoffmaister, Alexander W., and Jorge E. Roldós. "Are Business Cycles Different in Asia and Latin America?" *International Monetary Fund Working Paper* WP/97/09 (January 1997).

Hosono, Akio. "Economic Integration in Asia and Pacific: Experiences and New Initiatives." *Integration and Trade* 4, no. 12, IDB/INTAL (December 2000).

Jenkins, Rhys. "The Political Economy of Industrialization: A Comparison of Latin American and East Asian Newly Industrializing Countries." *Development-and-Change* 22, no. 2 (April 1991): 197–231.

Kuwayama, Mikio. "Open Regionalism in Asia Pacific and Latin America: A Survey of the Literature." *United Nations Economic Commission for Latin America and the Caribbean (ECLAC) Series in International Trade* 4 (December 1999).

Loayza, Norman, Humberto López, and Angel Ubide. "Comovements and Sectoral Interdependence: Evidence for Latin America, East Asia, and Europe." *International Monetary Fund Staff Papers* 48, no. 2 (June 2001).

Maxfield, Sylvia. "Capital Mobility and Democratic Stability." *Journal of Democracy* 11, no. 4 (October 2000): 95–106.

McGuire, James W. "Social Policy and Mortality Decline in East Asia and Latin America." *World Development* 29, no. 10 (October 2001): 1673–1697.

Meller, Patricio, and Gabriela Contreras. "A Comparison of the Export Baskets of Latin America and Asia." *Integration and Trade* 4, no. 12, IDB/INTAL (December 2000).

Palma, Gabriel. "Three and a Half Cycles of 'Mania, Panic, and [Asymmetric] Crash': East Asia and Latin America Compared." *Cambridge Journal of Economics* 22, no. 6 (November 1998): 789–808.

Paus, Eva, and Michael D. Robinson. "Real Wage Performance under Greater Trade Openness: Lessons from Latin America and Asia." *Journal of Developing Areas* 33, no. 2 (Winter 1999): 269–288.

Poon, Jessie P. H., and Edmund R. Thompson. "Foreign Direct Investment and Economic Growth: Evidence from Asia and Latin America." *Journal of Economic Development* 23, no. 2 (December 1998): 141–160.

Ramírez Bonilla, Juan José. "Inter-regional Approaches to Globalization: The Experiences of East Asia and Latin America." *Integration and Trade* 4, no. 12, IDB/INTAL (December 2000).

Ratliff, William. "Development and Civil Society in Latin America and Asia." *Annals of the American Academy of Political and Social Science* 565 (September 1999): 91–112.

Roett, Riordan, and Russell Crandall. "The Global Economic Crisis, Contagion, and Institutions: New Realities in Latin America and Asia." *International Political Science Review* 20, 3 (July 1999): 271–283.

Scollay, Robert. "Complex Intersections: East Asian–Latin American Trade Linkages in the Context of Recent Multilateral, Regional, and Sub-regional Developments." *Integration and Trade* 4, no. 12, IDB/INTAL (December 2000).

Smith, Peter H. "Japan, Latin America, and the New International Order." *Institute of Developing Economies, Visiting Research Fellow Series* 179 (Tokyo: December 1990).

Stockton, Hans. "Political Parties, Party Systems, and Democracy in East Asia: Lessons from Latin America." *Comparative Political Studies* 33, no. 9 (February 2001): 94–130.

Whitehead, Laurence. "Stirrings of Mutual Recognition." *Journal of Democracy* 11, no. 4 (October 2000): 65–79.

Wood, Adrian. "Openness and Wage Inequality in Developing Countries: The Latin American Challenge to East Asian Conventional Wisdom." *World Bank Economic Review* 11, no. 1 (January 1997): 33–57.

Index

Page references followed by *f* or *t* refer to figures or tables, respectively.

About the Contributors

Lily M. Bravo Castillo is a professor at the Institute of International Studies (IEI) at the University of Chile and a political analyst for the U.S. Embassy in Santiago. She has done postgraduate work at Keio University in Tokyo, and served as a consultant for the Chilean government on relationships with Asia and the Pacific Rim.

José Luis Estrada-López is a professor of economics at the Metropolitan University in Mexico City. He is affiliated with the nonpartisan Antonio Gramsci Center for Social Studies in Mexico City and his main research interest is comparative economic development.

Kotaro Horisaka is a professor of Latin American studies and Dean of Academic Affairs at Sophia University in Tokyo. He was for many years an economic correspondent for *Nihon Keizai Shimbun*, a business newspaper in Japan.

Akio Hosono is a professor of international economics at Kobe University in Japan. He has had a distinguished career in academia and as a consultant to the Japanese government and international agencies. He earned his Ph.D. in economics from the University of Tokyo and, prior to Kobe, was a professor at the University of Tsukuba.

Jiang Shixue is a professor and deputy director of the Institute of Latin American Studies (ILAS) at the Chinese Academy of Social Sciences (CASS) in Beijing.

His publications include *A Study of the Development Models in Latin America* and *Latin American Economic Reforms.*

Taik-Hwan Jyoung is the director-general of the Statistical Training Center for the Statistical Office of the Korean Ministry of Finance and Economy. He has a B.A. in business administration from Seoul National University in Korea and an M.A. in economics from the University of Paris.

Sayuri Kuwabara is a researcher at the Japan Center for International Finance in Tokyo. She holds an M.A. in Latin American studies from Georgetown University.

José Luis León is a professor of political science at the Universidad Autónoma Metropolitana-Xochimilco, and an adviser to the Minister of Foreign Affairs in Mexico. He received a Ph.D in political science from Columbia University, and he is the editor of *El nuevo sistema internacional: Una visión desde México* (1999).

Gilmar Masiero is a professor of economics at the State University of Maringá in Paraná, Brazil. He has held visiting appointments at Harvard University, the Institute for Developing Economies in Tokyo, and the Korea Institute for International Economic Policy in Seoul. His doctorate is in the field of business administration.

Shoji Nishijima is director of the Research Institute for Economics and Business Administration at Kobe University in Japan. He has written extensively on processes of economic reform, and he is coeditor of *Market and Government: Towards a New Development Strategy for Latin America* (1997).

Jaebong Ro is managing director of the Korea Institute for International Economic Policy in Seoul. One of his research fields is economic integration, and he has served as executive director for Korea's APEC National Study Center. He received a doctorate in economics from Cornell University.

Gilson Schwartz is a visiting professor at the Institute of Advanced Studies of the University of São Paulo, Brazil. A regular contributor and editorialist for *Folha de São Paulo*, Brazil's largest newspaper, he has a Ph.D. in economic theory from the University of Campinas. He is also editor of *Carta Asiatica*, a newsletter on Brazil-Asian affairs, and of Brazil Investment Link.

Peter H. Smith is a professor of political science and Simón Bolívar Professor of Latin American Studies at the University of California, San Diego. His most recent book is *Talons of the Eagle: Dynamics of U.S.–Latin American Relations* (2000).

Nualnoi Treerat is a member of the faculty of economics at Chulalongkorn University in Bangkok, Thailand. She is a frequent consultant to the ministries of commerce and of finance. She is coauthor of *Guns, Girls, Gambling, Ganja: Thailand's Illegal Economy and Public Policy* (1998).

Keiichi Tsunekawa is a professor of political science at the University of Tokyo, Komaba. He holds a Ph.D. from Cornell University and has been a visiting fellow at the Center for U.S.–Mexican Studies at the University of California, San Diego, and at the Woodrow Wilson International Center for Scholars in Washington, D.C.

www.ingramcontent.com/pod-product-compliance
Ingram Content Group UK Ltd.
Pitfield, Milton Keynes, MK11 3LW, UK
UKHW041103150926
475561UK00001BA/17

9 780742 523760